AS GOES BETHLEHEM

As Goes Bethlehem

*Steelworkers and the Restructuring
of an Industrial Working Class*

JILL A. SCHENNUM

VANDERBILT UNIVERSITY PRESS

Nashville, Tennessee

Library of Congress Cataloging-in-Publication Data

Names: Schennum, Jill A., 1956– author.
Title: As goes Bethlehem : steelworkers and the restructuring of an
   industrial working class / Jill A. Schennum.
Description: Nashville, Tennessee : Vanderbilt University Press, [2023] |
   Includes bibliographical references and index.
Identifiers: LCCN 2023012307 (print) | LCCN 2023012308 (ebook) | ISBN
   9780826505880 (paperback) | ISBN 9780826505897 (hardback) | ISBN
   9780826505903 (epub) | ISBN 9780826505910 (adobe pdf)
Subjects: LCSH: Iron and steel workers—Pennsylvania—Bethlehem—History.
   | Work—Social aspects—Pennsylvania—Bethlehem—History.
Classification: LCC HD8039.I52.U6 S346 2023 (print) | LCC HD8039.I52.U6
   (ebook) | DDC 669/.1097482—dc23/eng/20230624
LC record available at https://lccn.loc.gov/2023012307
LC ebook record available at https://lccn.loc.gov/2023012308

CONTENTS

Introduction

On a warm day in late autumn of 2012, I finally met Jack Franken, a steel-worker I had spoken to many times by phone.[1] Sitting in a cluttered ranch-house kitchen, I was aware I was in a bachelor's home—the kitchen was piled with dirty dishes, the spare rooms filled with junk, and the yard slightly unkempt and overgrown. Jack, a thickly bearded, messy-haired bear of a man, had recently returned to his family home in Bethlehem, Pennsylvania, after a career as a steelworker, first for twenty-three years at Bethlehem Steel's flagship mill, then for fifteen years as a transferred worker at the sprawling mill in Sparrows Point in Baltimore, commonly called the Point. Jack had just been laid off from his steel job in Baltimore when the Point closed. The afternoon I sat with him, he was living with his brother.

Jack's story is hard to hear, although he tells it without regret, shunning sympathy. After all, according to him, there are many workers in worse situations than his. After twenty-three of what he describes as rewarding years working in Bethlehem, he lost his job with the closing of the combination mills; the date, March 22, 1997, is engraved in his memory. He was forty-one years old.

Jack tried other jobs in the area, but either they were too low-paying, degrading, and demeaning, or they were downright dangerous. So when he received a letter proposing transfer to the Bethlehem Steel mill at Sparrows Point, he picked up and left for Baltimore, a three and a half hour drive from home. When he started work at the Point, he first lived in his camper, and then rented a basement apartment, commuting home when he had days off. His wife and stepchildren stayed in Bethlehem. "Transfers caused many divorces," Jack told me. "Absence does not make the heart grow fonder." It didn't take long for him to feel alienated from his family on visits home and in long distance phone calls. He and his wife argued, mainly about the kids, who were teenagers. "She wouldn't let me put a handle on those kids . . . long story short, that's what started the divorce," he recalls.

With his marriage in shambles, Jack threw himself into work. He put in long hours, worked overtime, and took extra shifts, making money while he could. This gradually led to better jobs at the Point, and the path seemed clear for completing the thirty years he needed for his pension.

Unfortunately, work was not easy in the new mill. Jack initially lost his seniority and found himself back in the grueling manual jobs that he had started in as an eighteen-year-old novice. His pay plummeted, he missed the camaraderie he had with his Bethlehem co-workers, and although he is white, he was shocked by the racism he encountered at the Point.

Jack's goal of working toward his pension ended abruptly on the day Bethlehem Steel entered the bankruptcy court, handed over its pension program, and sold what was once the second largest steel company in the world to a new upstart, International Steel Group (ISG). Jack had to decide whether to take a buyout from the mill's new owner or stay with ISG. Now divorced, he decided to stay and work in steel. ISG seemed a good company, and the pay was fine now that Jack had moved into a better job at the Point. But his stint with ISG was short-lived, as a series of sales and acquisitions of the Sparrows Point mill followed. ISG sold to Mittal, Mittal sold to Severstal, and Severstal sold to RG Steel. Finally, in 2012, RG put the mill on the market for scrap, ending more than one hundred years of steelmaking. In the fifteen years Jack worked at the Point, he had five different employers, a point he made clear to me when he lined up five hard hats on the kitchen counter, each with a different logo.

On that fall afternoon, Jack was still hopeful that some last-minute deal might be patched together to save the Sparrows Point mill and call him back to steel work. After all, it had happened before. Nonetheless, he admitted it was most likely a false hope, because just two months earlier he remembered encountering a stranger walking around the mill. "I looked at his hat and it said Art Brandenburg. And I got the chills. This is the guy that friggin' tore down our mill. I saw his name and I thought, oh my God, here we go."

Brandenburg was a demolition company that had torn down the steelmaking buildings in Bethlehem and sent them out for scrap. They shipped the machinery to steel mills from Wisconsin to China. If the same thing happened at the Point, Jack told me, the mill would never make steel again. And Jack was right; there is no more steel made at the Point. The mill was sold for scrap, steel jobs ended, and another steelmaking community fell into disarray.

Some might think of Jack's story as passé, an old story about US deindustrialization, a history of the 1980s. Or that it is about just a small sector of America—the fading and obsolete industrial working class. But today these many complex processes—shutting down plants, downsizing corporations, merging and acquiring businesses, outsourcing factories, using bankruptcy to strip away workers' assets—have resulted in increased insecurity, downward mobility, and a general erosion of life circumstances for many working- and middle-class Americans. It is devastating for workers to realize how little control they exercise over processes that affect every corner of their lives. To cope, they construct "hindsight," a contradictory psychological process in which they build the appearance of control through second guessing; they strategize as individuals and households to attempt to "stretch time" and access union-negotiated benefits; and they manipulate "retraining systems" for their own ends. But these individual and household strategies are not highly effective within a context of broad socioeconomic forces. Indeed, they often result in an individualizing of blame, an internalizing of anger, and an undermining of collective response, even as the legal system wipes out those benefits they managed to secure. Middle- and working-class Americans, much like Jack, struggle to find their footing in this new postindustrial landscape.

It is not just the loss of a suburban, middle-class lifestyle that many workers, including steelworkers, mourn. They miss the camaraderie and fulfillment built on the floor of the steel mill and the respect that US society gave them when steel production was seen as important to US economic strength. Bruce Ward, a former beam yard worker and rigger, summarizes the feeling: "What it meant to be a steelworker was a great deal of respect, not only received, but given. I think that respect was on both sides. Both for the fellows that I worked with, for the people that ran the plant, and for the people in the community. I think that that respect was what made it worth being a steelworker."[2] This satisfaction came from doing a job recognized by peers and management as difficult and well done, working in a role accepted by the country as central to production, and living as a responsible and dignified member of the community.

This book examines the decades-long period of transformation in the US, the steel industry, and at Bethlehem Steel, during which class relations were reshaped in the shift from a Fordist to a post-Fordist order. Through a focus on one cohort of ex-Bethlehem Steel workers (those hired in the period from 1963 to 1979), this book examines how these transformations played themselves out in the everyday spaces of people's lives and work, contributing to strategies of adaptation as well as changed understandings, values, and discourses related to class identity and class relations. These workers started work at the steel mill as young adults in the Fordist period of expanded expectations and opportunities. They then lived through a long period of downsizing and deindustrialization at the mill, and eventually they found themselves ejected from the mill into a new post-Fordist landscape. Workers struggled to hold on to hard-won Fordist rights and recognitions, even as they were being "schooled" in the new norms and morality of the post-Fordist order.

Over the past two decades, with the bursting of the "new economy" bubble followed by the shock of the credit collapse, the Great Recession, and then the Trump era, social scientists are showing a renewed interest in class analysis. For much of the late twentieth century, it was argued that class analysis, in the US, was increasingly irrelevant. Working people were often understood as either coopted into an affluent and quiescent Fordist middle class or defined as so undermined by post-Fordist processes as to have completely disappeared as a political force in the US. The first approach misrecognizes working-class power and possibilities of the 1960s and 1970s, and in doing so fails to recognize solidarities and dispositions that generate potentials for contemporary working-class critique and resistance. In the twenty-first century, new studies refuted approaches that downplayed or ignored the importance of class, using class-based analyses to understand the dramatically growing inequalities within the US. These analyses repudiate arguments that posit the end of class by documenting a very large, although changing, US working class.[3] Social scientists have examined the recent resurgence in organized working-class actions, they have analyzed changing working class participation in the political party system, and they are studying new sectors of a re-forming US working class, particularly women, new immigrant workers, and workers of color.[4]

With the election of Donald Trump, social scientists and the media became fixated on one fraction of the working class: white blue-collar workers. There are many conflicting explanations as to the extent of the white working-class contribution to Trump's presidential win, the reasons that *some* white working-class men voted for Trump, and how processes of deindustrialization contributed to this. The aging steelworkers who I spend time with overwhelmingly liked Bernie Sanders and Donald Trump in the run-up to the 2016 election. They were dismayed by traditional party candidates, including Hillary Clinton, whose husband symbolized the passing of NAFTA, a free-trade agreement that they understood as encouraging corporations to move industrial production out of unionized industrial areas to access cheaper, less powerful labor in the global South. Both Sanders's calls for a more egalitarian America, more protectionist trade policies, and regulated campaign financing and Trump's critique of free-trade agreements and argument for a strong infrastructural program that would create jobs appealed to them. While most of the steelworkers I knew ended up voting for Clinton, some simply didn't vote, and a significant minority voted for Trump in 2016. Trump won in Northampton County as the county flipped from voting for Obama twice.[5]

There has also been much recent discussion of the skyrocketing class-based inequalities within the US. This attention has focused on class stratification and the growth of inequality as measured through disparities in income, wealth, and educational achievement.[6] This book moves beyond static, stratification-based theories of class that enumerate characteristics through which classes can be defined and identified, to examine class as a fluid and dynamic social relation through which power is practiced and struggle enacted. Class relations are formed and exercised in social struggles in the factory, at the point of production, as well as in the community. They are embedded within broader cultural and political meanings and interactions, both on the shop floor and outside of it. These class relations generate shared ways of life, dispositions, and moral economies that can, at times, produce collective action.[7] This one cohort of steelworkers, experiencing a protracted process of deindustrialization, encountered what many contemporary working-class Americans are experiencing today—ongoing processes of class formation, dissolution, and re-formation related to the way in which flexible accumulation unevenly absorbs and expels fractions of the working class.

In this analysis, understanding class as embedded in relations of power in which capitalists expropriate the creative labor of the worker, thereby establishing class relations in which workers are situated in broader processes of capital accumulation and circulation, class politics and power are not understood as restricted to the workplace but are also related to "distributions of appropriated surplus labor as well as the form and extent of the appropriation."[8] Although my study focuses on work and people's understandings and experiences of life in and after the mill, work is only one site for the formation, dissolution, and transformation of class relations. Class relations are never static; they are constructed and deconstructed, reproduced and contested in the interactions of workplace, home, and community, and new relations are superimposed on and developed out of previous social and cultural formations.[9] Steelworker class identity, solidarities, and ways of life change as work relations are transformed through restructuring inside the Bethlehem mill; in the context of transfers to other mills; and as steelworkers moved out of the mills into post-Fordist flexible milieux of contingent labor, despotic management regimes, and insecure work. But steelworkers do not simply abandon prior social and cultural formations, habits, and sensibilities. Instead, these are incorporated into and challenged by new formations, generating critiques as well as fueling contradictions in workers' understanding and experience of the post-Fordist social order.

Class relations themselves include multiple individual and intra-household positions, both inside and outside the steel mill. For example, while white, male steelworkers held strong working-class identities at work, at home in suburban, middle-class neighborhoods, home ownership and mixed-class neighborhoods led to self-definitions for a significant period as "middle class." These middle-class identities are then challenged in the contemporary era, as processes of dispossession and disorganization erode middle-class positions. These transformations affect the class categories we have inherited from the Fordist past—of an affluent industrial working class in contradistinction to a poor or underclass.[10] We see that assumptions of a co-opted, affluent industrial working class were never entirely accurate—neither in the Fordist period nor, certainly, today. The industrial working class is situated within long-term historical processes that affect how steelworkers experienced and understood deindustrialization and the transition to a post-Fordist order over the past thirty years. Contradictory positions were generated both within and outside the mill, and solidarities and identities were built in part through exclusions that then became obstacles to collective action. It is through understanding the contradictions and continuities, as well as the solidarities, involving shifting inclusions and exclusions, all part of class shaping and reshaping, that we gain insight into both possibilities for and barriers to progressive collective action and identities.

Clearly, the institutional arrangements—inside the mill, within the company, and in the larger legal and institutional structures of citizenship rights and a public-private welfare state—shored up working-class consciousness and power in the 1960s, even as it channeled that power into the "appropriate" channels of union-mediated grievances, contract bargaining, and formal two party politics. The processes of deindustrialization, part and parcel of transformations in the regime of capital accumulation, undermined institutional supports and ate away at cultural expectations of a more egalitarian capitalism. This reshaped the industrial working class, dispossessing some, creating new pockets of poverty, moving others into devalued jobs in "low-road" manufacturing or the service sector of the economy, and maintaining a few in "high-road," restructured, skilled manufacturing jobs made more insecure by the threat of factory closure, capital mobility, and the surfeit of available workers. These processes produce contradictory identities as they play themselves out unevenly and seemingly arbitrarily across the industrial working class. Workers make use of moral economies forged in the Fordist workplace to evaluate and critique post-Fordist milieux, even as they also come to understand post-Fordist practices as a new social and economic reality. In apparently contradictory ways, processes of accumulation by dispossession heighten worker criticisms of corporate and governmental power while simultaneously directing anger inward, building resentment that may be harnessed by increasingly autocratic right-wing leaders and creating new fractures and hierarchies within the working class.

The "golden age" of the post–World War II period, while shorter and more fragile than often represented, embodied real progress for workers. Steelworkers like Jack Franken remember entering the mill in the 1960s and 1970s, when their work rights were codified and protected and their retirement seemed secure. Steelworker Ernie Lang describes his dad telling him to go to work at the Steel in 1972 because "it afforded us the opportunity to buy my house. It afforded us the opportunity to buy a new car every so many years, to buy appliances when needed. The biggest thing though was the benefits . . . the health care."[11] Carol Henn, who grew up in the 1960s in a steelworker family, says "one of the reasons Dad worked at Bethlehem Steel was to earn money that he knew would support his family and enable me to go to college. And certainly the benefits that unions won through the years added to the quality of life. It made a lot of things possible."[12] Within the community, steelworkers built a good life and secure future for their families. On a national scale, according to blast furnace worker Nick Darkach, in the mid-1970s "the steel industry was so big and so many people worked there that the whole country evolved around the steelworkers' pay. When we got a raise, other people got a raise." That this mature industrial working-class power posed a real threat to capitalist elites became increasingly evident in the 1970s and elicited a strong counter attack that undermined union power and displaced and devalued steelworkers.

The city of Bethlehem was a central place in Fordist America. It was the headquarters of a huge multinational corporation—the second largest steel company in the world. It was the steelworkers' community and the site of their "home" plant, the historic "flagship" mill where the Bethlehem Steel Corporation began its existence in 1904. They defined their mill as crucial to the success of the company, its contribution to national hegemony, and to the prowess of the city of Bethlehem. Workers lived in this small "global" city, making steel products used in the war materiel, infrastructure, skyscrapers, and autos that built American hegemony globally. They cite lists of the iconic sites built by Bethlehem Steel: the Golden Gate Bridge, much of the New York City skyline, and the George Washington Bridge, to name a few. By 1965, mill workers exercised power based on their predecessors' battles for union clout in the strikes of the 1940s and 1950s, power that was recognized by the formal institutions of the wider society—the courts, federal government agencies, the Democratic party. An entire private-public system of benefits had been legislated and enacted to ensure work stability and worker retirement (Medicare, Social Security, an expanded college and university system, employer-provided health plans, employer-provided pension plans, unemployment payments, supplementary unemployment pay). Workers entered the mill with confidence in their skills, the importance of their work, and their political power.

The Fordist Compromise

The fifteen-year period in which this cohort of workers entered the Bethlehem mill, from 1963 to 1979, came at the height of the "Fordist compromise" during which the US achieved global political and economic hegemony driven by a rapidly growing manufacturing sector characterized by large, vertically integrated corporations.[13] Fordism was organized around expanded reproduction, in which profits were plowed back into industries that were structured through a detailed division of labor, flow-line assembly, a rationalization of production, and a division of mental and manual labor that efficiently produced a variety of goods. Economic growth was fueled by an expanding domestic consumer market stimulated through suburbanization, government infrastructural investments, a robust welfare state, and a labor-capital accord leading to increased wages. In this Fordist system of accumulation, regulation theorists argue, the contradictions of capitalist accumulation were balanced through a set of Keynesian social and political policies that ensured a degree of stability in which a rising standard of living was defined as an economic and social good.[14]

The steelworkers I spoke with were the first cohort to work at the mill under a regime of middle-class wages. When entering the mill, a male steelworker anticipated making family-breadwinner wages in a life-long career that would enable him to live what he defined as the "good life." Millwright Sam Stevens said, "Most people who worked there had a job for life. There were lulls, you were laid off, but it paid well with benefits." A worker's wife could stay at home while the children were young; the family could purchase a house in a middle-class residential neighborhood; they would have good medical and dental care and financial security even in health crises; they could send their children (should they so desire) to college.[15] The worker could buy a new car when needed, his family could vacation together, and he could look forward to a secure retirement in his old age. Workers understood the middle-class consumption their wages afforded them as contributing to the economic vitality of their community and country. Craft worker Jerry Schneider said, "We had a reputation. We tipped the highest, we bought the best, we were generous to charities, we spread the money around. The economy of the Lehigh Valley counted on the steel*worker*, not the steel *company*." In the 1960s, for the first time this cohort of workers was better protected against the cyclical nature of the industry, as union-negotiated supplementary unemployment benefits ensured temporarily laid-off workers a living wage, and no-strike contracts seemingly ensured stable work. These protections enabled them to believe they could plan a "linear life narrative" that would not be knocked off course by periods of strike, layoff, and unemployment.[16] Carol Henn eloquently reminisces about what this meant to her, coming of age in the South Side neighborhood of Bethlehem in the sixties, in a steel-working family. She reflects that with

> the security provided by Bethlehem Steel and other employers, we had a kind of safety net that I didn't even recognize as such. There was a basic security in life. . . . We were free to be children, adults, parents, community. We had a freedom that we probably didn't appreciate or recognize at the time because it was just the norm for us. Half a century later, we look back and say "aha," there was a golden cast to those days.[17]

Although the terms *Fordist* and *post-Fordist* are prevalent in the literature, for the most part, the steelworkers that I spoke with did not know or use these terms. Instead, they described a more egalitarian period when they began work at the Steel, contrasting it sharply with the contemporary political economy. Steelworkers contrast the era when they could "choose" among secure jobs at a variety of large local industries where they could anticipate a lifelong career, experience internal mobility, support a family, have a middle-class standard of living, and expect to be cushioned from the vicissitudes of layoffs, illness, and injuries.[18] This choice of secure jobs among a few core industries may have been mostly restricted to men, but it did provide a real choice of stable, good-paying options. In addition, many of this generation could have considered college as their working-class parents began to realize the gains of the Fordist compromise. Many of these workers did not choose the college route. Some had started college and then dropped out due to marriage (often related to pregnancy), guilt over the cost for their parents, or not finding college fulfilling and engaging. Others eschewed college due to not being personally interested in it, often combined with limited parental expectations for higher education. For others, college was not a viable option—those whose families were more impoverished (by divorce, illness, or a spouse's death), or whose family circumstances led to greater barriers to higher education (as for the sons of first-generation Puerto Rican immigrants whose less-lucrative jobs combined with the Bethlehem School District's ethnically related tracking). For these, the possibility of fulfilling work and financial security in industrial jobs offered a viable career path.

Industrial labor is often characterized as highly alienating, deskilled work, an instrumental bargain enacted by workers in exchange for middle-class wages and benefits. But steelworkers refute this characterization. They describe much of their work as skilled, involving complex collaborative social relations, and generating dignity and meaning. For example, steelworker Ted Smith expressed pride in his productive maintenance work, "This is what I did. Everything is straight, it's plumb, it looks good, it works . . . they're good welds that'll hold up. That was fulfilling." He found satisfaction in "the camaraderie I had with the other men . . . I don't think I'll ever have that again in my life," and he found fulfillment in learning the complex skills he used as a senior maintenance worker. "One thing I learned in my life, no matter what I learned and did working here [at Bethlehem Steel], everything came in handy later. There was nothing I learned to do that didn't benefit me later with the knowledge bank I acquired."[19] A powerful moral economy of the mill gave value to labor. Work is important to Americans, and working-class culture is built, in part, through the habits, social relations, and material world of the work place.

As Antonio Gramsci points out, the Fordist regime is shaped not only through economic and political relationships, but also through the construction of a broader moral ordering that includes family relations, social behavior, understandings of self, and even forms of sexuality.[20] For many steelworkers, this more egalitarian regime molded individual dispositions in ways that contrast dramatically with today's post-Fordist flexible work. Tim Fuchs, an ex-steelworker currently employed as a skilled electrician, says, "When I worked at Bethlehem Steel, I made good money. You went to work and when you were at work you were in a good mood. You were at peace with yourself. . . . You came home, you were in a good mood, always. You weren't always worried like you are now." The stability and security of work produced fulfillment, freedom, and confidence.

This newly confident cohort of workers contrasted themselves with many older workers who were more reluctant to challenge authority, less assured of the protection of the union, and who held on to many practices that preceded unionization.[21] Curt Papp, who started at the Bethlehem plant in 1964, describes this: "Our forefathers, my father, worked in the blast furnace. Most of those people were under the conditions that nobody would want to work, and they survived. Because of them, when we came in—they called us the hippie generation—we started taking on all these issues: the safety . . . and we had arguments. Let's do it right this time—the 1970s." Historian Jefferson Cowie, in his study of working-class activism agrees, quoting a Lordstown plant union treasurer as saying in the early 1970s, "it's a different generation of workingmen. None of these guys came over from the old country poor and starving, grateful for any job they could get. . . . They've been exposed . . . to all the youth movements of the last ten years. . . . They're just not going to swallow the same kind of treatment their fathers did. They're not afraid of management. . . . They want more than just a job for thirty years."[22] The attitudes of this younger generation of workers, coming of age in the youth and civil rights movements and walking into a mill with strong and assertive union representation, were different than those of their fathers.

Ironically, these accounts of older, more quiescent workers are not describing pre-union workers. When the older generation was hired, in the early 1950s, the Bethlehem plant had been unionized for more than a decade. But the union was not as strong in some parts of the plant as it was in others, and the power of the union had not grown to its full extent within the entire plant.[23] While Bethlehem Steel recognized the union and signed its first union contracts in 1942, those initial agreements did not initiate tremendous growth in wages and benefits for steelworkers. Salary increases, as well as improved working conditions, had to be fought for through a series of steel strikes in 1946, 1952, and 1956, ending with the famous nationwide 116-day steel strike in 1959. Although each strike resulted in wage and benefit improvements, it wasn't until the 1960s, after the cost-of-living increases of the 1956 contract, that "for the first time union workers got wages that took them out of the working class into a decent quality of life and gave them the

promise of cradle-to-grave security."[24] In the late 1960s and 1970s, steelworkers' moved firmly into a middle-class standard of living, and their security
during layoffs, family health crises, and in retirement (through improved
pension benefits) was assured.

Jack Metzgar, whose father was a steelworker, describes the 1950s as a
period in which steelworkers had faith in "the direction we were going . . .
a rising tide was lifting all boats, raising everybody's prospects and expectations."[25] In contrast, the next generation, the ones I interviewed, understood
those possibilities as established social reality, a newly recognized social order. The most senior of these workers, hired in 1963, entered a work environment that for the very first time promised stable employment, a middle-class
standard of living, and strong protections overseen by the union. They were
welcomed in the mill, benefited greatly from the mentoring of older, more
experienced workers who understood not only the skills and jobs in the plant
but also the political system of the union, and they anticipated a career trajectory on the shop floor. Lester Brickly, who started as a laborer at the ingot
mold foundry in 1966, said, "I came to Bethlehem Steel because I was told by
different people that if you start at the Bethlehem Steel, you'll have a job for
life. You will never need to worry about going somewhere else."[26] Lester was
poised to learn new skills, bid into better positions, and see his collectively
bargained wages, benefits, and working conditions continue to improve.

Crisis in Fordism: Restructuring the Mill

Researchers and the popular media have long represented blue-collar workers of the 1960s and '70s—including steelworkers—as "ignorant, passive, and
conservative," a working class co-opted by their own affluence. However, more
recent analyses disagree with this representation, describing instead the many
ways that large portions of this cohort were "engaged, mobilized, connected
to each other, and motivated not just by wages and working conditions but
by belief in expansive versions of industrial and union democracy."[27] These
analyses show that this confidence and power threatened corporate elites,
eliciting a strong corporate offensive in the period of 1965 to 1973 against
which, in response, the younger generation of workers, who challenged bureaucratic unionism's focus on wages and benefits and its acceptance of management control of decisions related to disinvestment, fought back. These
workers pushed for more democratic working conditions.[28] These studies
examine progressive rank-and-file movements, including Ed Sadlowski and

the Steelworkers Fight Back campaign of 1977 that drew strong support from many workers in the Bethlehem mill's 1963-64 and 1973-74 cohorts. Sadlowski's campaign was run on a platform that was anti-war, anti–no-strike clause, and supportive of rank-and-file issues. The political power of an emboldened new generation of industrial workers clearly presented a political and economic problem to be confronted by corporate power, in part because those workers expected and believed in the promises of the Fordist compact of a new, more egalitarian capitalism. However, the post-Fordist strategies implemented by corporate elites were already beginning to undermine labor's gains. Workers hired in 1963-64 enjoyed only ten years of this order before processes of deindustrialization in steel became evident.

The Fordist period is often represented in the social science literature as a stable time during which an accord between business, labor, and government ensured a steadily growing economy. This shapes our understanding of the postwar US period as more solid than it actually was. Alternative analyses point to contradictions and contestations within the labor-capital accord. Davis, for example, describes it as an "armed truce" between business and labor (mediated by government), Winslow represents it as "a truce between business and business unionism" that was "partial and temporary," and Lichtenstein characterizes it as a "limited and unstable truce."[29] Ethnographers in the 1980s documented the "fragile affluence" of the industrial working class and the erosion of the labor-capital accord.[30] Historian Jefferson Cowie, in his study on RCA, argues that even in the 1940s industry's movements of capital show that "management may have been significantly less committed to its end of the [Fordist] bargain" than is commonly represented.[31]

US steel manufacturing was a core Fordist industry, but it also became a trendsetter in processes of deindustrialization paving the way for the emerging post-Fordist order. From the mid-1970s on, the steel industry attempted to restore high rates of profitability through reorganizing plants, restructuring labor relations, undermining union strength, extracting concessionary contracts, pursuing capital mobility, closing mills, arranging partnerships and mergers, and using bankruptcy strategies. As David Harvey points out, the emerging post-Fordist regime relied heavily on processes of accumulation by dispossession, "accumulation based upon predation, fraud and violence," including, at Bethlehem Steel, the shedding of jobs, the shredding of pension and health care commitments, the destruction of life insurance policies, and the devaluation of worker-held company stock.[32] Bethlehem Steel ultimately entered the bankruptcy courts to eliminate working-class assets and then sold its remaining steel mills to a vulture investor, who re-sold these leaner and meaner mills to Mittal Steel for a hefty profit. While these processes restored profitability to a transformed sector of the vertically integrated steel industry, they wreaked havoc on the lives of steelworkers as plants like Bethlehem closed and companies like Bethlehem Steel went bankrupt.

For many steelworkers in this cohort, while some of the real benefits of this period continued to be realized long into their work lives (the health care, decent wages, and the expectation of a pension), the imaginary that these were societally recognized entitlements—that their position in US society was secure, that their gains in the workplace were solid, and that this more egalitarian social order was realized and institutionalized in the US—began to be eroded and reshaped very early on. Workers' expectations of a secure lifelong career in steel came under attack within ten to fifteen years, at the most, of being hired. The benefits and working conditions they earned, as well as the available jobs, began to be whittled down as concessionary contracts, work restructurings, and department and plant closings ate away at worker power, devalued and depleted worker assets, constricted worker rights, transformed an understanding of worker position in society, and eroded workers' sense of possibilities. Within fifteen years of being hired, those workers hired in 1963 were already confronting a corporate offensive directed at transforming the steel industry and reshaping class relations in the US.

Contrary to popular representations, the post-Fordist regime has not been a successful or inevitable strategy for robust economic development.[33] Instead, it has been a "political project to re-establish the conditions for capital accumulation and to restore [and in some cases create] the power of economic elites," and deindustrialization has been inextricably tied to the growth of finance and merchant capital.[34] Within the steel industry, corporate elites struggled to maintain profitability in a broader political economy that favored the financial sector over heavy manufacturing. A steel industry threatened by increasingly ruthless competition aggressively restructured itself through practices that included shedding product lines, departments, and entire plants, pushing labor for wage reductions and speed-up and pursuing mergers, acquisitions, joint ventures, and bankruptcy. Known as rationalization, these large-scale processes of restructuring and deindustrialization played themselves out in waves of dislocation affecting varying industries and regions at different times and paces, manifesting disparate corporate strategies (which will be described in Chapter 1), and using tactics that play out unevenly even within specific communities and labor forces. Management structures, or factory regimes, develop and are implemented unevenly within the post-Fordist economy. Hegemonic and despotic regimes of labor control can operate side by side, and local labor market segmentation, the relation of contingent to permanent labor, the technologies of production, and the interactions between a new and an established working class all influence the development of post-Fordist manufacturing.[35] Even within the steel mill, expanded reproduction can occur simultaneously with processes of accumulation by dispossession, generating profits. Large-scale investments in the plant and new collectively bargained contracts, often with wage increases, may occur at the same time as downsizing, layoffs, and internal transfer.[36] These complex processes are experienced by steelworkers as disorienting and contradictory.

The last major hiring at the Bethlehem plant was in 1978-79. For these young workers, the tail end of the cohort I interviewed, a career in the steel mill was changing dramatically. Bethlehem coke worker Marc Ortiz explains that "being hired in 1978 was a different thing. Those workers had much more insecurity throughout their career." This last group was hired after Bethlehem Steel's 1977 Black Friday layoffs sent shock waves through the community, symbolizing the vulnerability of a company felt so recently to be indomitable. They were hired after waves of shutdowns had ejected thousands of workers from mills throughout the Monongahela Valley in Western Pennsylvania and from Bethlehem Steel plants in Lackawanna and Johnstown. Although Black Friday had a much greater impact on the corporate salaried than on the hourly plant workers, Tyler Wright, a salaried sales manager, told me "from 1977 on, there wasn't a week go by that you didn't worry about losing your job." Most workers hired in 1978-79 lost their jobs in the recession of 1982 and '83, a period during which Tyler says, "Bethlehem Steel came within weeks of going bankrupt."

This long restructuring of the Bethlehem Steel Corporation and the Bethlehem mill governed the work lives of the individuals I interviewed. Tyler Wright describes the process of Bethlehem Steel selling off assets that "began in a small way" in 1975 when the company "shut down fabricated steel and the alloy tool steel division" and continued until 2003, when the company was sold to the International Steel Group. According to Tyler, "we were constantly downsizing from 1975 to 2003." He describes almost three decades of restructuring, disinvestment, the closing of the Bethlehem mill, bankruptcy, and, ultimately, the demise and sale of the company. These decades explicitly showed workers how very short-lived and fragile Fordist "affluence" and security actually were, undermining their imagined ideal of a more egalitarian capitalism, and simultaneously generating both consent and resistance to post-Fordist restructuring. This was a Golden Age that was "less stable and uniformly prosperous than often represented," where steelworkers did not feel the full Fordist benefits until much later than commonly represented, and in which erosion through post-Fordist processes began earlier than posited.[37]

By the time these workers left the mill in the 1990s, often transferring to other mills and then being dragged through the experience of corporate bankruptcy, they had experienced a restructured, downsized, and eventually closed worksite and a bankrupt and defunct company. They left with eroded citizenship rights (both within and outside of the mill), limited retirement options, reduced health care coverage, devalued skills, and an uncertain future. They left in the context of a wider discourse praising the knowledge/information sector, high-tech industry, and the financial sector (and the "flexible" workers in these sectors) as the growth engines of the US economy while simultaneously attributing the failure of large industry to the arrogance, overly confrontational style, recalcitrance, and lack of foresight of what were represented as outmoded unions and outdated unionized industrial workers.

If we recognize this brief Golden Age as a moment of possibility, we can better critique the notion of an affluent, co-opted, white industrial working class, rendered quiescent and malleable by consumption and home ownership. A more egalitarian capitalism, a hegemonic order that values industrial labor, recognizes workers' citizenship rights, and supports participatory democratic processes, may empower workers to demand further change, as this generation of industrial workers did in many of the rank-and-file movements of the 1970s. The older generation was headed to retirement, satisfied with the gains they had made and looking forward to the pension and health care benefits they had earned. But this younger, assertive generation, growing up in families with heightened expectations and coming of age in a steel mill in which those expectations were formally recognized, was not willing to cede control of the workplace to management, nor to understand themselves solely as middle-class homeowners and consumers.

But there were potentials within the very possibilities of a more egalitarian order for the undermining of the Fordist compromise. Even as enormous steps were taken to build a more diverse working class within the steel mill (with changes initiated by the Consent Decree, which will be discussed in Chapter 4), disinvestment and downsizing threatened newly developing solidarities, accentuating fractures along lines of gender, age, and place and undermining the unity needed to effectively confront processes of deindustrialization. A bureaucratic, business unionism rendered labor less capable of fighting an ultimate plant closing, opting instead to stretch out the plant's life, pursuing pensions and benefits for retiring workers. A union focus on extending local plant survival contributed to expanded reproduction, increasing plant productivity even as large numbers of workers were laid off or retired in South Bethlehem and other plants. The local unions' focus on "home" plant workers made company- or industry-wide opposition difficult. And the failure of the union to encompass broader swathes of the working class, to unite with other social movements, hampered a more comprehensive opposition to processes of deindustrialization. Yet the importance of this period in the lives of the steelworkers I spoke with, the powerful imaginary of a Golden Age, demonstrates the transformative power of a vision of and belief in the possibilities of a more egalitarian capitalism.

In arguments that represent too-organized a transformation from Fordism to post-Fordism, steelworkers might be portrayed as naïve for not more actively planning out their transition to a knowledge-based economy through, for example, pursuing formal educational credentials that would pay off in more lucrative primary sector jobs. In reality, steelworkers often read the language of capital investment in mills to implement strategies—such as savvy manipulation or access to transfers available to a subgroup of home plant workers—for holding onto steel jobs, with the accompanying hard-won middle-class wages and benefits. These strategies may have benefited many steelworkers and their families, given the very long trajectory of restructuring and the accompanying post-Fordist erosion of the security, wages, and benefits of many "new economy" primary-sector jobs. But they also undermined broader collective action to confront corporate strategies of plant closings, the use of the bankruptcy court, and the sale of the company.

Much of the literature on deindustrialization has focused on sudden closures and worker and community reactions to such "shocks," experiences that can mobilize community and worker response, reflection, and analysis.[38] Indeed, for many communities and families, sudden job loss and mill closure was devastating.[39] But much of the restructuring at Bethlehem Steel did not take the form of sudden shock, nor was it codified into emotionally moving rituals (with the exception of the last cast ceremony at the Bethlehem mill), although there were multiple shocks along the way—the shock of Black Friday, the shock of sudden departmental closings at the steel plant, and the shock of what was once the second-largest steel company in the world entering the bankruptcy court. Yet, ultimately, for Bethlehem steelworkers, the construction of a new regime of advanced capitalism—a post-Fordist regime—followed a long trajectory of uneven social processes that were less-recognized, more uneven, highly contradictory, and often more confusing.

Structure of the Book

The first chapter outlines how the three-decade-long processes of deindustrialization played out in the city of Bethlehem, the Bethlehem Steel Corporation, the Bethlehem steel mill, and the lives of workers. Bethlehem Steel shaped the city's population, neighborhoods, and built environment, and throughout the city the corporate headquarters of the company and the giant steel mill were omnipresent, making this small city an important nexus in the global economy. The chapter also introduces the diversity of workers who came into the mill in the 1960s, discusses the beginnings of layoffs, shutdowns, and disinvestment in the late 1970s, and relates these processes to a broader restructuring in the US steel industry. I document the uneven processes of restructuring implemented by different steel companies, within the Bethlehem Steel Corporation, and inside the Bethlehem mill. I show how workers strategized and fought for their futures in this confusing and contradictory terrain, even as they contested dominant ideologies that blamed workers and their unions for steel's decline.

Chapter 2 examines the labor process within the steel mill, contextualizing this within Harry Braverman's analysis of the Fordist labor process, and Michael Burawoy's critique arguing that workers are active agents in generating a terrain of compromise on the shop floor.[40] I complicate this critique through showing how the internal state and internal labor market, while generated inside the plant, were shaped by and interacted with broader social processes from outside the mill. I show how the mill's internal social relations produced real rewards for workers, even while simultaneously manufacturing consent to the production process, and I explore particularities of steel work in the diverse and complex Bethlehem steel mill.

Chapter 3 shifts analysis toward the culture and broader moral economy inside the steel mill, connecting it to steelworkers' position within the broader social order. I investigate core concepts of citizenship, seniority, solidarity, and masculinity and their role in building a collective working-class moral order and identity.

This analysis is complicated in Chapter 4 through analysis of the exclusions implicit in building a white, male, industrial working class. African American, Latino, coal country, and women workers were denied the same access as white male workers to jobs and promotional opportunities. The largest EEOC settlement of the time, the 1974 consent decree, opened up plant-wide seniority for all workers as well as setting hiring goals and creating access to craft positions for women and workers of color in the mill, even as economic shocks and downsizing followed shortly thereafter. I document how, even with legally mandated opportunities, workers of color and women experienced obstacles in charting successful trajectories inside the plant.

Chapter 5 explores the effect of the long process of closing the Bethlehem mill and the bankruptcy of the Bethlehem Steel Corporation on steelworkers. Steelworkers used contractual agreements to attempt to best plan opportunities to transfer into other steel mills in an attempt to attain their pensions, even as in the uneven and confusing process of departmental closures, layoffs, and plant shutdowns, they lacked reliable data to make informed decisions. The bankruptcy of the Bethlehem Steel Corporation added insult to injury for workers, as the time clock stopped abruptly on pension eligibility and health care benefits were jettisoned, leaving workers bitter and disillusioned.

In Chapter 6, I argue that Bethlehem, unlike some other deindustrialized cities, has realized a revivified economy that includes warehousing and distribution, arts and entertainment, a robust tourist industry, and an expanding downgraded manufacturing sector. This chapter follows workers through retraining programs, internal and external transfers, and moves into new jobs in this post-Fordist Lehigh Valley economy, examining the ways industrial workers become defined as a reshaped working class. While this has ensured a thriving city, jobs for ex-steelworkers and a new, postindustrial working class are considerably lower-waged, more insecure, and have less worker control than steel jobs. This chapter delineates the strategies steelworkers implemented to re-locate themselves within this post-Fordist social order and the critiques steelworkers had of these new economy orientations.

CHAPTER 1

Bethlehem

The City, the Corporation, the Mill

The small, provincial city of Bethlehem housed the second largest steel corporation in the world, the headquarters of Bethlehem Steel Corporation, as well as a gigantic flagship steel mill that employed more than thirty thousand workers at its height, dominating the political economy of the region. This chapter places workers in the region within a longer history of the US steel industry, the Bethlehem Steel Corporation, and steel production in Bethlehem. Steel history shaped every aspect of the region: the demography, built environment, communities, experience of time, and structures of feeling of the city and its inhabitants. Many of the workers I follow grew up in steelworking families and were intimately familiar with the history of steel work in the Lehigh Valley. Through examining the place-specific history of the Bethlehem plant during both the growth of and crisis in the steel industry, I explore the ways Bethlehem Steel and the steelworkers reacted to threats to the Fordist order, and how these played themselves out in a decades-long process of restructuring and disinvestment within the mill. Bethlehem's revivified contemporary economy stands in sharp contrast to that of the rusted, depressed, and boarded-up landscapes of towns like Youngstown, Ohio, or Gary, Indiana, where sudden shocking and traumatic plant shutdowns threw workers out overnight into a harsh postindustrial labor market. The long process of Bethlehem's deindustrialization may initially be seen as an easier, softer landing for workers and may resonate more with how contemporary workers experience the incrementally increasing precarity of work than over-night shutdowns do. However, the uneven, contradictory processes of dein-dustrialization in Bethlehem were very difficult for workers and were con-tested and disputed by steelworkers, even while they strategized how to best weather restructurings within the mill.

The City

Bethlehem, a city of about seventy-five thousand people, is one of a trium-virate of cities stretching down the Lehigh Valley in Eastern Pennsylvania right up to New Jersey's border, where the Delaware and Lehigh Rivers merge. Bethlehem is nestled between the larger city of Allentown to the west and the smaller Easton to the east and is sometimes chauvinistically described by natives as "the rose between two thorns." The city is divided by the Le-high River, separating Bethlehem's north and south sides. The north side of Bethlehem, once an eighteenth-century Moravian settlement, features a quaint downtown with weathered stone buildings, a historic cemetery, and stately, nineteenth-century manses. Neighborhoods to the south of Bethle-hem's were sites of industry where worker-built row houses blanketed the steep South Mountain across from the massive steel mill. The steel mill and working-class neighborhood South Side is circumscribed on the south and west by the elite institutions of Lehigh University and St. Luke's Hospital, both heavily influenced by Bethlehem Steel.

Bethlehem remains a city split by its history. In the mid-nineteenth cen-tury, the first industrial magnates lived in Fountain Hill, a town bordering South Side. As the steel works expanded in the early twentieth century, upper-level managers moved to Bethlehem's north side, to "bonus hill"—named after the hefty bonuses that made up a significant portion of executives' salaries. In the latter half of the twentieth century, as steelworkers moved to suburban neighborhoods of single family "ranchers," managers moved out to Saucon Valley, close to the golf course and country club founded by Bethlehem Steel's elite, around which much of upper management's social life revolved.[1]

In contrast to the neighborhoods on the north side of Bethlehem, over the last 150 years South Side has welcomed ethnic immigrants who poured into the city to work in the growing iron and steel industries. This initiated dramatic population increases, as South Side expanded eastward. From 1870 to 1890 South Bethlehem almost quadrupled in size, jumping from 3,500 to 13,000 people.[2] Early immigrant groups of German, Irish, and English origin were followed by eastern European and southern Italian immigrants. By 1910, the census for South Bethlehem enumerated fifty-two nationalities, and 58 percent of the residents were either foreign-born or second generation.[3] When World War I and subsequent anti-immigrant legislation closed migration from eastern Europe and southern Italy in the 1920s, Bethlehem Steel looked for alternative sources of labor, recruiting Portuguese, Spanish, and Mexican workers to hot and hard steel jobs in the 1920s. Later, after World War II, Bethlehem Steel sought new labor in Puerto Rico, as agricultural workers moved to the South Side for jobs in the mill's coke works. The aggressive, ethnically oriented recruitment of laborers for the iron and then steel industries structured working-class communities in Bethlehem.

Until the 1950s, working-class families in Bethlehem's South Side could spend their whole lives segregated in their community—attending the vocational-technical (vo-tech) high school, going to the South Side library, doing their shopping in the thriving community of small businesses, and walking to work at the steel mill or, for women, the many textile and cigar factories. The north side seemed distant to many South Side residents. For years, South Bethlehem residents even had to pay a toll on the "penny bridge" to cross to the north side of town. Children in working-class families, while expecting to go to high school, often did not consider college, and many young men envisioned a future related to the steel mill. The public vo-tech school prepared working-class boys for work in the mill, and low steelworker wages made it hard for families to fund other career trajectories. Working-class neighborhoods were united through steel work, ethnic churches, lodges and benefit societies, sports leagues, and small businesses and saloons that supported vibrant community and street lives.

This began to change during and after World War II when the union was finally recognized and a series of strikes initiated collectively bargained contracts that began to improve steelworker salaries. During the 1950s, workers began driving to steel jobs from communities throughout the Lehigh Valley and beyond as growing salaries supported cars and homes outside the South Side. Parking lots sprang up across South Side areas near the mill. The vo-tech high school moved to the north side of Bethlehem, even while the tracking of students to the vo-tech and the "commercial" programs at the city's north side Liberty High School still kept working-class and white-collar students separate. Families became more likely to have some children heading into union jobs and others into lower management at the Steel, as growing sala-ries enabled steelworking families to send children to college.

Michael Kennedy, a sociologist who grew up in Bethlehem in the 1960s and '70s, describes the cross-class steel connections within his own family. His father went to college, began at Bethlehem Steel as a "looper" (or manage-ment trainee), and worked his white-collar career as a sales manager there. But his father's older brother, a favorite uncle, was a unionized steelworker in the mills.[4] Steve Donches, a public relations executive for Bethlehem Steel who became president and CEO of Bethlehem's National Museum of Industrial History, grew up on Bethlehem's South Side. Steve's father was a much-respected steelworker union activist who worked his way from welder to shop steward to staff member with the United Steelworkers (USW) inter-national. Steve went to college, came back and married into the local elite, and worked a high-level managerial career in Bethlehem Steel's corporate offices, often in an oppositional relation to the union. By the 1960s in Bethle-hem, splits between union and management, between steelworkers and steel managers, were playing themselves out within families like the Doncheses and Kennedys.

In 1963, when the cohort in this book began work in the mill, applicants to Bethlehem Steel came from a diverse area around the Lehigh Valley. Later, in the 1980s, as steel jobs began to decline and most steelworkers had long since exited the South Side neighborhood, new immigrants from Central and South America, the Dominican Republic, and Puerto Rico, and Latinos from New York City moved in. While to outsiders the Lehigh Valley appears a unified region, residents are sensitive to cultural distinctions embedded in the his-tories of microregions. When I met ex-steelworkers in the first decades of the twenty-first century, I drove many miles to visit long-inhabited single-family homes (ranch-style or reconditioned older homes) in and around Allentown, suburb-like communities on the north and west sides of Bethlehem, farming communities both north and south of the Lehigh Valley, industrial (zinc and cement) towns north of Allentown, suburban neighborhoods in Easton, and coal country communities further north, beyond the Lehigh Valley.

Most steelworkers with a long lineage of steel work—second, third, and even fourth generation workers—grew up in Bethlehem's working-class neighborhoods. For them, the sights and sounds of the gigantic steel mill framed experiences of space and time in the flow of childhood daily life. They describe the dust that dirtied laundry hung out to dry; the loud mill noises that punctuated their days and evenings; and the uneven rhythm of shift work that structured eating schedules, children's play, and leisure time.

Jose Achando, an older Portuguese machinist, remembers the city of his childhood:

> The sounds—we were deafened to them. You lived in the city of Bethlehem, you heard drop forges, you heard big saws, you heard big beams being dumped and you more or less, in your mind, you cut that all out. As a youngster, our cousins from Rhode Island started to come. . . . The first night they spent, in the morning at the breakfast table, they wanted to know, "What the heck was all that noise?" "What do you mean, what noise?" We were immune to it, because we grew up with it.[5]

Carol Henn, a steelworker's daughter growing up in the 1950s and '60s South Side, describes the living presence of the steel works:

> I simply remember the orangey, rosy glow that was in my bedroom in South Bethlehem at night. . . . There was no such thing as a dark house. . . . There was a constant noise. It was as though you were living near a living presence. . . . You had the sense that twenty-four hours a day Bethlehem Steel was vibrating and moving and making sounds and lights and everything else.[6]

Many workers have a strong nostalgia for the tightly knit working-class neighborhoods of their childhoods, even though they left these for single-family homes, manicured yards, and better public schools as their salaries rose. Nonetheless, they took many of their traditions with them. They continued planting the gardens that grew fresh tomatoes; they volunteered with their churches, local sports organizations, and community clubs; they attended union meetings and picnics; they participated in Democratic get-out-the-vote efforts; and they took seasonal hunting and fishing trips with buddies. And they moved with their strong identity as steelworkers who worked hard to make a living in the mill.

Even today, after the closing of the giant mill and the bankruptcy of the enormous corporation, the power and influence of Bethlehem Steel is embodied in the landscape of the city. As Walter Moore, an ex-plant patrol worker, points out, "When you look around the city of Bethlehem, old Bethlehem, you see Bethlehem Steel everywhere."[7] The transportation infrastructure of highways and railroads; built environment of corporate, research, and mill buildings; university and hospital; working-class and elite neighborhoods; golf courses and country clubs; sports teams and choirs; all of these were molded by steel jobs and the Bethlehem Steel Corporation.

The Mill

The city of Bethlehem was shaped by steel. Bethlehem Steel's South Bethlehem plant was originally an iron manufacturing plant. In 1863 the Bethlehem Iron Company was producing iron rails for the expanding system of railroads in the US; by 1873, they were rolling steel rails; and by 1890, the company was producing armaments for the US Navy.[8] Charles Schwab bought out this company, changed its name to the Bethlehem Steel Corporation, and parlayed that munitions expertise and technology into lucrative contracts with Great Britain during World War I and rapid corporate growth. Bethlehem Steel bought up, at various times, iron ore mines in Cuba and Chile, coal mines in Pennsylvania, shipbuilding companies around the US, and railroads and a fleet of ore carriers, and it added on to the original Bethlehem site by acquiring a stable of steel plants including Sparrows Point, Lackawanna, Johnstown, Steelton, Burns Harbor, and others. This geography of fixed capital shifted over time with purchases, sales, mergers, and partnerships. By the 1920s Bethlehem Steel owned six large integrated steel works, in addition to a slew of other assets, and was the second largest steel company in the US and worldwide.[9] Bethlehem Steel weathered the Depression and emerged from it as a "diversified steel company," a giant multinational corporation, and still the number two steel company in the world.[10]

During World War II, at the height of Bethlehem Steel's production, thirty thousand workers were employed at the Bethlehem steel works. The Bethlehem plant produced a wide variety of products including steel for the automobile and oil industries, consumer durables, and war materiel, and structural steel for skyscrapers and bridges. Bethlehem Steel entered the postwar period with a formally recognized union, having negotiated its first contract in 1942 under pressure from organized workers, a major strike, and state intervention. Large industries like steel forged agreements with unions to provide higher wages, regular salary increases, and good benefits in return for a stable, hard-working, quiescent work force. After the war, Bethlehem Steel continued to do well as productivity in core US manufacturing industries expanded, even as the steel work force in Bethlehem was reduced from its 1940s high to about sixteen thousand workers by the 1960s. The Bethlehem Steel Corporation also had corporate and financial assets—including offshore subsidiaries in the Bahamas and a bank in Curacao acquired in the 1950s—that helped the company avoid taxes.[11]

The steel industry was central in US economic development. From 1929 to 1958, the steel industry generated the largest percentage of US GDP growth.[12]

The two largest American steel companies, US Steel and Bethlehem Steel, came to control more than half of all steel plants in the US, as well as the majority of iron ore, coking coal, internal railroads, and ore carriers.[13] US political elites and corporate management developed a close relationship, and government inputs in the form of military contracts, capital for technology, and tax abatements helped to power the growth of the big steel companies.[14] Monopolistic control through price fixing, vertical integration of the steel-making process, exclusionary contracts with suppliers, and in the postwar period, collectively bargained labor agreements eliminating the strike threat and giving workers a bigger piece of the economic pie led to rapid increases in steel prices, growing wages for labor, and the elimination of competitors.

By the time the oldest members of the cohort of workers in this book entered the mill, in 1963, the Bethlehem plant was producing large quantities of a wide variety of steel products to fuel the growth of the country's suburban consumerism and expanding infrastructure. It was a diverse, vertically integrated mill containing all the components needed to make steel in a modern, rationalized fashion. The mill had its own railroad, the PBNE, to move goods internally within the gigantic plant. It had its own police force (the plant patrol), fire company, medical staff and pharmaceutical dispensaries, and power plant in addition to the myriad of maintenance and production workers to repair and build the machinery and buildings, as well as operate the machinery needed to produce steel. Workers described a city within a city within the plant, with a complex division of labor, a variety of spaces of work and leisure, and an ethos of production that imbued workers with a confidence that they could, literally, build anything the plant, and the country, needed.

Workers who entered the Bethlehem mill in the 1960s and 1970s talk about the "constant movement" at the plant, of machinery, of steel, of people, "the sparks flying all over the place, and the whistle blowing, trains are moving, everything was in constant motion here."[15] They describe shift changes that were so crowded it took an hour to get out of the parking lot, with people and cars flowing out of the gates. They portray departments with cranes, steel beams, and railroad cars moving every which way, a movement they imbued with danger but that also conveyed the importance and vitality of the plant during robust steel production.

In retrospect, we see that the steel industry was already encountering contradictions in the Fordist regime of accumulation, leading to a "crisis" in steel production and ensuing processes of deindustrialization in the 1980s. The steel industry confronted stagnant American productivity in the 1960s, when declining profitability was related to less robust economic growth (and much slower growth in demand for steel) as well as heightened competition in the domestic market from imported foreign steel and the expanding minimill sector. While global steel demand was already growing, US steel manufacturers were focused only on supplying domestic demand. In 1950 the US produced 40 percent of the world's steel; by 1970 it was 20 percent.[16] Declining profitability in the steel industry precipitated layoffs as early as the 1960s, which some workers feared indicated they would never work again.[17] In Bethlehem, some workers recall "old-timers" already warning them about these changes when they started working at the plant in the 1960s and early 1970s. Steelworker Peter Clarke, who began his career in the beam yard, reported, "When I first came into the department some of the old-timers said, 'Kid, this is no place for you . . . this place is going down. Get out now.' And that was in 1973."[18] Employment in steel in the US remained relatively stable during this period: in 1950 there were 674,000 workers and in 1970, 627,000.[19] However, strategies to reduce labor costs through introducing new technologies, contracting out, and closing shops were already producing structural unemployment in steel, and the United Steelworkers union was already negotiating around issues related to this job loss in the 1960s.[20] Although most benefits enhancing security were focused on the cyclical layoffs long endemic to the steel industry, some focused on structural job loss, such as bargaining for transfer rights between mills in 1977 and negotiating for increased pensions.[21] In 1973 the USW gave up the right to strike—even between contracts—in the Experimental Negotiating Agreement (ENA), which guaranteed steel a reliable labor force, without the threat of strikes and the accompanying cycle of stockpiling steel prior to contract negotiations followed by layoffs when the contract was signed. The USW bargained away the strike under affluent society assumptions of ongoing expanding reproduction in return for cost of living and wage increases.[22]

Imports were beginning to capture an ever-larger percentage of the US steel market, surpassing US steel exports for the first time in 1959, and attaining 20 percent of the US market by 1977.[23] But this increase in imports was not initially recognized as a major threat. Investment in the Bethlehem corporation and plant continued throughout the 1960s and 1970s. In 1961, Bethlehem Steel built a costly new corporate research complex, Homer Research Labs, on South Mountain in Bethlehem. It began construction of Burns Harbor—a brand new, integrated works on the southern shore of Lake Michigan—in 1963.[24] In 1968, ground was broken for Martin Tower, the company's new corporate headquarters on the north side, a twenty-one-story skyscraper that towered over the city skyline.[25] In south Bethlehem a new structural mill was built in 1968, and a new basic oxygen furnace was constructed, which required tearing down an entire neighborhood, "the Heights."[26] The early 1970s brought additional investment, bespeaking the economic strength of the Bethlehem Steel Corporation (even as imports were eating into its market) and of the historic Bethlehem mill. The company announced a major expansion plan in 1973, a banner year for Bethlehem Steel. In 1975, a new battery of coke ovens was constructed at the Bethlehem plant, and numerous pollution control technologies were added in the 1970s. There was a large hiring of plant workers in 1973-74. These investments, robust employment of sixteen thousand workers in the 1960s, management portrayals of a healthy steel industry, a thriving Bethlehem Steel Corporation, and a hearty and productive steel mill in Bethlehem obfuscated the very real threats to the industry.

The young workers entering the mill in 1963-64 came from all over the Lehigh Valley and surrounding area. They included third generation Bethlehem steelworkers who had grown up in tightly knit working-class communities on the South Side as well as newcomers to steel whose parents farmed or worked in other industries scattered throughout the Lehigh Valley.[27] They included "up-homers," the sons of coal miners from the north looking for the kinds of blue-collar jobs that had been disappearing with the decline of anthracite mining, as well as second-generation Puerto Rican immigrants to Bethlehem, many whose fathers had worked for the Steel. They also included some African American workers; a few of them were second generation, but most were finding jobs at the Steel opening to them for the first time. This was a diverse group of young men entering the mill, going into different shops and departments, and working next to seasoned old timers, many of whom still spoke in the accents of their home European countries.

Some of these young men had grown up dreaming of working in the steel mill, some simply fell into the opportunity of higher-paying work. Some were college dropouts who decided college just wasn't for them, and some were recruited by the Steel from the local vocational high school or community colleges for training as skilled apprentices. But most entered the mill with optimism, a feeling of opportunities and possibilities, a sense that they were in a position of power in their relationship to work. Al Trakas, who came to the mill from a town just north of Bethlehem, was getting married in 1964. He applied to the Steel because he needed a better-paying job than the auto repair work he was doing. Back then, Al recalled, "jobs were plentiful." Tom Oster, who went on to become a union president, agrees. "When I graduated from high school I had many options—Bethlehem Steel, Mack Trucks, PP&L, Western Electric—it wasn't a question of will I find a job, it was where do I

want to look for a job." For men from steelworking families who weren't in-
clined to college, the Steel was an ever-present option. Eddie Havela had more
than twenty relatives who worked at Bethlehem Steel. "It was almost like the
place to go to work. Being born and raised in a steel family, it was the thing to
do." And families saw a job at the Steel as a solid and secure career for their
sons. Marc Ortiz, whose father had worked for Bethlehem Steel, graduated
from high school and "one week later I was working at Bethlehem Steel. . . .
All the kids from high school were going there. That was the place to be." In
the Lehigh Valley, the steel company seemed too big, stable, and necessary
to the economic order to decline.

To the workers coming into the mill in the last big hiring at the Bethlehem mill, in 1978/79, the steel mill represented opportunities for young men,
and for the very first time, for young women in the Lehigh Valley region. Lisa
Szarko, a nineteen-year-old single mother at the time, moved from a lower
wage job to Bethlehem Steel in 1979, as mill jobs opened to women. She said,
"Bethlehem Steel, Mack Trucks, those were good jobs and money. You know,
it was nice money and I had a child to raise, so I applied. I figured, why not."[28]
Many women felt buoyed up by the women's movement and the opening of
steel jobs. Marlene Burkey started at Bethlehem Steel in 1979 at age forty, after being married and raising two daughters. She felt that opportunities were
opening for women: "Women's lib came out at that time and Gloria Steinem
said we can do a man's job."[29]

The Crisis

The excellent wages and benefits that Bethlehem Steel offered to high school
graduates and to women were impressive. However, times were changing. In
1977, Bethlehem Steel failed to post a profit for the first time since 1927, instead
posting a $448 million loss, the greatest in the corporation's history.[30] There
were major signs of trouble in the vertically integrated steel industry, at the
Bethlehem Steel Corporation, and within the Bethlehem plant. The 1977 plant
closings (many owned by US Steel) in western Pennsylvania's Monongahela
Valley brought strong local reaction and national headlines. That same year
in Bethlehem, on "Black Friday" eight hundred "shocked and angry" corporate workers in Martin Tower were precipitously laid off.[31] White-collar workers who thought of their jobs as secure, life-long careers were asked to pack
up their belongings and leave the office immediately, now unemployed. This
event was so traumatic that, according to plant patrol worker Walter Moore,

Bethlehem Steel's security workers were ordered to guard then CEO Donald Trautlein's home around the clock for fear of retaliation, not from the union workers but from white-collar staff.[32] Seven thousand plant workers were also laid off from other Bethlehem Steel mills the same year (although not from the Bethlehem mill).[33] The 1976 closing of the Fabricated Steel Construction division (related to the loss of the World Trade Center contract), along with the shrinking of the Johnstown plant in 1979 and the Lackawanna plant in 1977 were clear signs of trouble. Some workers from Johnstown found themselves transferred into other plants, including a few who ended up at the Bethlehem mill. The closures, bankruptcies, and mergers and acquisitions accompanying this growing crisis were realigning the landscape of steel production in the US by the late 1970s.

Shortly after the last wave of Bethlehem plant hires in 1978-79, recession hit the industry, and by 1982, "nearly 200 steel plants were closed nationwide, 200,000 jobs were eliminated and another 140,000 workers were laid off."[34] Declining rates of profit in steel, linked to the growth of the minimills, the increase in foreign imports, the lack of capital to invest in domestic plants, and processes of globalization all contributed to the crisis. In the first six months of 1982 111,500 steelworkers, or about 25 percent of the US steel labor force, lost their jobs.[35] Donald Trautlein, the new, financially oriented CEO of Bethlehem Steel, hired to rationalize the company, laid off thirty thousand Bethlehem workers from 1980 to 1982, one third of these at the Johnstown and Lackawanna plants.[36]

What had once been understood as cyclical ups and downs in the steel industry now appeared a more threatening decline. Foreign investment in European and Japanese steel after World War II, the opening of US markets to steel imports, the growth of steel production in newly emerging economies, and the support of the minimill industry, all "solutions" for capital, contributed to overproduction of steel, a "crisis of overaccumulation."[37] Steel did continue to be crucial to the global capitalist economy, but where and how steel was made changed dramatically, reshaping global steel production. This crisis continued in the 1980s as steel production grew in newly emerging economies like Brazil, South Korea, and Mexico. Government strategies under the Reagan administration supported the financial sector at the expense of industrial production. Steel expansion in newly industrializing countries (NICs) was financed through loans by banks in the US. The financial industry then lobbied for neoliberal policies that ensured a strong dollar and lowered barriers to imports, thus encouraging a flood of cheap steel imports and ensuring that NIC steel industries could pay off their debts.[38] While this benefited the financial sector, increased foreign competition combined with hard-to-come-by capital for domestic integrated steel hit the American industry hard.

A small minority of the workers hired in Bethlehem in 1978/79 managed to hang on to jobs at the mill through the 1990s. Those who survived either accessed apprenticeships or moved into specific departments that proved more stable. However, the majority confronted layoffs, recalls, and then termination in the 1980s. Within this group of permanently laid off workers, women were disproportionately represented, because most women mill workers were hired in 1979. Laid off workers faced difficulties finding their footing in the changing Lehigh Valley labor market of the 1980s, as local employers failed to recognize the steel layoffs as structural, long-term transformations. Regional employers expected that these Bethlehem Steel workers would be only short-term employees at their new jobs and would leave as soon as they were called back from what was defined as another cyclical layoff at the Steel. Lisa Szarko, hired as a laborer at the Bethlehem plant in 1979 and laid off two years later, describes the challenge of finding work after Steel, in the 1980s, in the Lehigh Valley:

> You never want to be a steelworker and get laid off. You can't find a job. Nobody wants you. You put Bethlehem Steel on your resume, nobody wants to hire you. Their mindset is—well when the layoff is over with and Bethlehem Steel decides to hire these people back, where are they going to go? They're not going to stay with us. They're going to go back to the steel.[39]

Workers themselves were ill-equipped to deal with permanent layoffs, as they also often interpreted these as cyclical downturns. Jill Ruch describes the gratitude she felt toward her foreman in the coke works, who told her clearly that she would never be returning to Bethlehem Steel. When she was laid off in 1981, he said, "You won't be coming back . . . go do something with your life, you won't be back." Jill said "I appreciated him telling me that, because without that I would have felt like I still have a shot at this. He helped me jump start the beginning of the next chapter of my life."[40] His advice propelled her back into higher education and a career in computers and finance.

Although the steelworkers in my study started working at the Bethlehem plant in the busy times of 1964, 1974, or 1978 when the plant had sixteen thousand workers, by 1980 declining profits in the steel industry were felt in many of the plant's departments. Many of the workers hired in 1978, with least seniority, were facing layoffs. Those who managed to hang on to their jobs spent the next eighteen years experiencing the effects of various approaches toward "restructuring" on the part of the Bethlehem Steel Corporation (negotiated often with the United Steelworkers union). Bethlehem Steel's long restructuring may have produced an "easier landing" for Bethlehem workers than for steelworkers at US Steel or other mills that closed abruptly. Anthropologist Christine Walley's father, for example, experienced what many steelworkers in Southeast Chicago and western Pennsylvania went through: He woke up one morning to find his mill closed and his way of life eradicated. Wisconsin Steel, the company Walley's father worked for, was the first steelworks to close in southeast Chicago. Her father related that after being told their jobs were safe, "he and other workers who were ending a shift were told to go home without further explanation."[41] Workers were not allowed to empty out their lockers, the gates to the mill were locked, and armed security guards patrolled the premises. In one short and shocking overnight period, workers were locked out of their mill, their work, and their respected role in the social order. Their entire lives were up-ended instantly. In contrast to this, the Bethlehem plant's decades-long restructuring played itself out differently. But, while better for steelworkers, this generated insecurities and tensions, simultaneously promoting hope and the fading promise of a secure retirement.

RESTRUCTURING THE STEEL INDUSTRY

While post-Fordist transformations threatened US industry and reshaped the US economy, US corporate elites were not a united force. Financiers had different interests (often being heavily invested in free-trade policies) than industrialists. Even among industrial elites, there were different strategies in confronting these obstacles. When the Reagan-era recession from 1982 to 1986 threatened the steel industry, the Bethlehem Steel Corporation, along with US Steel and other steel companies, was severely disappointed by the lack of government support for the struggling industry. But the two giant corporations responded differently to these challenges.

Mike Davis points out that the big steel corporations received billions of dollars in wage concessions from labor in the 1980s, as well as government support in the form of tax subsidies and concessions on environmental regulations.[42] But many companies—most notably US Steel—did not use that capital to invest in their Northeastern and Midwestern steel industries. Instead, it was used to diversify, invest in the Southern US, or invest overseas. Davis demonstrates that the regional shift in capital investment to the Sunbelt states was actively supported by the Reagan administration through military spending, agricultural credits, accelerated depreciation policies, and oil depletion rebates. State policies subsidized this geographical shift in capital investment, thereby creating the very Southern minimill competition that ate into vertically integrated companies' markets and exerted downward pressure on steelworkers' wages.

US Steel entered a period of major restructuring, focusing on diversification, the pursuit of foreign partnerships, and the "disassembly" of integrated steel production. Its 1982 purchase of Marathon Oil for $6.4 billion dramatically reshaped the corporation, as oil became about a third of the corporation's interests. US Steel also pursued an international division of labor in its integrated steel industry. It explored importing semi-finished slabs from Britain for finishing in its American plants. It used its capital to build foreign partnerships and sold some US assets to foreign corporations, even as it aggressively shut down and downsized its American steel mills in the 1970s through the mid-1980s. In 1986, US Steel sold its Fairless Works steel rod mill in Pennsylvania to China, initiating a massive deconstruction and transportation operation to move machinery to the Philadelphia port, across the ocean to Dalian, China, and then 125 miles inland. US Steel's international division of labor and its foreign partnerships and deals, combined with its diversification into oil, made the company much friendlier than Bethlehem Steel to free-trade policies and allied US Steel more closely with the interests of America's financial elite.[43] Although the corporation was headquartered in Pittsburgh, CEO David Roderick slashed operations at nearby Monongahela steel mills, throwing workers out of jobs and entire communities into disarray: "tradition and company loyalty seemed irrelevant to Roderick's cost-cutting."[44] The Homestead plant, "a symbol of US Steel's strength and dominance in the steelmaking industry" and a historic labor site, was unceremoniously shut down in 1986.[45] Garay argues that this closing of a works "so long the very heart of US Steel represented the company's concerted effort to disengage itself from its past. . . . Homestead was rationalized out of existence."[46]

The Bethlehem Steel Corporation took a somewhat different approach to restructuring in the 1980s, one that ultimately resulted in bankruptcy. The company attempted to reorganize management processes, introducing management-worker team endeavors; concentrate on what the company defined as its core products; and disassemble their integrated model. For Bethlehem Steel, this meant shifting away from the emphasis on a vertically integrated mill toward the "disassembly" of integration, using a statistical analysis of productivity—determining which plants, operations, and workers could be shed in order to modernize others, and maintain a profitable core of production. To do this, the company sold diverse assets and closed shops, divisions, and plants to narrow product lines.

Other steel companies also disassembled vertical integration, shedding upstream and downstream divisions and components, selling and closing upstream mines (the large producers sold off more than 70 percent of their mines) and outsourcing downstream steel service or processing centers that dealt directly with customers.[47] They also tried to increase productivity through the introduction of new technologies in "core" departments, new management regimes designed to enhance labor productivity, and contracts that eliminated union-defined job classifications. By 2000 this restructuring had resulted in US steel producers shedding 35 percent of the industry's capacity, while employment in basic steel simultaneously declined by 75 percent.[48] Bethlehem Steel went from a total of 130,000 employees in 1970 to less than 25,000 in 1990 (a decline of 81 percent).[49] These new strategies reduced labor needs at a much greater rate than they reduced production capabilities. US Steel's Gary Works, for example, was producing as much steel as ever by the late 1990s, but with a fraction of the workers, going from over 20,000 workers in the 1970s to 7,500 workers by 1990.[50] This was also true of the Bethlehem plant. Today, the only remaining steel facility on the Bethlehem works site produces nuclear forgings with slightly over two hundred workers (versus eight hundred when the facility was part of Bethlehem Steel).[51] The 1990s were often described as the renaissance of steel, as the US steel industry became more efficient and competitive. However, "the beneficiary of this intense focus on cost improvement has been the steel consumer. The loser has been the steelworker."[52] Steel's recovery has been built on the backs of workers' wages, job security, jobs, and health insurance and pension benefits.

The Bethlehem mill's gradual and incremental restructuring may also reflect Bethlehem Steel CEOs' reluctance to shut down the plant in their headquarters' city, given that many of them married Bethlehem natives, sent their children to Bethlehem schools, and became active members of the Bethlehem community.[53] In addition, "the chairman's work background may have been an important factor when plant closure decisions were being made."[54] Bethlehem's policies of promoting executives from within meant that many CEOs had worked in, and had sentimental ties to, diverse Bethlehem plants. This may explain why "outside experts"—from outside the corporation, the steel industry, and the region—like CEOs Donald Trautlein and Steve Miller—were brought in to initiate the most massive cuts and restructuring.

Bethlehem's Lackawanna steel mill was on the chopping block early on due mainly to the construction of the greenfield (i.e., brand new) Burns Harbor mill on the southern shore of Lake Michigan. Lackawanna was a huge plant, employing twenty-two thousand workers in 1963. But in 1982, Donald Trautlein, the outside CEO brought in to make deep cuts, abruptly shut down most of the plant (including the hot end, the steelmaking half of the plant) throwing 7,300 steelworkers out of work in a town of 23,700.[55] This was "one of the largest industrial shutdowns in the nation" and decimated workers and the town.[56] Only the coke works and a galvanizing mill across the street were kept open. Yet later, in the 1990s, south Bethlehem steelworkers were transferred to the Lackawanna coke works. Even within the corporation, some places were deemed more expendable as others were protected, perhaps not for entirely "rational" reasons.[57] Deindustrialization played itself out in seemingly irrational and contradictory ways—ways that often pitted one plant against another in an effort to increase profitability and maintain steelmaking and steel jobs in some communities.

US Steel and Bethlehem Steel may also have tactically altered strategies for downsizing and plant closings in response to strong working-class resistance. Uchitelle argues that steel companies changed their tactics of deindustrialization after the much-publicized community-based protest over the closing of Youngstown Sheet and Tube's Campbell Works and a number of US Steel works. After this, steel companies "got into the practice of shutting down a plant department by department, eliminating a few hundred workers in each action, spreading the process over months."[58] Hinshaw posits that this new, more incremental method of plant closings "impeded mass mobilization."[59]

Bethlehem Steel, unlike US Steel, also initiated a campaign to influence government trade policies. The steel industry understood that under US post–World War II hegemony, for example, capital was invested in Germany and Japan, supporting the development of their steel industries. New steel mills were located on greenfield sites, using the latest technology and design, and situated close to deep water ports. Developmental states in Japan and Germany supported the growth of the steel industry through subsidies, tax and tariff policies, extended loans, and minimum price laws. As these countries looked for markets for excess steel production, under Cold War politics geopolitical considerations often took precedence over domestic steel support in the US. The US opened markets to allies' imported steel, even as Japan and Germany protected their own steel industry from foreign imports.[60] In 1977, "the only open market in the world [for steel] was in the US."[61] Financial elites in the US, gaining power, lobbied for free market policies as crucial in ensuring timely debt repayments on the part of overseas producers. Imports claimed a larger and larger share of the US steel market, exerting even greater pressure on domestic steel producers during periods of global recession. State-level policies in the US also favored greenfield minimill investment over technological upgrading at the vertically integrated mills.

The steel industry found itself in the contradictory position of having to accept the tenets of a post-Fordist, free-trade model of development supporting the financial sector at the expense of manufacturing. Industrial elites could not argue for the federal subsidies, preferential tax treatment, and low-cost loans that many foreign-based steel companies received from their governments, because a developmental state model had become ideologically unacceptable in US discourse. But they could, and did, advocate for enforcement of WTO-sanctioned foreign trade laws. This led to tensions between Bethlehem Steel and US Steel in the 1980s. Bethlehem opposed strategies supporting free-trade policies, instead working with unions to lobby the US government to institute trade restrictions preventing the dumping of cheap imports from foreign steel producers.[62] This partnership in opposition to imports was visually represented by painting the slogan "Stop steel imports" on a giant I beam in front of Bethlehem's union hall, a sentiment both workers and management could support.

Both US Steel and Bethlehem Steel aggressively rationalized steel production through downsizings, shutdowns, and undermining the strength of the union. In South Bethlehem the steelworkers I spoke with experienced twenty to thirty-five years of this, years in which many managed to hang onto steel jobs and some of the Fordist wages and benefits that accompanied them. But this long, drawn-out process was painful, characterized by acrimony and disenchantment. In 1998, when Bethlehem Steel closed the Bethlehem coke works, the same I beam that allegedly represented management-union cooperation was repainted by a union officer to say "Bethlehem Steel new coke works—Peking, China" on one side and "steels coke works closing, Hank's big $$" (referring to CEO Hank Barnette) on the other. Jerry Green, the union president, stated at the time that he saw the corporation reneging on its former opposition to foreign imports, as they would now import coke from China to use in US steel mills, and that big salaries and golden parachutes to executives like Barnette were killing union jobs.[63] As far as the union was concerned, by 1995 cooperation and partnerships with management were dead. Instead, they were engaged in a fight to keep the mill open as long as possible to access pension-eligible retirements and hold onto jobs.

Bethlehem Steel's and US Steel's strategies restructured political and economic arrangements in the US (and globally) so as to strengthen capitalist classes, with devastating consequences for steelworkers. They displaced many workers from their jobs and created a system of lean production for remaining workers within steel mills that undermined union strength, sped up jobs, and outsourced productive work. The much-discussed conundrum of this strategy to increase productivity through reconfiguring the steel mills is that downsizing and layoffs drove up the legacy costs of the private welfare system (e.g., health care and pensions) agreed to through collective bargaining. This meant that there was enormous pressure on corporate elites to shed responsibility for legacy costs through aggressive accumulation by dispossession, to literally transfer the assets that working-class Americans had gained through the compromises of the Fordist postwar period to the new financial and industrial elites.

RESTRUCTURING THE BETHLEHEM MILL

The Bethlehem mill workers experienced this contradictory, long-term downsizing in varying ways, depending on their jobs, shops, and divisions. Frank Behum, in his 2010 book of interviews, asked workers when they first became concerned about the future of the Bethlehem plant; many referred to events of the 1970s. Manager Dick Adams points to Bethlehem Steel's failure to secure the contract for structural steel for the World Trade Center in 1970: "The thing that really rattled everybody's cage is when the steel for the World Trade Center was not awarded to the Bethlehem plant . . . the builders of the World Trade Center chose a Japanese supplier to provide structural beams that we were rolling in the Bethlehem plant. . . . We could see that the demand was being spread out across the entire world now)."[64] Bethlehem Steel underbid US Steel, but the Port Authority of New York and New Jersey opted for multiple contracts with steel companies, many of them using foreign steel to build the skyscrapers.[65] This led to the closing in 1976 of Bethlehem Steel's Fabricated Steel Construction division, which had employed seven thousand workers at six plants (including the one in Bethlehem).[66] The fabricating division was much respected in the corporation for its role in building such symbolic structures as the George Washington and Golden Gate bridges and the National Gallery of Art in Washington, DC.[67] The early closing of an entire division exemplified Bethlehem Steel's increasingly aggressive stance toward labor, as the company fought to lower labor costs in an environment in which fabricating was facing competition from smaller, more flexible independent contractors. When Bethlehem Steel demanded a 10 percent wage concession from Fabricated Steel Construction division workers, citing a decline in demand, workers rejected the proposal, offering concessions in health benefits instead. Much to the surprise of workers and the union, Bethlehem Steel responded by shutting down the division, throwing seven thousand laborers out of jobs and sending a strong message to workers and to the union.[68]

Lorenzo Quaryle, who started working in the fabricating shop in 1974 at age twenty, found himself laid off only two years later. He was unlucky in what had seemed like an excellent initial assignment. Lorenzo finally was called back to the steel foundry as a molder apprentice and was optimistic about his new position because "I was told you're safe here, you're not going to be laid off. Well, a year and a half later, I *was* laid off." After eighteen months of layoff, Lorenzo came back to the mill, but that did not last either. "Eventually, Bethlehem Steel decided to get out of the tool steel business," and he was laid off again. "There were several years," Lorenzo says, "that were very difficult years for me. . . . I was trying to keep my house . . . and I had a tough time of it." He was out of steel work, going through a divorce, selling appliances at Kmart, and it was hard: "my refrigerator was mostly empty at that time." Eventually, Lorenzo was rehired at the mill's boiler house, where he stayed, working as a millwright until its 1998 closing.[69] For Lorenzo, insecurity came early in his career, as he had the misfortune to begin in the very first department to be shut down at the Bethlehem steel mill, then bounced into two other early downsizings.

For many workers however, the realization of problems confronting Bethlehem Steel came later. Many defined the problem as foreign imports. For carpenter Carl Rieker, local events drove the point home: "I came to the realization that the plant was in trouble about 1985 . . . building that Comfort Inn with foreign steel while the Beam Yard was a mile and a half down the road. Now something stinks. Now that wasn't the union's fault. That was the company's fault. That was the people that built the Comfort Inn with foreign steel and foreign labor."[70] The company and the union, together, began to define the "problem" as foreign imports, and to combine efforts lobbying the federal government for import restrictions.

Other workers interviewed by Behum first saw changes within their own department in Bethlehem. Glen Snyder, a millwright, cited the 1981 closing of the Alloy and Tool Steel Division as the cause of his first anxiety about the future of the plant. "They said they went out of the alloy and tool steel business because there was no profit and there was no work. . . . How can you go out of a business when the technology and the demand for higher and better alloy steel is greater all the time?" Snyder attributes the decision to close the department to disinvestment—"the equipment we were using, was just really that ancient. And alloy and tool steel business, you should jump in with the latest technology you can get."[71] Workers resisted justifications of closures that focused on rationalization, arguing that the division was profitable, when it closed in 1981.

The first concessionary contract in basic steel came in 1983, after a long period of negotiation during which many steelworkers (including the local branches of the USW in Bethlehem) fought against granting concessions, interpreting the 1980 to '82 recession as a temporary cyclical downturn in steel demand rather than a structural transformation.[72] Many steelworkers remember this contract bitterly and link initial concerns about the Bethlehem plant to that event: "When they asked us for that money back. . . . And I hated to do that. That was my mortgage payment. And what happened with that? . . . What did I ever get out of that?"[73] These workers link the decline of the plant directly to Bethlehem Steel's strong offensive against labor in the 1980s. Ray Rosati, a maintenance worker, said he knew the plant was in trouble "when the air traffic controllers were squashed and fired. I knew this country was in trouble, and I knew the Bethlehem Steel was in trouble. They were breaking the union."[74] Many political and economic factors were mobilized in attaining the 1983 concessionary contract including using the threats of closing up entire divisions, closing down mills, and bankruptcy to demand union concessions.

The Bethlehem Steel Corporation, and the south Bethlehem steel mill, did not survive these processes of restructuring, of deindustrialization. At the Bethlehem mill, the hot end closed, with a poignant last-cast ceremony, in 1995. When the coke works shut down in 1998, the Bethlehem Steel Corporation ended its long history of production at the Bethlehem plant. The company filed for bankruptcy in 2001, shedding its pension and health care obligations to workers in the process and emerging ripe for purchase by vulture investor and New York financier Wilbur Ross. Eagerly building a huge steel company from the devalued plants of other companies emerging from bankruptcy, Ross represented himself as the savior of the vertically integrated steel industry. He had purchased LTV Steel a year before, after its bankruptcy, and in adding the Bethlehem plants, Ross' International Steel Group (ISG) became the second largest integrated steel producer in North America. The shock of the bankruptcy process enabled Ross to negotiate favorable contracts, further driving down labor costs through laying off workers at the plants, negotiating reduced job classifications, and cutting wages. Without the burdensome legacy costs of pension and health care commitments to retirees, the newly formed ISG became a valuable asset for international companies seeking access to US markets. In 2004 global giant Mittal purchased ISG, then merged with Luxembourg-based Arcelor (in a hostile takeover) in 2006, becoming the world's largest steel company. Some of Bethlehem Steel's mills are run profitably today under Cleveland-Cliffs, who bought out ArcelorMittal USA in 2020. But with the exception of the small Lehigh Heavy Forge—a press forge operating with a highly skilled, predominately white male work force of about two hundred—there is no steel production left at Bethlehem's massive works, a plant that once dominated the city.

WORKER EXPERIENCE OF RESTRUCTURING

In the steel industry, workers were dispossessed of assets gained in the Fordist period (secure jobs, living wages, health care benefits, and pensions) through processes of deindustrialization including layoffs, job loss, and bankruptcy. Although workers often find that there is little they can do to affect the long-term trajectory of the industry (or the corporation), they strategize as groups (through unions and other forms of collective action), households, and individuals to hold employers and governments to agreements made under Fordist contracts, to keep their home plants open, and to navigate successful retirement and transfer plans. As Katherine Newman shows, unlike laid off middle-class professionals, blue-collar laborers such as steelworkers do not blame themselves for their layoffs.[75] Workers do, however, simultaneously hold contradictory ideologies of individual responsibility, individual rational decision making ("free choice"), and the self-actualizing individual that can produce collaboration with management in attempting to make the works profitable and result in feelings of individual blame or shame when those efforts fail.

In the South Bethlehem plant, through restructuring in the 1980s and 1990s, Bethlehem Steel pursued what John Hinshaw refers to as a conscious process of "disinvestment and deindustrialization," in which layoffs; closing departments; attempted mergers, partnerships, and sales; introduction of new technologies; and new regimes for managing labor served to rationalize and intensify work in the mill.[76] Rationalization and intensification often went hand in hand with disinvestment, as, in the words of one former coke works supervisor, management "bled all the money out of the Bethlehem plant they could." These tactics were also very effective at undermining collaborative opposition, as the effect of downsizing played out unevenly across a variegated landscape of steelworkers. Older workers were able to retire early with benefits, as younger workers, with the help of their unions, focused their energies on cooperative efforts to make the works competitive, and on individual strategies of avoiding layoffs, hanging onto threatened jobs, and calculating transfer options.

Many studies of deindustrialization have examined the decline and despair of entire communities as factories closed, jobs were lost, people moved away, and houses and businesses were boarded up. Within Bethlehem, however, by the final closing of the plant in 1998 workers were spread out geographically, living in single family homes in residential city, suburban, or rural communities throughout the Lehigh Valley (or even further north, in the coal region). While the closing of the plant affected the entire city, it did not decimate Bethlehem's economy and infrastructure. Steelworkers' neighbors continued to work, businesses thrived, and the city government attempted to position Bethlehem for "development" and "progress." However, the daily lives of steelworkers were greatly affected. Their steelworks was in ruins, the culture of the workplace ended, the often multigenerational identity of the steelworker was gone, and steelworkers were out of a job. They grieved the loss of a cultural system forged on the shop floor, a sprawling plant with a complex division of labor, and a masculine world of dirt, danger, and hard work making products they could take pride in.

This long process of deindustrialization and disinvestment was at various times contested, resisted, supported, and finally accepted by steelworkers. Steelworkers and their union officials never saw deindustrialization as natural and inevitable, although that is how these processes are represented in dominant US culture. Instead, they fought long and hard, defining their struggle around the issue of keeping production going and jobs extant at their home plant. As Frank Behum explains, the title of his book *Thirty Years under the Beam*, reflects the feeling that "we [the workers] carried that plant for the last thirty years, doing everything that was asked of us." Although in some ways the struggle may have been narrowly defined, it strongly contested company and media representations of deindustrialization as a natural result of market forces, or a result of the intransigence of unions and over-the-top costs of workers. It also refuted the picture of steel production as a matter of engineering and managerial expertise, rather than workers' skills.

Kathryn Marie Dudley documents some ways that dominant ideologies blame blue-collar workers for not preparing themselves for a supposedly natural and inevitable economic transition. She shows that in Kenosha, Wisconsin, with the decline of the auto industry, autoworkers were told to simply "get on board" and position themselves for success through retraining and education as flexible workers in the new economy, rather than be stuck in what has come to be defined as an outdated industrial past.[77] The professional middle class in towns like Kenosha or Bethlehem cite steelworkers' disinterest in education, their unions' unwillingness to make concessions, and stereotypes of lazy, overpaid, workers with too much vacation time as evidence for the failings of workers.[78] In the cultural and economic environment of the 1980s, a professional middle-class "culture of the mind," environmental opposition to heavy industry, and media reports fomenting anti-union sentiment all contributed to a dominant discourse that denigrated steelworkers and mobilized sharp divisions between class factions in the Lehigh Valley. Jack Metzgar writes that in western Pennsylvania, "gone was that dense network of sympathies, power relationships and personal bonds with the larger community that had been so important in 1959 [when the community supported the steelworkers in their strike]. It was nearly impossible even to remember it."[79]

Workers, however, do not entirely accept these dominant explanations. Instead, they draw on values developed and legitimized in the Fordist era, as well as disillusionments forged in the process of disinvestment and deindustrialization of the 1980s and '90s, to articulate critiques of corporate strategies and of the government's role in them and to inform their own decisions and strategies made in reaction to these processes. Bethlehem steelworkers cite the contract between company and union, negotiated through collective bargaining and legitimated by law, as justly governing layoffs and promotions, establishing their rights to wages and benefits, and legislating work rules and processes. Workers also refer to their labor at the steel mill—the danger, the heat, the wear and tear on joints, the exposure to toxins—as moral legitimacy for their rights to wages and pension and health care promises. Workers talk about the sacrifices they had to make individually and in their family lives to produce steel—the swing shift, working holidays and overtime, commuting long distances—as evidence of the hard work they put in to earn wages and benefits. Citing the importance of industrial work for American security and economic strength, workers posit a value system in which thrift, savings, hard work, and deferred gratification should result in a middle-class standard of living for families.

Workers also point to the very real value of their steelmaking skills. Union officials like Tony Valeri saw enormous strengths in the Bethlehem plant, the greatest of which was the workers themselves, their skills and knowledge of steelmaking. Tony most regrets losing the assets of the Bethlehem workforce: "You've got to understand something, we had probably the best workforce in the steel industry. Because we're all foreign people that came from the other side. When they went to work, they wanted to make money. And that culture stayed with them, as far as I know." Creative destruction (deindustrialization and disinvestment), according to David Harvey and Eric Swyngedouw, is "not only the destruction of capital invested in places but also the elimination of local productive powers and capacities embodied in the skills, qualification levels, and know-how accumulated by generations of workers."[80] Tony understands these skills as transmitted intergenerationally, both inside and outside the plant. Inside the plant,

> In the coke works they were all Puerto Ricans. So when a Puerto Rican came in there, he talked the language of that guy, and that guy told him, "You'd better listen to me or you ain't going nowhere, I won't teach you nothing." That guy came up through the ranks, so the next guy came in, they were all educated the same way. We were educated the same way when I went in there . . . because that was the culture.

This knowledge and these attitudes, what Jack Metzgar refers to as "metal sense," built up over generations, is devalued and lost.[81] To Richard Moytzen, "it wasn't just one or two or a small group of people. It was everyone. Everyone that made this plant work. And unity, working together, was the power that made this happen. . . . It took us all being good at what we do to make that happen. And that plant ran for a long, long, long time."[82] These skills were valued and recognized by workers as the core capabilities that produced steel in Bethlehem for more than one hundred years.

As Bethlehem Steel downsized the Bethlehem plant in the 1980s and 1990s, workers attempted to hold onto their jobs and to continue steel production. In 1986, the company threatened to close the hot end, shedding 1,300 jobs in 1985, if the union did not agree to a restructuring that would eliminate 500 jobs.[83] This occurred in a local and regional climate of corporate plant closings. Locally, Mack Trucks had closed an Allentown plant, building a new one in South Carolina, and the entire Northeast was rife with steel mill closures. The union agreed to give up the five hundred jobs in return for modernization. The company did build a new mill, but it failed to come through with other capital investment, something that union officers are still upset about, averring, "they conned us on the modernization."

Union negotiations ensured that pensions and early retirement benefits were made available to workers whose jobs were eliminated. As the Bethlehem plant was downsized, older workers were offered "sweetened" retirement options, negotiated through the collective bargaining process. These included $400 per month supplemental pay to pad pension benefits until the worker reached the age to collect social security. This was a significant pension for workers.[84] Retired workers also maintained full health care coverage. Workers who retired with these benefits often did not need to find another job.

Pete Bondar, who retired from the beam yard in 1986, took advantage of the early retirement offer:

> I figured with the $400 of supplemental, it would carry me over. Later on, I realized that it wasn't that big of a deal because they would take taxes and stuff out of that. So it wasn't $400, it was more like $300 some. And then by retiring, the other guys, there wasn't enough guys to do a job, so these guys are working six, seven days a week, and they were making big bucks. And me, as inflation rose, my pension, which was a little over a thousand dollars, it's still the same.

Pete sees, in hindsight, that early retirement may not have been the best option. Had he continued working, his pension would have been significantly higher, as the "lean" remaining labor force made higher incentive pay and worked more overtime, thereby adding to their final pensions.[85]

Tony argues, "by giving up those jobs, getting the new mill, we kept the plant running for sixteen more years, we got sixteen more years of pension." But he also thinks "management was smart. Their strategy was reduce the work force, and let them work all the overtime they want. We don't have to pay the pension." This strategy of layoffs and early retirement combined with increased overtime leading to retention of a "core of high seniority workers" is documented in the Canadian steel industry as well.[86] Laying off younger workers reduces labor costs without adding legacy costs. But while early retirements reduce wages, and the increase to pensions resulting from overtime work strongly motivates more senior workers, both these strategies rely on inflating retiree health care and pension expenses in order to cut current labor costs. This is seemingly a nonsensical strategy without some expectation of underfunding pensions, or anticipation that something will happen to change legacy costs in the future (as it did, through the bankruptcy court in Bethlehem's case).

As Bethlehem Steel started closing entire divisions and departments, workers transferred internally to avoid layoff, using seniority to determine access to remaining jobs at the Bethlehem plant. As will be delineated in Chapter 2, internal transfer based on bidding on jobs in the plant had long been used to navigate career trajectories inside the mill. However, toward the end, as shops and departments were closed, laid-off workers used their seniority to transfer into those departments that were still operating. Many workers from all over the plant ended up in the coke works, the last department to remain functioning. The coke works was long considered the least desirable department because it was hot, dirty, and dangerous work and the air was full of noxious gases and by-products. Puerto Rican, Mexican, and Portuguese workers were over-represented in this division, as many white management and steelworkers were convinced "they could stand the heat."[87] White workers who had held skilled positions in more prestigious departments and divisions were disconcerted to find themselves at the end of their careers in the plant working in the racialized coke works. Barry Gorski, a white A-level machinist, said, "I never thought I'd end up down there. It was terrible. It stank. . . . But I did what I had to do." It was "the place no one thought you would end up in."

Union officers from this period also expressed the importance of getting workers their pensions. Curt Papp, a staff representative for the United Steelworkers International union, said, "I felt I could see the writing on the wall" in the late 1980s. "That was my theory at the time, keep the place going as long as I could, every year and every month someone became eligible for pension." Papp said the union kept encouraging senior people to take layoff and keep the young people working. "This kept extending the young guys to get more time. . . . Our goal was to keep the youngest people working at all times." Because business unionism had few tools to oppose departmental shutdowns, maintaining jobs in some departments, maintaining some steel production, and helping workers attain their pensions came to be defined as goals.

In addition to closing departments and eliminating jobs, Bethlehem Steel pursued hegemonic strategies to ostensibly incorporate workers into management decisions. As we have seen, unlike US Steel, Bethlehem Steel and some other steel companies attempted to institute participatory management practices in an effort to improve efficiency.[88] A joint labor-management team from the Bethlehem plant visited steel mills in Japan (and US minimills) in the early 1980s, looking for techniques to "streamline" production and reduce labor costs. The methods introduced by Bethlehem Steel, characteristic of flexible labor regimes, involved reshaping labor-management relations using paradigms of participatory programs in which joint labor-management committees underwent training in new techniques.[89] Management at the Bethlehem plant introduced the Partners for Progress program in 1984. Selected committees went through training in the Juran Institute, a "total quality management" approach that emphasized creating a "management-led culture of continuous quality improvement."[90] Joseph M. Juran and W. Edward Deming, the two management gurus of the post-Fordist total quality movement, had honed their approaches in Japan. Local union officer Tony Valeri remembers the Juran training sessions in which union and management personnel supposedly learned to "become the representatives: the company and the union. Everything was supposed to go through us . . . we were supposed to calm down the negotiating committee, and we were supposed to keep them from fighting." The forty-hour Juran course taught "decision making, interpersonal, and problem solving skills," encouraging workers and managers to collaborate on "teams."[91] Tony Valeri stated that Partners for Progress envisioned that "the union and the company will get together and start eliminating waste in the plant, eliminating down time, see what they can do to get the product out faster." Much of this effort was directed at cutting waste in time and materials, eliminating defects in product, and increasing productivity. Under Partners for Progress, he continued, "the union and management would sit down once a week and start different projects," cutting costs through "getting workers' input, and management's."

This new management regime was seen as an effort to increase efficiency, enabling Bethlehem Steel to respond to competitive pressures. There was a significant amount of support among workers for a program that sought labor's input in streamlining steel production, as workers felt that their contributions had never been sufficiently appreciated. Vince Baldi, a former union official, said, "They, the majority of Bethlehem Steel top management, probably enough of them knew about what Juran was, but none of them had the guts to mention this is what we should be doing. That we need these employees." Andy Vanek valued the Partners for Progress approach because he felt it was "the first attempt to actually recognize the net worth of the employees. . . . It was an attempt to mine the minds of the workforce to have a more efficient operation." This corresponds with Ruth Milkman's findings for GM autoworkers, that workers liked the ideas of greater labor participation in the design and quality of work, and a more humane and collaborative management.[92]

But just as Milkman found out with GM autoworkers, management at Bethlehem Steel failed to follow through on their commitment to the program. Although union leaders describe the initiative as important to corporate management, local plant managers had little incentive to institute real collaboration, often fearing it would lead to the elimination of middle management jobs. Workers complained that management did not reveal their true costs, obfuscating potential savings and putting workers at risk of bearing the brunt of cost savings or of losing their jobs if they revealed too much about their work load. Tony Valeri's analysis was that foremen and plant managers did not buy into the program. "People at the top said we should create a joint management/union committee. Every plant should have it. So, guess what? Management says we're dictated by the big shots across the river. We have to have a cooperative effort here, we'll do it. But if you don't have your heart in it, forget it!" Plant managers' lack of commitment to the plan, and their desire to have workers bear the brunt of restructuring, meant that the partnership was not a real "collaboration" and ensured that it was not successful.

Workers became disillusioned when, based on information they revealed in the collaborative process, cuts were implemented that affected their jobs and their departments. Some analyses argue that collaborative participatory models were thinly disguised techniques for using workers' knowledge to eliminate jobs, and many workers at the Bethlehem plant, some at the time and some in retrospect, agreed.[93] Wilbur Redline said that when Partners for Progress began he was willing, and even eager, to contribute to the participatory process in an effort to save the plant. But, ultimately, he was frustrated with the results of the program.

> We might have had six repairman, we were going to decide how many repairmen we actually really need in the power house to run the power house, because we didn't have everything running at the end. Do we really need a welder? Like they asked me, "Do you weld 40 hours a week?" Which, to tell you the truth, I was honest through that whole process . . . a lot of people lied through that whole process, union people included. All they did was try to save their jobs. I eliminated my own job. I went over to the blast furnace to work after that restructuring.[94]

Redline says, "I thought I was there to try to save Bethlehem Steel, and that's what I'm going to do here; I'm not going to sit and lie about nothing," but he ended up disillusioned, as he felt individual interests of both management and workers took precedence over saving the plant.[95] Frank Walton, a millwright, describes his frustration with the lack of recognition for worker contributions in the Partners for Progress initiative. Walton came up with an idea that would have streamlined part of boiler maintenance, and he told it to his foreman. "The repair foreman came to me and he said, 'Hey that idea you have? The engineer, he's drawing up plans for it. He's going to submit [them to] that program [Partners for Progress].' 'Oh, he is huh?' So I quick made a hand drawing and submitted it before he did." Rather than rewarding workers for new ideas, management attempted to coopt their innovations. To add insult to injury, Walton angrily related, "I got a letter that they appreciated my idea and it was a good idea. And they informed me I was eligible for a bond drawing [laughs]. That was my reward for saving them thousands of dollars."[96]

Walton's cynicism about Partners for Progress, built through this incident, prevented him from sharing later innovations. Other workers expressed
a more oppositional stance from the start, and were reluctant to reveal any
information to management. Some workers in the early 1980s were irate
with their union for negotiating concessionary contracts, giving up jobs,
and collaborating with management, and they argued for a more adversar-
ial approach.

There were, however, some other changes in the managerial regime that
workers were enthusiastic about. Most notably, toward the end of the Bethlehem plant, as more and more foremen were laid off, the union negotiated
the position of "working leader" with the corporation. Tony Valeri explained
how this worked: "They took the best incentive job in the shop and made a
working leader of the job, class 28. Up there pretty high. When the foreman
left, we replaced him and had that job permanently. It worked as good as
anything else. Workers had been there for twenty, twenty-five years, knew
just what the foreman was doing." Workers felt that this restructuring finally
recognized their skills and expertise, and resulted in a better, more effective
labor process. Dave Hrichak, who worked in the boiler house, thought the
working leader was good "because he was a union guy and couldn't really
side with management . . . you had to give and take from both sides." But,
he also thought plant foremen did not like this situation, and tried their best
to sabotage it.[97]

Some restructuring involved combining jobs, as John Pohanty describes
with the merging of two machine shops, ending up with "a much smaller shop
. . . so you wound up doing both jobs. They finally decided to save money after it was too late." By combining two jobs, as retirement ensured attrition,
the union negotiated an increase in job classification (involving a salary increase). The crafts were also combined toward the end of the plant's life, a
reorganization that many workers found highly effective. These strategies did,
however, foment some resentment on the part of departments that did not
get job combinations, and some resistance from workers who felt that they
should get the pay of two jobs for the merging of responsibilities, creating
fractions and divisions within the workforce.

In the 1990s Bethlehem Steel also pursued mergers, joint ventures, or sales
of pieces of the plant to maintain profitability. Today, workers harbor enormous resentment toward Bethlehem Steel for the failure of these corporate
restructuring strategies. One much-discussed potential joint venture at the
Bethlehem plant, in 1991 with British Steel, fell through after two years of
negotiations. The plan proposed closing Bethlehem's basic oxygen furnace

and last blast furnace (the hot end), instead sending structural beams from the Steelton plant for finishing in Bethlehem. Two thousand of the plant's 4,200 jobs would be lost. Union negotiations were crucial to the joint venture, as British Steel was seeking "a new standard for labor contracts" modeled after the nonunion minimill model of greatly reduced job classifications, more flexible labor, and salaries oriented around profit-sharing. British Steel blamed a recalcitrant union for dooming the deal, but union officials were not eager to emulate a minimill model in its entirety. One official describes visiting Nucor and Chapparal mills in the early 1980s.

> They were like working in the stone age. The problem is that there are so many other things that the union represented, not just wages. Benefits, work safety, we provided these for our workers. They [the minimills] had one guy, if that, that represented the whole safety program in the plants. They were dark, dingy, they worked 24 hours a day, had shanties that the company built. These guys would eat out on the job. It was a miserable place to work.

Union officials stressed safety and dignity at work, in addition to wages and benefits.

Each new proposal for restructuring the plant, whether it was closing departments, making capital investments, or contemplating sales and mergers, was accompanied by new corporate demands for union concessions and another round of blaming the union that generally played itself out in the local press. British Steel spokesmen blamed the union for failing to make sufficient concessions, but union officials regarded the lack of pension insurance and interplant transfer as unacceptable (enormous issues in such an uncertain and insecure context). Union officials and plant supervisors also speculate that British Steel lacked sufficient capital, that state support in England for the deal had waned, and that corporate Bethlehem and "the British" could not come to an agreement on how to restructure production functions. But it was British Steel's blame of the union that made the local news, contributing to dominant perceptions of steelworkers and their union as inflexible.

The final attempt to save steel production, after the collapse of the British Steel joint venture, was an agreement between the company and the union to restructure and modernize the plant so that it could compete with the minimills. This entailed cutting 1,500 of the remaining 2,500 jobs, dividing the plant into three subsidiaries, and modernizing (an initial investment of $105 million) by replacing ingot mold technology with a continuous caster and future electric furnaces (an additional $145 million). This agreement was announced—with the support of the city, the state, the union, and the company—with great fanfare in July 1993. Union officials, in a jam-packed meeting at Lehigh's Stabler Arena, convinced union members to give up jobs and make concessions to keep the plant running. Hank Barnette, Bethlehem Steel CEO at the time, said "we're seeing a new level of cooperation between labor and management." Don Trexler, president of Local 2599, was enthusiastic. "Getting a new caster was the greatest thing that could have happened. It was a sign they believed in us a little bit."[98]

However, a mere six months later, Barnette announced that due to mini-mill expansion, the company had reneged on its agreement, deciding not to invest in modernization at the Bethlehem plant. Pete Brekus, steelworker and editor of *Informer*, the Local 2599 newsletter, said "the company sold us a bill of goods about modernizing our plant while putting its investment eggs into its more profitable operations."[99] Resentment over this broken promise and wrath at Bethlehem Steel management was never overcome. Workers and union officials angrily remember that betrayal today.

Workers and union officials also continue to fault Bethlehem Steel for ignoring other viable buyout options from corporations like Noble Ventures and Pacific Gas and Electric for remaining portions of the plant.[100] Ed O'Brien, a former steelworker and USW district representative, could not believe that Bethlehem Steel would not consider these sales, especially as these were two well-funded companies. Noble Ventures had the capital of the wealthy Tisch brothers behind it. O'Brien relates that when the deal fell through "I got a call from Jonah Tisch, who is one of the Tisch brothers. A personal call. And like I said, these people are billionaires in New York. And he said to me that he had never been treated as shabbily in his life as he had by Bethlehem Steel." O'Brien fumes about these scotched deals. "We could have had 1,700 or 1,800 more people in here [the Bethlehem plant]." He speculates that Bethlehem Steel did not want a successful operation on their flagship site. "I still don't believe Bethlehem Steel wanted anyone to come in here and show the people on the outside that they could make this plant profitable."[101] The Noble Ventures proposal had strong support from workers, as Jack Roberts, a respected Bethlehem plant manager with considerable steelmaking experience, would have managed the steel operations.

But with the exception of a march on Martin Tower in response to Bethlehem Steel's rejection of an offer for the beam mill, this anger did not coalesce into a broader collective movement. It could be, in part, that as angry as union officials were, the only alternative they saw was to work with the company to save some jobs at the plant, to ensure that transfer rights to other plants were respected, and to attempt to roll as many workers as possible into pensions. In addition, as Jack Metzgar points out, there was not a thick web of public support for steelworkers in the community, with only a small core of workers remaining at the plant, a broader Lehigh Valley working class who were increasingly distanced from unions, and a new professional middle class planning for alternatives to steel production in Bethlehem.[102]

Dominant discourse faults industrial workers in steel and auto for not anticipating the demise of factories and the decline of the industry and preparing themselves for post-Fordist work. But the trajectory of downsizing and restructuring is a long and uneven process of concessions, promises, broken promises, and uncertainties. The terrain of disinvestment and deindustrialization, as played out over the long term, is not an easy one for steelworkers to "read," as many signals of the plant's health and of management's commitment to the plant are highly contradictory. For example, even as the plant lost jobs, departments, and divisions in Bethlehem, new technology was being installed in some areas in the plant. The $50 million upgrade of the Grey mill in 1988 and the $60 million upgrade to the coke works for environmental and efficiency improvements are two notable examples. In 1995 Tim Lewis, the Bethlehem plant president, said, "We intend to stay in the coke business for the ten-year planning horizon. In other words, in 2005, we'll still be in the coke business." But three years later Bethlehem Steel closed the coke works precipitously. Workers misread the $60 million investment, together with the words of management, as a commitment to production, often transferring into coke works from closed departments in order to get their final years until pension eligibility in at the plant. Dan Oates, a longtime worker in the coke works, was shocked by the timing of the coke works closing. "We were supposed to go to 2007, which would've given me plenty of time to get my pension." The convoluted process of buyouts, bids, and negotiations meant that even after an area, such as the combination mills, was closed down, negotiations were still in process that might restart jobs there. Laid-off steelworkers hung in a kind of limbo, awaiting the decision of Bethlehem Steel on the Noble Ventures' buyout of this mill, for example, which would have restored 430 of the 600 jobs.

The structural steel division closed in 1995, and by 1996, Brandenburg Industrial Services, a Chicago-based demolition company, was scrapping the plant, even as two thousand laborers remained at the coke works, combination mill, and Beth Forge and Centec.[103] These were the only areas still operating in the now almost-empty 1,800-acre plant, a quieter, ruined industrial landscape with small pockets of steel work. Workers watched the buildings they had labored in (and sometimes built) and the machinery they had run being scrapped by an outsourced company. Brandenburg did hire USW members, but workers harbored resentment toward some of the hirees, feeling that they had "sold their soul" to work for Brandenburg, tearing down the Steel. Anger was directed at Brandenburg and its workers. When Bethlehem Steel backed out of their deal with the union to install a continuous caster, Brandenburg was brought in to tear down buildings and "recycle the steel," either melting scrapped steel in Bethlehem's blast furnaces, or after the hot end was shut down, consuming it in its other plants. Bethlehem workers, struggling to preserve steel making at their plant, were furious at this cannibalization of the plant. Tearing down the buildings, shipping out the machinery, and scrapping the steel that constituted the built environment of their city made deindustrialization final, effectively putting an end to the possibilities of offers to restart parts of the steelmaking process. Years earlier in Ohio, the fight in Youngstown mobilized around US Steel's plan to tear down the Dorothy blast furnace, which was not even four years old, even as workers were scrambling to find ways to restart the plant. While Bethlehem did not have a labor initiative to take over the plant, workers hoped that buyouts could maintain some steelmaking there. As long as the mills and furnaces were there, standing, these buyouts remained a possibility. That ended with demolition.

It wounded workers to see their mill, the environment built, in many cases, with their own sweat and the sweat of their ancestors, torn down, the machinery that they knew intimately shipped off. The demolition, so antithetical to ideologies celebrating producing goods to build American strength, was condemned. The shipping of machinery to competing Bethlehem plants in Lackawanna, Sparrows Point, and Burns Harbor was derided. And the selling of machinery at fire-sale prices through brokers to steel mills in emerging countries with booming steel industries, especially to China, was criticized as downright treasonous.

When a number of skilled Bethlehem Steel workers took their pensions and went to work for Brandenburg, they encountered the raw anger of their fellow steelworkers. Tim Fuchs describes going to work for Brandenburg at the plant. "They used to scream at us and call us union scabs. They saw Brandenburg as an enemy, coming in to take their piece of life away from them." Tim thinks they were directing their hostility at the wrong entity, because "all these decisions were Bethlehem decisions. They used Brandenburg as a scapegoat," but the violent tension was real. "A guy almost attacked me, [yelling] why don't you tear Nucor's mill down, not our mill down." It was only when union officials appealed to steelworkers to respect their co-union members that tensions died down.

For the last workers in the plant, their mill, which had also been their city enlivened by the camaraderie of their co-workers, became a desolate and lonely place. Lorenzo Quaryle worked at the boiler house until 1998 at the very end, one of the last departments operating. He says that his last year, "was a very difficult time because where we worked, we were surrounded . . . by closed departments, empty structures that at one time used to teem with activity." He worked near the blast furnaces, which were

> once a hubbub of activity, making a very worthwhile product and with a lot of people. And that became a ghost town. And I always found that depressing. . . . I would occasionally walk into their welfare room. . . . It was a very haunting place because you'd see all these baskets where the workers would hang their clothes . . . all these baskets would be hanging down and the dust was accumulating and the darkness brought shadows that never existed before.[104]

Quaryle's productive city, the thriving, diverse, dynamic plant, was becoming a ghost town, an industrial ruin, before his very eyes.

Bethlehem Steel did agree to one final sale of a small remaining functioning part of the plant that had once been Beth Forge and Centec to WHEMCO. Workers argue that WHEMCO purchased this part of the plant in a process described as "asset stripping," as new corporations buy up old plants with the idea of either making them profitable or getting them at such cheap prices that they can make their investment back through the scrap market.[105] And ultimately, Centec went to the scrap market. But Lehigh Heavy Forge (once Beth Forge) continues to profitably forge huge steel components for the energy industry and the navy, and employs about two hundred steelworkers today.

Today the South Side's newly developed casino, ArtsQuest center, and public television headquarters, whose architect-designed buildings frame the historic blast furnaces, represent a reinvigorated city. Bethlehem now has a robust economy, is cited as an exemplar for creatively redeveloping the site of the old mill, and is considered a highly livable small city (see Chapter 6). The city's many industrial parks, including the most recent one on the eastern end of the steel mill site, attract small industry and call centers and have become a locus for logistics, warehousing, and distribution. The casino, with more than $1 billion of investment, anchors one end of the historic center of the former mill, and includes restaurants, retail shops, a hotel, and an events center. The dramatic, rusted blast furnaces stand as a colorfully lit backdrop behind the SteelStacks cultural center, ArtsQuest arts campus center, Levitt Pavilion outdoor theater, a public TV station, and a city visitors center—all built through public-private partnerships. An elevated walkway, similar to Manhattan's High Line, draws tourists and local residents to walk alongside the furnaces. This arts/tourist/entertainment complex has been much-cited for innovative renovation and economic development, receiving numerous commendations including a 2012 Pennsylvania AIA Silver Medal design award, a 2014 Urban Land Institute Global Award for Excellence and a 2017 Rudy Bruner Award for Urban Excellence. Officials from other deindustrialized cities, like Springfield, Massachusetts, have visited Bethlehem to study its successful redevelopment. Crowds of thousands turn out to the green spaces and pavilions beneath the blast furnaces to view the World Cup on jumbotron screens, to attend concerts on the outside stages, and for other events.

This contemporary picture stands in sharp contrast to other northeastern and Midwestern former steel cities, more commonly cited as representing depressed deindustrialization in the rustbelt. John Strohmeyer, for example, described Lackawanna, New York, in 1984 as "a city without a pulse. . . . Today, the plant lies ghostlike on the shores of Lake Erie. It is an industrial corpse, a cannibalized complex of lifeless smokestacks, black buildings, motionless and empty rails."[106] Bethlehem's Lackawanna plant was closed abruptly in October 1983, throwing 7,300 workers out of their jobs and decimating the town. Today, much of the Lackawanna mill's grounds are still unused and overgrown behind rusted fencing. These devastated landscapes of the former mills, the working-class neighborhoods, and the business districts of mill towns such as Lackawanna, Youngstown, Homestead, and many others stand in sharp contrast to Bethlehem's now-prosperous landscape and economy.

There is no steel mill in Bethlehem today. Ultimately Bethlehem Steel workers and union officials became disillusioned with the company's claims that it wanted to preserve steelmaking at the Bethlehem plant. Steelworkers in the know, especially union officials, have agonized over the reasons for Bethlehem Steel's intransigence. Why, they ask, was the corporation so unwilling to entertain and pursue viable plans for sale of some of the parts of the plant in ways that would allow some steelmaking functions and steel work to continue at the Bethlehem site? Some attribute this refusal to Bethlehem Steel's fears that competing companies might show up the once-giant corporation, generating profits where Bethlehem Steel had failed. Some attribute it to well-hidden but major environmental issues with the site lurking as a potential deal-breaker for any sale. Some cite pension issues—the desire of executives to loot the Bethlehem Steel pension fund for their own golden parachutes before the death of the corporation. Whatever the real reasons, in 1998, after years of concessions, negotiations, and shattered deals, steel work effectively ended in Bethlehem.

CHAPTER 2

The Labor Process at the Works

There is a complex labor process in the steel mill, an interaction between "productive forces, social relations, and mental conceptions of the world" that takes place on the shop floor.[1] We have seen that the steel mill occupies a central place in the post–World War II social order where steel production is at the heart of the industrial manufacturing that produced US hegemony. When workers entered the mill in the 1960s, they also entered a regime of social relations for controlling and directing labor. These social relations were formed and restructured in the forge of class conflict, consent, and compromise in which managers exerted control over workers' productivity, and workers resisted this control through their union, their collaborative pushbacks, and their creative culture. Under the Fordist regime, relations were governed through an internal state, functioning through the rules of the union contract and the grievance process, which defined rights and citizenship in the mill. Steelworkers navigated an internal labor market to plan out careers and predict futures, and they worked collaboratively on crews to creatively make and move steel. This chapter explores these processes, showing how they were generated internally but also interacted with relations of power outside the mill, especially "native" status, race, gender, and ethnicity.

During the 1960s and 1970s, the south Bethlehem plant was an enormous steelmaking factory. Its vast multiplicity of jobs encompassed thirty-two official job classifications, spread out across an intricate landscape of production, with shops and jobs contributing very differently to the manufacturing of steel and steel products. Although most steel jobs were divided into maintenance or production work, there were also "service" jobs (patrolmen, mailmen, nurses, delivery drivers) within the plant, as well as a nuanced hierarchy of management positions. This complex division of labor, the reliance on crew work, and the dramatic differences in production processes between departments and divisions made the labor process within the steel mill quite different from the Fordist model taken from automobile factories.

Workers, who initially began at the most grueling jobs in the plant, were awed by the nature of the work itself. Matt Nichols describes his first days: "It was pretty shocking to me to see the melt shop for Beth Forge. The size of the ingots we were pouring, and the work was something that was just, to me, phenomenal. I couldn't believe that work could be so hot and so dangerous." Charlie Joyce describes his first days on the labor gang in the blast furnace in the 1960s: "It was something different, something you never saw before." Jeff Hoffert describes beginning his job at the blast furnace: "It was very different than I'd ever experienced or thought of, it's a big place, a lot of things going on, and a lot of dangers. So it kind of scares you at first . . . you saw all the sparks and the heat and it made you wonder, did I make the right choice?"[2] Pete Petrovics still "wakes up with the shakes" thinking of the "near misses" he experienced working in the beam yard. Andrew Pingyar recalls his job in the ingot mold foundry, one of the dirtiest shops in the plant: "No matter what you touched, where you sat down, you got dirty. It was just black pitch dust all over the foundry and graphite unbelievable thick all over; and if one crane would bump into another one, the stuff would come down so bad that the people couldn't see where they were working or where they were going. It was that bad in there."[3] This "dirt" caused long-term health issues including silicosis and COPD. The scale of the mill, the dirt and danger of the work, and the enormous variety of jobs and products overwhelmed new workers.

The Structure of Labor at the Mill

Workers portrayed the steel mill as dramatically different from mainstream society, but the mill and the ways that labor is constructed within it are thoroughly embedded in wider regional, national, and global processes. The patriarchal structure of the mill; the privileges given to whiteness, masculinity, and native-born status; and the measurement of "skills" through testing and credentialing through formal education are just a few of the ways that hierarchies of mainstream society are made use of and reproduced within the mill. Indeed, the mill became more "different" from the "real world" as concessions won through union organization generated a middle-class life-style outside, where union workers and middle managers often lived next door to each other in neighborhoods far removed from the sound and sight of the mills, and as steelworkers developed identities as members of the middle class in their households and communities.

The gargantuan, vertically integrated steel mill was made up of a slew of departments and shops, many of which functioned independently of each other, even while flows of materials connected disparate processes in these departments. Jim Todd, a former foreman, explains that the Bethlehem mill "was a very special example. A specialty manufacturing plant on one end and a tonnage-oriented regular steel plant on the other end [the structural end]. It was really two entities in one." The plant had a reputation for being able to produce all kinds of specialty steel in addition to structural steel. This meant a great diversity of shops and departments, three local unions in charge of different areas, and an intricate array of jobs producing steel and maintaining a vast number of both new and antiquated machines. The complexity of machinery and the variety of shops was also related to the age of the Bethlehem plant, the historic flagship that had grown along the Lehigh River for over a century. When Jim first walked into the plant "I said, by God, this place is an operating museum." With sixteen thousand workers spread throughout the bustling mill of the 1960s, very few saw every shop and department or understood every facet of steel production there.

When the union won representation in America's steel mills at the beginning of World War II, the variety of jobs in steel plants across the country were organized, for the first time, into thirty-two classes, each of which carried a base rate of pay. This formal codification of earlier job categories was compiled by the United Steelworkers, to be agreed upon with the first USW steel contracts of 1942.[4] The classification process happened on a colossal scale, as US Steel alone had twenty-five thousand different jobs, each of which had to be assigned to one of the thirty-two classifications. These new categories were published in a thick job manual to be used by management and the union.

Complexity was heightened by different incentive pay rates attached to particular jobs and tasks. During the 1950s, steel plants in the US shed many unskilled jobs, and incentive systems were expanded in an effort to increase production while reducing the number of laborers.[5] In the Bethlehem plant, as in all steel mills, incentive payments supplemented base wages and encouraged greater productivity. Although incentives had been used in the plant for decades, they were extended to include many more jobs over the 1960s and '70s. In 1947, a minority of steel mill jobs received incentive pay, but by

1977, 85 percent did. Incentive pay, or piece-rate pay, set for a job by a rate setter (an industrial engineer) was determined by either a direct or an indirect relation to tonnage produced.[6] This pay could constitute a significant percentage of a worker's salary, sometimes more than 50 percent.[7] Rates varied dramatically depending on the job (production versus maintenance), the specific task being done, and the amount of work or demand within the plant in any given day, week, or year. Workers in those production jobs defined as central to the steelmaking process usually made higher direct incentive pay while maintenance workers made lower indirect incentive pay.[8] Thus, incentive pay (and therefore one's total salary) could vary dramatically between jobs in the plant and at different points in the fluctuating economic cycle. Although the USW fought to make these rates more explicit so that workers could accurately calculate and check their own incentive pay, the complexity of the system ensured that no one worker within a plant the size of Bethlehem understood the variety of rates attached to different jobs. In fact, it was only through experience that workers could assess the particulars of tasks with different rates, the ebb and flow of demand, and the speed at which jobs could be accomplished. Younger workers relied on information from more senior workers and from friends and relatives in other departments.

Differences in pay between production and maintenance jobs, which were both heavily reliant on incentive rates, therefore did not coincide with a neat distinction between "unskilled" and "skilled." In much of the literature on factory work, production jobs are represented as unskilled and maintenance jobs as skilled, but in a steel mill this is a false dichotomy, as the abilities necessary for production jobs were many and diverse. Maintenance and production did, however, entail different kinds of competencies. Production skills were not as easily transferable to jobs outside the mill as some of the maintenance skills, nor were they as tested, credentialed, and formally recognized within the mill. Maintenance jobs could offer better opportunities for upward mobility within the plant. Apprenticeship systems in the crafts offered opportunities to move into the ranks of foremen, although these programs were discontinued well before the closing of the Bethlehem plant.[9] High direct incentive rates in many of the production jobs, however, ensured greater pay for those employees than for craft workers.

Theoretical Perspectives

The Bethlehem steelworkers I spoke with were hired during the 1960s and 1970s, a period in which labor processes were structured under what scholars have described as a wider Fordist regime of accumulation. Marxist analyses discuss the shift within the factory from an earlier *extensive* regime of labor discipline in which the working day was coercively extended (through lower hourly wages and raising the number of required working hours) to a Fordist *intensive* regime where the introduction of new technologies and systems of labor organization resulted in concentrated production.[10] This shift has been characterized as moving from more "despotic" to more "hegemonic" factory regimes, as Fordist management techniques developed new systems of generating worker consent, as well as coercing workers, to intensify labor.[11] The capitalist must confront the problem, described by Braverman, in which the infinite "potential" of human labor is limited by the "subjective state of the workers, by their previous history, by the general social conditions under which they work."[12] The effective use of labor power in the actual process of production required shifting from "control of work to control of the worker," that is the activation and motivation of an entire human being, inseparable from his/her labor, in the transformation of labor power into labor.[13] Under Fordism, techniques such as speed up, the introduction of new technology, and new management practices resulted in factory regimes that intensified labor, increasing productivity. Regimes that developed out of the interaction of managerial processes of coercion and consent, while responding to workers' resistances, shaped the construction of a shop floor culture, labor practices, and worker subjectivities.

The 1974 publication of Braverman's *Labor and Monopoly Capital* generated a renewed interest in Marxist understandings of the labor process. Braverman described the way the development of scientific management, based on the time-motion studies performed by F. W. Taylor and merged with Fordist assembly line practices, created a new factory regime for intensifying labor. Practices of scientific management separated the conception of work from its execution (the mental from the manual), deskilling work (breaking work down into management's "mental" assessments of the division of labor and worker's "manual" work) and producing a detailed division of labor. This system, Braverman argued, intensified labor while simultaneously shifting power from the worker to management, reducing worker control over "craft" and the labor process and contributing to monotony and alienation. Braverman's discussion is particularly pertinent to Bethlehem Steel, as F. W. Taylor performed his famous time-motion studies with "Schmidt" (a Bethlehem steelworker) in and around the Bethlehem plant's No. 2 machine shop. Taylor was, however, fired from the Bethlehem plant, and Bethlehem never as fully adopted his technique as did the auto industry.[14] Steelwork, unlike assembly line work, proved more difficult to disaggregate into a detailed division of labor.

Braverman's emphasis on the alienation and dehumanization of workers through scientific management contributed to a general understanding of Fordist industrial work as "monotonous assembly line operations where 'deskilled' drones bide their time until the final whistle blows."[15] Researchers interviewing US factory workers documented dissatisfaction, finding that many assembly line workers did not like their jobs. Instead, they worked to have time off, to support and provide for their families, and to maintain a standard of living that included home ownership and high levels of consumption. This research described the compulsion to work as instrumental, driven by the need to maintain a culturally defined standard of living influenced by new forms of consumption and affluence in the Fordist period. This motivation, combined with values of sacrifice and deferred gratification, provided an inducement to work at alienating and dehumanizing jobs.[16] Given the perceived lack of meaning within work, many researchers turned their attention to the family and community, and tried to analyze the ways that market-structured consumption practices propelled people into working-class jobs. These researchers are interested in what compels people to work, how workers forge dignity in a Fordist regime that does not provide self-worth in the workplace, and why workers don't organize more resistance to such an alienating and exploitative environment.

In the late 1970s, social scientists responded to Braverman's analysis with an array of critiques. Critics disparaged his prioritizing of exploitation in the labor process while failing to give sufficient attention to the mechanisms through which hegemony is established in the workplace, what Burawoy called the "manufacturing of consent."[17] In the hegemonic management regimes of Fordist capitalism, Burawoy finds that labor is intensified not simply through the coercive disciplinary regime of scientific management, but through the building of worker consent on the shop floor using a variety of managerial practices.[18] Burawoy identifies specific structures at the point of production that generate worker cooperation with profit-oriented goals. He points to the importance of an internal labor market in representing to workers the idea of individual "choice" in jobs, a control over their own career trajectories. This was certainly true at Bethlehem Steel with its highly variegated work force and jobs at different incentive rates, classifications, and skill requirements. Burawoy discusses the role of the union-policed and regulated internal state, including the collective bargaining process and the grievance system, in individualizing worker dissatisfaction and limiting worker demands. According to Burawoy, the legally codified collective bargaining process removes the worker from negotiating (as he is represented by his elected union officials) and narrowly defines the issues available for bargaining, limiting them to wages and benefits. The grievance system is a labor union process, supported by the state, that transforms collective issues into individualized complaints. Burawoy also examines the importance of workers' agency in constructing their perceptions of choice through the use of individualizing shop floor "games" that make work more engaging but simultaneously function to increase productivity.[19] He argues that these characteristics of Fordist factory regimes generate worker consent to the labor process.

Burawoy's analysis directs attention to the importance of analyzing how consent is generated at the point of production, on the shop floor, not simply outside the mill through the affluent consumption practices of the Fordist worker. He shows that workplaces have been, and continue to be, powerful milieux for class formation and the shaping of class identities. The Fordist labor process that Burawoy delineates, with an internal labor market, an internal state, and workers' game-playing on the shop floor, did generate a system for mobilizing worker consent at Bethlehem Steel. The internal labor market at Bethlehem Steel functioned as an avenue for individual workers to exercise choice in bidding on jobs, and to generate consent to the labor process, even as individual choice was shaped and structured through gender and ethnicity. On the basis of union-regulated seniority, steelworkers could and did bid for jobs as they became available in the plant. Following Burawoy, this gave workers the perception of control over career trajectories, generating what Bourdieu would characterize as *amor fati*, an acceptance of the parameters of the existing system.[20]

However, in contrast to Burawoy's interpretation, the internal labor market did also produce real rewards and real management accommodations to workers. These gains construct dichotomous tendencies on the shop floor—on the one hand improving workers' lives inside and outside of work, but on the other generating a successful form of capitalist accumulation (contributing to workers' own exploitation). Halle, for example, documents how New Jersey chemical workers were able to exercise individual and household strategies in bidding internally for jobs: choosing jobs on the basis of variables such as pay, schedule, how interesting and how grueling the job was, and job security.[21] Bethlehem workers also weighed information about job classification; incentive pay; how "dirty," dangerous, and difficult the job was; work schedule; and variety and interest in the job in decisions on bidding. These variables were weighted differently depending on where workers were situated in the family or life cycle, and workers were influenced by their access to information and mentoring (often determined by gender, race, and ethnicity). The importance of different variables changed as processes of deindustrialization shrank the Bethlehem plant, as in later years job security, for example, became an increasingly important factor in bidding on jobs. But bidding in a robust labor market did allow workers to exercise some power over the linear narratives of their lives. Simultaneously, however, variation in pay and a structure that individualized the bidding processes could fragment working-class solidarity. It created interdepartmental resentments and conflicts over unequal pay, and generated individual rivalry, with workers keeping their bids secret from co-workers who were potential competitors for the positions.

Also contrary to Burawoy's assertions, the choices made in negotiating the internal labor market do not all happen at the point of production. Instead, the planning of a linear narrative for one's life is also shaped by broader residential patterns (such as home ownership), entrepreneurial opportunities and ideologies, and gendered understandings of household relations. There is a complex relationship between ethnic and gender identities constructed on the shop floor and roles and identities shaped outside of work (in household relations, kinship networks, school, etc.). Production workers, for example, often bid into or stayed in direct-incentive jobs precisely because they were some of the highest-paid hourly positions in the Bethlehem plant. Many production workers making direct incentive pay describe themselves as "hungry," willing to work long overtime and holiday hours. Part of that hunger is itself created through the production games of "making out" or competing with co-workers. When workers in the shipping yard, where steel is loaded onto railroad cars to leave the plant, say, "What do we make in the beam yard? We make money," *money* is not merely pay, it is also a measure of one's competence and respect. "Making money" is a way of demonstrating skill in manipulation of machinery, knowledge of shortcuts, and expertise in outwitting rate setters, and is respected by co-workers.[22] But the hunger to work at these production jobs is also produced outside the mill. Fred Bachman, in his role as the primary breadwinner, was a "hungry" worker, because, as he said, he had to support his stay-at-home wife and five children. Traditional gender roles within the household generated demand for the higher production wage. But gender relations outside the plant were also shaped by these production job choices, as swing shift work ensured that many wives of production workers could not work full time. The wives of beam yard workers—who volunteered for overtime opportunities in addition to regular swing shifts—had to take on the lion's share of responsibility for childcare, housework, and maintaining kinship relations, since their husbands put in such long hours at the plant. Bill Markus' wife describes running the household, doing housework, preparing meals, packing her husband's meals, and taking care of the children, all while working part-time outside the home. "There's never an equal sharing of work," she reflected, "that's just the way it is." While earning good salaries at the steel, these families were often least well-equipped to find other work after steel, as production skills and attitudes did not transfer to other jobs, and wives lacked marketable skills.

Internal Mobility at the Plant

Many workers charted careers at the Bethlehem plant in maintenance work, which they may have found more fulfilling than production jobs in the variety of daily tasks and opportunities to learn new skills. Maintenance jobs often had schedules that were more amenable to family life and to two-working-parent families and were less susceptible to layoffs. Many of these jobs also provided skills training that then helped workers to hold second jobs during periods of layoff or after work.[23] However, depending on the shop, maintenance jobs themselves could require shift work and overtime, and some did not easily transfer to smaller scale construction work.

Workers often made internal labor market decisions to accommodate family needs. Jerry Schneider, who worked as a carpenter (a maintenance job) for much of his career, describes working swing shift and volunteering for overtime hours. "I provided the best I could. I took as much extra work, even though the wife complained, took the shift work. It paid more." This decision brought more money into the household. But, Jerry's wife, Irene, ended up leaving her job in a garment factory. His wife "tried working for a while, but couldn't make enough . . . to pay a babysitter." Wives of men who worked swing shifts and overtime at all different hours found full-time work difficult, as their husbands' erratic schedules meant that they could not be relied on to assist with childcare.[24] These economic decisions interacted with cultural values about family. Jerry decided to go for the extra work to enable Irene to stay home because, "we wanted to raise our own children," rather than relying on daycare.

Feminist scholars have shown how shifting family responsibilities in the life cycle affect women's decisions about wage work.[25] While childcare responsibilities have a much greater impact on women's work, male steelworkers in Bethlehem also navigated an internal labor market with these needs in mind. For example, when Jerry's daughter was a teenager, he moved to day shift for a while.

> She [my daughter] was showing the fatigue of me not being there. The stress. She depended on me a lot. I used to make a thing when I worked on shifts, she'd sleep on the chair and I'd check her homework. So I took steady days for a while so that I could spend time at home. It helped. When she married and moved out, I went back to swing shift.

Jerry was not unusual. Often when kids were in high school, fathers felt the need to spend more time with them, going to their sports events, helping with their homework, ensuring that parental structure and support were there.[26] Louis Moran says he started taking Saturdays off when his son was playing high school football, and when his supervisor became irritated with this, he told him "God and family comes first, everything else is after that. If you think you're above those two, you're wrong." He says his supervisor understood and cooperated with scheduling during those years. Louis's ability as a senior, white, male worker to assert his needs for scheduling to meet family responsibilities stands in sharp contrast to the difficulty that younger, female steelworkers had in negotiating any scheduling flexibility related to their parenting responsibilities (this will be discussed in detail in Chapter 4).

The internal labor market was not limited to the many hourly production or maintenance jobs throughout the steel works. Workers also could attempt to move into supervisory positions, or aim for union officer positions. These other opportunities for mobility were also shaped and limited by a variety of variables (including class, gender, race, region, and ethnicity) produced both inside and outside the plant. Supervisory or foreman positions were often made available to workers in the apprenticeship programs, generally vo-tech graduates with some craft training, who were seen as potential supervisors. The apprenticeship program at the Bethlehem plant included extensive formal training, both in class and on the job, and before the programs were discontinued in the 1980s this was seen as a route for upward mobility into management. Some apprentices saw their trajectory at Bethlehem Steel as pivoting on a central choice between active commitment to the union, or moving into management. Charlie Richter, who started at the plant in 1951 as an apprentice, said, "I didn't join the union until I graduated from my apprenticeship. . . . Then I had to make up my mind to join or not. As time went on, in my early years, I got involved with the union and the company didn't like that. They did not like it. They put me on worse jobs." The choice between union activism or management was often quite explicit. Nick Koval, also a craft apprentice, describes working so effectively as shop steward in his department that he was approached by Bethlehem Steel management and offered a foreman position. "I was offered a foremanship, but I had to not file a grievance for a year, then they would give me the foremanship. I was a steward. I beat them on a real big grievance. They didn't want to deal with me anymore." As shop steward, Nick was the visible union representative on the shop floor, often acting as a mediator between management and workers, and was the point person for worker concerns and formal grievances. Management tried to coopt Nick, recognizing his considerable skills, so that they would not have to fight against him, but his loyalties were to the rank and file.

Work with the union, while possibly generating promotional opportunities, could also create obstacles to internal mobility. Carl Weiner describes these barriers when, as a shop steward in the electrical department, he bid on a maintenance position that required testing: "because of me being shop steward, when I wanted to get a C rate, they put some roadblocks in front of me. . . . When I took the test, they gave me a test with no relevance to what we were doing. I failed." Carl went to an outside attorney, sued, and won his case, securing the job assignment as well as back pay, but some workers felt they had to make a choice—between sticking with the union or attempting to take a route into management.

Becoming a foreman was not for everyone. Strong union ties and commitments, not wanting to take on additional responsibility, or simply not seeing it as advantageous prevented many from going this route.[27] Eddie Havela, who worked as a temporary foreman for much of his time at the Bethlehem plant, was offered a permanent foreman position but did not take it. "They quoted me an amount that was considerably less [than what I was making]. It didn't make sense" to take the job. In addition, the company often preferred recent college graduates over experienced workers for supervisory positions, and a worker might put himself in an emotionally vulnerable position by setting his sights on the job. Charlie Richter tells the story of when he and a friend, in 1975, were interviewed for a management job as cost accountant in the engineering department. Charlie expressed his ambiguity about the position, saying his wife told him "that's not for you . . . being dressed up every day . . . are you going to like it?" Three weeks later his co-worker and he got letters, which Charlie paraphrased as saying "'Sorry to say, we hired two college kids, but we'll think about you in the future.' . . . Did it bother me? Yes. To a certain extent. Did it bother my buddy? Very badly. It did." Many steelworkers would never be offered a supervisory job—social networks and/or ethnic or religious background advantaged some (mostly white Lehigh Valley natives) and disadvantaged others.

Some workers found opportunities to learn new skills and access power in their positions within the union, and becoming a union officer was another route for internal mobility within the plant. Work with the union could result in further education through coursework, travel, and the development of "white-collar" skills in mediation; the opportunity to exercise power in relations with management and with co-workers; and challenge and fulfillment in helping co-workers. But union positions were not open equally to all workers. Having a job like driving a truck that took the worker to a variety of departments could help in running for office. Being respected for formal craft work accomplishments could also be an asset. Rob Greer says an important decision in his career was taking the machinist craft tests, as "that gave me credit as a union rep. This guy is a machinist, he's got the rate, he passed the test." Being in a numerically strong department and having the right connections, such as ties with union officers, were also helpful. Curt Papp credits his success as a union official to a former union president who encouraged him to transfer into different shops to learn how they worked, making him a stronger union candidate and a better representative.

Scholars critiquing Braverman attempted to link specific factory regimes with an epochal approach to capitalism (associating different regimes with Fordist or post-Fordist orders).[28] In the epochal approach, much of the focus in labor process studies has been framed within an understanding of factory regimes under advanced capitalism progressing from coercion to consent.[29] Many scholars argue that more consensual regimes were instituted with monopoly capitalism and the accompanying Fordist systems of labor control, with assembly line technologies and practices of scientific management. Lee critiques this, asking social scientists to further explore "under what conditions is consent or coercion the key problematic for labor process analyses."[30] She argues that in an unevenly developing advanced capitalism, varied factory regimes may be related to different labor markets, and labor supply and demand may be shaped by gendered familial relationships as well as managerial ideologies.

Diverse technologies used in different industries may also shape regimes of labor control. Sociologist Ruth Milkman criticizes social scientists who elide mass production in monopoly capitalism with the Fordist revolution of the moving assembly line. She points out that in some industries, such as steel, "machinery did not exert sufficient control over labor," necessitating a greater reliance on incentive systems.[31] More recently, researchers have pointed increasingly to the competition and coexistence of various forms of labor control within different kinds of factories in regions and in countries in differing positions in the contemporary global economy.[32] The notion of a progress-oriented development of Fordist monopoly factory-based capitalism, managed through ever-more refined systems of scientific management, has been contradicted by the uneven geographic development of contemporary globalized capitalism. Harvey points out that today, "competition between different labor systems becomes a weapon to be used by capital against labor in the struggle to procure surplus value."[33] Neither Braverman nor Burawoy predicted the proliferation of these forms of labor control in advanced global capitalism and the resurgence of US sweatshops. Corporations use a variety of strategies to control labor, including the "spatial fix" of closing factories in the US and moving production into more despotic regimes overseas. Inside the US, they have increasingly used coercive systems of "management by stress" simultaneously with the "high road" expansion of consensual, team-oriented workplaces.[34] This produces a highly competitive terrain that often results in the devaluing of industrial labor through a "race to the bottom." The degree of coercion versus consent in factory regimes also differs in relation to ways "the broader political apparatus intervenes in the regulation and reproduction of labor."[35] Thus regimes of labor discipline are not constructed on isolated shop floors. The power of both shop-floor management and workers is embedded within wider systems of state control, and broader cultural and social processes.

The Plant as a Site of Social Reproduction

Burawoy does not sufficiently examine the way that internal labor markets are shaped by a gendered, racialized, and ethnicized industry-based division of labor. The proliferation of research on gender and work in the 1990s, including many studies of women factory workers in peripheral countries, explore these multiple means of degrading labor. These studies show that labor degradation is not limited to strategies of deskilling, and that the concept of skill is itself often constructed in racialized and gendered ways. They explore ways that racial, gender, and ethnic ideologies devalue labor through regimes that make use of broader social and cultural constructions of gender and ethnicity, and how, at the point of production, "that [societal] construction is constitutive of and constituted by power relations in the workplace."[36]

Bethlehem Steel, and the US steel industry, had a long history of organizing entire departments and shops at their mills along lines of race and ethnicity. Workers coming into the mill in the 1960s remember encountering the effects of this system. Historian Judith Stein shows that in the northern plants, "blacks and immigrants from Southeastern Europe" were concentrated in hot, dirty departments requiring manual labor. Stein also points out that the union was able to moderate the impact of essentialized notions of race and ethnicity on work assignments when its wage classification program raised pay rates for jobs in unpleasant environments.[37]

At Bethlehem Steel managers recruited labor using racial and ethnic stereotypes about the characteristics of laborers and suitability of labor pools. In the 1960s Bethlehem Steel used advertisements, employee recruiters, and kin-based networks to hire workers from both Puerto Rico and the Pennsylvania coal country for the least desirable jobs in the plant. Puerto Rican workers were defined as naturally suited for jobs in the coke works as they could "take the heat," and "up-homers" from the coal regions were seen as having a strong work ethic. In the plant's standard practices, new hires were either assigned to one department or were given a choice of departments. Those with fathers who worked at the plant (i.e., native-born Lehigh Valley residents), who had some relevant education related to manufacturing (at local vo-tech or college), or who knew people in management were offered more and better placement options and were able to evaluate them. Valley "outsiders" (from farming families outside the Valley or up-homers from the coal country) were not offered the same choices and lacked adequate information to assess their options. Non-white laborers were assigned to the very worst departments. Puerto Ricans, for example, were assigned to the coke works—a hot, dangerous, low-paying department—on the basis of race/ethnicity alone. Even when they were Bethlehem-born, second-generation steelworkers, Puerto Ricans were generally given the coke works as an initial assignment and usually were not offered any choice. Ed Ramos says, "when I went to apply, they read my name and said, 'You're the type of person that we need at the coke works.' I didn't realize what they meant by that until I got down there."

White steelworkers who came from outside the Lehigh Valley were also disadvantaged in initial assignments, although, unlike Puerto Rican applicants, they were generally given choices. Yet, because they lacked knowledge of the mill, they were not prepared to choose between initial departmental options. Rob Cuny, an earnest white steelworker, came to Bethlehem to find work after being laid off from a silk mill in his farming community west of the Valley. When he went into Bethlehem Steel, "they gave me two choices for work. I think it was iron foundry and the coke works. . . . I don't know why I picked the coke works. It was one of them things. . . . I didn't know anyone who worked at Bethlehem Steel at the time. Didn't know anything, going in blind." Rob could have made significantly more money at the iron foundry, but he had no knowledge of the plant on which to base his initial decision, so he chose the coke works.

To add insult to injury, after initial assignment to a department, internal mobility through transfer and promotion based on seniority was also differentially accessible. Workers had dramatically differing access to information about various job openings, and this information was crucial in navigating an internal labor market complicated by the incentive-based pay system. As a result, worker strategies vis-à-vis internal mobility were often convoluted, and options were not always neatly divided between production and maintenance jobs. Because different shops and departments, as well as the frequency of specific tasks, might influence incentive rates and schedules, this information was vital in planning the best career trajectory. Those with social networks inside and outside the plant connecting them to management or to union officers were advantaged in bidding on jobs. So were workers with positions that exposed them to different departments at the plant since they could discover factors—such as dirt, danger, the opportunity to learn new skills, the schedules, and the incentive pay—that would prove invaluable in deciding to bid on jobs. Access to this knowledge was heavily affected by gendered, racial, and ethnic divisions of labor, as minority workers were less likely to access advantageous social networks and more likely to be confined to jobs in less desirable shops. Thus, women, Puerto Rican, and African American workers relate very different experiences and understandings of mobility within the plant and the internal labor market than do white, male workers (see Chapter 4).

Prior to a 1974 consent decree mandating plant-wide seniority, internal mobility generally occurred within one's department, as seniority, and thus promotional lines, were departmental.[38] This meant that the department to which a worker was initially assigned overwhelmingly influenced his or her salary, promotional opportunities, and opportunities for learning new skills. Because of this, a number of law suits for discrimination were filed against Bethlehem Steel, US Steel, and the USW. In the suits against Bethlehem Steel, race-based discrimination at the Sparrows Point and Lackawanna plants was central. The suits resulted in court decisions mandating plant-wide seniority, bringing about the consent decree, filed by the Equal Employment Opportunity Commission (EEOC) in 1974 and applied to nine steel companies, including Bethlehem Steel. In accepting the consent decree, Bethlehem Steel acknowledged its role in racial discrimination and agreed to pay a settlement to aggrieved workers, to replace departmental with plant-wide seniority, and to establish goals for hiring minority workers.[39] At the Bethlehem plant, this resulted in the hiring of women for the first time since World War II and in granting plant-wide seniority to all workers (including Puerto Rican, Portuguese, and Mexican employees at the coke works). This ostensibly provided much better opportunities for minority steelworkers who could now bid on more desirable jobs.

However, the consent decree did not eradicate gendered and racialized barriers to mobility within the Bethlehem plant. Even after plant-wide seniority was mandated, most Puerto Rican workers did not transfer out of the coke works, or they transferred briefly, only to return. Puerto Rican workers describe encountering hostility in other departments and experiencing exclusion from the "camaraderie" of the workplace culture and from the mentoring that was crucial in learning new jobs.

Women hired in the 1970s who had worked hard to overcome initial resistance and hostility and develop collaborative and supportive social relations with co-workers found that transferring to a different department was very difficult, as they would have to once again work against sexist attitudes and practices. Women were also discouraged from applying for job opportunities by male supervisors who had low expectations for female workers (see Chapter Four). Black, Latino, and female labor was devalued on the shop floor, through the ways gender, race, and ethnicity were embedded in the wider community influenced the regional labor market and were used in the mill to create an internal labor market of segregated departments and unequal promotional opportunities.

The Culture of Labor

Braverman was also much criticized for failing to examine the role of worker struggle and agency in shaping factory regimes.[40] Burawoy's analysis of consent examines worker subjectivity and agency, but represents workers as too easily consenting to management's rules for interaction. Other social scientists emphasize the importance of worker resistance, exploring the many ways workers construct meaning in the labor process, build a work culture on the shop floor, gain knowledge of (and thus control over) the work process, and develop collaborative and egalitarian social relations. Newman argues that "the image of the factory as deadening does not capture the complexity of the Singer plant, which retained under one roof a mix of skilled and unskilled workers, of complex and routinized systems of production, of highly particularized work . . . and routine assembly line work."[41] Some social scientists also critique Braverman's dichotomy of "manual and mental" labor, instead pointing to the "skills and abilities" and kinds of cognition that are cultivated in "manual" labor.[42] Dudley builds on this more complex understanding of shop floor relations and production work, documenting a rich culture that is constructed by workers on the auto shop floor, but extended into the home and community, a self-worth "bound up with the kind of work we do," embedded in opportunities to demonstrate ability, and forged through collective, collaborative labor. The shop floor culture's alternative definitions of skill and ability give meaning and dignity to manual work and generate a "day-to-day experience of cultural solidarity" around shared goals of product quality and job security.[43] In my fieldwork in Bethlehem, workers expressed the complexities of a mill environment in which deskilling, exploitation, and alienation structured many aspects of work even while applying and learning skills and creative problem solving characterized others, and where a rich workplace culture provided meaning and fulfillment to many. To argue that this culture was only a means of generating consent to the exploitation of their own labor ignores the solidarity and worth that workplace culture generated. Making sense of these contradictions may require recognizing the possibility that workplace culture has different meanings for different participants. Identities and meanings play themselves out in relation to gender, ethnic, and class positions and may be related to the "attitudes" workers bring into the workplace, shaping their experiences of processes of deindustrialization.

There is a literature that attempts to understand industrial working-class identities that are "oppositional," in contrast to those that conform more closely to dominant cultural norms and expectations. Scholars of working-class identities in Europe and the US distinguish "street" versus "decent," "ear'oles" versus "lads," "hard living" versus "settled," "respectable" versus "no good," and "reputation" versus "respectability."[44] Some analysts locate this tension in the working class to dichotomies between a middle-class identity at home and working-class identity and experiences at work.[45] Inside the family, wives are often framed as more middle class in attitude; they often have non-blue-collar jobs that contribute to different identities at work and they may develop suburban gendered identities that are middle class. Ortner argues that gender is the locus for this contradiction between middle-class aspirations and values (more feminine) and working-class culture (more masculine), and Freeman explores how the polarity of gendered ideals of "respect" (more feminine) and "reputation" (more masculine) implies a "tension within and against which people conceive, define, and enact themselves."[46] Willis points to how at work, masculine shop floor culture and work relations produce a working-class culture and identity that is, to some extent, "oppositional."[47] Workers do not all share the same attitudes and ideologies about mainstream culture, social mobility, the value of education, masculinity, and work in the steel mill. And those workers who define themselves as more "respectable" are often better positioned—through their career trajectories within the mill, their attitudes about political and social interaction, and the structuring of their masculine identities—for life after steelwork.

These differing attitudes are evident in ex-steelworkers. While many workers I spoke with were happy to be out of Bethlehem Steel, there were many others who sorely missed their work and the work culture at the steel mill. Workers who were satisfied leaving the steel mill characterized their jobs as good ones for making money and having security, but also as entrapping and stultifying. Workers like Dan Torres did not want to return to the steel mill (although he deeply regrets the loss of salary and job security), and instead tried to forge new identities in a postindustrial milieu. Dan described running into an ex-steelworker:

> He said "if the mill was open we'd still be working there. You know that, right?" And I thought for a second and I said, "Yeah, you're probably right. I would still be there." It was one of those situations where I wanted something better out of life and I was having like this dilemma of how it is that we are not an environmentally friendly business, how we . . . our health is always in jeopardy and all those things, it was, it was starting to be a challenge. So for me, when it happened it was like somewhat of a relief that I didn't have to make that decision or have that fight within me anymore.

Dan stayed at Bethlehem Steel, even while not thrilled with his job, because he was "economically handcuffed, oh my goodness, and the security . . . there is a lot of value in job security." Although Dan went to work for Bethlehem Steel straight out of high school, and his father worked for Bethlehem Steel, he no longer strongly identifies as a steelworker, and would not want to return to the Steel. Many workers, if they were able to access pension and health care benefits as they took early retirement, relished the chance to leave the mill. For Ed Ramos "things went from bad to really good when the steel closed. The closing was good for me."

These workers describe an instrumental motivation to work, sounding similar to workers characterized by many researchers.[48] For them, work was primarily a means to provide a good life for one's family, and attain future benefits. Rob Cuny, who worked in the coke works, recalls, "it was hot and dirty, but I figured, well, I'd just keep doing it cause I wanted a good job and benefits and retirement." Many workers never wanted to work at the Steel; they envisioned themselves in other kinds of jobs and yearned for a different kind of life, one with a sense of alternatives. Luke Bauer "didn't want to work in an industrial place in the first place. When I showed up in the employment office, flowered pants, love beads, long hair, a beard, I was a 'token hippy.' They hired 'tokens' all the time. I thought I wouldn't get a job offer if I showed up that way." Luke wanted to work in graphic arts, but without a college degree it was difficult for him to find jobs in this field. He "didn't like industrial work" and defined work at the steel as "a deadening routine," but found that "Bethlehem Steel paid so well, I was raising a family, I couldn't afford to leave."

Some workers aspired to a different kind of life from that of their fathers. Will Hornack's father worked in the mill but "didn't want me to work there." There was a family history of two hundred years of work in the mill, and his grandfather was killed in the plant. Will's father "told me about the application there, but really didn't want me to work there. I mean he knew it was a dangerous place. It was a dirty place. And I think he wanted more for me than what he had." Will said, however, that once he started working in the mill "you kind of get stuck with the pay and the benefits."

But for other workers, like the one Dan ran into, instrumental motivations do not define the job. Many of the ex-steelworkers I spoke with would return to their jobs at Bethlehem Steel tomorrow, not solely because it paid well, but because without steel work they have lost a part of their identity, one they cannot recapture outside of the mill. They cite the feeling of fulfillment they got through the work and through the workplace culture forged on the floor of the steel mill. Jack Deutsch, who was a millwright, welder, and rigger at Bethlehem Steel for over thirty years, expressed how meaningful his work was:

> I'll tell you the funny thing about this is I still dream about the Bethlehem Steel. I swear to God, I'm the kind of person, I even ask doctors if some people do that, I have dreams all the time, dream about the Bethlehem Steel. . . . I'll get up at night, doing something, go to the bathroom. I run back to sleep so I can get back in the same dream. I missed it so much. I'll dream about things we did, at the beam yard, actually like we were there. . . . I dream so vivid, and so clear, that the guys and stuff, it's like I sometimes think I died and that's what it's going to be.[49]

Other workers also described ongoing, vivid dreams evoking the sounds, smells, and life of the mill. George Mark said, "When I dream about work, I never dream about where I worked for the last ten years. I always dream about Bethlehem Steel."

For some at Bethlehem Steel, the work on the shop floor created an alternative culture, forging social relations frequently described as entailing "camaraderie," where co-workers were "like family," drawn together by their efforts to attain some control over the labor process and maintain safety in a dangerous environment. Workplace culture was different from mainstream culture, corroborating David Halle's description of working men in the factory, leading middle-class lives in the community.[50] Jack Deutsch describes work at the mill: "It's a whole different life, you can't explain to people, you've got to be there to really see how nice it was, even though you're doing dirty, crummy, dirty jobs."[51] Andy Vanek loved his job in the beam yard. "Every day was different. You could never get bored working at Bethlehem Steel. Whether you worked for the company or the union [as an officer]. I'd work union [during the week] and weekends at the plant. . . . I'd work night or day shift. . . . I'd tell bosses if this guy wants off, just put me in there."

Carlos Rodriguez, a second-generation Puerto Rican steelworker who moved from a unionized mill job in the coke works to the offices at Bethlehem Steel, reflected on the enormous differences in the cultures of the two workplaces:

> I was a union worker for two to three years myself. Don't get me wrong. It's us versus them. The floor versus the office. That's the main thing. But it's a whole different world. There's like a . . . whole different attitude in the office. More professional. On the floor, in the mill, there's more crudeness. They play practical jokes on each other, use foul language. . . . It was like two different worlds. The mill was like living a whole, entire life.

White-collar workers and the professional middle class in the Lehigh Valley simply could not understand the culture of the mill.

Many workers got their jobs at the Steel because it was something that they and their parents aspired to, it was a family tradition, a trade that fathers had worked in, sometimes grandfathers, and often many extended family members. Their motivation to work was not merely instrumental but was rooted in family pride, skills, and expectations. That kind of intergenerational commitment to a trade is very different from the voluntary individual choice that workers are expected to make today in pursuing a flexible career, pursuing "lifelong learning" through ongoing higher education and certification, and jockeying for new opportunities and careers as they become available. Frank Havlicek recalls, "our fathers were all steel, you know. . . . It wasn't just a little whim, 'Oh, I think I'm going to put my application down the Steel.'" John Wister describes the family tradition and pride in steelwork in some Bethlehem families: "My grandfather worked in alloy. When I got my first check [from the Steel], we lived with my grandparents. He cried. He sat at the table and he cried because it was like, you made it. You've got a good job, good money, your life has just panned out okay. . . . Some people go to college and they don't have this." Shirley Macek grew up in a steel town, near the Lukens mill that Bethlehem Steel bought in 1998. She had a fierce desire to work in the steel mill that so many of the men in her family worked in.

> I came from a steel family, I came from a steel town, and I always wanted to be in the Steel. . . . I wanted to work in the plant. I wanted in that mill. . . . I just wanted to get in there and see, all this talk . . . and you would hear you have your life made if you got into the steel because you got paid well, you had the benefits, it was sort of like a respect in a steel town for steelworkers.

Shirley ended up getting in, not to the Lukens mill, but to the mill in Bethlehem.

Steelwork provided a common bond between generations and among extended family networks. Eddie and Mary Smith grew up in steelmaking families; Mary's father worked in the Steel, her first husband worked in the Steel, and her second husband, Eddie, worked in the Steel. They lived close to the steel plant, and many of their neighbors worked in the mill. Mary describes how her husband and her father "would sit there with their beers and they talk, it was always steel. . . . Everywhere you went the guys would sit there with their beers discussing the Steel. They loved the Steel. I mean it, truthfully, it was their second family . . . it was a life that you really got attached to." In this tightly knit steelworking community near the mill, steel work fueled masculine conversation and camaraderie, built masculine identities, and conveyed a shared commitment to the productive and valued work of steelmaking.

In Ruth Milkman's study of New Jersey auto workers, a group of younger, low-seniority workers accepted buyouts in 1986 and 1987 because of their concerns about future job stability and their dislike of working for General Motors. Milkman documents the complaints that workers had, characterizing auto assembly labor as monotonous and repetitive, with dictatorial management, and time that was controlled by the whistle. Workers found the environment loud and stressful, and complained that when you "find the shortcuts" in your GM job, and can do it well, "you get punished with more work."[52] They complained that the physical work was hard on their bodies. In addition, employment at GM in the 1980s was insecure, with the constant threat of layoffs. These representations of undesirable work, coupled with very desirable wages and benefits, evoke characterizations in the literature of factory workers with an "instrumental" approach to unfulfilling work.

Milkman admits, however, that this self-selected group of younger workers is not representative of all GM workers. The same was true at Bethlehem Steel. Bill Markus, a production worker in the Bethlehem beam yard says that when he was laid off, if he had not taken advantage of the early retirement offer, "I'd lose big money monthly for the rest of my life." He had the opportunity to retire while his earnings were still high (influencing the size of his pension) and with a $400 supplemental payment until he attained social security. So he retired. But, he says, many others did not:

> These guys stayed . . . some guys were just afraid to leave. You worked in a place like that for so many years, it's almost like an institution that protects you. You know, your wages are there, your living is there, everything, your whole life based on that. Some of those guys didn't have a life anymore, they didn't bother with their families, didn't go hunting anymore, they're just, you're into the steel company.

As Bill shows, many workers at the Bethlehem mill defined themselves through the close friendships they forged on tightly knit crews, the skills that were valued as necessary and respected, and the quality of the products they built, and they simply did not want to leave the steel mill.

Many workers who remained at the Steel in the 1990s had more seniority and had moved into more desirable jobs than those who took early retirement. But in addition, the work at a steel mill is very different from the work in an auto factory. The variety of shops, departments, and jobs within them; the opportunity to transfer; the option for learning new skills; the gang or crew work that forges strong social relationships; and the exercise of agency in making job choices all construct a distinct attitude toward steel work. Although there were workers at the Bethlehem plant who, like Milkman's buyout group, did not enjoy the work, who felt trapped at the steel plant, and who welcomed the opportunity to move into other jobs, there were also many, many others whose lives and identities were forged in the mill, and who found steel work highly fulfilling.

The culture of the mill contributed to the construction of worker skill and the creation of knowledge, the development of relations of solidarity, and a strong morality of rights and responsibilities. Although Fordist strategies were effective in circumscribing many aspects of workers' labor and knowledge, researchers have documented ways that workers struggle to retain knowledge, and thus a degree of control, over the labor process. William Kornblum, in his ethnographic study of South Chicago steelworkers, documented mill hand knowledge of the "idiosyncrasies of a particular mill" and the specific technologies and machinery used.[53] Experts, who do not work with the machinery every day, often don't have knowledge of these idiosyncrasies, and of the shortcuts and "grey zones" (in safety) documented by Halle, Dudley, and others.[54] As Harvey points out, "the perpetual problem of habituating the worker to such routinized, deskilled and degraded systems of work, as Braverman forcefully argues, can never be completely overcome."[55] Too much deskilling, Burawoy argues, can generate strong worker resistance and class struggle as workers become aware of the surplus value extracted, but too little and the capitalist accumulation of that value is threatened. Therefore, steel mill management recognizes and develops some skills in workers, even as workers struggle to attain their own forms of knowledge, skill, and a degree of control over the labor process. Sometimes, as Burawoy argues, that knowledge is used to consent to shop floor games that speed up production, increase productivity, and construct common interests for management and workers. But games can also collectively benefit labor gangs, as when workers in the beam yard create overtime work by slowing down and accumulating steel for the higher-paid work on holidays and weekends.[56] Knowledge and skills are also used to construct solidarity, egalitarian social relations, and a working-class culture on the shop floor as well as to free up leisure time within the working day to build these relations and inhabit the spaces of the mill.

Struggle, Knowledge, and Control

Approaches that overemphasize the hegemony of the workplace fail to pay sufficient attention to struggle. The autonomists argue that capital has to "struggle mightily" to control labor, as it is labor that has the creative ability to produce, and the ability to refuse to work, to block the labor process.[57] Workers were directly aware of this power to stop production at the Bethlehem Steel plant, and it contributed to the attitude of macho swagger and aggressive confrontation that production workers were known for. A commonly used metaphor at the plant compared it to the human body, or specifically the human digestive system—the beam yard (shipping yards) was the "asshole" of the plant, because if it closes its sphincter, everything stops. Steelworkers used this visceral metaphor to explicitly represent what Mario Tronti calls a crucial point of "blockage of the labour process."[58] In Bethlehem steelworkers grew up with a knowledge of the 1959 116-day strike. Production workers, like Al Trakas in ingot mold, expressed confidence in that power. Al was fully aware that the Bethlehem plant's ingot mold department supplied molds to a wide variety of steel producers in the US, including Bethlehem's Burns Harbor plant. This may have been an efficient means of production, but it meant that workers in ingot mold had a great deal of leverage at the point of production. Al lays this out clearly: "We used to just stop working, cut production in half or less. That [ingot mold] was the real nest egg. When you stop there, everything else stops right down the line. Like dominoes, it would fall down through all the plants including Burns Harbor." The knowledge of this ability to block production was exercised through workers' unions in demanding higher incentive rates and evidenced in the confident and assertive attitudes toward management held by production workers. Management could not operate through coercion alone, but had to grant concessions, such as paying the highest incentive rates in the plant to crucial areas like ingot mold, the blast furnaces, and the beam yards.[59] However, these confident and assertive—often described as confrontational—attitudes often handicapped production workers when they moved to jobs outside the Steel.

Although Burawoy critiques the "internal state" for generating consent through construction of narrow and individualized concerns, collectively bargained and grievable areas nonetheless included important concepts that validated worker culture and empowered workers. For example, safety measures in the contract supported values that workers constructed around craftsmanship. In the Bethlehem plant, individual skill was measured through the quality of work and through safety. The final product must be well-made, safely made, and of high quality, and workers took pride in the quality of the Bethlehem steel products they made. Richard Sennett argues that the craftsman, or steelworker, invests him- or herself in the object made "judging himself by whether or not the thing was made right."[60] Workers had to judge what was necessary regarding safety, they had to use their minds, not just their hands, to do the job effectively. Charlie Richter, who worked for more than forty years at the plant, describes this: "Them men used their heads, their minds . . . them men I worked with at Lehigh that didn't want to be foremen, these guys, there was nothing equal to them in using their mind and thoughts of a job. They used their ingenuity and their mind. Never did anything in a hurry, took their time. And they tried to explain it to you." For Richter, steel work was skilled work, requiring the merging of mental and manual labor and the sharing of knowledge.

Working safely, however, often contradicts the need for working quickly (and the use of speed-up as a technique of intensifying labor). In production jobs, speed was consented to through the game of "making out." The shortcuts that production workers use to display their skill and demonstrate their expertise at making money and outsmarting management are often in the grey area of what is safe. Part of the machismo of production work is centered in the willingness to push at those safety limits. Mike Wilson, for example, when describing working as a rigger, said, "I had to always show off, try to take shortcuts and stuff." Describing one such shortcut, he says, "I could have got disciplined, lost my job even, but I did it because I was a rigger, and let's just say it works. We were on contract at the time. The more you did, the faster you got the job done, the more money you made." Shortcuts became an issue for women working in production areas. Women crane operators describe themselves as very safe; they even prided themselves on their skill in safety. Jim Todd, a foreman at the plant, says that many women became crane operators, and "by George, they weren't reckless cowboys like the guys. Right off the bat they did a better job." But crane operator safety diligence did generate some resentment from co-workers who perceived the women as slowing them down.

Safety, like quality in craft work, requires methodical care, or what Sennett describes as "obsession."[61] Workers worried that the introduction of incentive pay to more and more maintenance jobs in the 1980s made work less safe (while also increasing individual competition between workers). Charlie Richter says,

> the craft never had incentive. That program didn't come until the mid-1980s, that they put us on incentive. And that should never have happened. . . . That's where men easily could get hurt. See. You're making the job go faster to beat your time, and you're not getting 100 percent of work. . . . Hurry up, that's good enough. Don't worry about that extra piece. You can't have that.

The craftsperson's care makes a safe, high-quality product used to "build America." A number of workers I spoke with brought up the 9/11 collapse of the World Trade Center towers as representative of the danger to the nation-state of inferior steel. The construction of the World Trade Center was highly symbolic in the life-narrative of the Bethlehem Steel corporation, as it was the first major construction contract that Bethlehem lost to foreign steel imports, symbolizing the beginning of the end for the south Bethlehem plant that produced the Grey beams used to build so many skyscrapers.[62] Bethlehem steelworkers often argue that the World Trade Center towers would not have collapsed if they had been made with Bethlehem steel, that the poor quality of Japanese imported steel, linked to new architectural techniques, contributed to the failure of those buildings, killing Americans and undermining US strength and hegemony.[63]

Conclusion

Burawoy represents the internal state as generating consent to an exploitative labor process through collective bargaining that defines labor issues narrowly, as pay and benefits.[64] Similarly, analyses of the growth of business unionism in the post–World War II period argue that unions conceded control of technology to management, limiting the definition of workers' interests to wages and benefits.[65] In these interpretations, business unionism constructed an identification of workers with business, articulated through the ideology that workers would do well if corporations did well. However, these analyses fail to recognize that collective bargaining continued to include many other issues that related to the labor process itself, and these could be mobilized by workers to support quality craftsmanship. The danger of the steel mill was one rationale for steelworkers' high pay relative to other industrial workers, and it was built into the collectively bargained contract as Article 14. This guaranteed individual workers a right to safety on the job, and the invocation of Article 14 could result in stopping the job, halting that area of production pending further investigation, and ultimately, in changing the requirements for the job permanently. Although a masculine work culture and shop floor games prevented workers from mobilizing Article 14 as often as they might, the contract did empower workers to challenge supervisors, even to the point of halting production.

We have seen that, within the mill, the labor process was a complex one. Many current representations of business unionism in the post–World War II period highlight the ways that unions failed workers, agreeing too readily to a system in which productivity and profitability in exchange for higher wages and benefits trumped all other considerations. But labor processes within the mill were more complex and contradictory than this representation. Inside the plant, the internal labor market and the internal state, mediated by the rules of the union contract and the grievance process, defined citizenship. While this "rule of law" did generate consent to the regime of production within the mill, it also constructed a more egalitarian culture there, encouraging worker voice, building solidarities, empowering workers as citizens, and making labor meaningful, fulfilling, and even life-defining for many, many workers.

CHAPTER 3

The Moral Economy of the Works

The South Bethlehem plant covered over 1,800 acres and stretched for more than five miles along the Lehigh River. Separated from the city of Bethlehem by fences and security officers, it was described as a "mythical place, at its peak [during World War II] a virtual city of 31,000 with its own police force and fire department, its own hierarchy and its own societal rules."[1] It had its own built environment and "natural" landscape, or "second nature" (including mountains, gardens, and orchards), its own sensations (sounds, sights, and climate); and its own vocabulary of vulgarity, slang, and arcane technical terms that were different from the outside world.[2] Connie Godfrey, one of the few women working in the plant in the 1980s, described the intensity, the danger, the scale, as "like a drug trip," and said that among "the flames and the danger, I felt I was on an escapade." It was "like Vietnam," in a "world of men," a world in which everything felt different.

Workers describe their initial experiences in the plant as disorienting and frightening. The habits of daily living—the showers, the clothing and "change around" (getting dressed), cooking food, and the schedule of sleeping—were all distinct from mainstream society. Workers I spoke with repeatedly said that "you couldn't understand" unless you were there. They said of their first days, "I thought I was on another planet," "It's like walking into a different country," and "[I felt I had] walked into 1930."[3] Bob Shoemaker says he would "walk through the gate and go down through the tunnel and walk into what we used to call 'the other world.' Like going down to *The Wizard of Oz* or *Alice in Wonderland* where you walk through the tunnel to another world. Another language down there too! I'd rather not elaborate on it."[4] Workers describe the noise, the dirt, the heat, the danger, and the scale of activities in the plant as initially being "overwhelming" and "scary." They recall the constant movement—of transportation (cars, buses, trains), of equipment (cranes, conveyor belts, larry cars), of people (flowing in and out of the gates at shift change)—in the bustling works of the 1960s and '70s. Bruce Ward, who started at the beam yard in 1973, remembered his first day at work:

> The scope of everything was huge! . . . It was a whole new world. It was this huge, huge facility with these overhead cranes, moving these I beams all over the place. And there were roller lines and beams coming out of the middle, and some of them glowing red, and some of them just moving along. And it was this loud, obnoxious noise, and these sirens going, and these whistles blowing. Actually, it was pretty scary![5]

Workers also describe the terrifying beauty of the steelmaking process. Dennis Mayer, who worked in the plant for years, eloquently reminisced, "the dirt, the dust, and the noise to me was like a big band, and poetry, and music, and everything else. I mean, it was just a fascinating place."

This was a masculine world, separated from mainstream society, to which most women were denied entry. Wives and daughters of steelworkers often never saw the inside of the plant. Mary Smith's father was a steelworker, and her first and second husbands worked in the mill, yet she never stepped inside the mill until one day in the 1990s, shortly before the hot end closed, when her husband got permission to bring her in on a Sunday to see where the men in her family had worked for their whole lives. Mike Holmes, who was hired in 1973 to work in the beam yards, said, "I always said every woman whose husband works at the Steel, she should come in for one day and watch what he does."

The male world of the steel mill had its own etiquette of eating, bathing, practical joking, and hygiene; its own understandings of proper social behavior; its own culture; and its own moral economy. For many, this was more real than the "real world"; the mill was a place where masculine working-class identity and solidarity were built through work and leisure in the spaces of the plant. This was different from the middle-class lifestyle that many had outside of the mill, where union workers and middle managers often lived next door to each other in suburban neighborhoods and where workers nurtured identities as homeowners, petty entrepreneurs, husbands, fathers, and volunteers in their communities.

The culture of the mill was informed by and embedded in wider regional and national processes as evidenced in the patriarchal structure of the mill; the privileges given to whiteness, masculinity, and native-born status; the measurement of skills through testing; and the credentialing of formal education. But the world of the mill also shaped a moral economy, a web of relationships of exchange and redistribution, often unequal, "that are governed primarily by morality . . . or by ethics governing a particular vision of the good life."[6] From these heterogeneous workers—with different skills, in different shops—through inhabiting and laboring in the city within a city, a collective white working class (that at times incorporated raced and gendered "others") and a citizenry of the steel mill was built.

The moral economy of the steel mill incorporated shared norms and responsibilities, an understanding of the economic roles of both workers and management and of proper and ethical behavior in the workplace.[7] These were compromises, informed by earlier regimes of morality (welfare capitalism, for example), and reached through social struggle—a "moving equilibrium" held together by shared understandings—and built through common institutions, habits, and practices (such as the grievance process and crew work). The political culture of the mill was transformed and formalized through mechanisms of collective bargaining and grievance; internalized in workers' belief systems and ideologies; enforced through informal reciprocity, obligation and redistribution; and materialized in redistributive practices such as cost-of-living increases and pension benefits. The union codified, built on, and validated some understandings of solidarity, seniority, and citizenship while ignoring others. This ethos, in turn, shaped worker interpretation of deindustrialization. Understanding this moral economy and its relation to the moral consensus in the broader society allows a deeper understanding of the indignation, betrayal, and affront that accompanied the long term processes of disinvestment, restructuring, and downsizing, and the eventual closing of the world of the mill.

Citizenship

In the US legal system, through the mechanisms of private property and the wage contract, the corporation is given privileged rights of citizenship. However, these have been tempered through a legal apparatus that recognizes the rights of unions as manifested through collective bargaining agreements. Through the wage contract, workers have what has been described as "economic citizenship," defined by Alice Kessler-Harris as "an independent and relatively autonomous status that marks self-respect and provides access to the full play of power and influence that defines participation in a democratic society."[8] Steelworkers attained economic citizenship, entitling them to benefits such as pension, health care, access to credit and mortgages, and the right to work. The economic citizenship of the family wage that constructed the "economic independence of self-directed 'earning,' as the ethical basis of democratic citizenship" gave steelworking men rights within their communities and families, with many women accessing a secondary "social citizenship" as mothers and housewives.[9]

Workers also had rights within the mill, thanks to the union and to the informal ways workers laid claim to the spaces of production and control over the labor process. The steel mill was set up as a distinct entity within which the corporation made most of the rules and laws, operating as a closed fiefdom within the larger city. The corporation did attempt to exercise tight spatial control—banning entry with gates and guards, barring photography, preventing workers from leaving during their shifts, and instituting all kinds of rules and regulations. As steelworker Will Weisner recalled, "it was closely controlled," and "once you walked through those gates, that was a whole other world."[10] In building spaces of everyday living as well as of production within the mill, workers constructed ownership rights.

Steelworkers were involved not just in producing steel, but in constructing the plant buildings; repairing, maintaining, and building plant machinery; generating electricity and water for the plant; patrolling the plant; delivering the mail; running the buses; and maintaining the grounds. They held political rights through the union, economic citizenship as manifested in the family wage, and inhabitance rights as dwellers within and builders of mill spaces. The corporate capital investment used for building materials was supplemented by the creative labor of steelworkers in constructing the spaces of production. Workers installed new roofs, maintained buildings and machinery, and constructed new buildings and mills throughout the plant. Although construction was sometimes entirely contracted out, at other times Bethlehem Steel workers raised the new mills and buildings, such as the 12- and 14-inch rolling mills built in 1975, or worked with outside contractors to do parts of the job. Charlie Richter describes working on this enormous 1975 job as a rigger: "A job like that is going to be day shift and middle shift. Very little night shift. Day shift was installing, excavating, and pouring concrete. And we would have to as riggers put the rebars in, and carpenters would make the form and that was a length of a football field. It was a very good job." Charlie took great pride in helping build this mill, in the new, innovative technology and the complex variety of workers' skills needed in building it. "This was going to be a first: belt driven and high speed. It was going to be spectacular. It was."

In those buildings, workers learned the intricacies of using the gigantic steelmaking machinery, as well as repairing and maintaining it. Dennis Mayer agreed that they felt an ownership of the mill, even though the corporation claimed it as their own, "even if you didn't build it, you earned a living on it." With a sense of ownership came pride in the massive scale of much of the machinery and the highly specialized knowledge required to run it. Workers delight in nuanced measurements (lengths, diameters) and weight capacities of machinery and the engineering details of furnaces and mills, and they highlight these in their descriptions of work.

Within the complex division of labor at the mill, certain production jobs (such as the heater at the blast furnace) were widely recognized as highly skilled, essential to producing quality steel, and demanding respect. Productive skill was also recognized and defined in relation to the skill of others, through collaborative crew work. An individual worker was not capable of undertaking major production, construction, or repair projects at the mill, but the knowledge that all workers had and the complex division of productive labor within the plant generated enormous confidence in their ability to successfully produce and build almost anything. Dennis Mayer says,

> At the Bethlehem plant we could have made an automobile with everything except the tires. We didn't have the means of producing synthetic rubber. But even the glass, we had sand that could have been manufactured into glass, our carpenters could have fabricated the dashboard, the steering wheels, things like that, the trim, the engine could have been cast in machine. Everything needed to build an automobile was there except the tires.

The immense power and self-sufficiency of the mill, in this example, emerged from the interdependence of workers with different skills laboring together to make a final product.

Workers in the crafts took pleasure in "the human delight in making useful things" and pride in the products that they created.[11] Tom Urban describes the work his father did, both at New Jersey Zinc and in construction projects around the town that they grew up in:

My dad used to, besides working at the zinc company, he learned how to lay brick, block, and stone, so there's lots of places standing that my dad built. And I just have a lot of admiration for that. And I kinda said to myself, jeez, there's nothing standing that I ever built besides my shed. But then again, there's my beads of sweat on some of the I beams in buildings, so that's something to look back on.

Workers mobilized a producerist ideology in which productive manual or mechanical labor, making the things that build the country, gives a "moral claim to the dignity of all work and to a decent living for anyone willing to do it."[12] At the Bethlehem plant, pride in productive work was linked with nationalism, as Bethlehem Steel products went into military production, skyscrapers, and bridges, building the landscape that represented US hegemony. The flagship status of the Bethlehem plant, as the birthplace of the second-largest steel company in the US and the producer of America's armaments and infrastructure, was a central component in workers' perspective and was mobilized by workers to legitimize the importance of their work. Steelworkers expressed this sentiment clearly: "you were part of the history, of the building of a nation, and that was part of your everyday life."[13] Workers cite the Empire State building, the New York City skyline, the Golden Gate Bridge, and a wide variety of military ships and weapons as evidence of the importance of the plant's production in building America, and they link the decline in America's strength, both at home and overseas, to deindustrialization, citing the 9/11 fall of the World Trade Centers as due to lack of support for the domestic steel industry. But even this claim varied within the plant, as Fred Bachman explained, emphasizing differences between production and craft workers. "The guys that melted the steel, forged, rolled the steel, they all take credit for building tanks, guns, ships, skyscrapers, Madison Square Garden. But the craft guys—you have to use your intellect, ingenuity, and experience to make order out of chaos."

A workplace culture that produced and prioritized values of seniority, citizenship, and solidarity meant that many workers did not accept the company's assertions that departments in the mill were not profitable. Over and over again, workers asserted that various departments at the South Bethlehem plant continued to be profitable, even as they were being closed. This was not just true of the Bethlehem plant but is characteristic of plant closings that both workers and the union believed that plants were profitable and productive and that it was workers' labor, skills, and knowledge that made them so.[14] A global upsurge in plant occupations and resistances to plant closings highlight this concern. For example, workers who occupied the Republic Window and Door plant in Chicago in 2008 refuted owners' claims that the plant simply was not profitable. Workers stated that they would "make money by keeping us open."[15] In Youngstown, steelworkers protesting plant closings in the 1980s argued breach of contract in court: that the company broke the promise it made to keep the plant open in exchange for concessions obtained from managers. Profitability was restored through union concessions and worker creativity, but the plant was closed anyway.[16] In these forms of resistance, steelworkers accept the capitalist profit motive, that the plant must make money. But they argue that their knowledge, skill, and labor are what make the plant profitable, even in highly difficult circumstances such as the failure of the corporation to invest in the plant. Barry Kirk, a worker at the Bethlehem coke works, argues, "Our coke was the best—in Bethlehem. Other plants were importing Chinese coke. It was cheaper, but not of the same quality. We had a customer base, we were selling to Ford's steel plant for the auto industry. We met the goals, but they still shut us down." Disinvestment is interpreted by these workers as antithetical to the basic premises of capitalism, and workers argue that even in the face of capital disinvestment and corporate managerial incompetence, their experience, skills, solidarity, and knowledge of the plant ensure productivity.

CITIZENSHIP AND SPACE

Workers struggled to control the space of the mill, the jobs they did there, and the time of the working day, although they did so within the terms and conditions of capital. The structuring of time in steel production—the swing shifts accompanying the continuous production of a steel mill—meant that workers were at the mill at all hours, weekends as well as weekdays, on holidays, and during blizzards. When demand increased but no new workers were hired, the mill demanded more overtime, and workers doing double shifts needed to catch sleep on the job, eat most of their meals at the mill, and reproduce their own labor internally to the plant. To this end, workers creatively used and constructed time and space at the mill.

The plant was a built environment as well as a "natural" landscape. Dennis Mayer says he would not have been happy working in a factory:

> I could never work in a factory. I liked the outdoors. That's why I chose forestry when I went to school. I didn't want to be confined. But the steel mill wasn't like

working in a factory—where you're making shirts, or making stoves, or making refrigerators. That was a big place. There was a lot of outdoor space and things. Between the buildings and things like that . . . we walked to most of our jobs.

The outdoor space of the steel mill, because it extended across so much land, embraced a variety of landscapes, including agricultural ones. Workers walked the land, they explored the geography (and they love to talk about the geography of the plant with co-workers, just as longtime residents of a city do), they took disallowed photos, and they kept material keepsakes from the plant. Charlie Richter describes the landscape of the plant:

> But them buildings out there at East Lehigh, when we were going out there in my time there was a lot of peaches, pears, and apples. Trees that were out there. Oh my God, lots of trees. It was all farmers fields before. They never tore them down. No, they let them grow, and they were good peaches. On middle shift we used to go out with our truck and pick peaches.

The East Lehigh section of the plant was an open, natural area with deer and other wildlife. Workers called this area "the cabbage patch" after the gardens that steelworkers cultivated on the hillsides in the summer time. Workers would fend off the deer and harvest and cook the vegetables that they grew there, especially on weekend shifts when there were fewer supervisors present.

Workers also literally constructed their own personal spaces within the mill, using their abundant steelwork skills. They built heaters to warm themselves in the winter, cook stoves to make elaborate meals, machines to brew their morning coffee, and "beds" on which they could lie down to nap. In "primitive," dirty, and unrefined places, workers built the technology to support their leisure activities and social reproduction within the mill. Using that technology, they often took on roles that, at home, were assigned to wives, such as cooking. Because middle shift was worked during the dinner hour, workers came up with creative ways to prepare elaborate meals. Although "the company" did not want you to have "no refrigerator, no stoves, nothing," men found ways to cook. "I saw guys bring bacon in to eat . . . raw bacon I saw men bring in. They put it on the radiator, steam heat, and they cooked the bacon, sliced bacon and it worked." The electricians would make elements for workers. "You had to know somebody. We had one made, five or six of them slots, steel plate, and then put a cover on like a grill, and on each end were the wires you plugged in." Coffee was made, out in the field, using these constructed hot plates. Maintenance workers on middle shift designed their own division of labor, in which some members of the gang went off to do repair jobs, leaving one to finish preparing their evening meal. Workers describe "one pot" stews, for which they would contribute ingredients or money, as well as more elaborate meals ("We even did a little bit of baking"). They often used leisure activities outside of work, such as hunting and fishing, to bring in ingredients for steel mill dinners.

When workers came in on holidays, meals might be more elaborate. Dennis Mayer describes Thanksgiving at the steel mill.

> Somewhere in the welding rod oven or somewhere, there's a turkey cooking. And you sit down with your other family, namely the guys you work with, from twelve until quarter to one or one o'clock, you're eating a turkey dinner with all the trimmings, because some guy was a good cook. A lot of times that fell on me, because from the Boy Scouts and stuff, I could cook on open fires. It wasn't hard in the steel mill to find a hot place that you could roast a turkey or a ham or something like that.

Cooking became a masculine activity, as it entailed building the cook stoves and cooking over open fires. The cuisine and style of cooking was masculine, with an emphasis on meat, potatoes, and wild game, and associated with the grilling that husbands did for family picnics at home, which they learned from their fathers or boys' organizations like the Boy Scouts.

In his study of Youngstown steelworkers, Bruno documents similar leisure time activities, finding that "time to eat, cook or throw ringers had to be stolen from productive space."[17] Informal economic activities such as sports pools and petty entrepreneurship also took place. There was even time to pursue hobbies—one Bethlehem worker designed and made special accoutrements for his Harley Davidson motorcycle in the machine shop. "Workers had ample opportunities to turn parts of the plant into places where they could satisfy their social needs" and leisure activities further built solidarity.[18] The more workers could exercise control over timing of work—by avoiding "make work," dividing tasks among crew members, and completing jobs quickly to produce leisure time—the more free time and public space they created.

Laborers who worked a great deal of overtime, or under extremely hot conditions, had to find ways to recharge and keep going. On many jobs, there were breaks in the work pace during the middle or night shift, when workers grabbed catnaps. They would use planks and boards as beds and grab a nap after an extremely hot job, or on a long night shift. To explain this to outsiders or bosses they used analogies of firefighters or managing a sports team—that it was important to be prepared to work when work was needed; that they needed to control the pace of their own work and not be given make-work to fill down time. In conditions of highly strenuous labor and during slow periods of work or long overtime shifts, catnaps were necessary. But workers' use of mill space for what society defines as leisure activities was not supported by the union, not written into the contract. As a result, workers had to negotiate their right to space and time with foremen, using rank-and-file strategies such as slow-down to educate those who were problematic.

The use of mill space for the activities of everyday living was turned against steelworkers by the wider community. Workers' cooking on the job and taking catnaps are still cited as proof of laziness and lack of motivation, exemplifying an attitude of unionized workers, that—in the most extreme manifestation of this argument—resulted in the demise of Bethlehem Steel and the closing of the plant. Lieber, in his book on National Steel's Weirton plant, quotes CEO Jack Redline as complaining that the plant "was being run by the union" with poor safety, and paraphrases Redline citing as evidence "that men were sleeping, drinking and holding 'steak-fries,' hot-plate barbeques in the mill during work."[19] This use of company space (private property) and company time (the wage contract) was cited as evidence of an undisciplined, unproductive work force. The very activities that Dudley describes as manifesting skill on the shop floor, and workers describe as reenergizing—for example wresting leisure time from management by finding shortcuts—are represented and perceived as laziness and inattentiveness to quality by the wider culture.[20] However, this seizing of leisure time also does build citizenship rights to the space of the mill, to the inhabitance of the city within a city, which, while often not recognized by mainstream society, was a powerful font of workers' feelings of citizenship rights. But this mainstream antipathy makes it very difficult for steelworkers to translate their feelings of a right to the mill through the appropriation of space for everyday living into a political stance in concert with wider community-based organizations or institutions. Instead, these practices were used to undermine community support for steelworkers in the Lehigh Valley.

When the Bethlehem plant was abandoned and being scrapped, and a casino was being built at one end of it, Will Hornack said he felt devastated. Who had asked him for his permission to transform this space? "When I drove by [the mill], it was kind of like, I can really compare it to, to the Indians when they were here. We took their land and did stuff, but driving by like that, you get the feeling, cause I was there for thirty years, you kinda feel like, hey, that's my land! Look what they're doing with it." These feelings of ownership mobilized political opposition to bringing Brandenburg Industrial Services in to demolish the plant and fueled opposition to some redevelopment efforts on the site of the works in postindustrial Bethlehem.

Workers at the steel mill attained formal citizenship rights in the steelworks through the Fordist capital-labor accord. This citizenship was recognized and legislated through the institutions and mechanisms of the "internal state," the collectively-bargained and union-administered rights of the worker. The business unionism of the 1960s and '70s recognized some workers' rights as citizenship rights, while simultaneously undermining other sources of worker power and creativity. The wider legislative structure of the "external" state, as well as the internally defined laws and institutions of the union, delineated a system of governance that defined which aspects of labor-management relations could be collectively bargained and formally adjudicated or grieved. The "right to work," the contract, earned the worker certain rights of citizenship inside the mill (a degree of health and safety, some control over work conditions, a fair wage) as well as outside of work (health care, pension, unemployment benefits). For Fordist workers, the union defined an internal citizenship within the plant that produced real power and benefits and that defined a moral economy of expectations, rights, and obligations in relationships with employers.

There is a significant literature that is critical of unions in the Fordist post–World War II order. Antonio Gramsci has a cogent critique of the role of unions in working-class movements, analyzing both unions and political parties as inextricably tied to the broader logic of the capitalist system and therefore unlikely to function as a material context for building counter-hegemonic good sense.[21] Gramsci contrasts working-class common sense—a fluid understanding constructed out of dominant discourses, traditional "traces," and experienced knowledges—to good sense—a system of thought that accurately expresses the interests and experiences of the working class. For Gramsci, the Italian unions failed to be sufficiently progressive, defining workers' interests narrowly as strictly economic. Therefore, although the trade unions began as more radical organizations, they ended up functioning to mediate relations between workers and capitalists within an accepted capitalist system, thereby aiding capitalist accumulation. Because they accepted the logic of the capitalist order, "trade unionism stands revealed as nothing other than a form of capitalist society, not a potential successor to that society. It organizes workers not as producers, but as wage-earners, i.e., as creatures of the capitalist, private property regime, selling the commodity labor."[22] Trade unions, through acceptance of the collectively bargained contract, assume as natural a legal system that recognizes a contractual relationship between workers and capitalists around wage-earning, fetishizing rather than questioning that relationship. Gramsci was also critical of unions for dividing workers into crafts (or into unionized versus nonunionized sectors) rather than uniting them into a broad working class, and for developing a bureaucratic structure that distances union leaders from the rank and file. Gramsci devoted much of his writing to questions of how to support, produce, and foster democratic, progressive forms of worker organization, to build on and develop a collective good sense within the factories. He explored factory councils, a form of organization that would be less bureaucratic, more democratic, and that "embraces the whole working class" as potential loci for worker political education, organization, and the construction of an alternative culture.[23]

Contemporary critics of the role of labor unions in what the autonomist school defines as the "Keynesian productivity deal" agree with Gramsci.[24] In this post–World War II deal between government, business, and unions, wage increases for workers (again accepting the premise of labor as a commodity) became tied to increases in productivity, and unions directed working-class struggles toward collaboration with capital. In this collaboration the unions defined their constituency narrowly (rather than using a broad-based concept of the working class), and through collective bargaining accepted the wage system, limits on what can be bargained for, and rejection of direct action such as strikes, demonstrations, sit-ins, and sabotage.[25] For the autonomists, this squelching of direct action is particularly problematic, as the refusal to provide the creative labor that fuels all capitalist growth is the real power of the working class. This "deal" is shored up with government legislation like the Taft Hartley bill, banning many forms of direct action and narrowly defining and circumscribing union powers.

Social scientists have built on this critique of business unionism. We have seen that Burawoy shows how consent is produced under the Fordist, union-regulated order of this period, as workers are motivated to increase capitalist productivity through competitive "shop floor games," speeding up production that union-approved piece work and incentive pay systems encourage.[26] Burawoy argues that worker solidarity is undermined through a grievance system that individualizes workers' issues, rather than treating them as collective problems. Other scholars recognize this as well, because the contract limits issues that can be bargained or grieved and broader-based solidarities and alliances outside the plant are discouraged.[27] They also argue that the bureaucratic structure of unions divides leaders from the rank and file, as union leaders become coopted through upward social mobility and shared interests with the professional middle classes.[28] In this bureaucratic system, leadership becomes more concerned with serving only the interests of the constituents that elect them, not a broader working class. In addition, union acceptance of the dominant definition of waged work divides the working class—splitting the waged from the non-waged and obfuscating the exploitation inherent in unwaged work within the factory (in the form of surplus labor value) as well as of non-waged workers like housewives or informal economy workers.[29] A "servicing" model for unions leads to longer-term contracts, negotiated by union officials and experts with little rank-and-file participation, and further distances union officials from the rank and file.[30]

Inside the plant, the union often amplified fractures and divisions within the working class, even while simultaneously building, at times, broader solidarities. At the Bethlehem plant, three locals represented different divisions, ensuring different elections and representation for most maintenance versus production workers, thus widening divisions between them. Departmental (as opposed to plant-wide) seniority legitimized pay and promotional differences along racial and ethnic lines until the 1974 consent decree. Defining wage bargaining in terms of percentage increases actually contributed to wage differences between higher-paid and lower-paid jobs, again often linked to racial and ethnic divisions in the plant.[31]

While these analyses point to serious issues with business unionism and are highly relevant to our understanding of union failure to effectively stop processes of deindustrialization, they do not recognize some of the real benefits that workers realized in the Keynesian productivity deal and some of the real struggles and resistances that continued within the plant. Worker gains from business unionism continued throughout the 1970s at the Bethlehem plant, including increases in wages and benefits; union-backed legislation that resulted in Medicare, Medicaid, the Occupational Safety and Health Administration (OSHA), and the Employee Retirement Income Security Act (ERISA); and improved working conditions. But these gains were often predicated upon rapid growth, an economy in which "there seemed to be no conflict between consumption and accumulation, labor and capital, equity and growth—the essential harmonies of affluence."[32] The hegemony of the labor-capital accord within (and outside of) the plant should not be reified. We need to understand this as a "moving equilibrium" in which worker struggle prompts responses from capital. For example, management speedup strategies in the 1970s were responded to by labor militancy, which then generated new management tactics that resulted in the concessions and restructurings of the 1980s.[33] This perspective recognizes an ongoing struggle, on a shop floor often not completely controlled by union bureaucrats, that defines or shapes labor-management relations. Even while power and benefits wrested by labor from capital in this process changed workers' lives outside the mill, contributing to suburbanization, homeownership, college education for children, and health and pension benefits, they also contributed to greater control over the labor process inside the mill (as described in Chapter 2). These real benefits to workers formed the basis for the legitimacy of the union and for a union-regulated moral economy through which workers understood fair and just relations.

The union-defined mechanisms of the internal state gave workers very real power within the mill, including control over not only wages and benefits, but also over many of the conditions of labor. Workers knew that they could use the grievance process to protest unsafe working conditions, changes in those conditions or in the expectations of their jobs, and incentive pay, all important aspects of control over their own labor. Although some analyses of business unionism have represented the grievance process as individualizing shop floor issues (and they often did do this), these grievances *could* be used to transform work conditions, not just for the individual grievant, but for all workers doing the job.[34] Labor terms and conditions were delineated in the collectively bargained contract, and workers felt empowered to control these working conditions. Jack Metzgar describes what this meant for his steel-working father. "Specific work rules and working conditions were crucial to him, and he had a way of dividing them from wages and benefits, a way that coincided with the split between work and family that was so much a part of 1950s culture. The wages and benefits were for the family; the working conditions, for him alone."[35]

In protecting workers' rights to bargain not only for wages and benefits but to also control many aspects of their own jobs inside the plant, the union ensured them citizenship within the plant, shoring up their self-respect and giving them opportunity for voice in the workplace. The granting of economic citizenship to skilled white laborers such as steelworkers tied many social benefits (health care, unemployment insurance, pensions) to jobs, and defined these workers as independent, autonomous citizens outside the plant, supporting families through the family wage.[36] Inside the steel mill, jobs and work conditions were protected by the contract.[37] This gave workers a "freedom" that they lacked pre-union. John Wister describes this feeling at the Bethlehem plant:

It wasn't hard for me to go to work. We had fun. We were just—it was like a happy group. Part of that, I'm sure, was because of the union atmosphere. I used to work for a personal friend of my father's. He yelled at me in a day more than I ever got yelled at in thirty-three years at Bethlehem Steel. There was a certain freedom about the work: freedom of speech, freedom to express yourself.

John felt confident that he could grieve an infringement on his working conditions, and in doing that, "the worst thing that can happen is everything stays the same. If you don't resolve it, you vent some of your frustrations."

Workers themselves contrast this freedom to an earlier period when "employment at will" gave bosses the power to schedule, promote, and fire arbitrarily. This squelched worker voice, freedom, and self-respect. The workers I spoke with had all worked with older laborers, or lived with older steelworking family members, who educated younger workers through stories about the mill before the union. These morality tales emphasized the favoritism exercised before the seniority system. Workers talked about the need to hold one's tongue in the pre-union days: "I would have been fired every day," with my "attitude" and "big mouth," and, "you couldn't say nothing or you're going on night shift, you're going to work every weekend. They had ways to control you." They also recalled that "before the union there was very little safety precaution. Very little concern for the men, I think. You were more like a, it was like having a mule in a mine; if you dropped they just got another one." Autocratic management styles undermined worker dignity and respect. There were many "general foremen that were not exactly what I would say polite when they talked to you, they would talk down to you. They wouldn't talk *to* you, they would talk *down* to you." Before the union, workers lacked legal recourse or backing to enforce rights; but with the union, "if I needed something or had problems, I went to the union." "The union were our lawyers, they were our defenders." While workers greatly appreciated the increased wages and benefits that came with union contracts, they also valued increases in their power, dignity, and voice in the workplace.

Union membership was a badge of citizenship. It codified skill and experience through seniority; it built plant-wide solidarity (post-1974) around common wages, benefits, and working conditions; and it generated a union identity in contradistinction to management. Al Trakas, who worked in the beam yard, said "the union gave you a self confidence that you had. You weren't just another number. You had rights and that type of thing." These rights empowered workers not only to use the formal mechanisms of the internal state, but to assert power informally as well. "When [the foreman] barked at me, I barked at him." Workers didn't hesitate to slow down work if unhappy to "teach" autocratic foremen lessons, or even to directly confront foremen with their physical and collective strength. Andy Vanek, an ex-beam yard maintenance worker, tells an illustrative story about a worker in the beam yards who was notorious for never taking guff from anyone. A problematic foreman ordered him and his crew to go down into an especially hot and greasy pit to work on an unnecessary job. The worker, a big, tough guy, grabbed an enormous chain, held it aggressively up toward the foreman, and said, "If we're going down there, you're coming with us." The foreman backed off, and the crew moved on to another job. Andy tells this story to illustrate the real power that some workers had to directly confront management, using physical strength, assertive confidence, collective solidarity, and the threat of violence. Although this incident took place outside of a union-mediated process (i.e., it was "unlawful" and the worker didn't grieve the foreman's actions), the worker's confidence in his own power was forged in an environment that recognized citizenship rights. These included the right to be respected, and if a foreman was seen as being disrespectful—in this case making an unjust demand—workers take action. Andy, who has worked at other jobs after the Steel, understands that this is a rare thing in neoliberal workplaces and that it is hard for outsiders to understand the moral economy of the mill. "You wouldn't believe this happened, but these things did happen at the Steel."

Unions fought to bring workers dignity and respect within their own mill. When F. W. Taylor, the expert who designed scientific management, worked at Bethlehem Steel to make labor more efficient, he described a German worker, "Schmidt," in terms one would use to describe an animal. Workers beginning at Bethlehem Steel in the 1950s recall this kind of degrading treatment. Frank Walton, a feisty millwright in steam, water, and air, recalled his early days at the coke works in the 1950s when the union was young. The men would dump a car into the hoppers, sweep out the car, and then have an unofficial respite before the next cars came in, "and we'd go down and have a sandwich. But the guys had to hide, they used to hide in their lockers and hide in the corner and hide stuff and eat." That didn't sit well with Frank, who found it degrading and dehumanizing. "So I went over and I'm sitting in the front of my locker eating the sandwich, and the general foreman come in and he did a double take." He chastised Frank for taking a break, but Frank held his ground. "The job's going on, nothing's being lost, and I'm not going to sit in the dirt and eat a sandwich."[38] Tom Petro, the former union president of Local 2598, took great pride in restoring dignity to work breaks. "When I come down here at the 35-inch mill . . . men had to sit down on the concrete to eat their lunch. There was rodents. There was all kinds of rats running around." Tom filed a grievance; "I said 'When you go home to eat, do you go home, Mr. Superintendent, to sit in a cellar, in a basement, where you eat your food?' He said, 'No, I eat off a table.' 'Well,' I said, 'we're going to eat off a table too. We're going to demand that.'"[39] The union recognized that steel mills were hot, dirty, and dangerous, but they did not need to be degrading to workers.

Although the bureaucratic structure of the union might distance rank-and-file workers from union officials, some union officers (like shop stewards) had more direct contact with workers, and the grievance system was often used creatively to change working conditions for the collective. Jack Metzgar argues, "When it works well a union steward system is a wonder of workplace democracy that blends thousands of face-to-face, grassroots encounters into a powerful national institution for collective action."[40] Mike Davis agrees, arguing that management, beginning in the 1970s, attempted to neutralize shop stewards as they were using grievance procedures rather than collective bargaining to actually transform jobs and working conditions.[41] Shop stewards at the Bethlehem plant give examples of strategies like flooding the system with grievances to change practices used by unjust foremen and citing Article 14 (safety) to bring production to a halt and cause re-evaluation of a job.

Charlie Richter recalls using the grievance system to express a critique of the very underpinnings of the labor-capital accord: the acceptance of the wage agreement, of the commodification of labor. Charlie describes an incident in the 1990s, when Bethlehem Steel decided to incentivize a big gas job at the coke works. The incentive system had been expanded to include maintenance jobs in the 1970s, but setting incentive rates for this wide array of jobs was a long, slow process and, in Charlie's experience, this was the first time a gas job had been rated. A multiple craft job (using pipefitters, riggers, etc.), it entailed doing welding and repair work on lines carrying highly volatile and poisonous gases. Those doing this work were required to have special training, special equipment (such as masks with piped-in oxygen), and special time constraints (requiring frequent spelling on jobs). Charlie's first objection, shared with many workers, related to the authority of rate setters' expertise. "How do you rate something you never did? Where does he get that knowledge? What the hell does he know about rigger work?" Although management reserved the right to rate jobs, and the union granted them that right, battles between management and workers over rate setting is well-documented in steel mills as workers, who have the knowledge of how to do the job, try to confuse or deceive the rate setter, resulting in a favorable job rate.

In addition, however, Charlie was outraged that a gas job was incentivized at all. He found it morally repugnant to put a rate on such a difficult and dangerous job; "Nobody in the world is going to rate my life!" He did the job with his crew, slowly and carefully, but grieved it. The grievance must have baffled the union and the company, as it wasn't a safety grievance nor was it a dispute over the rated amount. For Charlie, a gas job simply should not be rated. Workers on the crew need to work together, take their time, and ensure that the work is done well and done safely, that it is quality craft work. Rushing the job, or attempting to reduce crew size, common strategies used to increase pay on an incentive job, were antithetical to quality craft work and highly dangerous. Charlie's moral outrage at rating this job momentarily exposed the assumptions of the entire wage contract, of the laborer as a wage earner. "Nobody's going to put value on my life with gas. That's my assignment, and nobody's going to value it. . . . No. Nobody's going to do that to me or to the men that I work with." Charlie did not define this as a safety issue (Article 14), under which grounds he could have refused to do the job. He felt he and his crew could do the job safely, if they did it at their own pace. In winning the grievance, however, both the union and the company must have been nonplussed by Charlie's response. When company representatives asked Charlie how he proposed the men be compensated, he refused to answer, saying that pay was not his purview, "it's at the company's discretion." But the men had to be paid for their work, and how do you determine incentive for a job that cannot be incentivized? Charlie proposed that the company slip the pay into the men's paychecks, perhaps attached to another job, adding that "the men will know where it came from." Charlie had no solution for the pay, because although in most work he accepted the wage contract, this argument questioned the entire premise of wages for labor. Charlie's grievance may not have changed working conditions, since he says there were no other big gas jobs before the closing of the Bethlehem works, but it made powerful moral statements: that labor is more than a commodity, that craftspeople have the right to exercise their judgment and expertise in controlling the timing of the job, that there is no fair "wage" for a job like this.

Seniority

The principle of seniority was central to the organization of work at the Bethlehem plant. The institutionalized concept of seniority defined skill quite differently than the concept of ability that management preferred to use in structuring an internal labor market of promotions and layoffs at the plant.

The first union contract at the Bethlehem plant in 1942, along with developing a codification of job classifications, established a seniority system in which workers' access to promotions and protection from layoffs would be determined by length of time on the job. This principle became a crucial organizing concept for steelworkers, not simply because it structured access to jobs, but also for the ways it invoked values about work and skill and organized social relations within the plant.

Prior to unionization, steelworkers had long endured paternalistic systems of hiring and promotion that relied on favoritism to ensure exemption from layoff and access to promotion. Steelworkers were highly critical of these personalized systems, regarding them as disempowering workers and undermining the respect and dignity that working men should have on the job. According to John Strohmeyer, editor at the *Bethlehem Globe Times* for twenty-eight years, "Seniority had no standing as company policy. In fact, favoritism on job assignments at Bethlehem Steel was an open scandal tolerated by the company."[42] Nick Giacinto, who was ninety-two when I spoke to him and had started at the plant in 1936, describes relations with foremen before the plant was unionized. He says he would be afraid to be called before his supervisor, because "they could swear at you, spit in your face, you had to take it."

John Wadolny, interviewed by John Strohmeyer in *Crisis in Bethlehem*, worked for forty-six years in steel:

> At the Bethlehem Steel entrance off Emery Street, there were about twenty small wooden lockers reserved for foremen. The men who worked under them would come to work with eggs, chickens, half a hog, and so on and place them in their boss's [lockers]. It was expected at the time. If a guy wanted a better job, he was told to take care of his boss. And he did.[43]

Nick agrees. "There were a lot of farmers coming in in the 1930s. They could make more money at the Steel than they could on the farm. They'd bring stuff into the supervisors, they got the good jobs."

During times of scarce work, getting a job at the steel plant, and holding onto that job, was crucial, and systems of favors, payoffs, and patronage ensured jobs. Of course, this kind of access based on favoritism was also shaped by discrimination. Bruce Nelson quotes from a 1950 report by Joseph Badzar, a local union official at Bethlehem Steel's Steelton plant: those workers who were "recent immigrants or sons of immigrants, workers of the wrong religious denomination, workers who did not belong to certain fraternal lodges, and even workers who did not live in the same neighborhood as their foremen" simply did not get jobs.[44] Ethnic, religious, and community-based ties constituted social capital to be mobilized in attaining a job and in job mobility.

The ways this system of favoritism undermined worker dignity was symbolized through extreme, and perhaps apocryphal, stories illustrating foremen's power that are told and retold in the community. Strohmeyer relates one of these stories, as told by John Wadolny.

> But the one thing that turned me strongly toward the union didn't happen at the plant, it happened outside. Now, remember, I'm eighteen. I come from a good Catholic family. I'm working in a section with a bunch of guys mostly in their thirties. I was invited to a party at the Holy Ghost Club where they had bowling. What I saw turned my stomach. Two or three of the foremen were there. They were getting all their drinks free. The steelworkers' wives were there too, several of them really beautiful girls. The foremen would feel them up, right in front of their husbands. You know, fondle their breasts and everything. No one would say a thing. I thought to myself: "Is this the goddamn way you have to get ahead in the steel company?"[45]

Jack Metzgar the son of a western Pennsylvanian steelworker, relates a similar story, oft-told by his father to demonstrate the importance of the union:

> When work was slack during the Depression, before the union, foremen were in control of who worked and who didn't on any given day. . . . To get work, workers would vie with each other to curry favor with foremen and superintendents. One fellow who had a reputation as a particularly good worker had been employed steadily during one period; to ensure his employment, he cut his foreman's grass in the summer and shoveled snow for him in the winter without pay; he also brought homemade kielbasa and other goodies to the foreman on a regular basis. One day the foreman ran into this worker while the worker was with his sixteen-year-old daughter, a particularly beautiful young woman, as the story goes. The next day at work the foreman, a married man with a family and himself only slightly younger than his employee, asked the worker if he could arrange a "date" with his daughter. The worker said he'd see and would let the foreman know the next day. The next day the worker arrived with a particularly large supply of freshly made kielbasa, but told the foreman he would be unable to arrange the date. At this point he was summarily fired and was subsequently without work for the better part of a year.[46]

Both of these stories, extreme in the degree of humiliation communicated, were circulated over decades within their respective communities. The story in Strohmeyer's book came up a number of times in my conversations with people. The narrative was incorporated into Jay O'Callahan's one-man play *Pouring the Sun*, which depicted steelworking life in Bethlehem in the first half of the twentieth century and had a number of much-publicized performances in Bethlehem. These tales use graphic imagery to spell out a moral message. They depict a system that undermined a worker's masculinity, his independence, and his role in the family as a protector of women's dignity, respectability, and sexuality. The steelworker's job was constructed as a masculine job, requiring strength, toughness, and the ability to tolerate hard, dangerous, dirty work. But in the stories, the worker is emasculated by the foreman and caught in a double bind. The stories simultaneously expose the weakness of the company's argument of "merit" or "ability" as grounds for promotion and undermine the company's demand for "moral" workers.

Workers also describe the pre-union era as one in which solidarity was undermined by the lack of seniority. Before the union institutionalized seniority, many jobs in the mill were learned through informal apprenticeships. But often the more senior, experienced workers were reluctant to share their skills, to teach the younger workers. They were aware that their only guarantee of job security—of continuing in the more desirable, more skilled positions and avoiding layoff—was monopolization of steelmaking knowledge.[47] Bethlehem workers who started at the works in the mid-1960s recall older workers sending younger ones out of the room when they performed the tricky and skilled components of the job, continuing to work as if seniority did not protect their positions. John Wister remembers,

> the older repairmen there pre-union, my department one time was predominantly Pennsylvania Dutch, shipping maintenance, they'd talk Pennsylvania Dutch, and if they were discussing how to do a certain thing with a part, they'd go to Dutch or they'd send the helper, the young guy, "We need four bolts, go get them at the department." And you'd come back and the job would be done. "Oh, we got it, sorry." Pre-union, your job depended on your being able to do more than the next guy . . . there wasn't the sharing of vital information.

John contrasted that to the mentoring and solidarity built into senior to junior relationships in the plant in the 1970s and 1980s, "Now I walk in, an eighteen-year-old, first day. 'Come here kid, take this cap off, do this.' He's happy he can direct me. If there's a layoff, I'm going to be the first to go."

The moral is that union struggles that led to introducing and policing seniority allowed the worker to maintain his dignity on the job, to be a bread-winner and patriarchal protector, and to be further empowered in that role as the family ideal of the stay-at-home housewife and mother came to be partially realized by many steel working families. The union replaced "ability" and favoritism with seniority as the dominant principle structuring the internal labor market.

Seniority institutionalized the principle of experience—as measured by time spent on the job, in the plant—as paramount. Seniority became more important than the ability or potential ability measured by standardized testing or formal schooling, and was given value or cultural capital in mainstream, professional, middle-class society. Experiential learning, in which workers were schooled either formally through apprenticeships or informally in everyday working relations, develops skill. Richard Sennett, in his analysis of working-class culture, points out that although time and motion studies applied to the industrial labor process fragmented time into smaller units, long-term time was built into the institution of the factory through the valuing of these experiential skills in the principle of seniority.[48] Andy Vanek, a beam yard worker at the Bethlehem plant, describes his first day on the job as an eighteen year old in 1964, walking by mills rolling file steel. The worker taking him around said, "'Kid, you won't be working there. The only guys that work there are sacred cows.' 'Sacred what?' 'That's a guy with so much seniority that before the superintendent does anything, he talks to the guy to get expertise. Them guys really got whiskers.' 'They got what?' 'Whiskers. Seniority. Everything works by seniority.'" Ron Keschl says, "When you picked up a job down there . . . it took you years to learn that job . . . it was not just like an ordinary off-the-wall job outside some place."[49]

Respect for years of experience transcended the formalized union recognition of seniority. Workers revered the years that families had spent working at the Bethlehem plant. The "metal sense," or knowledge that is built up outside the plant, working with grandfathers and fathers in their leisure time, is recognized inside the plant as a family's "years of service." Nick Romero told me that many of his family members worked at the Steel. "Oh my God, cousins, uncle, my God. Oh my God, we probably got over five hundred years all combined." Richie Check's family is legendary in the community for having "441 years" of work (of father, brothers, and sister) in the Bethlehem plant, and Richie and his co-workers frequently cite that statistic as a way of validating Richie's knowledge of the Steel and his expertise in steelmaking, as well as the moral weight of his commentary.

This is not to suggest that seniority is the only principle guiding the internal labor market. Initial job and departmental assignments, and even promotions, were influenced by the cultural capital of formal schooling as well as performance on standardized tests. Management represented "ability" as crucial in promotion. And long after the union introduced seniority as a central principle, supervisors continued to use nepotism in promoting hourly workers. Andy Vanek criticizes management's notion of "ability," arguing that favoritism was rampant in the plant culture. "Their idea of 'relative ability' was if you're my relative, you're hired." And even with hourly workers, in the unionized workplace standardized tests were vulnerable to manipulation in ways that seniority was not. Black, Latino, and women workers relate ways that tests were rigged to make it more difficult for them to move into certain jobs. Eddie Perez, a second-generation Puerto Rican worker, described going for his welder's test. At that time, he said, "there were all Hungarians in that area. A Polish guy saw what was going on with the test, and took me aside. 'Try your hardest on that test. These guys don't want you to pass.' Well, I did and I tested higher than them. I had to prove myself and then they never bothered me—we were like a close-knit family."

Although seniority, for the most part, institutionalized a valuing of skills based in experience and learned through practice over time, the system was not perfect. As discussed earlier, departmental seniority, as initially designed by the union, "institutionalized discrimination" against black and Latino steelworkers.[50] Racial and ethnic minority workers were trapped in more dangerous shops and departments with shorter promotional tracks and fewer highly skilled positions. The mentoring necessary for experiential learning also could exclude marginalized groups, such as women who found it difficult to get men to teach them necessary skills. In addition, random luck might determine one's relative seniority within an "age grade" of peers. For example, if workers were hired on the same day, their birthday would determine seniority, and workers relate stories of making a "lucky" decision to start work a day early, thereby gaining seniority on a number of their peers. Bea Strahler, for example, did not follow her father's advice to start work immediately when called into the mill, but instead gave a week's notice at her retail job. She was trying to do the right thing, but she lost seniority during a period when thirty to forty steelworkers were starting at the mill each day.[51] This was not so important when steel production was robust, but with restructuring, downsizing, and internal and external transfers at the end of the plant's life, these small and arbitrary differences in seniority, totally unrelated to experience or skill, could have significant consequences.

Transmission of skills from more experienced, more skilled steelworkers to younger workers occurred through explicit instruction, as well as through observation, imitation, and practice. Charlie Richter says when he started at the steel mill right out of high school, a "big German guy . . . said to me, he called me schoolboy, and while he's talking he raised his hand with his finger, 'Schoolboy, you keep your eyes and your ears open and your mouth,' [Richter zipped his lips] 'you keep your mouth shut.' I did that for the next thirty years." Charlie also describes learning different jobs at the press forge through observation, "I used to watch the forger . . . and all they did was give him hand signals, how to make the press come down. The traveling table would take the ingot in and out so much of a distance. It was amazing to watch." Charlie recalls putting a crane up in the open hearth as a younger worker. The beams had to be put in up high, a dangerous job, so the foreman asked Charlie to stay on the ground the first day, and go up about 150 feet the second. The A leader took him up and said " 'I'm going to put you right here and sit in this spot and do nothing but watch us work.' . . . I watched them . . . I seen what was going on."

Young workers, or young pups as they were often called, were taught work skills and moral principles through participation and explicit instruction that included lessons on safety and attentiveness. Charlie remembers a rigger teaching him how to work at heights, climbing up with him, showing him how to climb and how to work up high, but also teaching him how to think about dangerous work. "He was right there the first time I went up, he taught me a lot," said Charlie. "Your mind has to be there where you are. No other place. Not with your girlfriend, not going on the weekend. When you're walking in the open, you have to be there." In addition to skills and attitudes, workers learned workplace morality through formal and informal interactions with more senior workers. They heard morality tales about preunion work at the plant, received lessons in how get along with co-workers, and learned techniques for putting foremen in their place. In short, they learned the moral economy of the mill.

Seniority also shaped social relations in the plant. Hirings occurred in large waves, when there were booms of demand in the steel market. At those times—in 1964, 1974/75, and 1978/79—large numbers of steelworkers started at the mill. These age grades of workers had similar levels of seniority, developed strong bonds as peers, and moved into the lower laboring jobs within the plant, allowing the previous age grade to move up into more senior positions. Respect for an older worker's seniority was part and parcel of the culture, and booms in hiring were welcomed by senior workers, as they allowed them to move into more skilled and less physically strenuous positions.

The centrality of the seniority principle shaped skill hierarchies within work crews. "Every team, every group that you worked with, the older guys were the brains of the outfit, more or less directed the job; the middle guys did the work; and the younger guys were the gophers, they did the hard climbing and the heavy lifting and pulling and pushing and stuff."[52] In addition, the middle age cohort played important roles in mediating conflicting seniority-based interests between old and young workers. In his book *Striking Steel*, Jack Metzgar describes the role of these middle workers in enforcing practices and inculcating a morality of solidarity:

> The ability to stick together was something that had to be cultivated and enforced over time. If a younger worker was working too hard or too fast, my father would explain to him that he was working himself out of a job: "If you're going to bust the rate, we're going to have to bust it too, and guess who's going to end up on the street?" Or, if you were an older workers with solid seniority protection, you were "working some younger fella out of a job."[53]

Bill Markus says that in 1979, when a lot of young guys came in, "it was like the bloom of spring. We loved it, you know, because we were moving up as these young guys were coming in and taking our place. It was short-lived."[54] After the 1979 hiring, no waves of younger workers came into the plant to relieve the more senior workers, and the plant's labor force grew older as it moved into the 1980s. John Wister said, "It put a big physical demand on the employees that were there, not having younger people. When I was younger, I would look at fifty, sixty, and think, Wow look how old these guys are. They would say [to the younger worker] can you swing the sledge hammer? We didn't have the younger guys. Physically, it put a strain on us."

For the younger workers, the hierarchy of the seniority system was difficult, especially as the plant downsized. Members of the "class of '79," the last large hiring of the plant, never lost their junior status. "The youngest got stuck in a position where I have twenty some years, but I'm still the youngest guy." Younger workers had always had last pick on selection of vacation time, were junior in bidding on jobs, and got last choice to be on crews for high-incentive jobs. When hiring effectively stopped after 1979, they were also deprived of opportunities to mentor newer workers in a setting where learning was a rite of passage into manhood, and teaching gave purpose and direction to older workers. Conflicts related to seniority resolved themselves in the expanding manufacturing sector of the post–World War II period, but in later years younger workers chafed at the prolonged deference expected toward more senior, more experienced workers in an environment that gave them no chance to move up. And as the middle age grade workers became senior, through retirements, there were fewer mediators to ensure that seniority interests did not trump solidarity. This, as well as extreme pressure on younger workers who were ineligible for early retirement, contributed to schisms in the Bethlehem plant.

Solidarity

Work in the steel mill is very different than work on the assembly line. The steel mill has a complex division of labor in which work is performed differently depending on whether one is in production or maintenance and what department or shop, and in which much work is performed cooperatively by small groups of people in crews or gangs. For some on swing shift, "a work group . . . may remain on the same turn for years, always working through the temporal sequence with the same co-workers and foremen."[55] Relationships with co-workers develop through collaboration over long periods of time.

Ties of solidarity differ depending on the ages of individuals, the amount of time the group has been together, the danger of the work, and its relation to steel production.[56] Feelings of camaraderie or solidarity are built into the social relationships—the dependence on members of the crew through a skill hierarchy and division of labor to get the job done effectively and efficiently (which might have a direct influence on pay rates), and to ensure safety. Crews entail a division of labor, as workers are not substitutable. Crew members are somewhat equal, but each has a different job requiring different skills, and all contribute to getting the job done. In dangerous assignments, safety depends not only on individual skill and awareness, but also on one's crew mates. Dave Campbell, who worked the same "turn" with his crew, was "with the guys forty hours a week. You'd see them more than your family—days, middles, nights. I'd come home from work night shift, go to bed, wake up for supper, go back to work. When I worked double shifts, I'd get home, eat, at three, I'd go right to bed and wake up at nine in time to go to work, with my lunch packed." Howard Kovarik, a beam yard craneman, describes the intimate communication that develops among crew members, saying he didn't have to wait for signals from workers that steel was chained up, since "I worked so long, you work so long, with a certain group of men, and you seem to know each other's moves and everything."

In production jobs, skill could be measured and collaboration built through safety and speed. Bill Markus, a maintenance worker in the beam yard, says, "Camaraderie is pride that we had . . . proud of our safety that the guy we worked with didn't get hurt." But he also talked about the shop floor games that workers used to measure skill:

> We were on incentive, but our pride was to beat the other crew. There's always that one-upsmanship, and we used to, like the crew over there at 16 saw, that was Paradise. And then someone would holler, "Trouble in Paradise!" There'd be an argument, whatever, someone don't agree, it wasn't going as smoothly as normally. They weren't all smiling. And then the other crew would pick up on that, and it would make them gear up a little more.

In the steel mill, the competition of the games, while serving corporate interests in speeding-up production, simultaneously and contradictorily built gang solidarity (unlike the individualized assembly line games described by Burawoy), working-class strength that could be used to resist, subvert, and oppose management demands.

Maintenance workers took pride in striving together to use skills of craftsmanship to make a quality product. Bill elaborates on camaraderie: "those guys were proud of fixing something, improving it. . . . I improved on [a machinery producer's] patent by adding a little piece, okay, something we worked without for years and all of a sudden some millwright, he welded up and said, 'I can make this better,' that's the kind of thing." Maintenance workers could get machines up and running so production workers could get back to their jobs; they could also innovate to make those production jobs easier. Fred Bachman, a rigger, explains, "I could *not* fix the crane, and shut the operation down. But most skilled craftspeople just don't think that way. They know we're going to fix it and not hurt production, because we'd be hurting our brother that was loading the steel, too." Solidarity is harnessed, in this case, to ensure productivity (i.e., used in the interests of the company), but it also builds strong working-class ties.

Principles of seniority (learning through mentoring and apprenticeship on the crew) and solidarity were reinforced through work on the crew. Charlie Richter, who worked more than forty years as a rigger, describes being a young apprentice:

> When I was in the gang, I did whatever I was asked to do. If I didn't know how someone showed me the right way and the proper way so I wouldn't get hurt. . . . After working a while I started to climb around, hang some rigging. You never went alone. Always someone with you. . . . I learned so much, especially [working] on the furnaces, the camaraderie with the men, talking with each

other, listening to each other, and helping each other. And who makes decisions on jobs. . . . They were always looking for the other person, that they didn't get hurt.

Key elements of gang work included awareness of and responsibility for co-workers. "We took our time, you have to. The other four men that were there with me, they were the best of buddies. You got to know each other. The camaraderie, it was there. That played a big factor in the riggers. The camaraderie that you had with the man." The camaraderie of co-workers ensured the job went smoothly and safely, even as the principle of seniority structured the division of labor within a gang. Young workers, pups, were also hazed by more senior workers in coming-of-age rituals that initiated them into the crew and to manhood. They were sent off to "get a bucket of steam" or a "left-handed wrench," or directed on circuitous wild goose chases through the plant. Many new workers to Bethlehem Steel left after a few weeks, unable to tolerate the hazing or difficult schedules and hard labor. But if they were able to make it through the hazing, they became a member of the group, and "once they accepted you, and you shown that you could cut the mustard . . . you became part of the family . . . both at work and over at the union hall. . . . You became a family. You became a close-knit family."[57] Workers look back on this process as a process of maturing, saying, "at the Steel, you had to man up," pull your weight in the group, and watch out for the safety of yourself and others.[58]

Jack Metzgar argues that although conditions in the steel mill were conducive to developing strong social relationships, "the ability to stick together was [also] something that had to be cultivated and enforced over time."[59] Work groups used various leveling mechanisms and informal sanctions to ensure that younger workers learned the moral economy of the crew. For example, a production crew might have to discipline an "incentive hog" who was working too fast, potentially causing a rate change that could affect everyone's pay or contribute to losing jobs. Such "selfish" behavior needed to be pointed out, usually first through explicit comments or teasing. If this did not work, the crew could mobilize "fellow workers to isolate, intimidate, and just generally harass the hog."[60] Thus informal sanctions were mobilized to enforce egalitarian standards for moral behavior on the crew.

Rewards were also built into collaboration. Being on a crew meant working together in a way that ensured the crew earned good money, worked safely, and did a good job, that they could take pride in production. Cathy Kovarik, a woman crane operator in the beam yard, describes the things she would do to make a crew member's job easier. She learned to break the chain herself so that her chainman didn't have to walk long lengths of the beam yard. In return, the chainman would ensure that she didn't have to climb down from the crane unnecessarily, saving her time and effort. Such continual instances of helping each other out were an everyday part of crew work and were reciprocal with co-workers, building strong egalitarian social relationships.

Even though these mostly male unionized workers took pride and gained prestige in the wider society as citizen wage earners who defined themselves as self-reliant and autonomous in social statuses of independent homeowners and family wage earners, they recognized their dependence on others in their wage work.[61] This was not experienced or defined as a weakness, in contradistinction to the dependence of women on the male breadwinner. In reality, of course, this male self-reliance at home was predicated upon the work of wives in childcare, meal preparation, housework, maintaining kin relations, and in most instances, wage work at various points in the life cycle. Dependence at work was defined as masculine and as a strength. An emphasis on danger, and the necessity of depending on one's co-workers for safety, was often stressed using military metaphors like "being in the foxhole together" or "watching my back." Such metaphors expressed the dependencies of solidarity within a masculine discourse of honor.

The moral compulsion to "look after the other person" and "help each other out" carried over into the more "private" living spaces of the workplace. Charlie Richter described how this worked in the welfare room, in the showers: "Anyplace you took a shower and somebody saw something on you, you were told about it. You had anything on your feet, arms, back, private parts, you were told—honest. And you'd better do something about it. You'd better. Otherwise, you're not taking a shower." Workers looked for any signs of infection or fungus that could spread in the shower, looking out for their own interests, but also for that of their colleagues. They also helped each other clean hard-to-reach spots. Charlie adds, "When you're taking a shower the dirt got behind your neck, down your back. Lots of times I was washing someone else's back with their washcloth, someone was washing mine. That was nothing new." Workers were especially solicitous of injured colleagues. "If guys would get hurt, and they'd need help in the shower, guys would help them. They would. If you got burnt or something." The most intimate spaces of everyday living and care that might normally be gendered as female and reserved for wives or girlfriends were sites of masculine reciprocity, where strong, egalitarian social relationships were built.

These relationships within the crew were also built outside, whether it was at the bar after work, or going to family picnics and weddings. Louis Moran, a worker in the beam yard, said,

I was just talking to a bunch of my friends about the Steel. It was a family. When you're associated with guys for so long, that was the hardest part, losing your, you know, you got away from your family. Because these guys, you grew up with them, you saw them get married, you went to their weddings, you saw their children grow up. You'd come into work, they'd say, "Boy, your kid did real good in football yesterday." Or your daughter, "Hey your daughter was in the paper for this." Whatever, you know. It was always a family thing.

Workers of the same seniority or from the same age grade went through life cycle rituals together, establishing reciprocal relationships. As John Wister said, "I'm a godfather for several guys, we've gone to each other's weddings. I started there when I was eighteen."

They also pitched in when someone needed help, as Louis Moran recalls:

I can remember one fellow getting hurt. And he actually got hurt and he had to put a new roof on his house. After work, we went over to his house, tore the roof off, put a new roof on. And we did this for a couple of days in a row, and got his roof done for him. He was hurt and couldn't do it, but he had to have it done. Because he was gonna do it himself. He had the material there, so we went over, and we did it. Which I think everybody should do. . . . This is things people should do for each other.

Scott Crewe continued his relationship with his gang after work at the Steel had ended. One of his post-Steel jobs, as an electrician, was at a restaurant/nightclub near his house. "I used to work there for tickets, I'd get so many tickets, they'd have a dinner show, like Jerry Reed, and I got us all tickets and we had dinner, and it was all on me. . . . I used to take all my pay in tickets, the best in the house, too. I made sure of that." Workers valued, and were taught to value, relationships of reciprocity both inside and outside the mill.

Workers who did not participate in this kind of reciprocity—whether it was helping each other on the work gang, buying fundraising tickets from co-workers when they were selling them, or sharing information and knowledge—would be sanctioned by the group through gossip, teasing, or withdrawal of friendship and solidarity. Charlie Richter tells of a co-worker who had special knowledge about shoeing horses. When a member of his crew asked him for advice, he responded, "I'm not going to tell you anything about horseshoeing," implying that this was his individual knowledge, attained through schooling that he had paid for and wouldn't give out gratis. Charlie asked, "Was that proper or right of him? To talk like that to his fellow workers that he's going to be with them for however long he's going to be there? Did it matter to him? He didn't care. But he did lose a lot of friends." Those "self-ish" workers developed a reputation that might hurt them in work where they had to rely on others.

Kathryn Dudley, in her ethnography of autoworkers in Kenosha, Wisconsin, found that solidarity was not limited to production workers, nor to one shop or department, but was built throughout the plant. In addition to the social ties of the crew, workers also develop "plant wide social ties characterized by this sort of generalized reciprocity" that is used to create an egalitarian workplace culture.[62] Generalized reciprocity ensures that workers cover for each other on "bad days" on the job. The union is crucial in supporting a broad, plant-wide working-class identity. The unionized workplace supported a culture in which workers cultivated a strong identity in contradistinction to management, pride in the product, and an ethos in which workers (both maintenance and production) helped each other to ensure that everyone could make a good living. Winnie Edwards, a woman who worked over twenty years as a machinist, says you "watch each other's backs." "The union created the culture that you look out for each other."

Both Dudley and Metzgar point out that on the shop floor, workers are allowed to be individuals, but within the context of an egalitarian working-class culture. Dudley argues that in dominant culture, "we think of skill or ability as a quality that is possessed by individuals," that can be "measured in some way."[63] But among Bethlehem workers, an emphasis on individual accomplishments is considered to be blowing one's own horn and is looked down upon as a lack of recognition that one's accomplishments are dependent on working with others. For steelworkers, "what counts is the kind of person you are, day in and day out. They look to their personal qualities on the job and off, not to specific things they have done, to define themselves. And these qualities always come in human packages that include unchangeable deficiencies, immutable weaknesses."[64] The formal credentials and achievements of professional middle-class culture are not recognized (and may even be denigrated) by steelworkers, but individual workers prove themselves on the shop floor. As William Kornblum found in his ethnographic study of steelworkers on the South Side of Chicago, this happens through "the skill and finesse through which he carries out his routine work" in a "complex team effort in which they [workers] perform as total personalities before a large audience of peers."[65] This skill and finesse is individual performance done in collaborative work with others. On the work crew, "your weaknesses were simply accepted because they could be offset by others' strengths, just as your strengths helped offset others' weaknesses. . . . Even if you could eliminate your deficiencies, you would have to define yourself as self-sufficient, a fundamental error that inevitably leads to both loneliness and an inability to be honest with yourself."[66] An individual's strengths would be an asset to the entire crew—"standing out as a particularly clever and skillful worker strengthens the solidarity of the group," and workers pitched in to cover for individual weaknesses and shortcomings, not expecting that any one worker will be perfect.[67] A hard worker without the same level of technical skills could also contribute to the crew. As Dennis Mayer, a pipefitter at the Bethlehem plant, says, "There was room for everybody in there . . . kids that quit school . . . could come in and get a forklift operator's job, make a decent living, and eventually retire and die with dignity. What does a guy like that do today?"

Cathy and Howard Kovarik, two married beam yard workers, discuss social mobility, and wonder if their own son, the next generation, fails to recognize this interdependency. His mother reflects, "To me he's very arrogant. I love him dearly, but he can be very arrogant." The dominant-culture emphasis on individual talent and merit as the grounds for social mobility is criticized by a culture that values egalitarian solidarity. As Cathy says, success is valued, "you're climbing that ladder to succeed, which is a good thing to do that," but it is never assured, and any one person might find him- or herself in a situation where they need those egalitarian and reciprocal ties. "Don't ever forget that small person down here, because that small person, if you fall down that ladder, you're going to need that small person to get back up and to succeed more." Cathy feels that her own son "forgets the little person down there. Don't ever forget that little person. You some day might need that little person again."

William Kornblum argues that the solidarities constructed through crew work and an ethos of collaboration in the mill could transcend racial and ethnic boundaries on the shop floor.[68] This might be difficult, as interethnic or interracial crews were not common in many shops in the Bethlehem plant, due to the segregation of workers by race or ethnicity. But, when black and Latino workers were able to successfully move out of segregated shops and to overcome more senior workers' initial resistance, ties of solidarity were created on the shop floor. Kornblum found that these ties did not often benefit minority laborers outside of work, which was also true for women workers at the Bethlehem plant. But my research shows that as white workers transferred into the heavily Latino coke works toward the end of the plant's life, enabled to do so by union rules of plant-wide solidarity, inter-ethnic ties were built through working together. And after initial periods of very strong hostility, ties of solidarity were also constructed in the context of gang work in stable shops for many women.

Building plant-wide solidarity was, however, more challenging than work gang or crew solidarity. As we have seen, there were all kinds of divisions within the variegated work force of the gigantic steel mill: between production and maintenance; between shops; and between different, often ethnicized and racialized, departments. These divisions were often formally incorporated into the internal state and regulated through the union contract. For example, in the enormously complex system of incentive rates, with various job classifications, and even particular jobs within classifications, receiving different incentive pay (direct, indirect, or secondary indirect) resulted in very different levels of pay between jobs and shops at the mill. One manager told me that "each machine in the machine shop had a different incentive plan." Sometimes single gangs or crews at the plant would have to overcome divisions within the workforce that were formalized through these systems. The distinction between production and maintenance workers, for example, could lead to tensions on the job. Ann Kovar relates working as a welder (a maintenance job on indirect incentive) in the iron foundry with a chipper (a production worker on direct incentive):

> A chipper who would be working side by side on the same job, and the chipper's getting good incentive, and I'm still getting my $40. And I used to tell him all the time, "This is so unfair." . . . I used to work side by side with the chippers, the guys that used to clean off the iron castings, and a lot of time they couldn't chip the stuff off. I had to blast it [with] an oxygen torch, and after I get done, he'd come in, chip a little, or chip outside or whatever, but a lot of times, him and I, used to work side by side and he used to tell me that "what they're doing to you ain't, ain't right."

Although these two individuals worked in unison, in their different job classifications (maintenance and production) incentive rate differences could breed dissension. Others give examples of dissension within maintenance gangs when incentive rates were introduced for specific jobs, as workers would lobby for the gang to have fewer members for the job (meaning higher incentive rates for each). This undermined the camaraderie of looking out for everyone, and encouraged workers to pursue individual interests, which coincided neatly with the production interests of the company.

Masculinity and Physical Work

Steelwork was also described as masculine work, and the steel mill as a masculine world. The dirt, danger, large-scale machinery, extreme heat, frightening heights, outdoor work, and heavy physical labor were identified as masculine, as was the culture of the workplace—the vulgar language, practical joking, sexual banter, and valuing of physical prowess. Masculine work and a masculine culture of solidarity included a valuing of physical effort, physical strength, and the ability to take physical punishment. Masculinity was not simply imported from the wider society (although masculinities constructed at home, in the school, and in the community were brought into the works), it was also actively constructed and produced in the mill. Pierre Bourdieu discusses the importance of a "valorization of physical strength as a fundamental aspect of virility" in male working-class culture and manual, industrial labor. He argues that resistance or opposition to dominant classes can only occur, for the working class, through the withdrawal of labor, through the strength of their fight, "which depends on the physical strength and courage of its members," and sheer numbers "through consciousness and solidarity."[69] Working-class strength, for steelworkers, was thus manifested directly in physical strength, as well as in solidarity.

Much steelwork involves difficult physical labor, and steelworkers cite this as a defining aspect of masculinity (and as grounds for excluding women, who are essentialized as physically weaker). Many steelworkers take pride in their physical virility as evidence of masculinity, and particularly for younger workers, physical strength and toughness are respected within the mill. Dennis Mayer relates an incident in which physical strength generated respect from peers when he was working on a job with a 650-pound valve:

> Becker and I picked that valve up off the floor and lifted it into place. That was normally a job where someone climbed up with a chain block and lifted it into place. Well Becker and I didn't say anything, but there were people there who saw it, and by the time we got to the washroom, "Hey, I heard you and Becker put the equalizer valve up without a chain block?" Well, you were kinda proud of it.

Jack Deutsch, a professional boxer who was much respected as a young rigger for his physical strength and toughness, says, "I always had to show off, try to take shortcuts and stuff. We'd do a job at the beam yards and working on the crane, and wait for the crane to come. I'd pick up a [extremely heavy] tank of acetylene and carry it up to the top of the steps."[70]

Physical strength was recognized, on the job, in people's nicknames—nicknames like Tree for a giant, strong steelworker or Tiny for a large man. But toughness was related not to strength alone but also to the ability to stoically take physical punishment. Those laboring in extremely hot environments in the plant, for example, were respected for their toughness. Dennis Mayer tells of walking by the soaking pits at the open hearth:

> As I come down, this guy jumps out from behind a column and with a very heavy Dutch accent he says "Hey buddy, you see them numbers on the columns?" I said, "Yeah, what about them?" "Them's the ones that stayed in the flues the longest." . . . Well, down underneath that access floor . . . someone had to go down in those flues and clean the soot. . . . I went in there when the lights would go out, I was in there already when the walls were still a dull red. Those laborers would be in there maybe twenty-four hours after the furnaces had been shut down. They had to wear inch-thick wooden shoes so their feet wouldn't burn up. And they were only allowed to work for twenty minutes, in what they call a twenty-minute spell. . . . This guy boasted about these guys whose numbers are on the walls. They stayed in the flues longer than the prescribed twenty minutes. They thought they were doing something great. But they were killing themselves. I don't know if there's an explanation for that. On the battlefield, that type of carrying on would be considered heroic. In the industry situation with the company knows it's dangerous, certainly you should know that it's not good for you, why would anyone be trying to look more manly by trying to abuse themselves more than they had to? I don't understand that behavior but it was there. I might even have participated in some of that stuff, being one of the bigger guys in the department, you know, lifting things that other guys can't lift. You know, there's some kind of incentive to act that way, even if I can't explain it.

Success at tough, physical, masculine activities outside the plant (boxing, excelling in other sports, heroic physical military performance, or honorable toughness in fights) generated reputation and respect within the plant. Jack Deutsch, the professional boxer, says,

> They all liked me. I was running, I was working out all the time. They all liked me. I never tried to push my way around like I was a tough guy, even though I was boxing all the time and all this tough stuff I was doing. I never, ever talked like I was tougher than they were. I just got along. . . . They were always nice to

me because I always acted like I was the toughest guy around, the strongest. And at the riggers, I probably was at the time.[71]

Of course, toughness and physical virility could also be measured through sexual conquests, and some men did gain reputations and prestige for sexual prowess. As Andy Vanek says, "steelworkers don't kiss and tell," unless, he adds, "you're around a whole group of men." This acclaiming of sexual "conquests" of women, while still joked about today, was a much more active component of social life and masculine conversation at the mill when workers were younger.

Taking risks and pushing oneself, even when afraid, was also evidence of masculinity. Although this could run contrary to considerations of safety, it was valued in the culture of the mill. John Baxter describes learning as a novice carpenter:

First day on the job I had to climb up a tower, 150 feet in the air. They wanted guys that could climb. It caused quite a disagreement. The seasoned vets didn't want a punk kid on his first day off the ground. They were worried about safety. The supervisors wanted to see if he could do it. They were arguing about it. There was a [senior] guy, I remember, he was complaining up a storm. At the end of the day he said, "I'll work with that guy any time." I was young and inexperienced, but that showed them. He was thinking they should work us in slow.

Although senior workers argued for safety, and for the training and experience in climbing that comes with on-the-job learning, they were nonetheless impressed with John's reckless daring.

The aging steelworkers I spoke with did have to deal with the loss of physical toughness and virility. Jack Deutsch says, "You think you're never going to get old, you're never going to fall apart, because you never drank, you never smoked, because you're the toughest guy around." And Dennis Mayer reflects on the toll that heavy, tough, physical work took on the body. As steelworkers age and manifest the effects of hard manual labor and toughness in their bodies, seniority privileges allow workers to transfer into less physically demanding jobs. Processes of deindustrialization—the long downsizing of the plant, the lack of hiring new younger workers, the movement of women into some of the less demanding jobs—eliminated many of these transfer opportunities, generating resentment and anger on the part of older workers who found themselves still laboring in physically demanding jobs.

Although some women lacked the upper body strength for certain jobs in the mill, women could condition their bodies to be more prepared for physical lifting. The women steelworkers I spoke with did not discuss learning to lift weights, but "hard-hatted" women interviewed by Molly Martin did talk about training with weights and having to "teach myself the proper way to lift heavy objects."[72] At the Bethlehem mill, women who stayed either transferred to other shops or were moved to jobs that did not entail such heavy lifting. Christie Radics relates being hired to work in the 48" mill, and working on roll changes, where "things were just heavy. So actually the girls that, a couple of us that were there, couldn't do the heavy part of it, so then we got moved to steam, water, and air, which I stayed for the rest of my time there."

Women were also tested around heights and for the gutsiness required to work up high. Although this was seen and defined as an innate difference between women and men, successfully negotiating heights is a learned skill, and women were often not given the training to do this. Shirley Macek, for example, describes her early experience working at heights in the boiler house. She says that she was deathly afraid of heights initially, but made herself do it. "I did know one thing, if you were afraid of heights you had no job. If you weren't willing to climb, you had no job." Larry Neff, an ex-rigger, described new rigger Brenda's initiation into climbing in his book. She was told to climb a 260-foot stack on the blast furnace before a large audience of men who turned out to watch this hazing. Neff relates that she made it up, one of a "select group of about ten" who ever climbed that stack out of the 170 riggers.[73] How one learned to experience and negotiate heights could be crucial to one's success.

Charlie Richter, on the other hand, got careful training on climbing and heights as a young rigger. Charlie describes a senior man teaching him how to climb:

After working awhile I started to climb around, hang some rigging. You never went alone, always someone with you. The first time when I went, I'm following this guy, up off the ground twenty feet, have to go another twenty feet, climbing, and he stopped. I stopped behind him. He said to me, "Charlie, you have to stop following me." I says, "How am I going to learn?" He says, "You'll learn, but how tall am I?" he says. I says, "Oh Jesus, over six foot, six foot two." He says, "Yeah, how tall are you?" "Five foot eight" He says, "You think. You and me, I'm climbing, and you're right behind me. When I grab ahold of something and you grab ahold, you better know it's there. When I grab it and you reach your arm out, you better know what you're grabbing. Otherwise, you know where you'll be? Laying on the ground. Don't follow me. Go behind me, but you're going to learn."

Charlie goes on recounting very specific, detailed, and embodied instruction from an older worker on how to climb at extreme heights. An experience that is frightening becomes knowable and manageable through supportive instruction. This opportunity was not given to women like Cathy Kovarik, when she bid on a job in the carpenter gang. Instead, the belief in women's innate fear of heights and avoidance of risk was used to haze and terrify Cathy and prevent her from taking the job (see Chapter 4 for more on this dynamic).

The masculinity produced in the steel mill inhabited a contradictory space in its relationship to class struggle over production and wages. Although working-class masculine identity has often been represented as "oppositional" to mainstream culture and gender identities, in the steel mill a working-class masculine ethos was mobilized both in service of and in resistance to capitalist accumulation.[74] Macho laborers would take risks, work in the grey area of safety, work under incredibly hot and difficult conditions, and not shirk from heavy loads to enact their masculinity in the mill. Paul Willis represents this as the "will to finish a job, the will to really work," which for workers produces masculine power; indeed, "masculinity is a power in its own right."[75] All of these demonstrations or practices of masculinity in the steel mill resulted in speed-up and increased productivity. But these macho attitudes could also be mobilized to confront managers and corporate policy, both outside the union-regulated internal state (as in the worker who threatened his foreman with physical violence) and inside the union-regulated system (in the assertiveness that fueled grievances and, in the past, strikes). These masculine characteristics that were needed in a dangerous job were used to define steel work as a male domain and to legitimize a right to higher wages for men. But the union- and shop-floor-defined expectation of a higher wage also contributes to an acceptance of the legitimacy of the wage contract—a fetishization of labor as a commodity—that accepts increased wages as the proper resolution for conflict over the labor process.[76] Defining steel work as masculine also excluded women from employment for years and generated enormous hostilities toward them when they did start to work in the mill. Men worried that if steel work became feminized, it could undermine their claim to a family breadwinner wage, so they forged solidarities in social interactions defined as masculine (for example, sexist talk that denigrated and objectified women), and developed self-esteem rooted in a masculine definition of steel work. In the Bethlehem mill, this conflict over gender exacerbated fragmentations and tensions within the working class.

The cohort of workers in this study, who lived through the long process of deindustrialization, began work in Bethlehem's mill in the 1960s and '70s. At that time the steel mill was a bustling city unto itself, with a rich workplace culture, a moral economy that guided work relations, and a complex division of labor. Steel production and steel work were seen by the wider society as central to US economic strength. Within the mill, the internal labor market and the internal state, mediated by the rules of the union contract and the grievance process, defined citizenship. A culture and moral economy of the mill made work fulfilling, enabled workers to live what they understood as a "good life," and defined their valued role in American society.

CHAPTER 4

Shaping the White Working Class

Uneven Exclusions in the Works

An industrial working-class culture of citizenship, solidarity, and voice was forged partly through outright exclusions of blacks, Latinos, coal-country workers, and women, and at other times, through uneven inclusions of members of these groups. These mixed patterns contributed to the building of a strong white, industrial working class but simultaneously limited its ability to effectively resist processes of restructuring and deindustrialization. In the post–World War II period, even as women were being ejected from wartime jobs, black and Latino workers were increasingly getting hired in the South Bethlehem mill. However, racialized understandings of the skills and abilities of black and Latino workers, and essentializing stereotypes like they "could withstand the heat," ensured that these laborers were disproportionately assigned to the hotter, harder, and more dangerous departments. These racialized and ethnicized jobs and shops, in turn, "devalued the worker and degraded the work," leading to a racialized definition of skill within the mill.[1] Heavily Latino departments like the coke works had less powerful local union representation, greater health and security risks, lower incentive rates, and a shorter promotional track (meaning workers could never attain the same level of "skill" and experience as in other departments).

In the Bethlehem Steel mill, union rules supported seniority systems, defined citizenship, and built solidarities. But these solidarities were constructed unevenly across departments and divisions; among the three local unions; among racial, ethnic, and gender groups; and between workers in different plants. The rules of the internal state, the recognition of experience-based skills and seniority, and the benefits of the worker citizen and mill inhabitant were forged through relationships that excluded African American, Latino, coal-country, and most especially, women workers. As anthropologist June Nash observed in her ethnography of General Electric workers, "The precarious security workers struggle to achieve" in the post–World War II period "is based on exclusions" of race, gender, and ethnicity; it is the creation of a white, male industrial working class.[2] While such fragmentation was often exacerbated by management in an effort to divide the work force and to cheapen labor, it was also produced by workers themselves who sought to control access to jobs and skills inside the steel mill. In a seemingly contradictory way, the processes that built a powerful white, working-class solidarity in the mill also limited those who were included in the industrial working class, as well as generating internal divisions and fractures within that working class. As these processes change and shift in varying geographic, historical, and economic contexts, working classes are formed and reshaped, and the "outer limits of the working class" and barriers to wider solidarities are constructed.[3] This was evident in the Bethlehem mill and was produced through broad, nationwide processes as well as local contexts that shaped solidarities differently in different Bethlehem Steel mills.

But even as unions excluded sectors of the working class, unionized industry also provided significantly more opportunities to black, Latino, and women workers than nonunionized industry. In the late 1970s, "unionized [companies] . . . had better racial records than nonunion ones."[4] Although black steelworkers confronted "exclusion, discrimination, and even segregation within organized labor," "no organization in this country . . . has done more to raise the living standards of black workers than unions."[5] The unionized jobs that Puerto Rican workers attained at steel mills were far superior to available options in nonunion industrial or agricultural work.[6] At the Bethlehem mill, black and Latino workers were brought in much earlier than women and were thus able to access the Fordist rewards of unionized work sooner. White women, however, could realize them through the family wage of industrial working-class husbands, which African American women had less access to.

Many of the workers I spoke with spent their entire careers in a South Bethlehem plant that included black and Latino workers, although they were likely to be segregated into specific departments. However, most had never worked with women in the plant before the last major hiring in 1978/79, when a large number of junior men and women entered the mill. This was somewhat different from other Bethlehem Steel plants. At Sparrows Point, for example, women worked in the tin mill and were thus able to transfer to other shops with the 1974 consent decree earlier than women in Bethlehem.[7] In South Bethlehem, women had not worked in the mill since World War II, at the end of which many wartime women steelworkers were let go to make room for returning veterans. The older steelworkers I interviewed had worked in a plant that totally excluded women for thirty-two years. For those workers and others, the large-scale movement of women into the mill in 1979 was a very difficult transformation.

Plant-wide seniority, imposed on the union and the company by an EEOC-negotiated consent decree, offered more job and promotional opportunities to black, Latino, and women workers, but also generated strong divisions and conflicts within the plant's working class. Interestingly, in the Bethlehem plant these conflicts were not as strikingly distributed along racial and ethnic lines as between junior and more senior white workers and between male and female steelworkers.

Race and Ethnicity in the Steel Mill

The steel industry in the US, and in Bethlehem, had a long history of racialized hiring. Workers defined through stereotyped Eastern and Southern European ethnic categories were hired into homogeneous departments and shops in the late nineteenth and early twentieth centuries. African American workers were hired in the steel industry as early as the late nineteenth century, and Latino workers were hired early in the twentieth century.[8] Steel mills included these workers in a growing and diverse steel working class, while also using racial and ethnic categories to shuttle them into shops deemed less desirable in terms of skills, danger, working conditions, pay, and promotional tracks. While there was broad consistency to these trends across the industry, there was also considerable variation in how they played out in local contexts.

Essentialized assumptions about race and ethnicity influenced initial job assignments and were then reproduced within the internal labor market. Within specific shops and departments, even with shop seniority, the more highly skilled jobs were reserved for white workers. Foremen, supervisors, and union officials were for the most part white and were exclusively male. These wages of whiteness were defended by the newly whitened children and grandchildren of eastern and southern European workers, who had gained access to these more skilled jobs in the steel mill in the postwar period.[9]

AFRICAN AMERICAN WORKERS

Many mills recruited African American workers during World War I and during and after World War II, contributing to the Great Migration of African American families from the South to the North, from agricultural to industrial jobs. At many plants, by the post–World War II period, African American workers were 25 percent or more of the work force.[10] In some steel mills, however, even in more urban settings (like Bethlehem), there were few to no African American workers. Historian Bruce Nelson cites data from a 1950 USW civil rights survey of steel mills to show that many mills in Memphis, Indianapolis, Youngstown, and several Pennsylvania steel towns reported never having black workers.[11] One local union official from Elwood, Indiana, reported no African American workers at the plant, saying "there has been a tradition that Negroes were not wanted here."[12] In contrast, Bethlehem Steel did recruit African American workers to Bethlehem during World War I. Historian Wandalyn Enix documents the founding of a "negro colony" of black workers, housing as many as six hundred African American workers near Bethlehem's coke works in 1917.[13] But these workers seem to have returned to the South during the post–World War I recession, and by 1923 Bethlehem Steel was actively recruiting Mexican, rather than African American, workers to the mill. However, the company continued to actively recruit African American workers to mills in other cities. In the 1960s, Bethlehem's Sparrows Point, Maryland, and Lackawanna, New York, plants had significant minorities of African American workers (about one third the work force at Sparrows Point and one sixth at Lackawanna), and in the 1970s Bethlehem Steel claimed that 12.5 percent of their total workforce at all their plants was black.[14] This is a sharp contrast to the few black workers at the Bethlehem works.

The most likely explanation for the paucity of African American workers in Bethlehem was the lack of a significant African American population in the region. In 1960, only 1.3 percent of Bethlehem's population was African American.[15] In addition, Bethlehem Steel's corporate elite, headquartered in the city of Bethlehem, may have been reluctant to exacerbate racial tensions in the city by recruiting black steelworkers after World War I. Certainly, they would have been familiar with a serious racial incident at Johnstown, Pennsylvania, a city somewhat similar to Bethlehem with a large Bethlehem Steel mill. In Johnstown, where blacks made up only 2.5 percent of the population, black workers did not join white workers in a 1937 strike and mill-wide walk out.[16] Black workers prioritized support for the Bethlehem Steel company over solidarity with their co-workers because of a 1923 incident when Johnstown's mayor responded to the crime of a black migrant killing two policemen by ordering every "Negro" new to the community to "pack up his belongings and get out."[17] In this tense confrontation, Ku Klux Klan members burned crosses on the hills around the city. But Bethlehem Steel refused to follow the mayor's order, standing behind African Americans in the Johnstown community, as the corporation had recruited these black workers.[18] The corporate elite, looking at Johnstown, may have read local cultural attitudes as resistant to recruiting African American workers and hoped to avoid racial tensions in the city in which they lived, had friends and neighbors, and were active in political and community affairs.

Before the 1964 Civil Rights Act, jobs in the Bethlehem plant and corporate offices were simply closed to most black workers. Only a few African American workers were hired in the Bethlehem plant in the 1940s and 1950s, and many of them used personal connections with Bethlehem Steel elite, either through a shared church or through domestic work in elite families, to secure those jobs. Also, race was a touchy issue for Bethlehem Steel's upper management, who were almost exclusively white and male. John Strohmeyer, former editor of the *Bethlehem Globe*, speculates about the role of "racial prejudice at the upper levels of Bethlehem Steel" as a variable in labor recruitment and relates a 1964 incident as illustrative of management's racist attitudes.[19] Philip B. Woodroofe, Bethlehem Steel's supervisor of municipal services, helped to organize an interracial, interreligious group designed to improve race relations and "forestall civil rights problems" in Bethlehem.[20] He was fired for his efforts (although accounts stress that it is unclear whether more bureaucratic reasons related to cross-departmental turf wars might have played a role). This story was picked up by the *New York Times*, gained national coverage, and became a black eye for the corporation.[21]

LATINO WORKERS

Without African American labor for some of the hottest, hardest, and most dangerous jobs in the plant, management at the Bethlehem plant sought labor elsewhere. During the booming 1920s, in a tight labor market, Bethlehem Steel looked to Mexico and Mexican labor. One Bethlehem Steel executive told social scientist Paul Taylor in 1929 that "the Mexicans are better, more dependable workers than the Negroes. The Negroes aren't there when you want them; they go south with the cold weather."[22] Mexicans were defined as not black (although not really white) and therefore preferable to African American workers. Taylor, in his book on Mexican workers, quotes a Chicago-area steel mill manager as saying, "When I hire Mexicans at the gate, I pick out the lightest among them."[23] They were also considered more "flexible" labor, as they could be expelled from the area because of their immigration status and lack of local ties. Bethlehem Steel recruited unskilled Mexican laborers in San Antonio, Texas and transported them by train to Bethlehem, without their families. Almost one thousand mostly single, male Mexicans arrived by train in Bethlehem between April and May of 1923. They were housed in a labor camp located next to the coke works, as well as a barracks in nearby Shimersville.[24]

Mexican men were assigned to hot departments, as it was thought they could take the heat, even though, as West points out, many of these Mexican immigrants came from temperate areas in Mexico. Maria, a Bethlehem-born Mexican American whose father came to Bethlehem to work at the Steel, says that Bethlehem recruiters "didn't want anyone that was educated. They wanted uneducated people, no schooling, no nothing. So they can use and abuse them." This echoes African Americans' experience in Bethlehem Steel's hiring at the Sparrows Point mill in the 1950s. Deborah Rudacille quotes an African American steelworker saying in 1955 that "they wouldn't hire anyone from Baltimore City, that they only wanted you if you were from the Deep South and wanted to get away from that rule."[25] Rural, uneducated, unorganized immigrants were seen as desirable unskilled laborers.

During the 1920s and the 1930s, especially with the slow-down brought about by the Depression, many Mexicans in the US were forcibly deported when their labor was no longer needed.[26] In Bethlehem many picked up and left, leaving a core of about fifty families, many of whom continued to work at the Bethlehem mill.[27] By the time the cohort of workers in this book started at the Bethlehem mill in the mid-1960s, Mexican American steelworkers were members of these core families, third-generation workers and long-term residents of Bethlehem.

Later, during post–World War II labor shortages, when Bethlehem Steel once again looked for laborers for the hardest, dirtiest, lowest-paying jobs, the company turned to Puerto Ricans. In much of Pennsylvania, the steel industry recruited African Americans heavily during World War II, almost doubling the percentage of African American steelworkers in the state (from 3.5 percent to almost 7 percent).[28] In Bethlehem, however, without African American networks to mobilize for labor recruitment and without the desire to recruit African American workers, Bethlehem Steel again looked for labor elsewhere, recruiting women and older men during World War II and turning to Puerto Ricans after the war. Dr. Sanchez, a local professor whose parents emigrated from Spain to work at Bethlehem Steel in 1950, said, "They weren't allowed to hire blacks at the [south Bethlehem] mill, so they hired Hispanics."[29] Puerto Ricans, like Mexicans, were hired as workers who were *not* black. A Puerto Rican agricultural worker who applied for work at a US Steel mill in Lorain, Ohio, in 1947 said managers had a clear profile for Puerto Rican steelworkers: "At the time in Lorain they would only accept tall people with white skin at the mill."[30]

The Puerto Ricans hired during this era first came to the US as agricultural contract laborers to work on eastern Pennsylvanian and western New Jersey farms in the late 1940s and 1950s under Operation Bootstrap programs. Rural male migrants from the tobacco and sugar regions in Puerto Rico worked for commercial chicken farmers, orchards, potato growers, and tomato producers near Bethlehem as seasonal laborers.[31] They quickly found that permanent industrial jobs at Bethlehem Steel were preferable to seasonal, low-paid agricultural contract work. Rather than returning to Puerto Rico at the end of their farm labor contracts, they stayed during the winters to work in the local factories and at the steel works. A study in 1950 showed that 89 percent of Puerto Ricans interviewed in Pennsylvania preferred industrial to agricultural work, citing higher wages and steadier employment.[32] Puerto Rican workers, unlike the Mexican workers who preceded them, moved into unionized jobs at the Bethlehem mill (although the union was still relatively weak). Although their jobs were on the lowest rung in the hierarchy of steel work, because they were unionized they offered better wages and opportunities than other factory or farm labor. Bethlehem Steel management then built on kinship, ethnic, and village networks to actively expand recruitment of Puerto Rican workers. Bethlehem Steel advertised in Spanish-language newspapers in New York City, asked workers to write to relatives at home, and sent a Puerto Rican recruiter to two towns in Puerto Rico, Corozal and Patillas.

This racialized hiring continued throughout the 1960s. In the Bethlehem coke works, Marc Ortiz, a foreman, reports that by 1970 the unskilled laborers were all Portuguese, Mexican, and Puerto Rican. In the more skilled jobs, there were only a very few Latino workers, and it was those that "did speak English, they didn't have the laborer's jobs, they had the more skilled jobs." Within the Bethlehem mill, a white male working class that excluded black workers and distinguished itself from the Latino coke works workers was constructed through these hiring, promotional, and seniority practices.

Consent Decree and Seniority

The union-managed internal state of the mill formalized seniority as a means of eliminating favoritism and recrimination in layoffs and promotions. Although seniority systems did recognize experiential skills, the departmental seniority of the 1950s and '60s ensured that workers assigned to less desirable shops had inferior promotional lines and opportunities, often looking at a lifetime of work at hotter, harder, lower-paying jobs. Because seniority was limited to departmental promotion lines, workers could not use seniority in bidding on jobs in other shops and were required to transfer in at the bottom of the job hierarchy. Because Latino workers were assigned to less desirable jobs, departmental seniority excluded them from the more coveted promotional tracks that led to higher-paid, more skilled, more varied, and possibly less dangerous positions.

The greatest challenge to the formalized, union-legislated and regulated system of seniority was the 1974 consent decree, which mandated plant-wide seniority in an attempt to eliminate exclusionary and racialized shop-promotional lines. It opened opportunities to transfer, with rate retention, to black and Latino workers who had been segregated in less desirable departments and occupational lines. Signed by Bethlehem Steel, eight other steel companies, and the union, it was an agreement with the federal government resolving many discrimination cases that had been filed with the EEOC. Civil rights suits filed by the government on behalf of African American workers at Bethlehem Steel's Lackawanna plant in the late 1960s and at the Sparrows Point plant in the early 1970s brought court or government-ordered solutions. The consent decree "put into place one of the most extensive affirmative-action plans in basic industry."[33] It mandated hiring goals for women and black and Latino men, put in place measures to increase their representation in craft positions, and restructured the seniority system from a departmental to a plant-wide basis.

Although the Bethlehem plant did not have a separate discrimination suit and had a very small number of African American workers in the 1960s, it was included in the industry-wide decree. For some younger workers this was beneficial, as they were able to transfer into more desirable departments. For others, however, already in desirable shops, plant-wide seniority hit them hard, as they could be bumped out of jobs by workers with higher seniority from other departments, or fall down in seniority in relation to layoffs and recalls. Changing the seniority system had major repercussions, and workers felt strongly about it, as "with the exception of the home, seniority represented an individual worker's largest investment."[34] Seniority was not only a financial investment determining one's status in the internal labor market, but, as shown in Chapter 3, was a codified system of values for recognizing skill, experience, and social status.

When the consent decree was implemented in the Bethlehem plant, many senior white workers moved into more desirable departments, knocking back younger white workers with less seniority. Jeff Scholl describes this in the electric furnace melt shop:

> In 1976, plant seniority came into effect . . . with the consent decree, and that just hurt me very badly. Because electric furnace melting was one of the highest paying shops in all the steel mill. And all of a sudden, in 1976, at the time I was running a stock yard crane. . . . I had three years seniority. . . . You had to have twenty years seniority to get into the shop, and everybody with twenty years seniority from the blast furnace and from all different shops bid in, and I was finding myself being laid off very often . . . the second there was any slow-down, we would be bumped down and out, and these men would just transfer in and take our spots.

In Jeff's department, none of the in-transfers were African American or Latino. They were all more senior white workers like Dennis Mayer, who transferred into the pipefitters from another department and was able to jump ahead of other pipefitters because of his seniority in the plant. While the new rules of the consent decree were accepted in the plant, they overturned the pre-existing order through which workers made decisions about internal mobility, and in some departments this exacerbated tensions between junior and senior workers.

Although senior white transfers were most common, workers were also affected by black and Latino transfers and quotas for black, Latino, and woman hires in apprenticeship programs. Greg Becker, who was hired in 1973, applied for an apprenticeship but was thwarted by consent decree policies "that knocked me right out." He says that black and Latino workers were accepted into the apprenticeship program, even though "they had less time" and "I had the scores to get it, but I couldn't get it." Greg perceives this as unfair, as he had both qualified for the apprenticeship and accumulated the seniority needed for eligibility.

Many white workers in Bethlehem had no memory of racial/ethnic minority in-transfers related to the consent decree, perhaps because many black and Latino workers, like Dan Oates, an African American worker hired in 1972, never took advantage of the shift to plant-wide seniority. Dan's initial plan had been to stay in the coke works for ten years and bid out. "But in ten years I was one of the youngest people working. You know, everybody with my seniority getting laid off in all the other departments. So I decided, I'm going to stay in the coke works, and that's what I did. I never got laid off in the twenty-five years I was there." For Dan, as for many workers, the effects of the consent decree coincided with the escalating processes of deindustrialization in the 1980s, and employment security became a more important consideration in bidding on jobs than pay, variety of work, or the opportunity to learn new skills. Dan recalls some workers transferring out of the coke works into more lucrative shops, but as shops were downsized, they were then laid off. This was risky because "if they were laid off for more than two years, they would lose their seniority." So when these workers came back, "once they got in the coke works they stayed there till the closing." This was true for many Puerto Ricans in the coke works. Even though they had finally attained plant-wide seniority, by the time this policy was implemented they saw the benefit of staying in their shop in a more secure and reliable job with fewer layoffs.

Racist assumptions also affected reactions to black and Latino workers moving into the higher-paying shops. Before the consent decree, it was difficult for Puerto Rican workers to bid on jobs in other shops, even when they were willing to give up their departmental seniority and had the union-recognized right to transfer. Marc Ortiz says when he first started in the 1960s, "at that time you couldn't get out of the coke works. I saw it with my own eyes, [the application for transfer tossed] into the garbage. . . . After the consent decree, and the union got stronger, it was easier to transfer with plant-wide seniority." Marc says that, nonetheless, many Puerto Rican workers did not transfer out of the coke works. "It felt uncomfortable being in those other places, felt out of place. They [the established white workers] felt that you were taking their job away." White worker resentment toward minority transfers, or what was perceived by some as special treatment for Black and Latino workers, made it difficult to build relations of solidarity and learn new skills through mentoring. Moreover, Carlos Rodriguez says there was a "feeling of community at the coke works. . . . To leave there was not comfortable for some people. Leaving would be difficult." Not only would transferring out make for uncomfortable and perhaps even dangerous work, but it could hold workers back from further mobility as a move into shops where white working-class solidarity put black and Latino workers at risk of serious accidents and generated barriers to promotion. Instead, at the Bethlehem plant, it seems that a major effect of the consent decree was that younger workers were bumped from desirable jobs by more senior white, male workers.

Moving out of secure departments into better jobs also sometimes backfired for black and Latino transferees, who, as more junior workers, found themselves in insecure departments or divisions. Walter Moore returned from the air force to a job at the plant in heat treatment. He was a second-generation, African American steelworker and had been a star athlete in high school. Walter aspired to less hot, dangerous, and dirty work, and applied for a job with the Bethlehem plant's internal security force, the plant patrol. As the first black candidate, "everyone said you can't get that job. You don't see any black security men here at the Bethlehem Steel. But I did. I got that job." Walter initially ran into racist attitudes from his co-workers, many from rural areas outside the city. Walter describes what he defines as archaic attitudes: "We had one guy, he was the closest thing to a black person they thought, before I ever got there. . . . He was a really dark Italian. . . . His name was Alexander, and they called him 'n' (I'm not going to say the whole word) Alexander. Everybody called him that."[35] While Walter thought this was a good career move and loved his job, it ended a few years later when, in 1984, Bethlehem Steel instituted a cost-saving restructuring by outsourcing their security work to a private agency. So, while he was a pathbreaker at Bethlehem Steel, Walter had also put himself into an insecure position, losing his steel job.

White workers were especially resentful of the back pay received by some black and Latino workers as a result of the consent decree. The EEOC demanded back pay at the last minute of negotiations, although this was strongly opposed by both the company and the union, leading to the withdrawal of Inland Steel and nearly undermining the entire agreement.[36] Judith Stein reports that I. W. Abel, USW president, was furious about the USW's $3 million obligation and argued vociferously that the "demand for back pay undercut systemic change" as it awarded individual rather than collective resolution.[37] White workers from the Bethlehem plant express resentment that all "minority" workers received back pay regardless of whether any individual experienced discrimination. White workers tell stories designed to rebuild class solidarity across ethnic and racial lines under the perceived threat of unjust pay. One such narrative is of a Mexican worker who received his back pay, told his co-workers that he couldn't keep the check, he didn't deserve it, and donated it to a local charity. Another is of a black worker who said he didn't deserve the check, that he should give it back, and was told by white co-workers to keep it and put it aside for his children's education.

The theme of the stories is that black and Latino workers should explicitly recognize that this was not pay that was rightfully earned, even if they ended up keeping the money. And of course, individual black and Latino workers (especially those working in predominantly white shops and departments) had strong motivation to deprecate these payments to their white co-workers, thus maintaining broader solidarities.

Black and Latino workers reported confusion around the back pay awards, as Gus Guerrera, a second-generation Mexican steelworker, recalls:

> I remember, one time they were giving money for minorities [as a result of the consent decree back pay awards]. A guy said to me, "How much did you get?" "What do you mean?" "For minorities." They were always joking. "No, over to the union hall, go over there to get money for minorities." "Oh, get out." . . . I see this one guy, he's Portuguese. He would always say he's white. I say, "What the hell are you doing here?" He says "I'm Portuguese, I'm a minority." . . . But when it came to money, I saw people I never knew that were minorities.

At the Bethlehem plant, management was unclear on who qualified for back pay and "minority" status. Women, African Americans, and Spanish Americans were considered minorities, but what about the Portuguese workers at the Bethlehem plant? John Strohmeyer quotes George Moore, the attorney for Bethlehem Steel's industrial relations department: "We couldn't get a definition out of the Justice Department or EEOC on what the hell is a Spanish-American. We were ready to pay the Puerto Ricans, but we also had a lot of Portuguese. Nothing was in the settlement about them, but we reached in our pockets and paid them too."[38] These stories reflect white worker beliefs that individual black and Latino laborers at the Bethlehem plant did not experience discrimination, even though race- and ethnicity-based initial job assignments affecting promotional trajectories were quite evident there. In the Bethlehem plant, where there were very few African American workers, awarding pay to ethnic minorities was quite contentious.

Black and Latino workers did express some discomfort around receiving the back pay. Gus Guerrera responded to my question about white workers' resentment of back pay by saying, "If they're giving money away . . . why doesn't this guy, just because he's white, why don't he get it? It's not fair. It's very hard. . . . I never asked for favors because I was Spanish. But when I did, I did figure, I'm going to get it. The heck with it." In some steel mills, activist steel workers refused to cash their back pay checks (which averaged only $300) because by doing so they would give up their right to sue for past discrimination, but this did not appear to happen in the Bethlehem plant.[39]

The consent decree also opened up opportunities to black and Latino workers and to women for apprenticeships and for promotions to foremen. Desirable apprenticeships that had been in practice closed to these workers contributed to the construction of skilled labor in the mill as white and masculine. But when black, Latino, and women workers gained access to these programs, they experienced heightened resentment and hostility from coworkers. This may have been in part because entry to apprenticeship programs was much more heavily constructed around formal credentials (vo-tech degrees and formal testing). Moreover, even as apprenticeships were opened up to candidates along lines of race and gender, the apprenticeship program itself was being dissolved, eliminating one avenue for becoming a skilled worker. By the mid-1980s there were no more apprenticeships at the Bethlehem plant.

Dan Torres, a second-generation Puerto Rican steelworker, moved into an apprenticeship as part of the consent decree's terms:

> Fifty percent of the jobs were going to minorities, fifty percent were going by seniority. I'll have to say that the company and the union in their wisdom were trying to do an honorable thing. But they didn't think it all the way through. Because no one checked with the workers to see if they would find this acceptable. . . . when you're an apprentice someone's mentoring you. So the person who's scheduled to mentor me the first eighteen weeks was the brother of someone who didn't get the job because of me. And in his most polite Pennsylvania Dutch format said to me in no uncertain terms I'm not happy that you're here.

Dan was so miserable that his father said, "Son, come down to the coke works. If it's that bad everywhere else, come down where at least you're with family." He did, and he stayed there for almost twenty years.

Marc Ortiz, a Puerto Rican worker, was offered a promotion to a sub-foreman position as a result of the consent decree and says, "They only did it because they had to, not because they wanted you." Then restructuring led to layoffs. "When things started turning around, getting rid of people was unfair," he recalls, adding that "you got kicked back down" on the basis of race/ethnicity. He reports being demoted earlier than white workers. "This was happening with management. The union, you couldn't do that. But management you could," because management positions weren't protected by union seniority guidelines that banned subjective and discriminatory decision-making around layoffs. Affirmative action programs designed to be effective in opening up new promotional opportunities in a booming steel industry were less effective, or even irrelevant, at a shrinking plant. Marc brought a lawsuit against Bethlehem Steel, charging discrimination in his demotion, but lost.

Even as implementing the consent decree in the Bethlehem plant exacerbated tensions between junior and senior white workers and between white and black and Latino workers in the short term, it may have resulted in broader solidarities in the long-term, building a union-recognized seniority system that included all workers at the plant (and had ramifications, to be discussed later, for transfer rights between plants).

It is ironic that at the end of the plant's life, the coke works became a desirable department to transfer into, as it was the last major shop up and running. Labor at the coke works also became safer, cleaner, and easier, thanks to activism on the part of workers, the union, and OSHA. Efrain Sanchez, a first-generation Puerto Rican steelworker who started working at the Bethlehem coke works in 1953, testified in Washington about the dangers of silicosis and was quite clear that the union and Puerto Rican workers who testified played a great role in improving those conditions. Efrain describes conditions when he started at the coke works as hot, dirty, dangerous, and difficult. He started at Bethlehem Steel with eleven other Puerto Rican workers, but by the end of the month, "there were only three left. People quit. It was too hot, and they didn't like working on Sunday (the holy day)." Over time, with environmental and safety upgrades, "they put in air conditioning, everything was done by machine, like remote control. It was easy. It was a good job when I left." Latino workers who found it hard to transfer out to other shops and departments were motivated to work collectively to change conditions in the departments they were stuck in, to use "voice" rather than "exit" strategies. By the time white workers transferred into the coke works, as the steel mill closed other departments, it had become a better job, safer, and a healthier place, although white workers still saw it as a lower-status job.

The plant-wide seniority introduced by the consent decree ensured that senior white workers could transfer into once stigmatized, but still open departments at the end of their careers in steel. In transferring in, they worked side by side, often for the first time, with Latino workers. Mitch Roberts, a white crane man who had worked in electric furnace melt, transferred into the coke works in the 1990s. He said his job as a lidman up on top of the coke batteries, was the toughest job I ever did . . . the coke works, the heat came up through our feet. It knocked you out. . . . The Hispanic population working down there were some of the best workers I worked with in my entire history in Bethlehem Steel. They were tremendous. I was pretty good at it, I could take the heat better than most. But these guys were animals, just downright tough.

In a masculine work culture that valued toughness, Mitch gained great respect for these hardy men. Jack Deutsch, who worked briefly at the coke works, said, "we became like a team to work together . . . they all liked me. . . . All those guys know everything. They've worked every machine there, and you're just a new guy coming there. You try to be on the QT and just listen." As the jobs at the coke works improved (through union activity) and the stability of those jobs became more appealing, and as white workers transferred into the coke works with restructuring, it became a more integrated department in the late 1980s and the 1990s, where white workers learned jobs from more senior Latino workers.

Many of the Puerto Rican workers I spoke with were second-generation steelworkers at the Bethlehem plant, hired in 1963/64 and 1974/75. This meant that they had long-term family connections at the Bethlehem works, and that most of them had seniority over the new women hires. Because of pre-Depression recruitment, Mexican workers in the 1970s and '80s were often third-generation steelworkers, able to boast of lineages at the steel as long as those of many white ethnic workers. Nick Romero, a third-generation Mexican American steelworker, boasts a lineage of "over five hundred years all combined" of family steel work at the Bethlehem mill, although he claims that his family's years of service do not get the same recognition as those of white workers. Although these family lineages, and the seniority related to their year of hire, gave these workers status over junior laborers, their Latino ethnic status lowered them in the skill hierarchy within the plant, and they continued to be recognized as Spanish or Mexican workers. Women, however, experienced the dual marginalities of being generally the most junior workers (hired in 1978/79) and being women in a male world. Mexican, Puerto Rican, and African American men were able to build solidarity with white co-workers through a masculine solidarity that women were unable to access. This was crucially important, as the hypermasculine culture of steel work shaped almost every interaction on the shop floor. Yet Mexican, Puerto Rican, and most especially African American workers were often unable to access a white working-class identity, and the wages of whiteness that accompanied that.[40]

Numerous accounts have pointed to the irony of affirmative action measures opening more desirable jobs and promotional tracks to black, Latino,
and women workers even as layoffs, restructuring, and downsizing in the
steel industry were eliminating opportunities. Less noted is that these same
opportunities were simultaneously being lost for younger white workers (in
the Bethlehem plant, those hired in 1973 and 1979). This contributed to a backlash mentality among some white working-class men, exacerbating hostility
toward black, Latino, and women workers.[41] At the Bethlehem mill, where
internal transfers preceding the mill's demise increased inter-ethnic solidarities, this hostility was dramatically evident toward women.

Despite the plant-wide seniority of the consent decree, discrimination continued to be practiced, albeit in less explicit ways. Black, Latino, and women
workers might find it more difficult, for example, to obtain special scheduling
requests (allowing them to meet family obligations, maintain second jobs,
or pursue schooling). When Fred Needham, a white worker, requested a special schedule so that he could attend his sons' high school football games,
his foreman acquiesced. When Marc Ortiz, a Puerto Rican worker, asked for
scheduling changes, he resented management's reactions. "When my sons
were going to college, and I wanted to visit the colleges, Bethlehem Steel,
they treated you like little kids. You need an excuse, you need this. I'm going
to Penn State or Temple University. They said, you can't do that." Ed Nobel,
an African American shop steward, describes a grievance he brought—that
he was denied access to a training program necessary to move into a higher
job because he would miss two weeks of it for his softball schedule. He later
found out that white workers were admitted to that same training and allowed
to take two weeks' vacation in the midst of it, so he filed a grievance citing
racial discrimination. Women found both foremen and union representatives
to be completely unsympathetic to scheduling needs related to childcare—
such as a child's illness or babysitting issues. Of course, women with young
children were more likely to also have very low seniority, but women report
that foreman responded inflexibly to childcare-related scheduling requests,
saying, "We hired you, not your child."

Even after the consent decree, skilled jobs still were not equally available to
black, Latino, and women workers. Ed Nobel described the difficulty he had
moving into a first heater position on the coke works heating gang. In order
to attain this position, the candidate needed appropriate seniority, an eight-
week training program, and a passing score on a written test. Ed suspected,
however, that white workers had greater access to the knowledge needed for
the test. "There was preferential treatment going on—how the hell did they

get all this knowledge?" Years earlier, this had been a position that was reserved for white workers; only one other black worker had ever attained it. In describing the fight that he had to go through to get this job, Ed says he "had to work harder than the next guy." Bobby Robinson also describes racial discrimination. "Sometimes, even with seniority, it didn't help you. You still got the dirtiest jobs."[42]

Union office and representation also were not equally available to black and Latino workers, although eventually members of these groups held some union offices. Ed Nobel says when he filed his two-week-off grievance, the union tried to get him to drop it and then followed up by attempting to kick him out of his shop steward position. He prevailed, involving the international office of the union. "I'm a die-hard union man" he says, "but it was the leadership within the union. They think they can do whatever." Local unions with predominantly white, male union officials were not always supportive of claims of discrimination. Yet even without equal representation, broader working-class gains won through the union did improve conditions for Latino and African American workers. Efrain Sanchez said, "If it wasn't for the union, we would never have got all the benefits we got. Not only we but all the steelworkers of all nationalities."

Workers of color expressed frustration that "the people at the top of the union didn't listen to you," and that "some of the union guys were worse than our own bosses, and they still are." Full citizenship in the plant, expressed through voice and political leadership in the union, status and prestige within the mill, and use rights to its entire space, was difficult for black and Latino workers to achieve. Danny Moreno said, "Latinos mostly didn't even run for [union offices], didn't even go for it. We had a couple of black guys that ran for shop stewards and stuff like that. The union presidents were all white." It was difficult for Latinos to get elected to union offices in shops that were predominantly white. Gus Guerrera said he was working on the crane once, unbeknownst to white workers in the shanty below, when a well-liked Puerto Rican worker came into the shanty. "He came in and said, 'I'm running for shop steward. What do you think?' They said, 'Sure, we'll vote for you. We've known you for a long time. Sure we'll vote for you.' He walked out, and they said, 'I won't vote for that goddamn pork chop.'" Some Hispanic steelworkers did become union officers, most notably a Spaniard and a Puerto Rican who became vice presidents and are lauded for doing a great deal for Latino workers. Manny Vega, an ex-union official, says he got involved because "some bosses would start belittling some of the employees, especially the Hispanics. And that ticked me off. . . . The union needed more Hispanic representation."

It is important to reiterate that the union, through mechanisms of the internal state that enforced plant-wide seniority and its importance in the internal labor market, was crucial in building solidarities across racial and ethnic lines. Many union leaders of color express the sentiment "I knew the union wasn't perfect, but I had to be part of this process to make things right. . . . We the people need to make the organization better." This solidarity was essential at the end of the plant's life when many white, senior workers found themselves alongside workers of color. Bill Markus, a white worker, described the importance of solidarity at the coke works, the last shop open, in the 1990s. "The camaraderie, you make it work. If you can't make it work, not only could you get hurt, you hurt others. And you lose your jobs. Because you won't have a place. This place will be gone."

Regional Exclusions

Although many exclusions were constructed along racial, ethnic, and gendered lines, a homogeneous white working class is not a given. It had to be constructed through processes that "whitened" ethnically defined immigrant workers. When the workers I interviewed started at the Bethlehem mill, many of the Lehigh Valley–born third-generation ethnic immigrants had become whiter, moving into positions in more desirable departments. But the rural northern workers from the coal regions were initially defined as a less educated, less cosmopolitan, inferior group.

During the 1950s and 1960s, growing labor needs put pressure on the company. As mentioned earlier, recruiters looked to Puerto Rican workers. But Bethlehem Steel also recruited aggressively in the anthracite coal region to the northwest of the Lehigh Valley, a region that had gone through its own decline, accelerating in the 1950s, as demand for anthracite coal diminished and the mines closed. Ed O'Brien, a former president of the local union, says "they [Bethlehem Steel] did a lot an awful lot of advertising [in 1963/64] when they had a tough time getting people. The ads in the paper would say, 'Do you have any relatives, friends, neighbors?' Bethlehem Steel was looking for people."[43] Sons of coal miners, in the late 1950s and '60s, were counseled by their fathers to "get the hell out" and look for jobs elsewhere. They did, even though for many, mining was "in my blood." The coal jobs were drying up, and young men saw the effects of regional deindustrialization on families and communities. Many looked to other unionized, blue-collar, industrial jobs such as those at Bethlehem Steel, although these jobs required commuting or out migration. Ed O'Brien, for example, recalls relatives moving to New Jersey and to Pennsylvania's Levittown (near US Steel's new Fairless mill), and commuting to the Lehigh Valley for stable union jobs.[44]

Speaking of Bethlehem Steel's efforts to find workers for some of its less appealing departments, Joe Privsek says, "You couldn't get the white guys to do some of this work. That's why Bethlehem Steel advertised in the coal region. They couldn't get local people to work in the ingot mold or the coke works." In this statement, Joe racializes the up-homers like himself as non-white, alluding to the privileged position of native Lehigh Valley white workers. Lacking opportunities in their region, up-homers were willing to work hard at these less desirable jobs. In addition, work in the steel mills was seen as preferable to the dangerous and unhealthy work in the coal mines. "[The] danger, I don't think I minded it. Coming from that area up there, and just knowing what my ancestors went through, this had to be a picnic compared with going down into a coal mine. That's the way I look at it."[45]

As with Puerto Rican laborers, the work characteristics of up-homers were naturalized and essentialized. They were perceived as willing to do back-breaking manual labor but also as rural hicks, not as intelligent, educated, or as likely as white Lehigh Valley workers to be candidates for apprenticeships and skilled jobs in the Bethlehem plant. In his book on working at the plant, Dave Kuchta, an up-homer, writes about interviewing for a job at Bethlehem Steel in 1952. He describes the interviewer asking "to look at my hands. Yes, he was disappointed. They weren't calloused and beat up from picking coal."[46] As a result, instead of sending Dave to the hardest jobs—as a general laborer, coke works, or ingot mold—the company gave him a better job in weldment.

Workers like Dave and other up-homers were not typical rural immigrant laborers, as many had long family histories of industrial work (many were third-generation coal miners), and often radical union experience. For example, Ed O'Brien attributes his strong union commitment to his "bloodline," as he had many relatives who were active in the United Mineworkers, and a great-grandfather who went on the run for his activities as a Molly Maguire.

Some of the up-homers moved down to the Lehigh Valley, meeting their wives there or marrying up home and making a family decision to migrate. Pete Bondar, for example, started working at Bethlehem Steel in the 1950s and commuted on weekends for the first six years. But after getting married, he and his wife moved to Bethlehem, raised their children there, and assimilated to urban life. Pete maintained a strong coal-country identity though, working with the union to ensure that he could help his community members, as those who were commuting "didn't have time to come to the union hall."

Others commuted from the coal country for their entire careers at Bethlehem Steel, earning reputations for driving through any kind of weather to make it to work. They opted to commute daily (or in some cases weekly) to maintain homes in the coal country and to preserve their identity as up-homers. Carpooling generated strong bonds of solidarity as "the trip took about an hour each way. . . . We would talk about everything under the sun."[47] Workers stayed in the coal region for a variety of reasons: because of wide social and extended family networks, inherited houses, and cheaper housing and cost of living; because "it was less hectic, [and had] less crime"; and because they loved "God's country"—the more rural towns and rolling country they had grown up in. Scott Crewe, who lived in New York City for a while, returned to his coal-country hometown, got a job at the Steel, and commuted for his entire career. "This is where I was born and raised, in this village. I never wanted to move."

Ethnic stereotyping was common in the mill, and was often used in joking relationships to build strong ties between groups, even while simultaneously denigrating them. Dennis Mayer says, "The guys from down there [the Lehigh Valley] they called us coal crackers in a demeaning way. But we took that as a compliment." However, resentments could grow when work became scarce. In the recession of the early 1980s, Pete Bondar remembers Lehigh Valley "natives" saying the up-homers "took their jobs. . . . 'Because of you up-homers we can't get a job.'" The very identities through which citizenship rights to the mill were mobilized (the intergenerational work of entire families within the plant) could be used to legitimize exclusions of newcomers—whether they were from the coal region, Puerto Rican workers, or women. Parameters for inclusion were unevenly distributed along racial, ethnic, and gender lines. Up-homers were white, but they were first-generation steelworkers from outside the Valley, whereas browner Mexicans might be third-generation workers and long-time Bethlehem natives.

Management mobilized stereotypes and differences in an attempt to pit workers' groups against each other. Charlie Joyce says the company "would use up-homers coming in to work [in bad weather] as leverage against the people from the city who didn't come in during bad weather." The naturalized regional characteristic of "hard work" was used to pit workers against each other and led to demands at times from Lehigh Valley natives to young coal region workers to slow down.

However, many up-homers were able to move into skilled jobs at the steel mill, often using training from the military to access craft jobs. Building on shared white, ethnic, masculine solidarities with native Lehigh Valley workers, up-homers were able to overcome stereotypes and assimilate into a broader steel working class. This gave them access to the internal horizontal labor market, mentoring in the plant, and robust solidarities with other white steelworkers. Strong commitment to unions contributed, for many, to participation as shop stewards and union officials, offering additional avenues for internal mobility.

Women in the Steel Mill

The 1974 consent decree mandated that 20 percent of all new hires nationally in steel mills be women and laid out the goal of getting more women into the crafts and skilled trades.[48] At the height of their employment in basic steel in the US (about 1980), women held 14,500 maintenance and production jobs, increasing from 1.8 percent to 5.8 percent of basic steelworkers from 1974 to 1979.[49] By 1984, after massive layoffs in basic steel, there were only three thousand women in basic steel work. This constituted a higher percentage of women steelworkers, but much lower overall numbers as layoffs displaced thousands of workers, including most of the newly hired women.[50]

Like all workers, women entered the steel mill with low seniority. The bulk of women hired for shop floor jobs arrived in the plant's last wave of hiring in 1978/79. Like their male counterparts in that age grade, women never experienced the opportunity to mentor younger workers and, with low seniority, they found limited opportunities for moving into better jobs, especially during industry contraction in the early 1980s. In fact, many women hired in the late 1970s lost their jobs in the 1980s and never returned to work in steel.

Most women workers shared a white, Lehigh Valley identity with most of their male age-grade peers. (I did interview one African American woman who came into the mill in 1979, and she believed that the antimony toward women trumped racial hostilities in her experience.) However, the hypermasculine environment of the mill ensured that most men were initially very hostile to the idea of women steelworkers. With the exception of the most junior men— those coming in at the same time as women—male steelworkers had never worked with women in the mill. Men argued that women did not have the physical strength to do the hard manual labor in the mill, with its risk, dirt, and heat, and that they were technically incompetent and incapable of working with heavy equipment. Moreover, women confronted overt resentment that they were taking the "family-wage" jobs that steelworkers fought for and that unions pushed as necessary for maintaining the ideal male-breadwinner nuclear family. The postwar exclusion of women from what was defined as male work in the auto industry, the steel industry, and the Bethlehem mill helped legitimize and maintain the family wage.[51] Women's paid work was defined as supplemental, while women's unpaid work as housewives and mothers was defined as primary, even though most steelworkers' wives held waged jobs at various times. The family wage served to reproduce gender inequalities at home as women were refused entry into jobs defined as male and denied access to male wages, but it also ensured security and benefits for steelworkers and their wives and families.

Shirley Macek, who started at the Bethlehem plant in 1979, had a boss whose son didn't get into the plant, "and he resented that. He said that the jobs were for them [the men]." Cathy Kovarik says, "We would hear comments like, 'You oughta stay home, you oughta take care of your kids.' You know. 'You should be home making babies. You should be taking care of us, making dinner.'" Even other women, often relatives and neighbors, expressed disapproval. Catherine Cooper's aunt chastised her for applying to Bethlehem Steel—as a single woman—in 1978, saying, "Well, don't you feel guilty taking a job away from a man who's supporting a family?"[52] Women may not have taken explicitly feminist perspectives in applying for steel jobs, but they very quickly had to develop and refine counterarguments legitimizing their presence as they confronted sexist stereotypes.[53] Shirley responded to her boss, "I didn't take this job from anybody. This job was my job." Understandings of citizenship rooted in the right to work were not extended to women in the mill. Instead, women were seen as behaving immorally, as "taking" or stealing a male job. Later on, as some women married other steelworkers, they also confronted resentment that one family would monopolize two family wages. A moral economy that emphasized solidarity structured around preserving jobs for as many workers as possible interpreted this as selfish, immoral behavior. This perspective did not recognize that many of the women working on the shop floor of the mill were single mothers seeking the better pay and benefits of steel jobs, or wives working to supplement their husbands' less lucrative wages.

Many men in the Bethlehem plant also resented the consent decree's civil rights emphasis for taking precedence over what they defined as the central moral principle of seniority. Fonow argues that this contributed to the hostility that women experienced on entering steel mills as they "entered the industry under an unpopular court order at a time when court orders regarding affirmative action and desegregation were generating considerable hostility and backlash in white, working-class communities across the United States."[54]

Access to valued apprenticeships was an especially contentious issue. At the Bethlehem plant, Ben Weyer believed his electrical apprenticeship was "taken away from him" by prioritized women, arguing that affirmative action should not trump seniority. Bess King described the pushback that she ran into on being admitted to a millwright apprenticeship program:

> I took the test for the apprenticeship program, the millwright program, and then I passed that test and I got chosen to be one of the millwright apprentices. There were a couple of guys that were resentful because of the fact that I was a girl and they thought that's what helped me get into the apprenticeship program. I was indignant about that. I said 'I passed the test like everyone else.' I didn't really think that maybe I was being given special treatment because I was a girl. But I thought, well, what if it was true? It should be so, because they denied you having a job there for how many years because you were a girl? I thought, well, turnabout is fair play.[55]

Workers also resented the loss of "preferred labor jobs," which were physically easier jobs and traditionally reserved for older, weaker senior workers. Howard Kovarik describes such a job: "When trucks came in to get loaded, they used to back in to wherever they were going, so we had a person called a truck walker that would precede the truck and kept it aligned. They started giving this preferred job to women only. Well that got my dander up, because that's not seniority. Assign this job to the senior person that wanted the job." Howard's wife Cathy, a crane operator, saw this problem as more complex, relocating it within gender-based discrimination. She responded, "But it wasn't the women that necessarily wanted the job, it was the men that insisted this is what they wanted them to do. Because the men didn't want the women to be the crane operator, the chain person, the loader." In Cathy's interpretation, these less physically demanding jobs were also lower-prestige, lower-pay, and less-skilled positions. Giving them to women preserved more skilled jobs as male.

Because seniority was the central principle formalizing and structuring skills and experience and organizing hierarchical social relations in the plant, a rights-based discourse and civil rights legal structure were seen as threatening and immoral. This blue-collar critique of affirmative action is very different from a dominant professional middle-class objection centered in the idea of innate talent and merit. Professional middle-class opposition to affirmative action is based in the argument that these programs lead to the promotion of less talented, less intelligent, and less qualified people since "quotas" do not respect the "normal" criteria for measuring merit, that is, standardized tests and educational credentials. The shop floor culture does not give the same authority (in fact shows considerable skepticism) to formal credentialed merit, instead valuing experience encoded in seniority.

Although the consent decree gave women jobs in the steel mill, there was little in the ruling that enabled them to "challenge sexist practices on the shop floor" and to protect them from harassment and discrimination.[56] Bethlehem Steel had done almost nothing to prepare for women's entry into the mill. There was no training around sexual harassment or discrimination, no education of workers or foremen around new hires, and, at the Bethlehem plant, there were not even suitable washroom facilities for women. Building solidarity among women workers was difficult, as women were located in disparate departments and shops spread across the mill, and women had difficulty mobilizing union support for issues such as childcare, pregnancy, sexual harassment, and sex-based discrimination. One of the few women who held a union position, Cathy Kovarik, is critical of local union officials' lack of attention to women's issues and their resistance to including women in union positions. She says, "The union definitely did not know how to handle the women. They did not know how to fight for the women . . . they had no clue how to deal with the women." She tells a story of a new washroom built for women to illustrate these issues. As shop steward, Cathy went to inspect it and found that, although the company was insisting the women move to the washroom that very day, there were no walls on the toilet stalls. Cathy went to her union representatives and "invoked an Article 14. . . . I thought it was unsafe." She stated her complaint as a gender issue, that women (unlike men) needed toilet stalls for privacy. Local union officials, while unsympathetic, did file the grievance, and set up a meeting with company officials that evening, at the washroom, only to find that the stalls had been completed. This made Cathy look foolish. Cathy's husband says, "They set her up. The company and the union set her up." The male union officials *had to* file a grievance that she had grounds for, but the union and company collaborated to ensure that the bathroom was completed before the evening meeting, thereby undermining Cathy's power, authority, and standing as a shop steward and negating the validity of women's issues in the plant.

Lacking solidarity and union support, women often had to resort to individual strategies to deal with sexist discrimination at work. They attempted to overcome discrimination and harassment by countering male stereotypes of women workers, constructing solidarity with sympathetic male co-workers, and mobilizing gender-neutral moralities of respect for seniority and skills and a valuing of collaborative work. As women could not effectively mobilize arguments for their right to citizenship through the family wage, they instead had to prove their value as productive laborers and contributors to the gang or crew.

Women disproved male assumptions by demonstrating how hard-working, physically adept, and tough they were. Ann Kovar and a woman co-worker worked under a foreman who was initially hostile to women. He assigned them to the very hardest manual job of anyone on the labor gang, digging under a railroad track for days on end. Ann and her co-worker did it, and at the end of this job, the boss "actually took us aside and he told us that, he actually apologized to us. . . . He said 'you girls outperformed some of these guys by a hundred to one,' and he thanked us. He apologized to us for the way he was treating us up to that point, and pretty much after that we didn't have any problems." Shirley Macek, who worked in the boiler house, says "many of us, I think, tried to prove ourselves. The ones that didn't left." Shirley describes her strategy:

> Basically every job that they gave you, you know, you learned it as well as you could. You made sure that you did everything you were supposed to do. And I always tried to do one thing extra, just one little thing. I'd get a can of paint out and paint something. Or just do one little thing extra, fix something that, you know, nobody else would do.

Some women felt very strongly that they were setting a precedent for women in steel work, and that it was their moral obligation to prove that women could do the work. Karol Keglovitz's father laid out her responsibilities as a pioneer for other women very clearly before she started work in the plant. "My dad said to me, 'Just remember something Karol, you're one of the first women working in that place and you're going to set a precedent for Bethlehem Steel whether or not they're going to hire anyone.'"[57]

Women also used other strategies, including toughness and vulgar language, supporting co-workers in trying circumstances, and refusing to adhere to male stereotypes of feminine workers, to build solidarity with male co-workers. Cathy Kovarik tells the story of working on a crane in the beam yard, with "hungry" crew on direct incentive, who were giving her grief, keeping the work pace relentless and fast.

> Normally when there was breaks, maybe the one guy down here would go up in the crane and give this guy a break and so forth and so on. I didn't get no breaks

that first day. That first day they just kept pushing and pushing. . . . There was no let up. And I kept up with them. I was not going to let them discourage me.

Cathy says she did the work, and she did it well. But at the end of the day, as she left the crane and walked into the shanty, she looked at the five guys in the crew and said,

> "I hope to God when you go home tonight you can't get a hard on, because you'se fucked me all day." Now that broke the ice I think. That broke the ice with these guys, because I let them know what they did to me. But yet, on the other hand, I wasn't angry at them and I wasn't really cursing . . . believe me, I didn't curse at work, I really didn't.

Cathy felt that by standing up for herself, by not "taking crap," she showed these men, using their own language, that she was willing to work hard, but expected to be treated respectfully, as they treated each other. She was not going to go to the boss, as the ethos of solidarity dictated that problems between co-workers be dealt with between workers, not taken to management. But she showed that, although she was not masculine, she was tough and would not take their harassment. After that incident, according to Cathy, things went much better with the crew.

Women also built solidarity through relationships on the job with age-grade peers, as junior workers experiencing hazing together. Cathy Kovarik relates that with the major hiring of both women and men in 1979, many junior workers started together in the beam yard, doing "muley" jobs that required working together. "We'd have to synchronize pulling it together and dropping it" to make the job move more easily. New workers, men and women, were sent together to this crew work. Their age, seniority, and place in the life cycle, "became a bond. These guys took, helped take care of the women. The women took care of the guys. . . . They enjoyed the company, a lot of them, they became friends. Not just in the plant, but outside the plant. You would hear them talk about parties at so-and-so's house."

Women struggled with how to define respectable femininity in a masculine work culture that required tough behavior from them. Ideas about women's roles at home generated stereotypes about women working in nontraditional jobs—either they were willing to participate in a masculine environment because they were not respectable (of loose morals), or they were not sufficiently feminine (i.e., too masculine). To be characterized as loose would be highly problematic for a woman, leaving her open to overt sexual harassment. But in an environment in which discussions of sexual conquests, ribald commentary, and vulgar representations of women were a part of the everyday discourse from which masculine solidarity was built, women were denigrated and excluded.[58] Cockburn found that among unionized printers, "women are the subject of a traffic among men that serves the purpose of forging solidarity within the workshop and giving meaning and strength" to the union.[59] Women, therefore, had to focus on building solidarity with male co-workers in other ways.

Those women who managed to transfer into receptive departments (sometimes at lower pay rates) or to move beyond the long initial period of hazing and harassment developed strong relationships of solidarity with co-workers, although many did not and left. Shirley Macek, who worked in steam, water, and air, described a rich camaraderie at the plant, "we lived our lives there. You know, we knew each other. We knew the families. We knew the ones that died, the ones that lost their jobs, the ones that lost family members. You know, our lives were intertwined." For Shirley, at the steel mill, "everybody looks out for everybody else. It's one thing I seemed to notice. We did try to take care of each other." Christie Radics describes the strong relationships she developed with the male crew members she worked with on the same turn at the boiler house. "The people on your shift, you got to know so well. I mean we talked about everything and anything. They were just like having a girlfriend because that's you know, I was the only girl on my shift . . . and we just got along so well."

Many women, however, left steel jobs because the harassment they experienced was too great, the schedule was too difficult (for mothers the swing shift, posted anew each turn, made scheduling babysitting close to impossible), or the physical labor was too grueling. Of course, many men who started work at the Steel in the 1970s also left. And, as women were just beginning to gain some seniority and the opportunity to bid on better jobs, the recession of the early 1980s produced large layoffs of junior workers, and many women were let go, never to return to steel work.

Women often stayed in shops in which they had proven themselves and had built strong social bonds, rather than transferring to higher-paying departments where they would have to prove themselves once again. Cathy Kovarik, who bid into a coke works job as a carpenter, describes the hazing that she went through in her first day on the job in this new department. Cathy readily admits that she is afraid of heights and says, "If they don't want you, this is what they do to you . . . " She describes working, her first day, on a swing scaffold far above the ground, where male steelworkers kept jimmying the scaffold so that it was frighteningly crooked as she hung on to it. Cathy's co-workers did not mentor her or acclimate her to climbing, unlike Charlie Richter's, for example, who tried to protect him from climbing his first day on the job (see Chapter 3). Instead they made the heights seem as frightening as possible, causing her to transfer out of the department. Such tactics resulted in a certain amount of occupational segregation within the plant, as women preferred to remain in lower-paying jobs rather than transferring to new shops where they were dependent on learning skills from more senior workers.

Women also sought jobs they could excel in (women gained a reputation, for example, of being good crane operators). They avoided jobs that required extremely heavy lifting as well as direct-incentive production jobs with a more macho, fast-paced, and risk-taking culture. Cathy describes preferring crane work on a maintenance crew in the beam yard, rather than on the same production crew day in and day out, even though it meant less money. She felt excluded, as a woman, from the masculine solidarity of the production crew, where skill was defined by making money, working very rapidly, and using shortcuts to speed up the work. Cathy prided herself on safety as a crane operator, but this value conflicted with the shortcuts taken by the macho work crew. She describes receiving a "discipline" while working as craneman in a beam yard production crew. She said she carefully followed safety guidelines, waiting for the signal from the chainman before lifting steel beams. But her superintendent "said he thought that I was slowing production down because I wasn't moving fast enough." The discipline she received assigned her to working with maintenance crews, a work that was less pay but that she enjoyed more as she could work more carefully and safely, "I did not move unless I had a signal from them." She equated this work style with feminine gender roles, "I think being a mom too, you always, being a mom you know you're a little more, you don't want your boys to get hurt. And I think I was always that mom. I don't want my boys to get hurt so I'll, I'll do things." Cathy felt her skills, which she defined as carefulness, quality work, and safety, were underappreciated in the masculine production crew, which excluded her from the solidarity of the gang. In the maintenance crane job she felt included and appreciated, and could build relationships of solidarity, but she sacrificed pay in so doing.

Social scientists have shown how women factory workers build solidarities with other women workers, making use of feminine values and practices of kin work, social networking, and family-oriented rituals to build relationships that transcend racial and ethnic differences.[60] But in the steel mill it was difficult for women to build everyday ties with other women, as in such a large plant, with so few women on the shop floor, women were often physically isolated. Cathy says, as a shop steward, she tried to get the union to better represent women:

> I tried to call and get a hold of the women . . . so that we could get a meeting just for the women, to let them know that there was somebody there, and union representation for them. Let me tell you, it didn't work. . . . I can remember calling and riding out, and I think there was about thirty-two or thirty-five women that I got a hold of to come to the union hall. You would not believe what went on. It was more like "Why are you trying to start a problem? . . . You know, we don't need this here. . . . Already we're having a hard time, we don't need somebody to come to stir up a problem."

Cathy found this frustrating. "So that was shot down. It was everybody for yourselves I guess after that." The women Cathy spoke with may have realized that the tension between individual rights and union-supported values of seniority and masculine solidarity would render their attempts to organize around gender counterproductive. Organization could generate even greater resentment on the part of male co-workers, fueling a backlash of sexist stereotyping of women as needing special, protective treatment. The physical isolation of women within the plant meant that they had to rely on solidarity with male co-workers, and gender-based forms of organization that threatened those ties would be injurious to their work lives.

Women workers especially resented other women who did not work hard to prove themselves in the mill. Shirley talks about women co-workers who "didn't really want to learn, didn't want to do the jobs, and caused a lot of problems. . . . We resented those women, because it made it bad for you. All the hard work that you do and all the stuff that you do. They just undermine everything you've done." Some men assumed chivalrous and protective attitudes toward women who came to work in their departments, and some women encouraged this, mobilizing feminine imagery to solicit assistance and special treatment. Bill Markus describes his objections to this: "I didn't have much contact with women in the beam yard. But some guys ran over and did their work. It was impossible. You can't serve two masters. They'd pull the hook out for the women. How many times are you going to do that? Our incentive's going down the toilet." Chivalry undermined group solidarity as it slowed the entire work crew down, and co-workers' responsibilities toward other men on the gang took second place to paternalistic impulses. Those women who struggled to "prove themselves" realized that chivalry would only contribute to protectionist ideologies and heighten sexism on the shop floor. Cathy gives an example of a woman who came down to the beam yard. "She got those real long, red fingernails, this makeup and stuff like that. There's no way that this woman, no way that she would have fit in doing chaining." Cathy resented her, "because there we are trying to make a way, and now you come in . . . and you want to walk around like you don't want to get dirty. Where there're some of us, are in the ditches, and we're getting dirty. So it made it even more difficult for some of us women." This worker did not succeed in the beam yard, but Cathy says, "I think she came in and they wound up putting her in the office to carry mail, and yet a lot of the guys didn't fight her." She was moved into a cushy job, the kind traditionally reserved for old or injured senior men, but viewed as more "gender appropriate," thereby generating even more resentment. There were also a very few women who were sexually active with a variety of co-workers. Although they were a minority in the mill, stories about them abounded. This behavior enraged most women workers as it reinforced stereotypes of "loose" women propagated by men and encouraged the sexual harassment that accompanied those ideas in the mill.

While the moral economy of the plant, codified into internal law by the union, prioritized seniority in determining access to promotions, in reality race/ethnicity and gender affected workers' access to job openings. Other accounts of women in steel mills document a pattern of foremen discouraging women from bidding on jobs and assigning women to hard jobs, resulting in lower pay and harder work.[61] This was true at the Bethlehem plant as well. Ann Kovar relates how her bosses discouraged her from bidding on better jobs, but she went ahead and bid eventually, citing her union-backed seniority. She also describes one boss as "another one that was down on women, very down on women." She says, "I used to set up on my job [as welder], then he'd bring one of the other guys over and tell them, 'you're taking that job.'" This was insulting to Ann, as she would be moved to a lower paying position after having done all the work setting up her job. In this case, Ann went to her union shop steward and he advised her. "One time when you're with your boss alone, read him the riot act. Tell him anything you want to tell him." He advised her to not "take crap" from her boss, to use masculine language and an aggressive, masculine attitude to put him in his place. Ann did that:

> I made it known point blank that he is not going to say one more thing to me.
> . . . I told him I'd put up with this long enough. And pretty much I would say,

after that he leveled off. I think it just took me to stand up to him and tell him what I really thought. And normally, I'm not like that. I more or less just go in, do what I'm supposed to do, and go home at the end of the day.

In this case, Ann was given the confidence to deal aggressively with management, because she knew that the union supported her, even though she resolved her problem outside of the formal grievance system. Her union officer's advice was to handle this as a man would, through a confident, aggressive attitude at the point of production.

Masculine solidarity was built outside the plant as well as inside, through family activities such as picnics and weddings, but also through male activities—hanging out in bars, going on hunting trips, and playing sports. Most women I spoke with at the Bethlehem plant did not socialize with co-workers outside of the plant, and this is the case with women steelworkers in other mills as well.[62] When I asked about these activities, Christie Radics said, "It just didn't interest me to do it. And I don't really know of anybody that did do it. The girls that I worked with never did. And there's a lot that the guys' wives weren't thrilled about us being there." Mary Fonow documents at the Wheeling-Pittsburgh steel mill in Steubenville, Ohio, a near-picketing by wives when women were first hired in the mill. Bethlehem women workers corroborated the dissatisfaction of wives.[63] Shirley Macek said,

> their wives would never stand that you're friends. You're not looking to steal their husband. Like, my god, you crawled around in piping with these guys. You put your life on the line everyday with these guys. But you're not out to steal them. But you have so much more in common with them than I think anybody else could ever know. But you can't maintain this relationship without there being a problem [after the works closed]. So we got more cut off.

The tensions that women experience with the wives of steelworkers may be more than simply sexual jealousy (although clearly the stereotype of female steelworkers as loose played into this). Ellen Israel Rosen, for example, in her 1980s study of working-class women, documents their resentment toward women moving into male, family-wage jobs. These women are seen as

> depriving another wife of her rightful due. Working-class women therefore hurt themselves as women by claiming equality with men. Terry Sullivan, a garment worker, expressed this dilemma quite forcefully when she said, "When I see the women go and drive the bus or deliver the mail, when there are so many

young men who need jobs, I think men should have these jobs, not women. I think women hurt themselves by being equal to men."[64]

In the Lehigh Valley, this resentment was exacerbated by sexual jealousies and tensions rooted in stereotypes about the loose, nontraditional, blue-collar woman; wives' understanding of the masculine culture of the steel works; and the mill as a separate city off-limits to wives. Male steelworkers used various strategies to assuage wives' fears. Karol Keglovitz says that she was never invited to co-workers' weddings:

> because some of the guys they told me . . . if they ever see me at the store I should keep moving . . . I'm serious. He says, "Don't say hello to me 'cause I told my wife . . . she knows there's women down here, and I told her you were big, fat, and very ugly. And if she sees you walking over and say hi, I'm dead."[65]

Women also framed their femininity carefully in an effort to avoid sexual harassment. The masculine shop floor culture was built, in part, through a portrayal of women as sexual objects, discussions of sexual conquests, and a tacit understanding that "running around" was acceptable, perhaps even desirable, and would never be mentioned to wives. The representation of women as disreputable put women at risk of harassment. Jeanne Brugger tells a story of when she started at the mill in 1973. On her very first day in the plant, "some guy came up and told me the only reason I must be there is I must be a two-dollar hooker looking for some extra money." For Jeanne, this comment seemed to come out of nowhere, and she reacted strongly: "I was so shocked, I really was shocked . . . I still lived at home." This kind of role assignment legitimized, for men, their sexual harassment of women workers, including making up stories that undermined their reputations. Christie Radics, for example, says, "They make up stories about you. I just remember one time, the only thing I can think of, somebody must have saw me and my niece, and this one guy says 'Oh, so how's your daughter?' I'm like, 'What are you talking about?' and he went through the whole story." In implying Christie was an unwed mother, he was undermining her respectable reputation. Women combated this treatment by highlighting kin connections as daughters, girlfriends, and wives, emphasizing intergenerational ties to steel work—grandfathers, fathers, brothers who worked in the mill. Some women did get protection within the mill through these familial connections, although it was often tempered by their assignments to very different shops than their relatives worked in. Lineages of steel work that understood metal sense as patrilineal—passed from father to son—undermined the status of intergenerational steel work for women. Women also might mobilize a relative's prestigious working-class accomplishments (achievement in sports, for example) to earn respect. Bess King tells of moving into a new group of men in her apprenticeship, a potentially difficult situation. She describes an event that earned her acceptance:

> A couple of the guys I worked with had motorcycles. They were talking about it one day and I said "My brother-in-law used to paint motorcycle tanks." . . . They asked me who he was and I said his name was Barry Omaha and they fell all over themselves. They were hugging me. "Oh, guess who her brother-in-law is?" . . . They were very excited about that, and after that, I was like their best buddy.[66]

Workers' respect for her relative's achievements outside gave Bess prestige inside the mill.

Although upward mobility into supervisory jobs was problematic for all workers, as solidarity with co-workers in contrast to management discouraged individual mobility, it was especially problematic for women. The consent decree included goals that 25 percent of supervisory promotions would be obtained by women and black and Latino workers. This became an issue for women who worked hard to prove themselves to male co-workers and build relationships of solidarity. Ann Kovar describes working at the coke works when one of the women, Donna, became a labor leader. "Many of the guys resented that big time." So, she says when the general foreman came to her

> he came out to me and he says "Ann, I want to make you a foreman." They needed more minorities into management positions. I don't know if that was NOW mandated or that was just steel company mandated, but they wanted to do this. And I remember all the stuff Donna went through, and I said to him, I says, "Well, if I work up to the job, I'd take it. But," I said, "I don't want it because you need a woman in a supervisory position." And he says, "Are you sure?" I says, "That's exactly how I feel."

Ann would have liked the supervisory position, but she didn't want to be given preference as a woman. "I said, 'I'm sticking true to me.' So I never, I never took a foreman's job. I just felt that I needed to work my way up there." Within a moral economy that valued seniority and denigrated affirmative action, Ann interpreted the offer as unethical, and realized her co-workers would as well. She probably also realized that without the support of male co-workers, the foreman's job would be untenable as senior, experienced workers had multiple strategies to undermine the efficacy of problematic foremen.

Women in the mill also claimed citizenship, a right to the city of the mill, but in ways that were different from men. I never once, for example, heard women talk about cooking in the mill. Cooking appeared to be a man's job, although women could bring food into the mill, wives packed lunches, and women workers baked cakes at times. In fact, Mary talked about the men feeding her as she walked around the plant, "middle shift, night shift, I could go the whole plant and get coffee, donuts, sandwiches, anything. They'd be cooking." Gender roles around cooking and feeding were reversed in the spaces of the mill.

Women also viewed the large, open spaces of the works differently. Where men found autonomy and leisure time in hidden, unsupervised spaces, women frequently described these spaces as a bit frightening. Mary Keenan recalls being scared at night in the No. 2 machine shop, a large, empty building with strange sounds. Jeanne Brugger, who walked around to many different shops, describes seeing a man and a woman worker having sex once in the mill. Her reaction was, "anybody could do anything down there. After I saw this, I just thought, anything could happen. I better really start watching my back. 'Cause before, I always thought things were jokes that they did to me." Rather than representing an autonomous life space, this scene made the masculine space of the mill more frightening to her, raising the threat of sexual violence. Similarly, the aggressive use of highly explicit pornographic posters to claim spaces as masculine—a practice that Jeanne Brugger says increased exponentially after 1979, when most women entered the mill—transformed benign, shared spaces into threatening ones. Unlike the men I interviewed, women do not report sleeping or taking catnaps as, again, this might feel unsafe. Like men, women came to have an understanding of the geography of the mill, and some enjoyed its natural spaces, talking eloquently, for example, about releasing a snapping turtle into the river. The beauty of mill spaces was appreciated, but the danger of gendered violence in empty spaces was omnipresent.

The washroom, a place for building masculine camaraderie, was a physical space of conflict and exclusion for women workers. Since the company had done nothing to prepare for women entering the mill, they had to scramble to carve off bathroom and showering space from men's facilities or bus women long distances for bathrooms. Either solution bred resentment toward women, who were either seen by male co-workers as taking what had been male space, or taking what was work/crew time to make it to distant showers. These washrooms became points of contestation. Ann Kovar took a bus to the new washroom where she had to change when she worked at the iron foundry, "'cause they never had washrooms for the women, you had to go a long way to take a shower." Women saw each other in the washrooms, so some solidarity could be built there, but the isolation of the washrooms also made them sites of harassment. There are a number of reports of men creating peep holes to spy on women taking showers, and then using the private information they gleaned to denigrate women to a broad audience of co-workers in the public spaces of the mill.

Women took on ownership of mill spaces in different ways than men and did kin work, the gendered work of sustaining kinship relations, there. Shirley Macek developed an elaborate lineage diagram of steelworkers in her department, steam, water, and air. During the 1990s she created a wall in the power house, with light shining on it, on which "all these names were put in one, a block, that was painted in gold, and then preserved and stuff. Of everybody that was in our department from the beginning." Shirley said that this project resonated with workers. "You would have people that would come from all parts of the plant just to look at the wall and maybe find their name, make sure their name was there." Shirley put over three hundred names on the wall, and the piece attracted workers from all over the plant. She felt bad about excluding workers. "We had a lot of what you would consider brother, sister departments that we worked so closely with . . . but there was only so much room." Shirley translated her gendered skills into celebrating "family" connections and doing kin work to build an artistic representation of the meaningful social relationships in the steel mill. The kinship chart codified the principle of seniority, depicting the influence of more senior workers on junior ones, and it aesthetically engraved the names of workers, as the people who created the steel and the spaces of the mill, on the very walls of the plant.

Some women workers benefited from the early retirement incentives that were offered in the 1980s, as these freed up permanent jobs in departments by getting workers out of the labor pool and creating positions that involved working for short periods in different departments. Those women who stayed at the mill tried to get permanent jobs that allowed them to build relationships of solidarity with their male co-workers, something they could not do when they kept moving from department to department. Julia Mueller, an ex-steelworker, says, "the company started offering the rule of 80 [a retirement incentive]. That freed up permanent jobs in departments that were staying

open. They [women workers] could move off the labor gang and quit bounc-
ing around so much." However, as deindustrialization and downsizing in the
1990s shrank opportunities in the mill and heightened competition, women
once again encountered increased levels of hostility and harassment at the
end of their careers. Some of this hostility coalesced around the perception
that women were receiving favored treatment regarding medical disabilities
and external transfers to other plants (Chapter 5 will discuss this in more
detail). And some of it centered on the obvious and explicit junior status of
women, for the most part hired in 1979. For example, Julia explains that in
some departments, if a male worker was laid off from another department,
he couldn't bump a junior worker above a certain job classification. This
protected junior workers, and women were "marked" as junior in those departments in a way that men weren't. As Julia says, "in the power house, if
she was still there, someone laid off from the machine shop, they can't bump
her off in the power house because that job rises above the bumpable level.
That already started hostility. Men thought, 'These girls barely got here and
they're still working and I'm out of a job?' That began in 1988 or 1987 already.
Guys were getting bumped out." Men hired in 1973-74 knew, simply by looking at a woman, that she was junior to them, and they greatly resented these
departmental rules that forbade them to bump the more junior workers.
These resentments, generated by the stress of seniority-mediated layoffs,
exacerbated hostility toward women.

Conclusion: The Limits of Diversity in the Steel Mill

African American, Mexican, and Puerto Rican men historically experienced
multiple forms of exclusion in the steel mill. These changed with unionization, the civil rights movement, and the 1974 consent decree, but even as
these black and Latino workers gained opportunities, the restructuring and
downsizing processes of the 1980s and 1990s displaced them. Categories of
race, ethnicity, and gender also interacted with other variables important to
building inclusivity into the industrial working class, such as people's claims
to citizenship through native status in Bethlehem and lineages of work at the
mill. Coal-country workers, as non–Bethlehem natives and first-generation
steelworkers, also initially lacked social capital to access the full opportunities in the mill. However, as white men they could build bonds along shared
ties of race and masculinity—very important in the white, male mill.

Women had the most difficult time entering a plant in which working-class solidarity had been defined as centrally and inherently masculine. For one thing, they arrived with the last major hiring wave, in 1978/79, making them the most junior workers in the mill. Because of this, some male steelworkers downplay the role of gender-based discrimination and attribute these difficulties to seniority, interpreting them as the normal hazing that junior steelworkers experienced in their interactions with senior men. This view renders invisible the discrimination women steelworkers faced within the internal labor market in the plant. Also, unlike other workers, women were brought into the plant under the auspices of the consent decree, a major affirmative action program that prioritized race and gender over seniority and threatened the male power structure. Despite resistance, racialized, ethnicized, and women workers began to build solidarity, establish citizenship rights, and attain seniority. Yet even as they realized these gains, processes of deindustrialization began to erase them, eliminating apprenticeships, promotional tracks, and jobs. As insecurity and competition over jobs increased within the mill, women once again encountered hostility from male co-workers. Ironically, however, internal transfers into the coke works created strong interethnic bonds of working class solidarity. As workers fought to keep their own mills open and to slow down closures, exclusions and divisions prevented them from effectively building broader alliances within the community, with other industries, and even within the steel industry and the Bethlehem Steel company. This handicapped the unions in resisting restructuring and plant closings, leaving workers to instead manage the effects of these on their own.

CHAPTER 5

Closing the Plant, Killing the Corporation

Shifts and Shocks

As shops, departments, divisions, and, eventually, the entire Bethlehem works closed down in a process that lasted nearly three decades, workers and their families scrambled to respond. Many eligible workers took early retirement to gain their pensions and health care coverage. Others transferred internally or to other plants, hoping to continue working at Bethlehem Steel long enough to qualify for their benefits and retire. However, in 2001 when Bethlehem Steel entered the bankruptcy courts and the Pension Benefit Guaranty Corporation (PBGC) took over the pension plan, people's career-long paths toward pensions were abruptly ended. When the bankruptcy court then allowed Bethlehem Steel to abandon its health care responsibilities in 2003, workers and their families were hit hard again. These capitalist processes of accumulation by dispossession, supported by broader state policies, played themselves out unevenly across the lives of steelworkers and their families, with enormous consequences.

Workers were keenly aware of the significance and value of their defined-benefit plans. Steelworkers made household decisions, designed family strategies, and took collective action with the aim of attaining their pensions. The more junior steelworkers, hired in 1973 and 1979, were in the greatest danger of losing this benefit as they were still ineligible for retirement when their shops closed. Bethlehem Steel was a historical forerunner in both the development of worker pensions (through a struggle headed by the United

Steelworkers union), and in the elimination of those pension and health care obligations through Chapter 11 bankruptcy.

The exact value of a worker's pension was often difficult to determine because payments were calculated on either the "best five" earnings of the last ten years of employment or as a percentage of the final salary. Nevertheless, the overall value of monthly pension payments was clear, ranging from $1,000 to $4,000 per month over potentially decades of retirement, a crucial benefit. Workers were intent on receiving their pensions, and the union made this a clear priority in structuring downsizing and layoffs. They felt fiercely that the pension was not a "legacy cost" or a form of welfare, it was their due, earned through years of hard, dangerous, and dirty work. Jose Rodriguez pointed out, "We gave up our safety [health and environmental, due to the danger of the job] for security . . . we expected security" in return. Workers emphasized their citizenship rights to their defined benefit pension—both in terms of what Ghilarducci defines as "deferred wages" (collectively bargained in lieu of wage increases) and as "payments for depreciation," earned through the hard, hot, and dangerous work that takes a lifelong toll on the worker's body. These were not "legacy costs," they were "legacy benefits."[1]

As restructuring downsized the Bethlehem plant, older workers were offered sweetened options, negotiated in collective bargaining, to encourage retirement. These included a $400 monthly supplemental benefit to pad the pension until the worker was eligible for Social Security. This resulted in significant pensions (although these varied relative to earnings), and retired workers maintained full health care coverage. People who retired with these benefits could live comfortably without working. Or they could supplement their pension with part-time work, secure in their salary and benefits. Curt Papp, a staff representative for the United Steelworkers International union, said, "I felt I could see the writing on the wall" in the late 1980s. "That was my theory at the time, keep the place going as long as I could; every year and every month someone became eligible for pension." Papp said the union encouraged senior people to take layoff, and keep the young people. "This kept extending the young guys to get more time. . . . Our goal was to keep the youngest people working at all times." Because the union had few tools to oppose plant shutdowns and maintain steel jobs, and most Bethlehem steelworkers were older, attaining retirement and the accompanying pension and health care benefits came to be the central goal for the union and for workers.

In the broader Lehigh Valley, there was little sympathy for workers' demand for their defined-benefit pensions, thanks to the broader societal shift to more "flexible" defined-contribution plans. Today, most American workers lack defined-benefit plans. As a smaller and smaller percentage of workers (generally unionized, and often in the public sector) continue to have defined-benefit pension plans, public support for these pensions has shifted, and middle-class Americans are often jealous, rather than supportive, of these workers.[2] Both Republican and Democratic governors across a wide swath of states are today using the ideology of neoliberal austerity to attack public-sector benefits. Private-sector workers who pay substantial monthly fees and co-pays for their health care plans and need to set aside monthly income for 401(k)s are encouraged to resent teachers, transit workers, and autoworkers with better health and pension plans. In Bethlehem, white-collar resentment toward steelworkers who were perceived as being well-paid, receiving great benefits, and having secure and stable jobs without having gone to college were fueled through media and politicians' representations. Recent politics that shift the focus of accumulation by dispossession onto public-sector worker pension and health benefits play on people's interests as tax payers, stockholders, and homeowners and foment resentment toward unionized higher-paid workers, arguing that their wages and benefits do not reflect the "market-determined reality" of low-wage post-Fordist work.[3]

External Transfers

As shops and departments closed down in the 1990s, those Bethlehem Steel workers who were not eligible for retirement were laid off. These workers had four options: they could attempt to get back into the steel plant, transfer to another Bethlehem plant, access their pensions through medical disability, or forego the pension and look for jobs outside of steel. Many were candidates for transfer to other Bethlehem plants. According to the USW contract, when workers with more than twenty years of employment were laid off for more than two years or due to plant shutdown, they were eligible for either a shutdown pension or "suitable long term employment" at another Bethlehem Steel plant in the region, within a two year period. But Bethlehem Steel disputed how "the region" was defined, hoping to avoid paying early pensions by offering transfers to more workers. To this end, much to the disgust of many workers, Bethlehem Steel and the USW renegotiated criteria for plants falling within transfer range, adding the Sparrows Point, Maryland, works (a three-hour drive from Bethlehem) and the Lackawanna, New York, steel works (a five-hour drive from the Lehigh Valley) to the existing Steelton option (Harrisburg, Pennsylvania—a little over an hour). In 1998 Bethlehem Steel purchased the Lukens Steel Company, adding mills at Conshohocken and Coatesville, near Philadelphia, as potential transfer sites. Jeff Hoffert, who transferred to Sparrows Point only to miss his pension by eight days when Bethlehem Steel went bankrupt, is quite critical of this process.

> When this place [the Bethlehem plant] shut down, nobody had the rule of 65 [pension eligibility], so they arbitrated. They had an arbitrator decide our fate. And he decided we can go to different plants—Sparrows Point or Lackawanna. He was sitting in the room, all dressed up nice, and decided, "Hey now, you can change your lives and go to a different place." Which was not easy.[4]

Corporate management then tried to find transfer options for as many laid off workers as they could in an effort to delay pensions.

Workers had some input into transfer decisions. A worker could decide to accept a forced transfer, volunteer for transfer to a specific works, or reject a transfer. However, in the incremental, extended downsizing of the Bethlehem plant, shops, departments, and divisions closed at different times, and steelworkers often had a limited number of plant transfer options at the time of their layoff. Some steelworkers volunteered for transfer, requesting Burns Harbor, Indiana (so far away that they could not be forced to transfer there), Steelton, or Sparrows Point. Workers attempted to design best-option strategies for themselves and their families. But in navigating the variegated and shifting terrain of deindustrialization, they did so with limited access to formal knowledge. They relied on networks of steelworkers, union contacts, and for some, information from extended family members or friends who were managers at Bethlehem Steel. Workers, depending on one's job in the plant, union position, race, gender, and ethnicity, had access to varying information. Workers who traveled throughout the plant in their jobs or held union offices (and these were disproportionately white men) were more likely to have access to relevant information.

Workers might elect to voluntarily transfer in order to select a plant closer to home, as Dave Baker did when he volunteered for the Steelton plant. This allowed him to commute daily from his home in the Lehigh Valley. In contrast, some workers chose to transfer long distances—to Burns Harbor, for example—on the basis of information about high income and steady work at the plant. Barry Gorski described his decision to go to Burns Harbor: "It's the furthest plant of all that they had. But I figured I'd put in my sacrifice, five years, and work as much as I can as far as overtime. I heard from other people that transferred out there that they were making very, very good money. Our pension here was very low, this plant didn't have a great pension because of the difference in money." Barry weighed his options, given the information that he had.

> Should I go to Sparrows Point and make less money, or to Steelton and make even less money? I was hearing that one of them was going to close down, too. A lot of rumors were going around. I decided I should go to the best plant, and make good money. They were going 100 percent at that plant [Burns Harbor], it was always going 100 percent.

Barry stayed at Burns Harbor until International Steel Group bought Bethlehem Steel after the bankruptcy, and didn't make it to retirement, so he took a buyout and returned to Bethlehem in 2003.

While workers exercised some choice and control over transfers, in reality the company held the power. Laid-off workers waited for official letters to arrive offering them transfer. Although rules of seniority were supposed to dictate the timing of forced transfer letters, there was a degree of uncertainty and arbitrariness to the process, and therefore, a visceral element to the physical arrival of the letter. John Moore describes receiving his letter, which arrived by certified mail at his home. "It was like getting a draft notice. My heart sunk when I got it." Although workers would call the union hall to find out where they were on the "list," the timing was always uncertain.

Once the letter arrived, families held anxious discussions to decide whether or not to accept the transfer. Workers and their families visited the new site, workers had physical exams, and families agonized over transfer decisions. Workers called colleagues who had visited or transferred to these plants, visited the union hall (a gathering site and informational network), and gleaned information from their initial site visits. Some workers, generally white men, had access to more information than others. Workers weighed variables such as abundance of work, pay, and overtime hours; the condition of the plant; and commuting distance in constructing family strategies.

In considering transfers, workers' understandings of place clashed with neoliberal assumptions of a mobile, flexible workforce. Workers' emphasis on place, in which workers and their families inhabit a "life space . . . functioning in the context of their cultures and communities," as opposed to capital's mobile flow across spaces, was evident in these decisions.[5] First, most workers did not move with their families to the city of the new job. Instead they designed alternative plans to maintain their homes in the Lehigh Valley while working at transfer mills for enough time to gain their pension. The lack of younger workers at the Bethlehem mill meant that most workers had less than ten remaining years to reach pension eligibility. Maintaining Bethlehem as a home base and defining transfer as a short-term strategy meant that commuting distance was a key consideration. Steelton, and later Coatesville and Conshohocken, were Pennsylvania plants that could be reached in a daily commute. Sparrows Point and Lackawanna were too far for that. Many workers with sufficient seniority, such as Dave Baker, volunteered to go to the Steelton plant in Harrisburg. Dave talked to his wife about moving to Harrisburg to avoid the two-and-half-hour daily commute, but "she said absolutely no." As for setting up a household in Baltimore or Buffalo and commuting home on weekends, Dave said "my wife would have divorced me." Ellen Bream said she "cried and cried" when she heard that the transfer options for her husband, Rich, were Burns Harbor, Indiana, or Sparrows Point, Maryland. She told him, "I've never flown, and I'm not going to start now." Ted Smith poignantly described the enormous stress of transferring to Sparrows Point and commuting home to Bethlehem on weekends:

> Taking that move was probably one of the hardest things I've ever done in my life. I would have done anything in the world not to have done that. And my first probably three or four Sunday nights, you know, I'd always leave on a Sunday night to go down there [Baltimore], when I'd come home on a weekend. And my wife would be in tears and bawling. I actually would have to push her out of the car and leave. Which was hard, because I had to do it.[6]

Contemporary members of the professional middle class, inured to dominant concepts of flexibility and independence, find it difficult to understand the intimate violence, so well-described by Ted, inflicted by these semi-forced moves. In a contemporary, post-Fordist worldview, long commutes, frequent moves, and the necessity of managing periods in which husbands and wives live in different places in order to work are normalized and even valued. But for working-class steelworkers, ties to place are profound, and family ties and relationships are structured through everyday practices of proximity. Men felt they had to accept these transfers to hold on to Fordist wages and benefits, but it was heart-wrenching to do so.

Workers' ties to place were not strictly symbolic or emotional but also produced social capital that could not be reproduced in the new cities of Lackawanna, Baltimore, or Harrisburg. These included kin and friendship networks that could mobilize collective labor (for babysitting, or household improvements, for example), facilitate home ownership, and support job opportunities. Extended kin networks, including blended families, were maintained through women's kin work. This "nontransferable capital in homes and land, kin and friendship" provides important supports for working-class families.[7] Steelworker families also valued their role in providing social and material support to children and grandchildren. They provided housing when necessary, childcare, and financial and emotional support. Many families with grown children chose not to move so they could continue to be near children and grandchildren, and those with teenagers did not want to disrupt their schooling and social networks. In addition, wives held a variety of jobs that they were reluctant to give up for a short-term move, as secure jobs with health care, pension, and vacation benefits could not be easily replicated in new cities. One wife did take a six-month leave of absence from her job as a health care professional to join her husband in Lackawanna, but she returned to work in the Lehigh Valley at the end of that time, unwilling to give up her secure, well-paid position with seniority for a short-term relocation.

Another consideration in transfer strategies was the viability of the new plant. Mark Nowak decided not to volunteer for transfer to Steelton, but instead to wait for a letter forcing his transfer to Lackawanna, because of the poor condition of the Lackawanna plant. Mark knew the plant had been through an extended downsizing, and, in his judgment, it would soon close down. "I wanted to go to Lackawanna, since it was down to the coke facility. It was in bad shape, the facilities were falling apart. I thought that the rules would say that after the second shutdown I would be eligible for my pension." Tom Urban also waited for the Lackawanna letter: "I played the odds. I had a feeling that the place in Buffalo wasn't going to last much longer, especially after I got there and saw the condition of the place. I knew that was the next place to close 'sooner or later.'" Workers acquired information on site visits, using their educated assessment of machinery to determine the extent of recent capital investment. They then used this data in an attempt to predict the uneven process of deindustrialization within the corporation.

Workers also had to calculate the possibility of long layoffs as they moved to unstable workplaces where they lost seniority. Dave Baker said, "In transfer, there was no guarantee that you were going to stay there. It was just to get you off the pension list. That's what it was all about." Dave's wife was reluctant to move because of this insecurity. "Brenda said, 'Who's to say they don't do to you out there what they did to you here?'" But, a long-enough layoff could roll a worker into pension benefits, and this would be desirable. The potential insecurity of jobs at transfer plants, within a corporation and a steel industry undergoing massive restructuring, was also an important factor in the decision to commute rather than move permanently. Selling one's house, having one's wife leave her job, and moving children to new schools, all for the tenuous promise of steel work, was not usually a viable option.

Given this unpredictable terrain, workers, in hindsight, questioned the decisions they made. They tried to make rational decisions with the data they had, but that information was often limited. They didn't know Bethlehem Steel's long-term viability; the time frame for shut down of shops, divisions or plants; or the likelihood of entering bankruptcy court. They couldn't predict the effects of bankruptcy—the end of their seniority, the 2001 takeover of their pension benefits by the PBGC, the loss of retiree health care benefits. Which works would the corporation close next? Was closure inevitable? What was the likelihood of layoffs, and for how long? In what time frame would this occur? Yet even as rational individual choice was not always effective, perhaps even because of this, workers were simultaneously internalizing common-sense understandings of contemporary work as inherently insecure, unstable, and unfulfilling.

Transfer was also unpredictable because the union rules governing seniority could become confusing in the process. As departments and divisions shut down, workers were laid off, thus becoming eligible for transfer. But the arbitrary nature of department shutdowns combined with the uneven availability of job openings at various plants meant that junior workers might get more desirable transfer options than more senior workers. This irked Jim Wojcik, who argued to the union, "Wait a minute . . ." Why should a Bethlehem plant employee junior to him get a more desirable transfer simply because his department closed earlier?[8] George Dent, for example, recalls arguing for a transfer to Steelton on the basis of seniority, but later regretting it. "Little did I know if I kept my mouth shut, I would never have went anywhere." George simply lacked the information to predict that the closing of the Bethlehem plant's coke works, after his voluntary transfer request, would throw a number of lower-seniority workers into the transfer pool, making it more likely that he could have avoided transfer entirely. Had he waited, he could have spent two years on layoff and then rolled into his pension. These processes contradicted the moral principle of seniority, although not the union-negotiated law governing the transfer process, and thus made company transfer decisions appear arbitrary and unjust in the eyes of workers.

Despite its risks and uncertainties, the decision to transfer was clearly necessary for most workers in order to complete the years needed to attain their pensions. Since all of the workers at Bethlehem's plant were relatively senior, for them this was not an extended period of time. Over and over again workers voiced this motivation—"I went up to do my time for pension eligibility." "I had twenty-six years at that time; I needed four years." "My goal was three years and out," and "I was not going to turn it [the transfer] down. I would've went, no matter where, I would've went. I wanted to get my thirty years. I wanted to take care of my family." Most workers did not want to move. They felt, as crane man Frank Havlicek did, "I'm a Bethlehem steelworker. Bethlehem's my plant. It's always going to be my plant, and I live in Bethlehem . . . this is our home. That's not our home up there. We're only going up there cause we have to, we have no choice. We're doing time there. We're coming home here though." Workers' goals shifted from keeping their home plant alive to that of "doing time" until they were eligible for pensions. Work that had once been fulfilling became a means to an end. The moral economy of the home plant—the values of seniority, citizenship, and solidarity that guided relationships and practices, made work meaningful, and gave work dignity—was displaced and overturned in a new plant that did not recognize workers' seniority and citizenship rights, which undermined solidarity. For many workers this transformed work into something alienating and unfulfilling. For the most part, workers were putting in time to earn their retirement benefits, and when their time was up at the host plants they returned home to Bethlehem.[9] But again in a somewhat contradictory way, the carrot of increasing their pension benefit did motivate workers to put in long hours at their new plant, thus increasing plant productivity and increasing their anticipated pension payments.

THE COSTS OF TRANSFER

Once workers got to the new plant, they confronted a harsh new labor regime in which they lost many seniority benefits, a loss with psychic as well as material consequences. The local unions had differing agreements on transfer workers from other Bethlehem Steel plants, as US labor unions had frequently negotiated collective agreements that "distinguished between home plant workers and trans-plants" as a part of the price of company-wide recall rights.[10] As a result, other plants did not fully recognize workers' South Bethlehem plant seniority. In material terms, this meant that workers had to take whatever job they were assigned, often moving from prestigious, skilled positions to jobs as common laborers, work they had not done since they were young men. Tom Urban describes his new position at the Lackawanna coke works.

Well, we had to start at the bottom. And when you were not the bottom, that's where you went. Things moved pretty fast. . . . I had twenty-six years when I went up there and it was twenty-six years this guy (the boss) threw out the window. He gave us two months seniority. Which means I had to go to the top of the coke ovens. And I was forty-five years old. Young kids were doing the fish dance up there, and I was forty-five. It was so hot I thought my brain was on fire.

The shift to laborer jobs stung all the more as the Bethlehem transfers watched younger native workers move into more skilled positions. Larry Stewart transferred to the Steelton plant near Harrisburg, Pennsylvania, a distance that was within a daily commute. While this was desirable, allowing Larry to continue living at home in the Lehigh Valley, he found his new unskilled work demeaning. "I hated the job. I couldn't stand my job. This was working on an assembly line, grinding the welds. I've never done that in my life. You couldn't even leave the line unless you raised your hand like a kindergarten kid." Going from a skilled welder who controlled the pace of his work and the structure of his jobs to a disrespected cog in the machinery was an alienating and degrading experience. Although USW contracts laid out conditions for compensation at lower rates, or time limits for promotion into more skilled jobs, many transferred workers felt hostile bosses at their new plants denied them opportunities as long as they could.

Workers also lost seniority when it came to requesting days off, vacation times, and work schedules. Barry Kirk describes being unable to commute with fellow Bethlehem workers, as Steelton bosses deliberately put them on different schedules. This meant greater expense, less collegiality, more difficult commutes, and less time spent with other workers. It also became more difficult for these once-senior workers to arrange time with families, including for important family events.

As we have seen in Chapter 3, seniority was a crucial concept for Bethlehem steelworkers, Losing seniority meant a loss of value and respect for experience and craft skill, and of the lived recognition of that status in relationships with co-workers. Jerry Blazek recalls, "When I went to Baltimore I started out as if I just came off the street. There were kids eighteen or nineteen years old that had higher paying jobs than me." This upsetting of the accepted moral economy of the mill was demeaning and alienating for Bethlehem workers.

Demotion at the new plant not only violated moral principles of seniority, it also was highly inefficient for production, as the company failed to best use skilled workers. Fred Schneck, a foreman at the Bethlehem plant's blast furnace, describes the under-use of Bethlehem transfer workers at Sparrows Point:

> I'm going to tell you something. Edison Morales was one of the best welders that I ever worked with in my life. That man could be blindfolded, one arm tied behind his back and hang him upside down, and still put a perfect V underneath the bell cylinder on the blast furnace. I mean it, you couldn't get a better guy. I come down there [to Sparrows Point] and he's in the washroom as a janitor. I go over to the blast furnace that day, because they were down, and I'm up on top of the blast furnace and we're waiting because they had a contract out. Because they need a 6G welder to fix the job that they had on top of the furnace. I went down to the manager on maintenance and I said, "You have a 6G welder down in the washroom right now." I said, "He could get you going in an hour." They didn't put him up there. This is where it was so unfair to our guys.[11]

In the case Fred discusses, company management outsourced work, costing the plant money, because of its failure to properly value transferred workers' status and skills. Demotions also contributed to tension and hostility between the home-plant workers and the transferees, ensuring that workers would be hard-put to collectively fight closing the new plant.

Solidarities, identities, and forms of political organization within a plant are localized, preventing the development of a broader working-class solidarity. In some of the receiving plants, Bethlehem newcomers confronted the resentment of local natives, reversing a central worker identity as experienced, senior community members in the Lehigh Valley to that of short-term, transient residents in new cities. They also lost the value of their lineages of intergenerational experience at the Bethlehem plant and the claims this service gave them to the space of the mill and to intimate knowledge of its machinery and technology. In addition, workers were cognizant of the uneven unfolding of deindustrialization across space and time, tracking Bethlehem Steel's decisions regarding capital investments in various plants and correlating them with long-term plans for those plants. This bred competition between various Bethlehem Steel mills and between USW locals over corporate capital investment that indicated long-term commitment, as workers fought for the survival of their home plants. Partially as a result of this competition, officers of union locals often favored their constituents, the native workers at the home plant, over the new transfers from Bethlehem. In this competitive climate, most Bethlehem workers expressed dissatisfaction with their new union locals.

Steven High describes the tension between "home planters" and the "shut-down veterans" who are transferred from previous plant closings, but does not sufficiently emphasize some of the very real material causes for these tensions.[12] Workers in Lackawanna and Sparrows Point believed the new Bethlehem workers were taking jobs from their relatives and that they had come to shut down the plants. Bethlehem transplants were viewed as wrong-fully holding their jobs, not having full citizenship rights in host plants, and lacking the valued seniority that shaped work and social relations inside the plant. But host workers' fears were also accurate, as jobs *were* opened for transferees, reducing overtime opportunities for native workers, the prob-ability of junior workers being called back from layoff, and the demand for new hires. In a shrinking steel labor market, host workers resented priori-tizing transferees over more junior natives—often the brothers, sisters, and nephews of senior native workers.

At Lackawanna, where many Bethlehem transferees landed, native work-ers were long familiar with job insecurity dating back to the 1968 opening of the greenfield Burns Harbor plant.[13] As early as 1970, steel production at Lackawanna was cut in half and the workforce was reduced from eighteen thousand to about nine thousand workers.[14] The long, drawn-out process of deindustrialization at the Lackawanna plant, similar in many ways to what happened at the Bethlehem works, meant that Lackawanna workers had been struggling for decades to keep their plant alive. Like their Bethlehem plant counterparts, these steelworkers had lived through contradictory pro-cesses of layoffs and expansion.[15] Large numbers of Lackawanna steelwork-ers had been laid off, and Bethlehem transferees were seen as stealing jobs that should have been theirs. These workers did not accept the neoliberal naturalization of mobile, flexible labor. Instead, they made intergenerational claims to industries and industrial jobs as rooted in and historically tied to the community. Such claims, illustrating ideologies of long-time competition of one plant against another in the attempt to stay alive, were encouraged by management.

In addition, natives often correctly read a lack of commitment to host plant productivity on the part of transferees. In truth, transferees often hoped that their host plant would close, giving them access to their pension through the second-shutdown clause in the contract. While home-plant workers strove to ensure that their plant stayed open, transferees were not so motivated, and may have even worked against plant survival. I heard one story, from a Bethlehem retiree, of an attempted sabotage at the Lackawanna coke works, in which a Bethlehem worker almost precipitated an oven-closing accident. This would have closed the coke works, thrown workers out of their jobs, and moved Bethlehem transferees into a shutdown pension. Events such as this, along with general suspicion of transferees, pitted workers against each other and weakened their ongoing opposition to restructuring, downsizing, and concessions.

Transfers also put enormous strain on steelworker families. There was the economic pressure of sustaining two households, the emotional stress of maintaining marriages and other long-term relationships while commuting, and the constant worry that workers weren't providing the guidance and support that their teenage children needed. Family and friendship ties and habits of everyday life in Bethlehem shored up a moral terrain in which gendered roles, enacted through daily practices, maintained families. Once unmoored from the family ties and kinship networks of the Lehigh Valley, many workers' second homes in Sparrows Point or Lackawanna became male-focused. Workers would room with other Bethlehem steel workers, sharing apartments and townhouses, cooking and (when possible) commuting. Many workers dealt with this unsatisfactory home life by working as many over-time hours as they could. But in periods of limited overtime, the masculine culture of the steel mill, brought home at night to workers' home lives, could threaten once-stable family relationships. Co-workers did not condemn peers who ran into marital trouble. Instead, they recognized the difficulty of main-taining marriages under these circumstances. Without the constraints and supports of household gender relations and family structure, marriages suf-fered. Norman Brist, who transferred from Bethlehem to Lackawanna, feels that "the guys who did the best are those who stuck together and did things together. Guys that lived by themselves didn't fare well at all. They went out on the town, picked up girlfriends, had a hard time dealing with everything. It was an emotional issue. Having a wife at home, a girl there. One guy com-mitted suicide because of that." Workers also recall some wives at home who started "running around" when their husbands were absent. Many marriages ended in divorce as the demands for a flexible, mobile workforce disrupted the habits and routines of everyday family life and the deep social networks and connections of the Valley.

Workers felt the strain of absence on other family relationships as well. Norman Brist believes his daughter didn't finish college because "I wasn't there for [her] . . . the father support wasn't there. . . . I would be the strict one.

Donna would have it easy on them. Fathers are more strict than mothers."
Male workers transferred to fulfill gendered wage-earning responsibilities
within the family, fully aware that they could not make steelworker wages
and benefits in the Lehigh Valley labor market. But in doing so, they experienced damage to family relationships and a diminution of their defined
roles as father and husband. The gender-based division of labor within the
household changed as wives did more yard work, snow shoveling, and home
repair, and more discipline of children—roles that had formerly been defined
as masculine. The circumstances of transfer forced men into the narrower,
less fulfilling role of breadwinner, which alienated and marginalized many
of them within their own families.

PENSION-SEEKING STRATEGIES

Workers used every available resource to plan the best strategy for attaining
their defined-benefit pension, but most transferees did not reach this goal.
The closing of the Lackawanna coke works in July 2001 threw many out of
work. Bethlehem Steel's entry into Chapter 11 bankruptcy that same year, followed by the PBGC takeover of the pension on December 18, 2002, resulted in
many workers failing to get their pensions. Workers tell of being six months,
three months, and in one case eight days away from rolling into their pensions at the time of the PBGC takeover, which abruptly severed carefully calculated pension time frames. Most Bethlehem workers at the Sparrows Point
plant missed their pension because of the PBGC takeover, became International Steel Group employees, and had to stay with ISG or accept a buyout,
giving up rights to employment. The seemingly arbitrary date of the PBGC
takeover, an event completely out of workers' control, determined whether
individual and household strategies for pensions were effective or not. Without the power to make decisions as to plant closings and downsizings, and
without access to insider information, strategies based on individual rational
decision making are difficult. When John Caputo went to the Sparrows Point
union, angered and upset that he did not get his pension, "the big union guys
there" were not sympathetic, saying there was nothing they could do, it was
due to "the luck of the draw," not solid moral principles or savvy individual
choice. This left John tremendously angry at the union, at the company, and
at the government.

The option of transferring to another plant is seen as an important benefit, and one that many steelworkers in western Pennsylvania or southeast
Chicago never had. The transfer process, using Fordist-generated contract

recall rights, did enable many Bethlehem steelworkers to access retirement benefits that most contemporary workers no longer have. Yet the process was also an uneven aggregation of Fordist and post-Fordist practices that produced both speed-up and sabotage, critique and consent. By creating geographic and generational fractures in the working class, emphasizing individual and household strategies to attain benefits, and devaluing what was once creative and meaningful work, interplant transfers undermined broader collective resistance to a downsizing process that ultimately resulted in accumulation by dispossession. While real Fordist benefits were generated for some, in the end steelworkers failed collectively to protect their benefits, many of which were simply erased in bankruptcy, a move that shocked the workers and their unions.

MEDICAL DEFERMENT

While most workers who were ineligible for retirement had to either forego their pensions or accept transfers to other plants, others successfully used individual strategies to access retirement benefits without transfer, mobilizing a post-Fordist morality that emphasizes short-term gain while lauding risk-taking and one's ability to manipulate the system. Workers with strong contractual knowledge and/or social networks linking them to expert knowledge were better-positioned to pursue these strategies. For example, some workers exaggerated medical issues to avoid mandatory transfer and roll into their pension monies. As we have seen, when a worker was laid off, the company could make a transfer offer within two years. At that point the worker either had to accept the offer or relinquish their claims to pension and health benefits. One could avoid this choice only by proving a medical disability that would preclude working at the new plant. When Bob Hale was finally laid off from the steel mill due to departmental shutdown, he knew that because he didn't have seniority to get his pension, he would be transferred to another plant. When he received a letter for transfer to Lackawanna, he was working in a good health care job and did not want to move. Bob had pursued a nursing degree while at Bethlehem Steel, had the credentials to make a career shift, and wanted to stay in the Lehigh Valley. Nonetheless, he went up to visit the Lackawanna plant for a tour and a physical. He was irritated by the attitude of the nurse and the doctor in the Lackawanna dispensary, and he filled their forms out in great detail, writing down every ailment he had ever been diagnosed with and deciding "we're going to jerk [the doctor] around more . . . the faster he talked, the slower I'm going to talk." Although in Bob's story, the decision to attempt to get a medical deferment was rooted in the rudeness and insensitivity of the medical staff, it clearly was also a decision that could benefit him tremendously.

Because of Bob's health care career, he had connections to expert knowledge in the Lehigh Valley. First, he went to his family doctor, who listed Bob's medical restrictions. These were rejected by Bethlehem Steel. Next, he went to specialists to get more detailed work restrictions sent to the company. Bethlehem Steel then asked him to come up to New York for another physical. Bob countered their proposal with a little-known union rule stating he could have his physical exam locally. Bethlehem Steel approved that, and granted him a three-week hiatus while their doctor was on vacation. Even if not ultimately successful in attaining a deferment, Bob's time-stretching tactic could be useful. The time that he was able to gain through delaying tactics translated into less time needed to work at the Lackawanna plant, and it was all time toward his pension eligibility; it "squeezed another week out of them." The local union advised Bob to go to Lackawanna, but he resisted: "No, you're never getting out. It's like going to hell, you'll never get out." Finally Bob received a phone call that he describes emotionally, his eyes tearing up as he recalls his anxiety in seeing the "red light on the answering machine," and his overwhelming relief—at not having to quit his job, leave his family, and commute to New York—when he heard their message: "You are unfit to work." Bob avoided the transfer and rolled into his pension. He could continue in his new health care career, live with his family, and have a secure income and benefits.

Although workers like Bob were able to use education, connections, and health care knowledge to attain medical deferments, it was still very difficult to predict whether these things would influence the decision of the Bethlehem Steel company doctor. Lorenzo Quaryle related his own experience applying for a medical deferment to exempt him from transfer to the Lackawanna plant. Like many steelworkers, Lorenzo did not want to transfer to upstate New York. He had a small business in Bethlehem and had "heard stories of marriages going under and suicides . . . and this is a very sad and difficult time, if you can imagine what we were going through." He had long-term back problems and other medical issues, so he "armed myself with documentation from my doctors showing all these problems." With a folder full of documents, he and his wife headed up to Lackawanna, and he went, by himself, into the clinic to speak with a doctor and have a physical examination. During the exam, Lorenzo felt at a disadvantage: "I had no way of reading his [the doctor's] train of thought, how he was thinking. I was just wondering, what does he think?" Lorenzo was then asked to go outside and wait, so he did.

> And I think it was a good twenty minutes, twenty-five, maybe a half an hour, and then the doctor came out of the room and handed the nurse a folder. And the nurse opens it up and starts looking. And I'm staring at her and I'm focusing my eyes on this nurse because I'm not seeing her face, because she's looking down at this document. After what seemed like an hour, which I'm sure was about ten or fifteen seconds, but it seemed like an hour to me at the time. . . . I remember her looking up at me with a straight face. And then she couldn't hold a straight face anymore, and she had a smile from ear to ear and she said, "You failed." [16]

Lorenzo knew that he had carefully prepared his paperwork and had serious medical issues, but his entire future was wrapped up in the company doctor's decision, and the suspense of awaiting that decision was almost unbearable.

Many workers were critical of the manipulative tactics that resulted, for some, in medical deferments, as they felt that the rules of the collectively bargained contract should be followed. The contract was the bible, it was the rule of law, and it spelled out benefits earned through hard and dangerous work at the steel company. Manipulating the system runs counter to the moral economy of the mill that understands medical or unemployment benefits as not to be misused or abused by the undeserving. Yet the situation does not always lend itself to such moral clarity. John Moore and his wife, while talking about the hardship of transferring to Lackawanna—the emotional hardship on the family, the difficulty of the new workplace, the loss of seniority—reflected on the medical-disability strategy that some workers used. John said, "Seeing a doctor, that worked for them. There was a lot of people said they were unable to pass the physical. They're all working today. That got under your craw." But, after working for four years at Bethlehem's Lackawanna plant, John found himself laid off again in 2001, without a pension. As he considers this, he clearly feels conflicted about adhering to the moral system, the rule of law of the union contract. He sees that the company, the state, and even the union tried to cheat him out of his rightfully earned pension, ignoring the rule of law even as he played by the rules. This betrayal causes him to almost reevaluate his tactics. His wife, however, reassures him: "You did it the right way."

Critiques of medical deferment also had a gendered cast. Although some women were hired in 1974/75 and were eligible for pensions when laid off in the 1990s, most were hired in 1978/79, had low seniority, and were not pension-eligible. However, most women avoided transfer to another plant (I heard of only two women who transferred). In the 1990s, during the final closing of the Bethlehem plant, women workers were perceived by many as receiving special consideration and more likely to qualify for medical defer- ments. Perhaps the plants to which transfers were available did not relish the notion of integrating women into their workforces, and some may not have had proper facilities for women. Nevertheless, male workers perceived this as unjust treatment, and hostility toward women escalated in the last few years at the Bethlehem plant.

Some women simply turned down transfers, opting instead for retraining and pursuing new jobs, often outside of steel. Others pursued their transfer options. Ann Kovar went to visit the Lackawanna plant, although she had already decided not to transfer there. She describes her feelings at the time: "I like my little town of Bethlehem . . . if they take me, I'm probably going to say pass." She brought with her MRIs and doctors' reports detailing the in- juries she had acquired through years of welding—carpal tunnel syndrome, an injured right knee, and a lower-back injury. The Bethlehem Steel doctor in Lackawanna determined that her work restrictions would be too great and granted her a medical deferment, allowing her to roll into her pension. Ann remains a bit uncomfortable with this today. "I don't like to tell anybody. I felt bad about it, but yet it's due to me. . . . I did my dues there." Injuries like Ann's are part and parcel of steel work, especially for older workers, but many male steelworkers felt that the Bethlehem Steel doctors at Lackawanna and Sparrows Point were less likely to recognize men's injuries as problematic.

Cathy Kovarik, a crane operator, injured herself in the early 1990s while still working at the Bethlehem plant. She becomes highly agitated as she talks about angry reactions of male co-workers with whom she had built strong relationships of solidarity. Cathy describes her injury as related to a job as- signment, a "tight end job" involving upper body strength that put women at greater risk of injury. She badly pulled something in her arm and shoulder, damaging nerves in her arm and leading, she believes, to fibromyalgia, a de- bilitating condition that has often been thought of as a psychological wom- en's disease. When Cathy was placed on an office desk job in Bethlehem, her male co-workers reacted angrily, threatening to damage her car, and placing a noose on her desk.

Many of these guys that had given me grief at the end, I shoveled next to them. . . . I shoveled more than Tom shoveled just so that the guy can rest, and yet the guy . . . gave me grief. I asked him, Why did you do this to me? I took care of you many times. . . . These were the men I worked with for years. They were angry because the place was closing.

Cathy felt crushed that these men perceived her disability as emblematic of special treatment to women (thereby undermining the rules of seniority) and as an unethical manipulation of the rule of law (eligibility for medical disability).

A few workers were able to attain disputed pensions through collective action. When Bethlehem workers were laid off from the coke works in Lackawanna due to its closing in the fall of 2001, they expected to receive their pensions under the second shutdown criteria. Unlike the native New York workers, they were thrilled to see the coke works shut. Tom Urban, a transfer millwright at Lackawanna, describes an executive from Bethlehem's corporate headquarters coming to Lackawanna to reassure the workers, paraphrasing him as saying, "You'll be fine, you'll get your pensions. This is the second shutdown." However, he was wrong. When the PBGC took over Bethlehem Steel's pensions on December 18, 2001, in bankruptcy, they recognized the Bethlehem transferees as laid off rather than shut-out workers and therefore not eligible for their pensions. The Lackawanna transferees were furious at this decision, claiming that the only option available to them, the small, still-open galvanized mill across the street, did not actually have jobs for transfers and was not the same facility. While they worked at the Lackawanna coke works, "we could never bid on a job over in that area, in that mill, because they said it wasn't part of them." When workers protested this decision, they got no support from their local (New York) union, the Bethlehem local union, the international union, the PBGC, or Bethlehem Steel. Lackawanna transfers viewed this denial of their pensions as highly immoral and unjust, especially once they started comparing their cases to those of other Bethlehem workers, such as office workers and transferees to other mills. Transferees to Sparrows Point and Burns Harbor who did not meet the pension criteria at bankruptcy were offered buyout monies designed to downsize the workforce from Bethlehem Steel, making for a more attractive purchase by the International Steel Group. But the Lackawanna transferees got nothing.

The Lackawanna transferees began a collective letter-writing campaign. Various Lackawanna transferees reported writing "letters to the editor, to the PBGC, to politicians. We submitted them to the Lackawanna newspapers, to the *Morning Call*. We talked to people in Martin Tower and tried to get them to say something off the record." For these workers, collective action was important, "it helped keep our sanity" in a struggle in which "you're up against Bethlehem Steel, and PBGC, and all their lawyers." These workers remain angry with the union—"the union itself, after being so strong and saying they're for the working person, for them to drop us the way they did, it was totally unfair." The local union in New York felt little commitment to the Bethlehem transferees. The Bethlehem local claimed the issue was not in their jurisdiction, and the International said the collective bargaining agreement did not cover these pensions. The decentralization of the union thus left transferees, who no longer had a home plant (as theirs had closed), without strong protection. Finally, through collective pressure on their then state senator Arlen Specter, these workers received an appeal hearing. As a result, in 2005, the PBGC ruled in favor of second shutdown pensions for the Lackawanna transfers. For these workers, receiving the pension was a tremendous financial relief, even though ultimately it was much-reduced. As Tom Urban said, "In spite of my low-paying job with the state, and the pittance that I get from my pension, I'll be at a livable level. [Although] I'll never be able to retire, I'll have to work for the rest of my life." John Moore's wife recalled receiving notice that the appeal was in their favor: "I opened the letter from the PBGC. I handed it to him. He turned white. . . . He was jumping up and down."[17]

At the Steelton plant, a proactive local union called steelworkers into a marathon session on December 17 (one day before the PBGC takeover), presenting the option to take a layoff, which would let the workers claim "early out" pensions, before the PBGC takeover. This strategy, based on a restructuring plan designed to produce a downsized labor force for an International Steel Group purchase, enabled the USW to shed workers who didn't have thirty years' service and weren't sixty years old—which included many of the Bethlehem transfers. Sam Chase, a union official, describes the meeting. "We sat at a table for fourteen straight hours. People brought their wives, daughters, sons to talk about this. What are my options? What's the impact of my decision today?" Sam said it was difficult to lay out the future. "There was so much uncertainty with our plant at the time. . . . Will ISG buy Bethlehem Steel? What will happen to the pensions? . . . We didn't know." Nevertheless, Bethlehem workers were encouraged to take layoffs that day and most of the transferees to Steelton attained their pensions.

The PBGC takeover was not the end of the story for workers and their families. For those who did manage to roll into pensions, Bethlehem Steel used bankruptcy court to jettison health care obligations and turn responsibility for already awarded pension benefits over to the PBGC. This strategy yielded a new "lean and mean" company, without costly legacy expenses, to be purchased by the International Steel Group. ISG negotiated new contracts with the USW (eliminating past practices rules and creating multiskilled jobs), and then sold the restructured assets to Mittal Steel Company for a neat profit. These actions were justified by neoliberal representations of legacy costs as welfare-like entitlements that need to be removed, thereby "freeing the political economy to behave more flexibly."[18] Even with the most careful plans, many workers were stripped of the assets, rights, and benefits that were due them. Workers used the parameters and rules codified in union contracts and legitimized through strong values of experience, hard work, and senior- ity to plot rational strategies to protect their benefits. They found, however, that through arbitration, corporate counterstrategies, the use of bankruptcy court, and the sale of the company, the best-planned, rational, individual, and household strategies were, all too frequently, ineffective.

Bankruptcy

Bethlehem Steel workers who transferred to other plants or retired with "sweetened" pension packages were shocked when they discovered that the company had filed for Chapter 11 bankruptcy in October of 2001. Workers were disgusted with Robert "Steve" Miller, the "fix it" expert brought in by Bethlehem Steel's board a week after 9/11. Miller had helped Chrysler obtain a large federal bailout, had experience with bankruptcies, and was selected, ostensibly, to "turn around" Bethlehem Steel. Instead, he took advantage of the "shock" generated by the terrorist attacks of 9/11 to bring the company into bankruptcy court, filing for Chapter 11 protection within a few weeks. Steelworkers denigrate the contemporary accolades for executives who gen- erate quick profits through restructuring, layoffs, and corporate dismantling. Most steelworkers today are extremely cynical about Steve Miller, dismissing him with comments such as, "All he wanted to do was sell it [the company], that's all he was here for the way I seen it," and, "He did nothing. He sold the place. Anybody could have done that."

The steel industry in the US was a trendsetter in first establishing the benefits (later defined as legacy costs) of pensions and health care.[19] Later, the steel industry also became a trendsetter in the strategic use of bank- ruptcy to jettison these health and pension obligations. In the 1980s, LTV Steel's bankruptcy became the first large pension claim faced by the PBGC (of $2.2 billion). Negotiations around this case led to changes in bankruptcy and pension laws and set important legal bankruptcy precedents.[20] In 2001,

Bethlehem Steel's pension fund became the largest (at $4.3 billion) at that time to be picked up by the PBGC.

By the time Bethlehem Steel entered the bankruptcy court, the meaning of "turnaround" had changed in the US as corporations increasingly began to strategically use Chapter 11 to eliminate legacy costs and reorganize corporations, thereby generating profits for financiers, managers, and corporate buyers. In 1989, books like *Turnaround: Avoid Bankruptcy and Revitalize Your Company* still gave corporate executives advice on steering clear of a heavily stigmatized bankruptcy process.[21] But by the time Steve Miller wrote his autobiography in 2008, *The Turnaround Kid: What I Learned Rescuing America's Most Troubled Companies*, he was touting his role in bringing Bethlehem Steel into bankruptcy, defining this as a creative turnaround strategy. Thus today "turnaround" refers to intentionally going into bankruptcy court as a way to strategically restructure the corporation through gutting union contracts, dumping legacy commitments, and using the rule of law to protect the corporation from civil claims and lawsuits. Miller described bankruptcy as "a growth industry," and wrote, "I had also contributed, along with Wilbur Ross and Leo Gerard and many others, to the transformation and preservation of the American steel industry."[22] Miller represented the steel industry as hobbled due to "health care . . . pensions, high-cost labor contracts, and intense competition."[23] In his formula, therefore, getting rid of these obligations, workers themselves, and the rules written into contracts would render the industry fit to compete internationally. The use of the bankruptcy courts to restructure the industry was "a success story" in which "we may even have set an example" for other businesses.[24]

By 2009, restructuring through bankruptcy had come to be referred to as a "quick rinse," and was juxtaposed to the more thorough "cleanse" of restructuring through corporate takeover. In her ethnography of Wall Street, anthropologist Karen Ho quotes a British corporate raider describing the "cleanse" as a strategy to "let the market free, and . . . cleanse through market action a structure which was wrong."[25] For corporate powers, workers' benefits are legacy costs, and defined as unnatural, rigid restraints on corporate profitability, constraints that can be washed away by the natural processes of "the market." In this language, bankruptcy can drain the legacy costs of old-line industries (such as steel, airlines, and auto manufacturing), allowing the emergence of the corporation as a "new" entity, no longer responsible for previous contracts or commitments to workers. These quick rinses, or "pre-packaged bankruptcies," cancel debt obligations and exert pressure on unions to agree to concessionary contracts with the restructured corporation.

In the Bethlehem Steel case, International Steel Group (Bethlehem Steel's buyer) was able to negotiate a contract with the United Steelworkers union with a reduced number of jobs, fewer job classifications, new work rules, and without previous health and pension benefits by threatening liquidation (as opposed to sale). International Steel Group became an attractive and profitable steel company that Wilbur Ross was able to sell for $4.5 billion to Mittal Steel in 2004, just a year and a half after buying Bethlehem Steel, realizing a $267 million windfall. Social scientist Eileen Appelbaum points out that Ross's profits "almost exactly equal the losses sustained in the pension and health care programmes for retirees."[26] Clearly, there were profits to be made in steel. But this contemporary financial economy, created through deregulation, laws favoring speculation, and a culture lauding shareholder value, continued to rely on dispossessing workers of their assets and driving down wages to generate profits made through bankruptcies, takeovers, and mergers and acquisitions.[27]

Although steelworkers had foreseen the eventual closing of the south Bethlehem plant (if not the timing or abruptness of the final shut down), they did not predict bankruptcy. And even when Bethlehem Steel filed Chapter 11, many steelworkers saw the bankruptcy process as a restructuring, not as the end of the corporation. Even union officials like Ed O'Brien, former president of the United Steelworkers local, did not predict the bankruptcy.

> That is one thing that I could never foresee. I certainly, with many, saw the Bethlehem plant shutting down. As far as the company going in complete bankruptcy, even as it was headed that way and people were coming to me with concern about their pension and benefits—and of course the pension is partially covered by the PBGC, the benefits are gone—I never, never, in my wildest thoughts did I ever think you would see that happen. Never, never. Things could have been handled different if you knew you were on the edge of a bankruptcy. I don't know who saw that coming.[28]

The filing for bankruptcy, and the bankruptcy process, including the court-approved termination of promised health care coverage, unfolded rapidly and stunned steelworkers. Don Booth had just transferred to Bethlehem Steel's Coatesville plant. He had been there two weeks and went to the office to fill out his paperwork for the new job.

> I'm talking to this lady, and she says, "Hurry up. I got to get you out of here. Bethlehem Steel just filed for bankruptcy and we have a meeting in an hour." My second week there! The first week, I could have gone back to Lehigh Heavy

Forge. I'm thinking, I'm screwed. I'll just go with the flow. . . . Oh man, I didn't see that coming at all . . . I just thought Bethlehem Steel would be there forever. . . . I thought Bethlehem Steel was too big to fail.

The shock of bankruptcy disrupted individual worker strategies. As a result of the bankruptcy, Don wasn't eligible for his pension and spent a few years trying to regain his steelwork job at Lehigh Heavy Forge.

Workers struggled to understand the purpose and process of corporate bankruptcy. When Steve Miller was first hired, he held a meeting with workers at Sparrows Point to assure them he was there to save the company and restore profitability. Days later, the company filed Chapter 11 bankruptcy. Management used a medical metaphor with workers, representing bankruptcy as a cure for an ailing corporation. But steelworker Manny Vega found that bankruptcy was, instead, analogous to death. Manny Vega was still working at Sparrows Point when Bethlehem Steel filed Chapter 11 bankruptcy. "We thought it was like [the company] going in the hospital. Go in, get fixed up, and come out. But they didn't tell us you come out on the other side of the door, where they put you in a box [coffin]." At the end of the process, Manny was shocked to find the corporation defunct, his pension clock ended, and International Steel Group in charge of the remaining assets.

Bankruptcies, under Chapter 11, allow companies to reorganize and restructure. In order to go through bankruptcy, a company first must get capital through financiers who are awarded the status of "debtors-in-possession." These secured creditors, who stand to earn large sums through high-interest-rate loans and exorbitant fees, are guaranteed their monies back and are given a great deal of decision-making power constructing the plan for reorganization. Often, corporations can *only* get financing through the bankruptcy process. Steelworker Richard Moytzen explains, "and then the filing for bankruptcy came. They had to do that because they owed money and they needed more money to keep operating and the only way anyone would loan them money, which was GE Capital, was if they would file bankruptcy."[29] In addition, upper-level managers petition the court for special incentive pay, required, so they argue, to maintain key managerial staff during this difficult process. Bankruptcy lawyers who guide corporations through this process also stand to make significant amounts of money. Legal fees, financial fees, and executive bonuses are generally approved by the bankruptcy court. Steelworkers like Tom Jensen question these expenditures: "The bankruptcy judge says they need these qualified people to have an 'orderly shutdown.' Give me a break!"

Workers are not defined as important stakeholders in bankruptcy proceedings, but as unsecured creditors. In addition, labor contracts forged through collective bargaining can be changed or eliminated in the bankruptcy court. After a short period of good-faith bargaining, "management can petition the bankruptcy court to implement a labor agreement unilaterally."[30] Many ex-steelworkers are highly critical of the bankruptcy system, in which the laws of the court trump labor laws protecting their collectively bargained contracts. Louis Moran, a worker who lost about 40 percent of his pension and all of his health care coverage as a result of Bethlehem Steel's bankruptcy, explains:

> People would say, "You have a contract and you're in good shape." But when a judge says, "This is what you're going to do," you can tear up that contract right there.... Once it goes to bankruptcy court the judge controls it. It doesn't matter if the employee has been working there for forty years, they pay the creditor of six months first. It is supposed to be guaranteed, this is a contract. But *this* contract is not the same thing. People are treated differently.

In court, the contract of the "debtor in possession" loan is prioritized and honored by the bankruptcy court, and the labor contract is nullified.

During the bankruptcy process, Bethlehem Steel petitioned the court to eliminate its pension liabilities by having the PBGC take over its underfunded pension obligations. The PBGC intervened suddenly (on December 18, 2002) to take the fund over, much to the surprise of Bethlehem Steel, the International Steel Group, and the United Steelworkers union, to prevent additional under-funding that would have created a greater financial responsibility for them. ISG, Bethlehem Steel, and the USW had plans to allocate early retirement incentives through shutdown payments to thousands of steelworkers prior to the PBGC takeover, thereby trimming the most expensive component of the workforce. This would have passed those early retirement obligations directly to the PBGC, while simultaneously reducing labor costs, making an ISG purchase more palatable and creating an additional $500 million to $1 billion in claims on the PBGC.[31]

The PBGC was mandated to insure "core" benefits, not early retirement benefits, so many steelworkers lost the early retirement packages they had accepted in the 1990s. In addition, PBGC pension caps are significantly lower for newer workers, so they suffered large pension cuts. Finally, the PBGC did not fully recognize Bethlehem Steel's agreement to increase pension benefits annually from 2000 to 2004. Therefore, most retired steelworkers experienced cuts in their pensions with the PBGC takeover. These reductions affected many of the steelworkers I interviewed and could amount to losses of as much as 40 to 50 percent of monthly pension payments. Workers who were most at risk of losing significant pension monies were those who were younger when they retired, those who received a $400 early retirement supplemental pension benefit (until Social Security kicked in), and workers whose pensions exceeded the PBGC cap.[32] In addition, because the PBGC did not recalculate rates until about eleven months after takeover, some workers received a letter a year and half later telling them of mandatory give-backs of pension monies (which would be deducted from future checks). Matt Nichols, for example, worked as a millwright in the Bethlehem plant from 1965 until 1997. When he was initially laid off, with his pension, $400 per month supplement, and full health care coverage, his family was fine, although he did continue working. When Bethlehem Steel claimed bankruptcy, he lost his health care benefits (then had to pay more than $1,200 per month for family coverage), his life insurance policy, and, when PBGC took over the pension plan, his $400 supplement. Overnight, the bankruptcy "cost me about $1,800 a month." To add insult to injury, Matt received a letter from the PBGC stating that they had recalculated his pension payments, and he would have to pay back extra monies. When I spoke to him, "they [hadn't] changed" his monthly pension payments, and he says if they do, "the house, furniture, everything will go on the market. We're making it now, that's all we're doing."

The date of the PBGC takeover determined the end of the pension clock. Many workers who had transferred to other plants specifically to earn their pensions failed to do so. Some were days away from receiving their pensions, but if they had not reached their pension date by December 18, 2001, they were instantly ineligible. Dave Campbell compares his experience at Sparrows Point, commuting and working for three and a half years only to be denied his pension, as similar to US soldiers "going to Afghanistan and Iraq. They feel like they're torn away, that they have no options. I could have said no. [The soldiers] didn't have any options. They're getting shot at, those poor sons of bitches. But, in my case, you're not allowed to shoot back. Who do you shoot?" Dave made a commitment to transfer, made sacrifices at his new job, and still found himself metaphorically attacked and helpless to respond when he failed to make his pension. Steelworkers who had been looking at a secure retirement, perceived as a just agreement between employer and employee that recognized the grueling nature of steel work and the need for early retirement, found that contract decimated in the bankruptcy court. What had once been a smart career decision (for example, opting for steel work as opposed to college) leading to a secure retirement was now highly insecure. Many workers were propelled back into the labor market to look for work to supplement reduced or eliminated pension and health care benefits.

Workers are cynical about the role of the bankruptcy court and bitter about the effect of the PBGC takeover. They question the inequality of pension re-muneration, wonder about the pensions that salaried workers and manag-ers walked away with prior to and during the Bethlehem bankruptcy, and are highly critical of the losses they experienced with the PBGC takeover. Bill Civ-ick says, "I lost my pension. I lost my health care. . . . That made me bitter. . . . You had the golden parachutes for the executives . . . that's not the way to treat a workforce that was good to you people." Suspicions of golden parachutes are well-founded, as reports increasingly document the hidden pension and re-tirement packages of top executives at firms. Firms going through bankruptcy attempt to protect corporate compensation and increasingly try to hide enor-mous executive pensions as popular outrage at executive compensation has grown.[33] One way to increase corporate pensions is to add "phantom years" to pension plans. In Delta Airlines' 2002 bankruptcy, the board of directors tacked sixteen phantom years onto CEO Leo Mullin's service, resulting in a greatly inflated retirement package. Phantom years are added to executive pensions, even as real years are wiped out from worker pension plans. The idea of phantom time is predicated upon the principles of seniority—that years of work experience translates into pension monies—but turns it on its head. Executives simply invent their additional years. In a corporate culture that rewards speculation, "creativity," and the ability to manipulate the rules, these fictional years are more real (they certainly earn many more benefits) than the real years of the workers. Workers' long years of hard work are erased through strategies such as freezing pension plans, switching to cash balance plans, and jettisoning pension obligations through the bankruptcy courts. Worker strategies to "stretch time" to realize their pensions pale next to ex-ecutives' ability to create time out of nothing.

Another strategy that received some media coverage is the purchasing of life insurance policies, payable to the corporation, on workers and ex-workers. This is an appealing strategy for corporations as tax-free life insurance bene-fits on workers go directly into "informal pension funds for executives" that function like "big, nondeductible IRAs." In addition, gains on investment of this money are reported as income, thus "reducing the drag that executives have on earnings" each quarter.[34] This much-used system essentially pits cor-porations against the very lives of employees, as corporations are "betting" on their deaths. Just as executives like Steve Miller bemoan the longer lives of employees as they assess "legacy costs," so life insurance policies bet on early worker deaths to fund the lengthened pensioned retirement lifetimes of executives.[35] These supplemental executive retirement plans are often preserved during the bankruptcy process, even as workers' pensions are being reduced and turned over to the PBGC.[36]

The huge sums paid through supplemental executive retirement plans (SERPS) and deferred compensation programs are becoming a considerable percentage of corporate profits. These executive payments point to the hypocrisy of claims that it is workers' legacy costs that are killing corporations and the overriding moral importance of creating shareholder value, since much value is eroded in these gigantic payoffs. Executive pensions rose an average of 19 percent in 2008, even as company share prices declined an average of 37 percent.[37] At General Motors, executive pension obligations exceeded $1 billion in 2006, even as GM was blaming workers' legacy costs for killing the company.[38]

BANKRUPTCY AND HEALTH CARE BENEFITS

As a part of the post–World War II contract between labor, business, and government, unions had negotiated robust private health benefits for workers and their families that included eye care, dental coverage, and prescription medication. Retirees also had coverage for themselves and their families. Although the 1974 ERISA legislation shored up private (employer-provided) pensions by establishing the PBGC as a public pension insuring agency, no such entity exists for health care. As a result, when Bethlehem Steel used the bankruptcy courts to eliminate their legacy costs, workers who had qualified for retirement found at least part of their pensions covered by PBGC. But in March 2003, when the bankruptcy court approved the eradication of health benefits, retired and displaced workers suddenly found themselves without any health care coverage.

Ironically, ERISA contributed to the vulnerability of large corporate health care plans in bankruptcy court. Language in the legislation was interpreted as supporting tax benefits for self-insured corporate health care policies, thereby encouraging large corporations to set up their own employee health care coverage policies in the 1980s. Doing so saved these companies as much as 50 percent in benefit costs.[39] ERISA provided substantial public support for health care benefits offered through what is thought of as the private sector, and favored large corporations over smaller businesses. These changes contributed to employers, not insurance companies, becoming the major health risk bearers.[40] But this also meant that as employers sought ways to increase profits in the 1980s and '90s, they looked aggressively to savings in health care coverage. They raised employee and retiree premiums, copay amounts, and deductibles; instituted caps for coverage; restricted coverage; created high-risk retiree groups; and eliminated health care coverage all together. Unionized retirees across the US were especially hard hit by these health care cuts.

Bethlehem Steel was able to use the bankruptcy process to eliminate health care benefits for all retirees because by 2003 business-friendly bankruptcy courts in New York and Delaware were assisting corporations in shedding legacy costs, and because Bethlehem Steel had a self-insured health care plan. Americans think of employer-provided health care coverage as a "private" benefit. In reality, however, private health care, like private pensions, is actually embedded within a much larger "public-private welfare regime."[41] Public health benefits, such as Medicare and Medicaid, were developed to fill gaps in private employer-provided and insurer-purchased benefits. And private benefits relied on public state legislation, court systems, nonprofit insurers, and tax subsidies. Jacob Hacker points out that heavy US reliance on employee-generated private health care coverage has resulted in lower public accountability, scrutiny, and discussion of these benefits. Employer-provided benefits are represented and understood as under the purview of the private corporation, and as such, are not constructed through public or democratic processes. The lack of public discourse around private erosion of benefits ensured that the ongoing cuts and reductions in health care are "played out family by family, workplace by workplace, debate by debate."[42] This privatized production of benefits means that rather than pulling Americans together in a response to health care displacement and insecurity, "for most, insecurity is a private experience," and strategies for piecing together health care coverage happen at the individual and household, not collective, level.[43] In addition, the patchwork quality of publicly provided benefits, a result of this regime in which public programs are added on to cover gaps in employer-provided coverage, and the growth of a "medical-industrial complex" in private coverage, makes the health care system very difficult for Americans to understand (as we saw with the Affordable Care Act), invites cost inflation, and excludes many Americans.[44]

Bethlehem Steel entered the bankruptcy court in 2001 with $3 billion in health care obligations. ISG was unwilling to purchase the company unless it successfully sloughed off those obligations (in addition to the pension costs already transferred to the PBGC). The bankruptcy court's approval of this clinched the sale. This shedding of benefits is an egregious example of accumulation by dispossession. Thomas Geoghegan argues that slashing pension and health care benefits "did more than any wage cut to increase income inequality in the US," resulting in an enormous transfer of wealth from working Americans to financial elites, an increasing impoverishment of the working class, and a corresponding greater reliance on debt for working and middle-class Americans who lost their jobs, their pensions, and their health coverage.[45]

Because there was no national insurance program for health care, unlike pensions, the loss of health care hit steelworkers hard. Steelworkers said, "The most heartfelt thing of losing was the medical benefits"; losing the health insurance, "that was hard." "I lost my pension. I lost my health care. I would have given up one or the other but not both. . . . Losing my health care. That hurt. That made me bitter." Steelworker Ann Kovar says the loss of health care affected widows a great deal and "that was a sin." Sam Ackermann, a union official, describes working with retirees after the elimination of health care benefits. Elderly retirees came to the union hall, escorted by adult sons and daughters, confused about why medical bills were arriving at their homes, with no idea that they had lost their benefits in bankruptcy. Sam had to explain to them that their Bethlehem Steel health care benefits had been wiped out by the courts.

The effects of losing health coverage played themselves out unevenly. Bethlehem steelworkers had to be pension-eligible (i.e., an acknowledged retiree) to receive health benefits upon leaving their jobs. Some of the younger workers, whose pension clock ended with the bankruptcy, never realized those benefits. Many workers, even with pension payments, sought new jobs, generally at lower wages than at Bethlehem Steel. Families in which spouses (usually wives) had good health coverage through their jobs added husbands and children onto their insurance policies, although generally at additional expense. Richard Moytzen, for example, explained, "Fortunately my wife had health care, so I'm covered by that. But phew, if I didn't have that, I'd be in dire straits."[46] Others (depending on age, history, or disability) could find alternative sources of public insurance (Medicare, Medicaid, veterans benefits, and later ACA plans), although they often had to find a supplemental policy and prescription plan, and ended up with much-reduced quality of coverage. And some were forced to deplete savings, sell houses, and/or go without insurance, putting themselves at risk of financial ruin and of serious health crises.

The uncoordinated and uneven patchwork of public programs available often made accessing benefits quite difficult. In March 2003, just two weeks before the elimination of benefits, the *Morning Call* published a guide to health care for the twenty thousand Bethlehem Steel retirees and dependents in the Lehigh Valley. But even in this complex guide, there were many un-certainties. For how long would COBRA coverage extend? Would the state of Pennsylvania have a Blue Cross plan available? Would that plan be available if the worker allowed coverage to lapse? Would the International Steel Group set up a trust fund to help with health care? What would this trust fund cover? The confusing panoply of health care options (all of them expensive), and the arbitrary and unpredictable trajectory of this loss meant that steelworkers couldn't calculate its full implications and had difficulty generating effective strategies to ensure health coverage.

As a part of the bankruptcy settlement, Bethlehem Steel workers and re-tirees had access to COBRA benefits, initially for six months, and then, when the International Steel Group sale was finalized, for their lifetime. But as health care price increases continued to outpace inflation, monthly prices for insurance through COBRA went up, and these policies were simply too costly for most steelworkers.

Seeking Work for Benefits

The loss of health benefits propelled many Bethlehem workers back into the labor market. One strategy was to find a job with coverage, which often meant rejecting private-service-sector jobs and pursuing public-sector positions. Ron Kosek said that after the bankruptcy, "It started to cost me my pension to pay for my medical benefits for my wife and I (the kids were out). The $400 supplemental was taken away . . . so I went back to work." For Steve Jaros, when Bethlehem Steel dumped legacy obligations, "I lost everything. I had a part-time job, and that's what forced me to go full-time for benefits." For Barry Kirk, who managed to qualify for his pension just fourteen days before the PBGC takeover, "health care became most important in looking for jobs."

Many steelworkers found jobs driving or monitoring school buses for local school districts. This strategy—finding a part-time, public-sector job—could work if the retiree had sufficient pension payments to supplement low wages. The Bethlehem Area School District (BASD) ensured that ex-steelworkers were covered by the school district health insurance policy, even as part-time workers. The bus drivers union did, however, run into enormous problems in their first contract negotiations after the Affordable Care Act was passed. The BASD argued that if workers worked under thirty-five hours, the dis-trict no longer had to provide them with employer health care. The union pushed to maintain health care with success, but the negotiations left them highly critical of the Affordable Care Act. Some workers would have preferred to work part-time but found themselves working full-time to obtain health coverage. Dan Oates, for example, was offered a part-time bus monitor job, but he would have had to wait out a three-month probationary period before being insured. With a sick wife at home, Dan couldn't do that, and instead got a full-time job.

Some workers found private-sector jobs with health coverage. However, spiraling health prices, particularly for small businesses ineligible for the tax advantages of self-insured corporate policies, resulted in employer cuts to health benefits. Barry Kirk, a coke works carpenter who had transferred to Bethlehem Steel's Coatesville plant, found himself moving from job to job after the bankruptcy because of insurance issues. In 2005, Barry's wife, Lynn, had health coverage through her job, but she described her plan as very bad, with high deductibles and a high premium for adding Barry. She also was not at all certain that she could add him to the plan. Barry had experienced arterial blockage and recently had a stent put in, and Lynn was afraid her insurance plan would refuse him coverage due to a preexisting condition. Barry, therefore, needed his own employer-provided plan. He found a job he loved at a hobby store, but when this small business cut back on its health care policy after four years, significantly increasing his premium, Barry had to resign and re-enter the labor market. Barry's next job, at a company that did hydraulic assembling, ended when they changed to a plan with a $5,000 deductible. Barry's wife was upset that this low-paying job had such poor health coverage. She said, at "$12 an hour plus paying for health care with a $5,000 deductible, all you're working for is health care." Barry found himself back on the job market.

Eddie Smith, a former Bethlehem Steel crane man, found his truck driving job no longer tenable when his employer announced to the workforce that he would be dropping health care coverage, instead giving them cash. "I worked for them for a few years and then they came up one day and says, 'We're not going to have no more insurance for you. We're going to give you $250 a month, do what you want with it.'" The $250 didn't come close to covering the monthly $1,200 he would have to pay for insurance for himself and his wife. His wife, Nancy, was angry about this abrupt elimination of Eddie's health care, as the sudden change made it impossible to find the best alternative. "When his company dropped the insurance, if they would have told us . . . we would have saved money already with his Highmark Blue Cross. We didn't know that." The insecurity of employer-based health care made planning for coverage very difficult.

Employer-provided health care today is covering less and costing employees more. Pat Daly says of the large food manufacturer he now works for, "You get health coverage, but it's not as good. It's like that everywhere. They keep making it worse and worse. You pay more and get less." Even as workers' real wages remain stagnant, their costs in employer-provided health care go up, lowering their standard of living and driving many workers into debt. None of the workers I spoke with described their current health coverage as being as good as that offered through Bethlehem Steel.

Seniority and Health

Some workers, like Jerry Schneider, retired with their pension and health care benefits. Jerry, who worked as a carpenter at Bethlehem Steel, took an early retirement package in 1995, deciding that the pension and health care would be sufficient and believing it was better that he retire than that younger workers were laid off. Union officials said, "If you don't go we'll have to lay the younger guys off and they ain't going to get nothing. I said ok. My house is paid for. Hey, some young guy with a family, let him keep working. So I left." But the pension and health benefits he planned on to support himself and his wife in retirement were gutted by the bankruptcy court's decisions. Losing health care was devastating for Jerry, as his wife was chronically sick with diabetes and didn't work. They decided to continue their health care coverage through COBRA, but were paying $1,200 per month. Jerry says it cost them his "PBGC pension plus $100 to pay for health insurance. We were living on social security. I couldn't afford taxes and maintenance for the house . . . I couldn't afford it. . . . So I lost my home." For Jerry, "health care darn near wiped out my savings. Until my wife turned sixty-five and could go on Medicare . . . I have a sickly wife . . . I couldn't drop it." Jerry and his wife sold their house, moving into one owned by their daughter.

Pensioned workers between ages fifty-five and sixty-five were eligible for the Trade Adjustment Assistance tax rebate. The TAA program had a 65 percent health benefits subsidy written into part of the 2002 revised Trade Adjustment Act passed by the Bush administration. This subsidy was a compromise that "says much about the politics of selling free trade to a skeptical public."[47] Bush added this program to assure Democratic congress people that they could vote for free trade without abandoning organized labor. Many claim that the resulting program is unnecessarily complex. For example, in 2007 only 11 percent (or 28,000 of 250,000) of those displaced workers eligible for a federal tax rebate or subsidy for health insurance took advantage of this program, even though the subsidy was quite large (for many workers, more than $900 per month).[48] When the *Wall Street Journal* asked why that was, they concluded that the rules were too complex, 35 percent of the premium was still too expensive for many families, and the insurance coverage did not start until after a sixty-day period. In addition, the Trade Adjustment Assistance program did not cover every displaced worker in the Bethlehem plant.

Workers over sixty-five could access Medicare, although they did have to worry about Medigap insurance and Medicare B premiums. In addition, in 2005 workers became eligible for United Steelworker–negotiated VEBA prescription benefits, a program that helps considerably with the ever-growing expense of pharmaceuticals. And some workers were able to access veterans' benefits, although it was often difficult to obtain them and they did not provide coverage for spouses.

Younger workers were at high risk of losing health care. They had their pensions cut significantly by the PBGC, and they were not covered by the TAA subsidy. Therefore, if they could not find a job with health benefits and/ or were not married to someone who could access benefits, health insurance was simply too expensive. One such worker, John Caputo, went without any health insurance from the time he left his steel job at Sparrows Point, spending money out of pocket for clinic visits. The Affordable Care Act of 2010 was a great benefit for John, who was able to sign up for subsidized health care. It "was much better than having no coverage." It did, however, force him to limit his working hours as a driver to maintain eligibility for subsidized health care.

CONSEQUENCES

The insult of losing health care is exacerbated by workers' many health issues related to long careers working in the steel mills. Bethlehem Steel was a loud, dirty, and dangerous work environment. Many jobs involved heavy manual labor that stressed backs and joints, accidents that resulted in injuries, and environmental issues such as exposure to asbestos that created long-term health problems. Many workers I spoke with had back and joint injuries related to their work at Bethlehem Steel, most had hearing loss, and one welder had problems with his eyesight from "being flashed." Many workers had been diagnosed with asbestosis and were members of an asbestosis lawsuit. Some of these workers were able to receive medical disability, but the majority were simply faced with more expensive health care needs.

In addition to suffering health issues related to their steel jobs, many workers also suffer health consequences from displacement—the stresses associated with losing one's job or seniority, or of transferring. Although it is difficult to document the impact of displacement on health, a *New York Times* article cites studies indicating that heart attacks, stroke, diabetes, arthritis, and psychiatric issues are exacerbated by the trauma of layoff.[49] Research has shown correlations between unemployment and overall mortality, deaths from cardiovascular disease, liver cirrhosis, arrests, suicides, and imprisonments.[50] Studies cited by Russo and Linkon find higher levels of depression, increases in family violence, declines in physical health, and increases in mortality rates associated with job loss.[51] And economists Case and Deaton point to an increase in "deaths of despair" caused by overdose, suicide, and alcoholism among mid-life, white, working-class people.[52] Lack of access to health care, or insecurity of access, often prevents workers from getting the care they need during unemployment, displacement, and devaluing, thus exacerbating these issues.

Workers feel strongly about health care and they vote, in part, on the basis of this issue. Their identity as union members also continues to shape their participation in formal politics. Almost every worker I spoke with cited health care as a high priority for political action and reform, and supported both Hillary Clinton and Barack Obama in the 2008 election in part because of their health care proposals. Most workers support a public option in health care, and many workers support a national health care system. Workers, for the most part, supported the Affordable Care Act, but many still feel it did not go far enough. Dan Oates, an African American steelworker, says that health care is a crucial political issue for him, since "I know how good health care can be" from working at Bethlehem Steel. Fred Needham says, "They have a very good health care system in Canada," where he summers in his trailer home. Fred says Europeans he met "could not believe what we do here. European countries are way ahead of us in that." For Barry Kirk health care is the most important political issue: "The government has to have something available like Medicare to someone who makes $12 an hour but can't afford $890 a month [for COBRA]. You can't afford to pay $11,000 for health care. You cannot afford it." John Caputo, who was without health coverage in 2009, said his major political issue is health care. It "needs to be fixed. There needs to be a program that covers people who cannot afford high monthly payments." Steelworkers fought hard for health coverage through their unions, and they understand the right to health care as an earned right associated with hard work.

Conclusion

As workers and their families struggle with the consequences of the bankruptcy court decisions and deal with medical issues related to their hard work at Bethlehem Steel and to the stresses of displacement, most do not describe themselves as angry. Instead, they describe themselves as bitter. Jerry Schneider is highly critical of the bankruptcy process:

> The executive board went to the bankruptcy judge, said we have to pay all these board executives their bonuses or they'll walk away. The bankruptcy judge approved their bonuses. Millions of dollars. That was money that would have been our health care and pension. Bethlehem Steel could borrow from our pension at 2 percent. They took our money. As soon as they got their checks, they bailed. The place went down the tubes. I'm bitter.

Jerry says that he is doing other things now: "I'm doing community work, I'm relaxed, I feel good, I'm earning honor." Through a schedule filled with community volunteer and political work and with helping to raise his grandson, he feels fulfilled. But does he have "big bucks? No. Social security and pension? No. My daughter gives us a rent free house. I have a good life. All of that bitterness, yeah." George Dent says, "Losing my health care, that hurt. That made me bitter." Norman Brist recalls, "In 1999 and 2000 I was very bitter. In 2001 I had enough. I gave up fighting. It took a lot out of me, and I got very depressed." Norm says he was helped to recover through counseling, scouting with his son, and the satisfaction he gets out of his current job overseeing maintenance at a community college. "It could have turned out a lot worse, had my wife not been supportive. Many wives were bitter and fought often. My wife was my rock."

The feeling of bitterness comes up over and over in interviews and conversations with steelworkers and their families. Bitterness is not anger. To be bitter is to be cynical, disillusioned, and hurt by the perceived injustices of the plant's closing and the bankruptcy. Steelworkers are bitter that corporations can fire them at will, after a long trail of broken promises and commitments. Steelworkers are bitter that the bankruptcy court can wipe out contracts that were forged in legally recognized union negotiations. Steelworkers are bitter that the government did not intervene to help the US steel industry to survive, even as other industries (e.g., auto) and sectors of the economy (e.g., financial) are now assessed as "too big to fail."

But bitterness, unlike anger, does not fuel empowered action. It is turned inward to feelings of depression, rancor, and disempowerment. Bitterness is not shame, as blue-collar workers (unlike many displaced white-collar workers) do not hold themselves directly responsible for their displacement.[53] Nonetheless, workers convey a deep disillusionment and disempowerment, a criticism of corporations, the courts, the government, and even the union that has no formal forum, no community-based organization, or clearly articulated ideology through which to express itself or to mobilize collective action. The bitterness, turned inward, can fester as stress emerging in health consequences like high blood pressure, digestive problems, and cardiovascular disease, in psychiatric issues like depression and suicide; it can eat at families (leading to domestic violence and divorce); and it can fuel substance abuse.[54] It can be expressed in withdrawal of commitment to wider institutions—the union, political parties, corporations—a kind of privatization of pain (although the church can provide some solace). It can generate individual strategies focused on getting what one can in an unjust system (through tort law, medical disabilities, or lying for Veterans' benefits). And it can be turned into a resentment that fuels a turn to the Right. But bitterness rarely fuels progressive collective action.

Unlike professional middle-class workers, who often blame themselves for layoffs, steelworkers do not blame themselves for being fired as they reflect on their "choices" and strategies in responding to industrial restructuring. They do, however, second guess the decisions that they made along the way. In hindsight they are able to map out better scenarios. They reflect on alternative individual choices that could or should have been made. Should they have kept the job they attained during a layoff and not returned to Bethlehem Steel? Should they have stayed in the Lehigh Valley and not transferred? Should they have volunteered to transfer to Burns Harbor or to a different plant? Workers are bitter toward the company, the bankruptcy courts, and the government—understanding the role of these institutions in their loss of pension and health benefits. But many also internalize some aspects of dominant cultural ideologies that blame blue-collar workers for the "bad choices" of "failing to get a college degree" or retraining or not otherwise better positioning themselves within the new "postindustrial" economy.[55] Societal discourses emphasizing individual choice and personal responsibility shift blame from societal institutions to the individual and family. In hindsight, workers wonder if they made bad choices. If only they had made different decisions, could they have attained their earned pension and the stability of a secure retirement? Given the uneven, rapidly shifting, and enormously contradictory processes of deindustrialization in Bethlehem, it is highly unlikely that workers could have made "better" decisions, but the doubt embedded in hindsight erodes workers' anger, turning it inward in self-blame and bitterness, individualizing understandings and experiences of dispossession, and undermining solidarity.

Because loss and dispossession play out unevenly across steelworking families, there is a general feeling among most steelworkers of still being better off than someone else. Over and over again I heard steelworkers describe themselves as "lucky" or "fortunate," knowing that there are others who are worse off. Robert Kaufmann says, "I was one of the fortunate ones, I was always able to find a job," even though his jobs entailed an enormous reduction in pay and a loss of many health benefits. He says, "Health care destroyed my pension. I was lucky enough to get social security to make ends meet." It seems ironic that Robert describes himself as lucky by virtue of accessing an earned benefit on the basis of his age alone. Mary Keenan and her husband lost pension payments and had to struggle to put together much more expensive health care coverage. "I have no complaints. I think we were lucky. . . . It's really hard to survive, but we did. We're still here, and I'm still alive." Jerry Schneider lost his house and his savings paying for health care, but he says. "I was lucky." Why? Because he received a pension through the PBGC and sold Bethlehem Steel preferred stock before it lost all of its value. The uneven processes of dislocation and dispossession (affecting pension, health care, stocks, housing, and savings) mean that these processes hit unequally across steelworkers and their families. Steelworking families spoke with each other and generally found that there was at least one area where they, unlike someone they knew, had been spared from total dispossession. Even Fred Needham, who lost all his savings paying for health benefits, describes himself as "lucky enough to get social security to make ends meet." He knows that there are younger workers who have not yet accessed social security payments.

Will Wagner was one of the rare workers I spoke with who described himself as unlucky, having lost his house, gone through personal bankruptcy, and been laid off from a series of manufacturing jobs after Bethlehem Steel. He worries, "Am I going to have a job tomorrow?" and says he wonders, "Do you have a monkey on your shoulder with this bad luck?" But still, he says, when he runs into guys who are "devastated" by a layoff, he and his wife "say it'll be okay. We've been through this." Rather than anger, Will and his wife have developed a kind of pride in their ability to survive.

Whether one accesses a public program, is married to someone with health coverage, or finds a job with coverage, access to health care is not represented as embedded in a moral economy. Steelworkers do not discuss this in terms of "deserving" or "undeserving." Instead, they talk about luck. Access to coverage appears to be arbitrary, unpredictable, and insecure. Although there is a strong emphasis on thrift and savings and a bit of blame for those who continued to squander earnings as the Bethlehem plant downsized, for the most part, workers refuse to generate explanations for steelworkers' trajectories post-layoff into categories of deserving and undeserving. In a system in which one's promised access to health care is simply eliminated by the rule of law and one's eligibility for a pension determined by a court-mandated date, an understanding of dispossession as arbitrary and unpredictable, determined by factors outside a person's control, and supported through broad societal institutions simultaneously generates both a deep bitterness and a feeling of still being better off than someone else.

It is not only health care, wages, and pensions that have been eradicated by the bankruptcy court. Instead "the whole message of unions—save, put it away for your retirement—had been discredited."[56] Even workers who did not love working for Bethlehem Steel had clear goals for the future, "of retiring at sixty-five," "of working thirty-five years, then retiring." Workers can no longer articulate those kinds of goals. Instead, they see themselves as continuing to work forever. The future seems uncertain, insecure, and arduous. Even the benefits that ex-steelworkers and their families managed to secure are tenuous, as unpredictable and arbitrary future processes might eliminate those. Workers are concerned about financial insolvency of the PBGC as ever larger pension plans are dumped on it. Workers worry about the insecurity of public- and private-sector jobs. Workers are anxious about the health insurance benefits they have managed to attain, and the rising cost and insecurity of these benefits. "It makes me bitter, but . . . you put all them years in and you . . . but then, who knows? With the social security too? Is it going to be there? It's scary." And those steelworkers who went into public-sector jobs are becoming increasingly concerned about their defined benefit pension plans and health care benefits as US politicians, citing state "budget crises" as the cause, take aim at these plans under new austerity programs. The tenets, understandings, and expectations of the old negotiated order have been turned upside down, and workers struggle to make sense of and survive in a new, insecure social order.

CHAPTER 6

The New Economy

During the 1980s, the city of Bethlehem appeared to be spiraling toward economic disaster as shocks from downsizing both the steel mill and Bethlehem Steel's corporate offices reverberated throughout the city. But by the end of the 1990s, the regional economy had rebounded, generating new jobs and attracting new businesses. In fact, today Bethlehem is lauded as exemplifying a diverse, postindustrial economy and an ideal small, urban living place, unlike many other steel cities. Social scientists highlight the varied and irregular economic and social trajectories of deindustrializing communities, contrasting the devastating decline of cities such as Youngstown, Ohio, or Lackawanna to the economic renaissance of cities like Bethlehem or Pittsburgh. But these stark oppositions are often exaggerated, as they ignore deep class divides in access to "new economy" jobs. Steelworkers and their children run into many of the same obstacles and frustrations in planning new futures in Bethlehem, Pennsylvania, as they do in Youngstown, Ohio.

As Bethlehem Steel downsized dramatically during the 1980s, the city and the surrounding area suffered. With the loss of thousands of steel jobs, unemployment in Bethlehem reached an official high of 12 percent. Shops and businesses closed on the city's South Side, parking lots stood vacant, and each year the steel plant grew quieter and emptier. The wider region shed manufacturing jobs, losing 44 percent between 1970 and 2000.[1] Manufacturing losses began in the garment industry in the 1970s, followed by losses in steel, auto, and other manufacturing in the 1980s and 1990s. These losses affected every sector of the economy, from small businesses, to local bank branches, to housing markets.

In the 1990s, however, the economy in the Lehigh Valley expanded again, with a diversified base of high-technology companies, warehouse-distribution centers taking advantage of the area's proximity to eastern seaboard cities, back-office and call center functions, a growing service sector with a large health care component, a tourism and entertainment industry, an expanding retail sector, and a large construction industry related to housing and population growth. By 1999, the *New York Times* described Bethlehem as experiencing a renaissance, citing its economic rebirth as a "high-technology phoenix . . . rising on the steel shards," and celebrated Bethlehem's success in attracting businesses and expanding employment.[2] In the 2000s, the redevelopment of the historic center of the Bethlehem plant site—with the opening of a casino, hotel, TV station, and arts center—further rejuvenated the city. In 2008, Bethlehem was described by *CNN Money* as a revivified city and selected as one of the "best places to live and launch," a city that is "bustling with tech and biotech startups."[3] Bethlehem was voted one of the hundred "best places to live" in a 2012 *Money* magazine ranking and was ranked by *TravelMag* as one of the "most charming towns and small cities in Pennsylvania" in 2021.[4]

The Lehigh Valley's economy shifted from heavy reliance on manufacturing to a postindustrial service and knowledge-based economy. In 2007, the Lehigh Valley was declared "the hottest job market in Pennsylvania," adding 27,000 jobs since 2002, a rate far exceeding job growth rates for the rest of the state; by that year, five of every six jobs in the Lehigh Valley were in the service sector of the economy.[5] Of course, the service sector is a broad category, as anthropologist Jane Collins has pointed out. Collins distinguishes between "labor intensive" and "knowledge intensive" service-sector jobs—two categories with very different schedules, benefits, wages, and working environments.[6] Ex-steelworkers are likely to find themselves qualified for the labor-intensive, low-wage, insecure jobs, but not the better paying, knowledge-intensive service-sector jobs.

Sean Safford, a Harvard business professor, compares Youngstown, Ohio, to the Lehigh Valley, arguing that while in 1975 both were middle-sized industrial cities dominated by manufacturing, by the 1990s Youngstown was a depressed rust belt city, while Bethlehem had transitioned successfully to a postindustrial city with a robust economy and charming urban aesthetic.[7] He attributes this successful transition to the dense social networks facilitated by a strong regional alliance of political and business elites. This alliance, he argues, was able to mobilize local capital, generate strong political supports, and develop public-private partnerships to jump-start vigorous economic diversification.

But social science claims that this "new economy" has generated modern, skilled, knowledge-information jobs for middle-class workers in cities like Bethlehem are belied by the family trajectories of displaced steelworkers.[8] Although some displaced workers were able to access middle-class jobs in the expanding health care sector, construction industries related to growing housing markets, and high tech sectors of the Lehigh Valley economy, the majority of ex-steelworkers turned to lower-paid jobs in warehousing, manufacturing, or the service sector; sought out public-sector jobs; or turned to small business ownership. Most workers lost salary, benefits, and job security in this transition. The healthy postindustrial economy of the Lehigh Valley was constructed through the displacement and devaluing of the industrial working class, the accompanying creation of a more female, black, and Latino new working class, and the transformation of regional class relations.

A regional upper-class alliance, which initially included Bethlehem Steel executives, worked to reinvigorate Bethlehem's economy in an inter-urban environment that has become increasingly competitive as capital becomes more mobile. In order to attract capital, regional class alliances must outcompete other urban regions by offering appealing environments for both production and consumption. Pennsylvanian projects such as "toolboxes" of tax breaks, enterprise zone incentives, technical assistance, public-private partnerships, low-interest building loans, and infrastructural improvements attempted to attract businesses, many from New Jersey and New York, to the Lehigh Valley. This alliance has actively recruited smaller corporations to the Lehigh Valley by building forty-two industrial and corporate parks, beginning in 1959, with an emphasis on economic diversification. Industries in these parks now employ some twenty-four thousand workers and involve millions of dollars of private investment.[9] There are now seven industrial parks in and adjacent to Bethlehem, the most recent as of this writing opening on the eastern end of the former Bethlehem steel works site. These parks have successfully attracted light manufacturing, financial back-office operations, and warehousing/distribution centers.[10]

Warehousing and distribution is a major growth industry in the Lehigh Valley. The construction of transportation infrastructure, combined with location marketing, the above-cited tax rebates, and easy access to major markets on the East Coast—highlighted in Lehigh Valley advertising as "within a one day truck drive of one-third of the US market"—led to the opening of many warehouses in the area.[11] The twelve million square feet of warehouse space in the Lehigh Valley in 1995 had expanded to one hundred million square feet by 2021. Infrastructural improvements, including highways—the completion of I-78 in 1989 and the Route 33 spur in 2003, and the expansion of Route 412—have contributed to this growth. Food warehouses that use refrigeration in food distribution throughout the northeast and internet sales-oriented distribution centers have moved into the area. The former Bethlehem Steel land on the eastern end of the plant now houses multiple giant warehouses and an intermodal facility. Although these facilities are immense and have substantial land and infrastructure needs, they do not generate a large number of desirable jobs. Most warehousing jobs are not unionized, pay averages around $17 an hour, and there are limited opportunities for advancement. Many warehouses hire temporary labor through organizations like Manpower, although some do provide more secure jobs. In addition, the warehouse industry was hard-hit by the Great Recession, as decreased demand for products led to decreased deliveries. The industry has recovered and is now expanding in this region with recent additions of Walmart and Amazon online shopping warehouses; it was buoyed even further through the pandemic.

Bethlehem's industrial parks also attract smaller manufacturers, although manufacturing continues to decline as a percentage of the Lehigh Valley labor market. While manufacturing still produced thirty-four thousand jobs in Lehigh and Northampton counties in 2019, this is down from thirty-nine thousand in 2004 and is a huge reduction from the 50 percent of the Lehigh Valley workforce who worked in manufacturing in 1950.[12] Manufacturing continues to be an important sector of employment, but the current, smaller manufacturing often offers nonunion jobs, low wages, and reduced benefits, and is subject to frequent closings and layoffs. Unionized manufacturing jobs in the Lehigh Valley, and the higher salaries accompanying them, have declined significantly.

Bethlehem's regional elite, through participation in organizations like the Lehigh Valley Partnership, also work to construct an economic environment that emphasizes new economy, high-tech start-ups, service industries (including health care and education), and tourism and entertainment. Regional elites lobbied hard for the Ben Franklin Technology Center, a public-private partnership located at Lehigh University, funded with state monies, and set up to support high-tech and biotech start-up businesses. This incubator site, located at Bethlehem Steel's former Research and Development Center, provided a home for successful local electronics and biomedicine start-up companies like IQE and Orasure. Start-ups were effectively linked to a private venture capital company that tapped into regional capital as well as to local banks.[13] More recently, Factory LLC, a private equity/scale up organization supporting entrepreneurs in the food and beverage industry, opened in Bethlehem Steel's mill depot building. While these start-ups fuel economic growth, they tend to create professional middle-class jobs requiring a college or postgraduate education.

Another aggressively marketed growth area in Bethlehem is the tourism and entertainment industry, highlighting the city's "emerging identity as an entertainment destination."[14] A regional "growth coalition" elite builds on existing festivals, Bethlehem's Christmas City reputation, and historic preservation and tourism efforts in North Bethlehem. The wealthier, Moravian north side of Bethlehem had long been regarded as a historic tourist destination, but the tourist/entertainment economy has now expanded to the South Side of the city, developing in competition with entertainment venues and gambling milieux (such as Atlantic City) in New Jersey. Bethlehem's casino, originally built by the Sands and now owned by Wind Creek Resorts, aggressively advertises its location as closer to both New York and Philadelphia than New Jersey's rival casinos, and has successfully outcompeted them over the past few years, contributing to the dramatic decline of the gambling industry in Atlantic City and the city's resulting semi-bankruptcy.

Between 2000 and 2020 the Lehigh Valley's population expanded, fueling a construction and housing boom and a growth in the higher-end retail sector. Rising real estate prices in New Jersey and Philadelphia made the Lehigh Valley a preferred place to buy homes. Many newcomers were willing to commute longer distances to their work in order to access more affordable housing. This influx of professional middle-class immigrants fueled a housing construction boom and drove up the "market basket of goods and services" in the Lehigh Valley by 24 percent over the four years preceding the Great Recession.[15] While this growth was desirable for some, such as those working in the housing construction industry, real estate developers, and large corporate home builders, it was less advantageous for many steelworkers and their families. The growing cost of goods, increased traffic congestion, and urban sprawl changed the feel of the area and are often highlighted by steelworking families as serious problems in the Valley. While construction and housing were hard-hit by the Great Recession, they grew again in the past decade, with a lot of new urban development projects and a housing market further fueled by the pandemic.

The redevelopment of the site of the Bethlehem steel works is also an important part of economic development efforts. The 1,800-acre site constitutes about 20 percent of the city's taxable land. In the late 1990s and first decade of the 2000s, even as projects like the Lehigh Valley Industrial Park VII began successfully redeveloping some areas within the sprawling grounds of the former mill, the historic center of the site remained in ruins. This area, highly visible from major thoroughfares and bridges, was "weedy and surrounded by a chain-link fence."[16] The buildings were rusted, overgrown fields spread out where other buildings had been torn down, and the giant blast furnaces rose, cold and dark, out of the ruins. The site became an attraction for "industrial explorers" who broke in to sneak through the wreckage, taking photographs of industrial blight. This eyesore acted as a symbolic drag on Bethlehem's revitalized image.

Redevelopment of this site—what was once the largest brownfield site in the US—has been a long-term project.[17] Bethlehem Steel was an active force in the redesign of the site in the late 1990s, until bankruptcy. The corporation worked with the state of Pennsylvania, the Lehigh Valley Economic Development Corporation, city government, federal government, and private developers to develop a plan for the site.[18] Bethlehem Works (BethWorks), an organization initially established in 1997 by Bethlehem Steel, was devoted to redeveloping the site. When Bethlehem Steel declared bankruptcy and sold the land to the International Steel Group in 2003, this project seemed in jeopardy. However, in 2004 ISG sold a core 124 acres to Bethlehem Works Now, a group formed predominately by Newmark Knight Frank, a major New York City developer. Shortly after this purchase, local newspapers revealed that Las Vegas Sands was a majority shareholder in the development group and that the Commonwealth of Pennsylvania would, for the first time, be issuing a limited number of gambling licenses within the state. The Las Vegas Sands Corporation, a Fortune 500 transnational corporation, was headed by Sheldon Adelson, the single largest campaign donor in the 2012 presidential elections, and a major contributor to Trump in 2016 and 2020. Although there was strong opposition to building a casino, mobilized through community-based organizations and religious groups, BethWorks Now and Sands were able to overcome this through fostering key allies, notably the area's political and economic leadership. Sands assured allies that through the company's political connections, they were guaranteed one of Pennsylvania's casino licenses.[19] These developers also wooed local nonprofits, donating land to ArtsQuest, PBS, and the city; spread around cash donations; and offered office space to the Steelworkers' Archives. They promised union jobs for casino construction, they assured the community that historic adaptive re-use of buildings and preservation of the blast furnaces was a crucial component of their plan, and they promised both skilled and unskilled jobs to local residents. They also brought the prospect of significant financial investment to a site that needed a capital-rich anchor, and by 2012 they had invested more than $800 million. The Bethlehem City Council voted to allow gambling on the site, the Sands won the state casino license, and work began on the promised casino, hotel, retail center, and convention facility.

In the midst of the casino construction, the Great Recession of 2008 hit the highly leveraged Las Vegas Sands Corporation hard. The Sands had to halt billions of dollars of construction in Macao, as well as stop construction on the hotel and retail component of the Bethlehem project. Simultaneously, the Sands worked all the faster to complete the Bethlehem casino for a spring 2009 opening designed to fuel cash profits. Pennsylvanian approval of table gaming in 2010 contributed to increased revenues at the casino, and by 2014 the Sands led all Pennsylvania casinos in table game revenues. In 2010 Sands resumed construction on the hotel, which opened in May 2011, and built a retail mall and events center. In 2019 Sands sold the casino to Wind Creek Resorts, a Native American gaming corporation headquartered in Alabama. While temporarily sidelined by the pandemic, Wind Creek has recently completed construction on a second hotel at the site.

The transformation of the oldest section of the steel works to a tourism and entertainment center continued. In 2011, ArtsQuest completed a $36 million "cultural and recreation center" called SteelStacks, offering a variety of venues for concerts and entertainment. PBS built a $17 million broadcast center on the site. A Smithsonian-affiliated museum, the National Museum of Industrial History (NMIH), redeveloped the Bethlehem Steel electrical repair building for a 2016 opening. The city built a visitor's center in the old stockhouse and opened an elevated public walkway along the Hoover-Mason Trestle, once used to move materials to the blast furnaces. These venues build on the heritage of the site and incorporate adaptive reuse of Bethlehem Steel buildings into design plans. This new development, anchored by the casino, is represented as a dynamic tourism/entertainment center for Bethlehem's economy, designed as a destination for New Jerseyans and New Yorkers. The construction and redevelopment at the most historic part of Bethlehem Steel's flagship mill offers visitors an exciting contrast to the bulldozed and rusted mills in eastern Pennsylvania, with new public and private venues nestled beneath the backdrop of the towering, brightly lit blast furnaces.

Of course, entertainment growth in Bethlehem is predicated on competition with surrounding states, and revenue flowing into the casino is certainly related to the devastating decline in revenues in Atlantic City. While jobs are generated in this service sector, many of the jobs are lower pay, with worse benefits, and lack the union protection of the steel jobs they replaced. Steelworkers had varied responses to the building of the casino. Some gambled and looked forward to having a casino in town. Many steelworkers wanted rejuvenation of the site, and hoped for preservation of some of the oldest buildings and of the blast furnaces. Since the omnipresent landscape of rusted and decaying buildings was a constant reminder of the blow of Bethlehem Steel's demise, many wanted job-creating economic development. But steelworkers remained highly critical of the ability of a casino—so symbolic of the new, speculative, financialized economy—to replace what they defined as the productive work and good jobs of the steel industry.

Bob Burkey, a former steelworker and founding member of the Steelworkers' Archives, fought for the opening of the casino. Burkey was a strong supporter of the casino because he liked to gamble, he hoped casino taxes would lead to decreased property taxes and ease the strain on ex-steelworkers with limited income, and he wanted the casino to preserve buildings on the steel site. The support of ex-steelworkers was a powerful voice in legitimizing the casino, and the casino built a bench with a view of the construction in memory of Burkey. This bench, emblazoned with a plaque, commemorated his advocacy for the casino and was memorialized as being a place to watch the Sands build the future.[20] After the construction was completed and the casino was in full operation, this bench mysteriously disappeared, never to be replaced. The casino cited job production for Lehigh Valley natives as proof of its value to the community, and the casino has many lower-paying, service-sector jobs in food service, maintenance, and security filled mostly by locals. But most of the higher-paying casino jobs (e.g., management and dealers) have been filled by out-of-towners moving to Bethlehem from other casino cities. Steelworkers are also critical of the casino's lack of follow-through with historic redevelopment of the oldest part of the former steel mill, as many buildings still stand empty.

Some steelworking families also resent the entertainment venues, feeling they result in expensive entertainment they cannot afford to attend. Some steelworkers are critical of the growing expenses attached to ArtsQuest's Musikfest, an annual event that relies heavily on the strong spirit and tradition of volunteerism in the community. They argue that even as Musikfest generates higher profits each year, participation for regular people becomes prohibitively expensive. There is worry that the "campus" developed on the steel works, and now being used as a site for Musikfest events, will exclude the less affluent, catering to outsiders and to the regional professional middle-class. Steelworkers are also critical of a restrictive covenant, attached to the land around the blast furnaces given by the casino to the city and not-for-profits, banning any union organization or speech "offensive to a reasonable casino owner" in this public "town square." Many believe this represses the voice of working people. This elicited a large protest in 2012, with the local USW, ex-steelworkers, and community organizations playing a major role.

In 2008, the Great Recession hit the Lehigh Valley economy hard, slowing down housing development and migration to the area, producing an unemployment rate of 9.5 percent in 2010 (higher than the state average of 8.8 percent), and eliminating job growth in all sectors except education and health care. The Valley regional elite's emphasis on tri-state competition—attracting New Jersey professional, middle-class homeowners and commuters, as well as businesses—ground to a halt. The housing market went into a tailspin, new construction stopped, and many sectors of the economy experienced layoffs, shedding jobs and closing businesses. By 2019, unemployment numbers and job numbers had returned to their pre-recession levels, only to fall precipitously again with the COVID pandemic. These economic crises have contributed to broader structural effects on a displaced and devalued working class, including increased job loss and job insecurity for ex-steelworkers. Ongoing economic restructuring has provided an opportunity for regional elites to intensify attacks on unions, attempting to widen the wedge between working- and middle-class property owners and public-sector unions.

Steelworkers in the Contemporary Labor Market

As Bethlehem Steel continued to close shops and departments, shutting down the last shop in the Bethlehem plant in 1998, the final plant workers were laid off with early retirement or transfer rights. Some workers took retirement and looked for other jobs, some transferred to other plants, and some turned down transfer and found themselves on the job market. Later, after Bethlehem Steel's bankruptcy in 2001 through 2003, many retirees and transferees found themselves back in Bethlehem and back on the job market, as retirees needed income after losing health care and pension monies and as transfer jobs ended. Workers moving into other jobs often found the experience of getting and keeping new jobs in the "flexible" postindustrial labor market bewildering and demoralizing.

Workers' initial reactions to retirement or layoff in the late 1990s varied dramatically. Many workers described their initial layoff or retirement, with pension and health care coverage, as a "happy time," a "good time," a "fun time," although "short-lived." Workers who accessed their pension had sufficient pension and health care benefits to either not work at all or to work part time or pick up odd jobs to supplement their income. Manny Vega, who worked until age fifty-two at the Coke Works, said, initially "things in my case went from bad to really good when the Steel closed. The closing was a good thing for me." Some workers in hard, hot production jobs, or workers in less desirable departments, felt relief at being able to retire early, and jumped at the opportunity.[21] When Marc Ortiz was offered early retirement from the Coke Works in 1995, "I stood up so fast. I stayed, not because of the salary, but because of the health benefits." Marc had been investing money in real estate since the 1970s, and with an early retirement pension and health benefits, he was eager to devote himself, full-time, to his real estate business.

Other workers transferred to other plants, but after working for years still found themselves without a pension (thus needing work) or with a reduced pension with the company's bankruptcy. They were, therefore, back on the job market in the early 2000s, after thinking they would never need to work again. The loss of health care benefits also propelled many workers back into the labor market. As we have seen, the effect of these losses was unevenly distributed, as those workers whose wives had jobs with comprehensive health coverage or who were Medicare eligible were more able to manage the health care loss. Others, even with sufficient pension payments at layoff, describe themselves as being in their forties or early fifties when their jobs at Bethlehem Steel ended and "too young to quit working." Many steelworkers expressed a strong desire to work, defined themselves as good workers, and prided themselves on having a strong work ethic.

As steelworkers looked for jobs, they encountered a postindustrial Lehigh Valley economy and labor market of the late 1990s and early 2000s that was dramatically different from the labor market of the 1970s, when they had first landed jobs at Bethlehem Steel. The depressed Lehigh Valley economy of the 1980s had recovered, and a diversified economy generated new jobs, but most of the manufacturing jobs that had fueled the area's economy in the 1970s were gone. Although by the 1990s the economy in the Lehigh Valley had again expanded, the kinds of jobs available for ex-steelworkers were limited in pay, benefits, and promotional opportunities. Workers entered this revivified economy in the late 1990s and early 2000s as they were expelled from the plant or returned from transfer jobs at other plants.

RETRAINING PROGRAMS

After layoff from the mill, many workers took advantage of a variety of government programs designed to retrain workers, provide further education or skills training, and reorient workers for job search in a postindustrial labor market. Uchitelle points out that the federal government put a significant amount of resources into retraining workers "dislocated" through deindustrialization. While retraining monies provided benefits for workers, including education and extended unemployment benefits, federal programs put monies into retraining rather than into government support that would have enabled US manufacturing to remain competitive.[22] The Clinton administration provided "subsidies for education and training and . . . 'portability' for health insurance and pension benefits" instead of policies protecting US industry.[23] Government programs and policies approached layoffs and downsizing as an inevitable effect of globalization and a necessary component of economic development in a post-Fordist economy. Thus, federal programs were designed to "reskill" what were defined as obsolete industrial, "dislocated" workers. Under the Bush administration, however, even these job training programs and unemployment benefits were cut significantly, resulting in even greater difficulties for laid-off workers.[24] Instead of supporting unionized manufacturing, federal policies stimulated rust belt deindustrialization through encouraging industrial development first in the right-to-work sun belt and later overseas. The effect of these policies on the steel industry is well-documented (see Chapter 1).

As many social scientists have demonstrated, social service programs such as job training or workfare, in addition to teaching concrete skills, also disseminate ideologies of personal responsibility, personal flexibility, a positive attitude, and the necessity of ongoing retraining. Retraining programs construct a discourse about the importance of personal growth through "flexibility and constant change" in the contemporary economy, reinforcing an "instrumental, individuated, competitive understanding of job loss and economic adjustment."[25] Much of retraining focused on individual attributes—individual skills, resumes, personality, and job-seeking strategies—rather than collective processes.

While failing to support manufacturing in the Northeast, the social wage was simultaneously slashed with the evisceration of the welfare state. Cuts in the social wage (such as reductions in unemployment insurance, food stamps, housing, and Social Security) propel workers into the low-wage labor market.

Frances Piven shows how neoliberal social policy has developed in conjunc-
tion with this shift in jobs, contributing to declining wages, insecure jobs,
unsafe workplaces, and a lack of benefits.[26] These state policies are linked to
economic processes that "increase worker vulnerability."[27] State policies that
intensify labor discipline are complemented by corporate strategies such as
the long-term fight against unions, the use of threats of mobility and downsizing to generate concessionary contracts, the recruiting of cheap immigrant
labor, and the transformation of secure jobs to insecure, low-wage positions.

It was often difficult for workers to access retraining programs. Ted Smith,
for example, encountered enormous obstacles in coordinating his federal
Trade Adjustment Assistance (TAA) benefits between two different states.
Ted was eligible for federal TAA funding since his job was determined to be
lost to foreign imports. After transferring to Sparrows Point, Ted was laid off,
and elected to take a buyout from ISG after Bethlehem Steel's bankruptcy. He
decided to continue his education in nursing, as he had been taking courses
while working at Sparrows Point, but ran into frustrating barriers. In attempting to register for a nursing program in Pennsylvania, "I had to deal with the
state of Maryland as well as the state of Pennsylvania as well as the federal
government. So I had three bureaucracies I always had to contend with, and
sometimes they were conflicting." In addition to a pile of other paperwork,
Maryland needed a letter of intent from Ted's Pennsylvania college, which he
had difficulty procuring within Maryland's time frame. Ted felt overwhelmed
and was close to giving up, as he struggled with coordinating his government
benefits through these three separate government entities. Ted persevered,
with the strong encouragement of his wife, and ultimately did succeed in accessing government support and finishing his nursing degree, but someone
with less confidence and emotional support might have failed to do this.[28]

Retraining and re-education directed at downsized professional, middle-
class workers differs from that for blue-collar workers. Until Obama expanded
the Trade Adjustment Act, this federal program did not recognize white-collar
workers as displaced by foreign imports. Therefore, unemployed white-collar
workers were immersed in a privatized, for-profit marketplace of job coaching, networking seminars, and attitudinal workshops. Middle-class workers
are bombarded with guides that describe job loss as an "opportunity for self-
transformation," are embedded in networking strategies to mobilize social
capital, and are sold career coaching services. Ehrenreich cites the title of a
2004 business self-help book by Harvey McKay, *We Got Fired! . . . And It's the
Best Thing that Ever Happened to Us*, as exemplifying the middle-class "attitudes" taught through white-collar retraining and networking sessions.[29]

Although blue-collar retraining does include motivational and attitudinal workshops, monies made available through TAA and union contracts ensure that community college, vo-tech, and proprietary college courses geared toward attaining new marketable skills are a key component of blue-collar retraining programs. In addition, as government monies were put into retraining programs for blue-collar workers, workers could access concrete monetary supports including extended unemployment benefits and tuition payments.

As the hot end of the works closed in 1995, a union-run dislocated-workers program for Bethlehem Steel workers (and USW workers from two other local plant closings) opened near the steel plant. This program offered worker retraining through a variety of federal funding sources, and a number of steelworkers took advantage of it.[30] Workers attended workshops, signed up for courses and programs, received job search assistance, and accessed extended unemployment benefits, and 65 percent of these participants found new jobs. The average starting wage, however, was $11 per hour, less than half the average wage of workers at Bethlehem Steel.[31]

Because a patchwork of state and federal programs provided benefits, unemployed steelworkers were split and divided in seemingly arbitrary ways. Extended unemployment benefits and tuition funding varied substantially by department and job within Bethlehem Steel. Some jobs, those deemed lost due to foreign imports, were eligible for federal TAA funding. At Bethlehem Steel, production jobs were more likely to qualify for TAA monies than maintenance jobs, and certain divisions qualified while others did not. This eligibility was partly determined by the company, who reported to the government on the percentage of production displaced by foreign imports. But Norm Mitchell, a former craft worker at the plant who worked with many displaced workers in the retraining program, found that this reporting was arbitrary, varying from shop to shop, affecting workers unevenly, and occurring irrationally. "It depended what department shut down at the time that you got laid off, whether you were deemed TRA or not." For workers, this eligibility for extended unemployment benefits, significant retraining monies, a stipend, and a health care tax rebate appeared to be arbitrary—the luck of the draw.

The dislocated workers program offered practical courses such as resume design and interview preparation, but also included counseling-oriented workshops such as "the seven stages of grief after losing a job." The *Morning Call* described program staff saying they taught workers "to shed the sense that all jobs should be like the ones they had: high-paying jobs for life."[32] In these workshops, retraining prepares workers to accept the new post-Fordist labor market as natural and inevitable, teaches workers to generate individual strategies for employment (often in what comes to be accepted as devalued work), attempts to convince workers of the inevitability of downward mobility, and naturalizes the loss of value of what are defined as "manual" skills.

For some workers, attending classes or retraining was not easy. Many workers had not taken a class since high school and found it challenging to be in a classroom setting. Steelworker Mark Castor transferred to Sparrows Point, commuting back and forth from the Lehigh Valley to attain his pension. When Bethlehem Steel declared bankruptcy, he returned to the Lehigh Valley and looked for a job, but he found that "when we got out, finding another job wasn't easy. My age was against me. I had only a high school education, no college education." He took HVAC classes at a proprietary business school through the dislocated workers program. He found the classes difficult: "I only had a high school education. They tried to have you do your math on the computer. I didn't know the first thing about a computer. You had to know algebra and different geometry. I was lost. I had a hard time with that there. . . . There were twenty-four of us in the HVAC course, and only half of us made it." He quit the course and found a job in maintenance at a nursing home, accepting that this lower wage job was the best he could do, given his lack of college credits. Going through retraining stressed the value of formal schooling, devalued skills and experiences learned on the job, and redefined him as a worker only deserving of low wages. Mark ended up accepting this as a new reality. "I'm only getting half of what I got pay wise," but "with a high school education and my age, sixty, where am I going to find a job?"

Retraining programs also covered only career training or community college, that is, training defined as suitable for blue-collar workers. Workers acquired commercial driver licenses, HVAC certification, computer training, forklift licenses, and massage therapist licenses. Those workers who wanted a BA had to pay for college themselves, or begin college earlier (while still working in the steel works) through a Bethlehem Steel tuition reimbursement program negotiated by the union. Taking advantage of this was nigh impossible for many workers, however, due to their lack of control over shift scheduling. William Brown, for example, attended computer classes, but says, "I would have liked to work in safety and health, but the training for that would be too long." But retraining programs generally did not lead to jobs with comparable wages to steel work.

For those workers who did attain a BA, even a college education did not ensure high-paying jobs or job security in the region's postindustrial labor market. As political scientist Jacob Hacker points out, "high levels of education may be a prerequisite for success . . . but they are no means a guarantor of middle class security."[33] Older steelworkers, even with college degrees, confronted obstacles of age, union background, and lack of white-collar experience that worked against them in moving into white-collar positions.

Some workers found white-collar positions, but not at the salary or the hours they desired. Louis Moran, a maintenance worker in the machine shop, had always felt conflicted about his career at the Bethlehem plant, as his parents and uncle (who worked at the mill) "would've rather seen me go to college. [My uncle] discouraged both of his sons not to work there . . . my parents were—well, they wanted me to go to college." Louis's girlfriend got pregnant, he married at nineteen, and he found himself working at Bethlehem Steel. Louis had no confidence in his academic abilities, and didn't find until much later, when he attended college while at the mill, that he was quite talented academically. He enjoyed college tremendously and did well. Louis planned ahead for his post-Steel retirement, taking college classes. "I just knew that I wanted to get out with a thirty-year pension. I had always planned that." Because Louis worked steady night shifts, he was able to take advantage of the tuition reimbursement program and complete his BA, all while working at the mill. He wanted to become a math teacher, but the money he was making at Bethlehem Steel by then was far superior to an entry level teaching salary, so he stayed until his department closed down. After the plant's closing, Louis obtained a white-collar job at a government agency. But even with his education, Louis has been working for significantly lower wages ever since leaving Bethlehem Steel and is "looking for another job . . . it doesn't pay very well there. And there is something about, and this is my stuff, there is something about having a college education and using it and getting paid less than [half my Bethlehem salary] . . . considerably less. So that's a part of it." Louis, while proud of his college degree, was discouraged with the salary, the management style, and the lack of opportunity for promotion at his white-collar job.

Successfully completing retraining did not ensure jobs for all workers, as even newly acquired skills were not marketable, or resulted in jobs with much lower wages. For example, many workers used the program to train for commercial driver licenses (CDL) with the goal of getting trucking jobs. However, not one of the workers I interviewed was happy with these trucking jobs. Even as workers pursued their licenses, the trucking industry in the US was undergoing restructuring. The industry was deregulated in the early 1980s, and, as a result, more than three hundred companies closed and many new small trucking companies entered the market. Sociologist Stanley Aronowitz argues that the deregulation of transportation under Carter was "the most anti-working-class measure of the postwar era" as it created an enormous nonunion sector in the trucking industry.[34] While unions retained a foothold in long-distance trucking, short-haul trucking became predominately nonunion, and "costs and risks were increasingly transferred to workers in the deregulated environment as small firms contracting work out to owner-operators began to replace the larger, unionized trucking companies."[35] Winnie Edwards, who worked for thirty years as a machinist at Bethlehem Steel, attained her CDL through retraining. She soon discovered, however, that this restructured trucking industry did not provide satisfactory jobs. She accepted a job driving cross country,

> but it is a bad, bad life. . . . They never put runs near your home. The dispatchers run you when you should not be driving, you're too tired . . . everybody's log books lied . . . our companies weren't unionized . . . you're all over the place, you get vacation but can't go anywhere cause they can call you anytime and be ready to get on the truck. . . . And you never get enough sleep.

She became a "flexible" worker with few rights and protections, underpaid, working in unsafe conditions, whose personal time (including her commitments to kin) was eroded by the need to be constantly on call to her employer. Winnie hated the job—"it's not a good life"—and quit.

Retraining programs are developed under an ideology that defines workers' existing skills as obsolete or nonexistent. Programs advocate the acquisition of entirely new skills to ensure success in the postindustrial labor market. But because neoliberal jobs themselves are increasingly insecure, generating a growing "precariat" of workers that share an experience of instability, then retraining is itself no guarantee of jobs or of job stability.[36] Many workers simply could not find a job in the field in which they were retrained. Bart Novak went through TAA retraining in computer work—"I thought computers might be the fastest way to get back in the job market"—but he could only find a part-time job in the field and kept searching in unrelated industries for full-time work. Many ex-steelworkers moved into highly insecure jobs. Bob Allen graduated from HVAC training with an associate's degree in 2005 and got a job at a company that installed clean rooms for pharmaceutical manufacturers. His job had a low salary ($11 an hour), but many of the jobs he was sent on were protected by prevailing-wage regulations mandating payment of a wage set by the Department of Labor and Industry on publicly funded jobs. On those jobs, about half he worked on, he made about $50 an hour. Bob "loved the job," and felt that he was learning, gaining skills and competence. But at the end of his first year of work, just prior to eligibility for vacation, he was laid off when his entire department was eliminated. Bob claims "they decided we were making too much money with prevailing wage," and he found himself thrown back into the labor market.

Job insecurity was also generated when employers cut benefits. Barry Kirk, for example, found a job he loved working for a small business, a hobby store where he managed the model train division. The job used many of his skills. "It was my hobby. I knew a lot about it in all aspects, the history of the railroad, the railroad today, the technology of the hobby. It related to my Bethlehem Steel job." He was able to use the electrician skills acquired at Bethlehem Steel and his knowledge of railroading to excel at a job he was interested in. But when the small business owner dropped health care coverage for his employees, Barry, whose wife did not have a health care plan, had to leave the job. Many workers were repeatedly pushed back into the labor market by reductions in employee health care coverage or by layoffs, and many workers bounced from one low-wage manufacturing job to another.

Workers, of course, do not always accept retraining programs' discourses of personal responsibility, the need for education and retraining, and the re-orienting to what is seen as inevitably devalued work. Many steelworkers, as well as ex-union officers who worked as counselors in the dislocated workers' program, made pragmatic use of these programs to extend unemployment benefits under TAA funding. As long as workers were enrolled in college or a skills training program, they were eligible for extended unemployment benefits. Some workers used this strategy to give themselves more time to search for the right kind of job. Unlike "welfare," these benefits are seen as legitimate, earned through a lifetime of hard work, and available to workers because of unjust foreign competition. While this critical perspective enabled workers to use these resources pragmatically, it also encouraged workers to understand deindustrialization as solely a result of foreign competition. The TAA "required workers to blame their troubles on foreign competition" rather than on domestic restructuring and a corporate offensive against labor.[37]

POST-FORDIST WORK

When steel workers lost their jobs in the mill, they were shocked to be spit out into a postindustrial labor market that de-valued their skills and experience. At the Bethlehem mill, skills were defined through experience, and understood through the principle of seniority. As described in Chapter 2, seniority shaped work at the Bethlehem plant, incorporating values of skill, organizing access to jobs, and structuring social relations at the plant. As workers looked for jobs outside the plant, seniority was devalued, read as "old-age," not experience, and assessed as a liability, not an asset. Workers were dismayed to find that the very criteria defining worker value at the Bethlehem mill became detriments in the post-Fordist labor market. An emphasis on gaining new proficiencies defined steelworkers' deficits as lack of skills, rather than lack of jobs, and posited the solution as retraining. And a contemporary labor market that valued youth and flexibility devalued the seniority that coded for skill, expertise, and prestige inside the Bethlehem plant. Many ex-steelworkers entering the Lehigh Valley labor market in their late forties and fifties found that their age put them at a big disadvantage. Danny Moreno, a Puerto Rican worker, describes looking for work in 2002, after he left the Sparrows Point plant. "People do not want to hire a person in the grey zone. You're too high risk when you start hitting your fifties, upper fifties, they tell you, 'Sorry, we can't use you. When you get social security you're not going to stay. You're older, you'll break down quicker.'" Eddie Havela sent out hundreds of resumes and attended multiple job fairs. He describes an interview in which the interviewer clearly was not interested in him, looking right past him to two young guys. "They weren't even dressed nicely, they were wearing old raggedy T-shirts. I was dressed pretty neatly. He wasn't interested in an old guy. At the time I was fifty-two, but he wasn't interested in me. That was a good lesson for me about job discrimination, although some deny it. All my experience didn't matter. They just wanted some young blood." Andy Vanek, who finished his bachelor's degree after losing his job, found "that nobody wants to hire a fifty-three-year-old ex-steelworker. If they had six applying, all those others just having graduated [college], they'd never hire me. They couldn't bullshit me like they'd bullshit the other five. I felt it was age discrimination." These workers understand that age becomes interpreted as weakness—poor physical condition and health and a less compliant attitude—rather than as seniority—skills, experience, and heightened responsibility.

Within the mill, the capital accumulated in seniority insured that older workers could move into less physically stressful jobs inside the steel works. Outside the mill, the wear and tear of years of manual labor aged workers' bodies prematurely, making them even less suitable for postindustrial manufacturing work. In blue-collar jobs requiring manual labor, injuries and illnesses acquired over a lifetime of steel work limited the jobs workers could apply for. Barry Kirk, an electrician, injured his ankle in a fall at Bethlehem Steel's Coatesville plant. The injury affected the feeling in his foot and his balance, limiting his ability to climb on electrical jobs—"That made my job search harder." Andy Vanek, who looked for a job in business logistics, found "by that time my knees were shot and I couldn't work in logistics." At a thriving Bethlehem mill, but without workers' Bethlehem seniority, their age, union experience, and physical condition worked against them in the labor market, pushing them into low-wage jobs in the downgraded sector of manufacturing even as the devaluing of their skills and knowledge, legitimized through a dominant discourse describing manufacturing as a "dinosaur," cheapened their labor in the marketplace.

Workers also confronted a labor market saturated with ex-steelworkers (particularly in the shrinking manufacturing sector). Many workers sent out hundreds of applications, and received countless rejections, often settling for underemployment (working part time), temporary work (for agencies such as Manpower), a long period of unemployment, or jobs at much reduced wages. This unemployment is not cyclical, as often represented in news coverage, instead, it has a long term or permanent effect on laid-off steelworkers, as manual labor is devalued and made flexible. As Danny Moreno, a now unemployed steelworker from the coke works put it, "For me, it's been a recession ever since I left Steel." People like Danny are the "shadow unemployed," the discouraged workers who have given up looking for jobs.[38]

Steelworkers found that macho attitudes that were effective on the shop floor constituted barriers to employment in service sector or office jobs that require a manner of "enthusiasm, initiative, and flexibility."[39] Some of the most confrontational, macho dispositions on the mill floor were found in production jobs where time is money, and where workers had confidence in their power to halt production. These assertive masculine stances produced results on the shop floor. Worker assertions were often backed by collectively bargained rules and adjudicated (if necessary) by the grievance system. In the nonunion, postindustrial workplace, these attitudes were highly problematic and could get workers fired. Andy Vanek and Al Trakas both describe getting fired from jobs because of their "big mouths." Al says that he lost a job in manufacturing "because of my big mouth . . . it's just that I had that union instinct in me, what the difference between right and wrong was, and I used to point out specifically what was wrong." Al describes a job in downgraded manufacturing—a company reclaiming mercury from light bulbs—where workers' health and safety was endangered every day. When he tried to make changes, he was fired. But Al does blame himself, in part, for having an "attitude" that does not work well in the wider society. Andy is also conflicted in discussing being fired from his job at a local college, after he pointed to problems with his boss' policies and challenged his boss' authority in staff meetings. Andy sees his firing as unjust, but also recognizes it as the reality of the neoliberal workplace. He blames himself, that it's his "big mouth," that "it is my fault." He is aware that the contemporary workplace does not have the kinds of protections that allow workers to speak frankly. It is "employment at will," and without the backing and protection of a union, speaking out puts one's job at risk. Steelworkers relate this very clearly to the lack of a union. Winnie Edwards, an ex-machinist, is highly critical of her son's job at a nonunion pharmaceutical warehouse, "You can't do anything. You can't say anything. They have to sign a paper that they agree they can be terminated at any time." But workers also accept this as being the reality of the contemporary workplace. If they want a job, workers have to adhere to the standards of this new, unjust reality. Bill Markus describes his initial interview at a local college:

> [The college] had no union. They didn't want to hear that. They were reluctant to hire people from the steel company. I was the first one hired at [the college] from a union, on the outside like that. They took a chance with me. I had a credit check. They put me on probation. My boss said "I hear one thing about a union!" "You're not going to hear that. I'm done with that. It's a whole new life I'm starting."

Bill realized that he had to accept the anti-union tenets of the "new economy" workplace.

Bethlehem production workers used their confrontational, assertive attitudes at the Steel to attain results. They threatened to slow production, file grievances, and undermine the authority of foremen unless management made concessions to demands. With the backing of the union, these strategies were effective, although they did not lead to promotion into management. But in the contemporary workplace, this assertive approach is interpreted as belligerent and defensive and is subjected to discipline. Without a union to support them, workers lose their jobs, and without a broader ideology to make sense out of these interactions, workers partially blame themselves. They understand the injustice of these work relations, but they also accept this as the new neoliberal reality. This sets them up for failure. Either they will fail by exercising their "big mouth" in a world where they know that is not accepted, or they will "exit" a situation that requires that they be acquiescent, either voluntarily or involuntarily. Barbara Gogol voluntarily left her job as a welder at a small, family-owned plastics plant after being fired. She enjoyed welding there, but found that the owner "used to hire and fire people at will. Whatever, something he didn't like, he'd fire the whole crew, and then the next day they'd be called back." When Barbara's crew made a gun box for his pickup truck, and it didn't fit correctly, she said the whole crew was fired. When they were all called back the next day, Barbara said, "I'm not coming back . . . I'm not going to be treated like that," and went to work at McDonalds for the next two years. Barbara was able to do that because she had no children, no debt, and was collecting a pension from Bethlehem Steel. Less common in interviews with workers was evidence of steelworkers organizing collectively at their work sites to change the new work realities. An exception to this was the dynamic organizing efforts of the Sands Casino security guards, some of whom were ex–Bethlehem Steel workers, to successfully form a union in an intensely anti-union environment. For the most part, however, the disciplining processes of transfers, job loss(es), retraining, and an often long and difficult job search, as well as the real power contemporary corporations have to squelch union organization, impresses on workers the new reality of post-Fordist work.

Workers also had to adopt a demeanor and style that did not "come naturally" to fit into mainstream culture in service-sector work. They had to learn how to "act" like a white-collar worker. This often made workers uncomfortable in their jobs. Mainstream culture demanded polite, enthusiastic, and servile dispositions that were construed, by blue-collar workers, as hypocritical. Bill Markus contrasts the work environments at a college to the steel mill: "At the steel company we had our own language, shop talk that we were allowed to get away with. At the [college], you had to watch what you say." The language of the shop floor, with its vulgar jokes, crude language, and assertive attitude, was quite different from that of office and service work. Gus Guerrera, who worked in retail, said, on his new job, "you had to watch yourself. You had to be polite, clean, and you had to produce totally differently." This meant either code-switching to act properly in a different context, or transforming oneself to fit the ideals and mores of mainstream middle-class culture. But code-switching could be perceived as a betrayal of one's true self, of those characteristics of personality that were valued in the mill. Sociologist Pierre Bourdieu describes this for the French working class, where politeness and posturing are seen as "a substitute for substance, i.e., for sincerity, for feeling, for what is felt and proved in actions; it is the free-speech and language of the heart which makes the true 'nice guy,' blunt, straight-forward, unbending, honest, genuine, 'straight down the line' and 'straight as a die.'"[40] One's character is established through actions, and acting like a service-sector worker may not be as easy as simply code-switching for the context. This can undermine one's valued character, be interpreted as duplicitous and insincere, and be read by oneself and others as immoral action.

Many service-sector jobs were seen as feminine, requiring subservient or conciliatory attitudes, or emphasizing intimate or care work demanding middle-class norms of etiquette. Many steelworkers shunned these jobs as not sufficiently masculine. A few workers did, however, decide to use retraining monies to enter the expanding field of health care. Bob Hale, an intensely energetic machinist who put himself through college while working at the mill, decided to go into nursing to take advantage of the glass escalator for men, when his fellow students told him "for a man it's great." But he took a lot of abuse from co-workers for pursuing what was defined as women's work. In the hyper-masculine culture of the mill, Bob reported, "They called me a queer. 'You're going to do enemas, you're going to do enemas.'" But Bob knew how to take their razzing and give it back to them through the confrontational, masculine joking common in the mill. He described his response to one particularly persistent co-worker: "I said, 'How long an enema takes, it depends how big the asshole is. Depends. In your case, it would probably take about eight hours.'" For Bob, nursing is a valuable "profession" requiring training and skills; "if caring is all it took, anyone could be a nurse. It's more than that." But he also finds it fulfilling—"the most gratifying is helping someone that really needs the help." Brian Stephens, a coke worker who became an X-ray technician (a more "masculine" health care job) when his HVAC training program was cut, found that he loved working in health care. At the coke works, "I felt I was hurting the environment, environmental issues, every smell, in the press was the coke ovens . . . so you almost felt like a criminal working there. In medicine you felt you were helping people." As a more masculine health care worker, he felt his work in health care was higher prestige than steel work in his middle-class, suburban community. For these men, health care jobs with benefits and promotional tracks provided fulfilling opportunities to help others in an expanding service-sector industry. But most masculine steelworkers eschewed this feminine work.

In her study of GM workers taking buyouts, sociologist Ruth Milkman found that many workers were successful in moving out of the plant after a buyout into a postindustrial labor market. But the self-selected group she studies is a group eager to move, with dispositions, orientations, and skills that may be more suitable for work in the post-Fordist workplace. These workers are more successful than those who chose to stay behind. In the case of Bethlehem Steel, those workers who had craft skills, who had less confrontational masculine attitudes, and who had more formal education and accreditation through standardized testing were more likely to successfully move into postindustrial jobs in the Lehigh Valley. Craftspeople were more likely to have developed dispositions that enabled them to accommodate to the world of white-collar service work. Many craft workers at the steel had formal training and coursework within the mill, took standardized tests, and worked in "servicing" the machinery that production workers used to produce steel. Depending on the shop, this could result in a less confrontational, more conciliatory attitude and approach toward solving problems, more suitable to postindustrial work.

In service-sector jobs where flexibility was valued, steelworkers were also often at a disadvantage. Ed Zalenka lost his job at a funeral home when he refused to come in to work in response to his boss's last minute request he work on the next day, a Saturday. It was not the weekend work that bothered Ed—steelworkers were well-accustomed to working weekends—it was the expectation of scheduling flexibility without the pay that made flexibility at the steel mill a "choice" of the worker. Overtime at the steel mill paid well, and "hungry" production workers volunteered for overtime at every opportunity. Don Booth liked the incentive pay at Bethlehem Steel, because "you could actually control your own destiny"; the worker had some power and control over his salary. Flexibility in the service sector removed the agency of the worker, eliminating the choice embodied in the collectively bargained exchange of overtime work for additional pay.

Workers also understood flexibility—the need to be constantly "on call" to employers' needs—as undermining their autonomy and eroding their control over the timing and pace of work. Steve Jaros, for example, objected to the expectation that his time was flexible, that he was continually on call to resolve maintenance problems in the nursing home he worked in. He contrasted that with steel work: "At Bethlehem Steel they're not going to call me off the crane to say, 'This don't work. Come down here and fix this.' I'm already doing my job." The autonomy at work at the mill was not the idealized individualistic autonomy of the contemporary professional. In the mill, doing crew work, self-direction and autonomy took place within a context of doing work well in collaboration with co-workers, the expertise of one worker complementing the effectiveness of others on the crew.

Workers also objected to the need to cater to service-sector demands that they found unreasonable, irrational, and simply lacking in common sense. Workers, while recognizing formal educational credentials, are highly critical when education does not generate common sense understandings. Some steelworkers are baffled by the lack of knowledge among educated college students, or the lack of mechanical awareness of nurses in the nursing home. Steve Jaros, now a nursing home maintenance worker, says,

> You can't be an idiot to go to nursing school. You've got to have somewhat of a brain. But you think, "Now, how did they make it through nursing school if they're doing something like that?" They have lifts that lift patients off the beds, they've been working with these lifts how long? And in nursing school they teach them how to work these lifts. But if you don't click the battery it's not going to work. They call maintenance.

Steve felt nurses had "book knowledge" but lacked the common sense to solve a simple mechanical problem. The "general public" is also described as lacking common sense. Matt Nemeth describes his job as a driving instructor, working with teenagers and their parents: "the general public has no common sense . . . they're stupid." At Bethlehem Steel, workers understood how their co-workers would act, but Jack Hardy, a Lanta bus driver, found the public unpredictable—"it changes from day to day." Even though the steel mill was dangerous, Jack finds driving bus much more dangerous, more stressful, because "in the public world, people driving their cars, everybody is out for themselves." Common sense—the ability to work sensibly with others, to think about the safety of yourself and others, to have mechanical knowledge that leads to "smart" work—is more highly valued than book knowledge.

Workers also long for the feeling of satisfaction that came from using their skills to produce a tangible, useful product. Workers mobilize a producerist ideology in which productive manual or mechanical work, making the things that build the country, gives a "moral claim to the dignity of all work and to a decent living for anyone willing to do it."[41] At the Bethlehem plant, pride in productive work was linked with nationalism, as Bethlehem steel products went into military production, skyscrapers, and bridges, building the landscape that represented US hegemony. But workers also feel accomplishment in making solid, physical products with real, practical uses.

Ted Smith, for example, might be represented as a worker who "successfully" made the transition from industrial work to the new economy. Through much hard effort and perseverance, Ted attained his bachelor's degree and became a registered nurse. While Ted takes great pride in the hard work and determination in this, he nonetheless waxes eloquent when reflecting back on his work in the mill. He vividly recalls an assignment where he had to modernize a train car. "It took like a year and it was really a big success.

. . . At the end of the day, this is what I did. Everything is straight, it's plumb, it looks good, it works, the welds are nice, they're good welds, they'll hold up. And that was fulfilling." Steelmaking brought greater satisfaction to Ted than his nursing job.

> Overall I would say my job as a steelworker, especially my last days at Bethlehem, were more fulfilling in that I had a job where I worked with another person and I thought out of the box. I made things. I was proud of what I was doing. I could sign my name there, "Hey, I made this. . . . This works." And in nursing, you don't really have that fulfillment. There's so much stress. There're so many time constraints and liabilities.

The car he redesigned worked beautifully, improving production processes at the mill in an immediate and tangible way, unlike the more amorphous nursing care he provided.

Workers' experience working with the union was also often seen as a negative in the Lehigh Valley labor market. Their knowledge of workers' rights, safety regulations, and union contracts was seen as a threat, and many companies were reluctant to hire assertive Bethlehem Steel workers. Eddie Smith describes a new refrigeration plant that opened on the former Bethlehem Steel site: "They would not hire anybody because they didn't want an organized union down there. They were afraid that if guys like me went down there [they'd organize]. . . . So they took your application but there wasn't a chance you'd get hired." Tom Oster's sister knew of a job in a plastics factory but was reluctant to tell him about it, assuming he would not work in a non-union plant. But he had to work, he had children in college. When he interviewed for the job, his interviewer asked him about his union involvement. "His questions were geared at, he had a fear that I would try to organize this plant to become union. At the time, I just thought, I've got to work ten years, I have two kids in college, I've got to do something." Tom answered a barrage of questions from two interviewers before they hired him, reassuring them that although he was a strong union supporter, his union organizing days were behind him.

Many of the new jobs had no unions at all. Ex–Bethlehem steelworkers were critical of the effect this had on employees, relating it to the dampening of employee voice, autonomy, and solidarity. Tom Oster says at his shop, "I was old enough, collecting a pension. I could be a little bolder. I always spoke my mind. We only had one shouting match. Others would not exchange their thoughts. They would say, 'I can't believe you talk like that to the boss.'" It worked for Tom, but for others this assertive stance could result in being fired in the neoliberal workplace.

Workers are also disillusioned with the lack of solidarity in their new, postindustrial workplaces. Leach points to a new "culture of competition" in redefined manufacturing work that includes "greater management control and surveillance of work and a workplace culture of individualism and competition."[42] Hal Rouse describes going to a craft workers' reunion and hearing that

> someone was saying that they were working at a place and there was such a jealousy among the workers that they were at each other's throats. He said, "We would never have been like that at the steel." His co-workers were always looking to hang you. He said, "Now I'm working with guys that are not acting the way we would act with each other at all." He found that eye opening.

Winnie Edwards, an ex-machinist, says that with a union, workers "watched each other's backs, you looked out for each other's safety." This doesn't happen in a nonunion workplace like the warehouse where her son works. Tom Oster commented on the lack of camaraderie at the plastics factory where he worked for ten years after leaving the Steel: "At Bethlehem Steel, within a short time of your being hired, you acquired a nickname. If you screwed up, it might not be the nickname you would have liked. But ten years at [the plastics factory], I was Tom when I walked in and Tom the day I left." Ron Keschl attributes this lack of camaraderie to heightened surveillance and a despotic management regime: "You get on the outside, and I'm talking about on the outside of Bethlehem Steel . . . and that's exactly what you get. You got people that don't even talk to each other. You could work alongside somebody and they won't even talk to you. They're afraid somebody's watching you and they're going to jump on you or whatever the hell it is."[43]

Workers found this lack of solidarity not only in contemporary manufacturing, but in public- and service-sector jobs as well. Ed Zalenka describes his work as a zoning officer in the public sector, where his co-workers were "like chickens in a pen with a handful of feed, each person for themselves." Gus Guerrera found that they were "funny people" working in computer sales at a large retail store. "It's the same thing when it comes to sales and commission, it's dog eat dog. . . . They [co-workers] weren't telling me the right stuff to explain to people." Gus said his co-workers misled him and withheld information so that they could out-compete him on sales. Unlike Bethlehem

Steel, at his new jobs, he says, "I don't trust anybody." Bill Markus describes an environment at the college he worked where "just 'cause they worked at [the college] they'd squeal on you." Workers contrast the supportive relationships of solidarity within the mill to the cut-throat, competitive work environments in precarious, nonunion workplaces. Not only does this loss of solidarity lead to fragmented, individualized workers, but it makes work itself less fulfilling.

Downgraded Manufacturing

While the decline in manufacturing jobs in the Northeast US has been well-documented, the ways that US manufacturing jobs have changed is less examined. Manufacturing had declined significantly in the Lehigh Valley, but it still remained a viable sector of the economy, generating $7 billion in annual output and providing eighty-six thousand jobs in 2003, when transferred steelworkers were returning to the area.[44] But the good jobs in the manufacturing sector of the economy—jobs at Bethlehem Steel, Mack Truck, Western Electric—were being lost and replaced with lower wage, less secure, less safe jobs with limited benefits in a downgraded manufacturing sector. As we saw in Chapter 2, different factory regimes are often related to different labor markets and technologies of mass production.[45] These regimes can be characterized as the "low road" of structuring manufacturing—intensifying control over labor through the use of piece rate pay, heightened surveillance, and a "primitive Taylorism," all in a nonunion or weakened union environment.[46] This is contrasted to a high road of manufacturing that emphasizes team work with trained, multiskilled workers receiving seniority and benefits to maintain a skilled work force.[47] The growth of a low road in which "manufacturing by stress" is the management regime created jobs in the downgraded manufacturing sector.[48] In fact, of late pundits have lauded the return of manufacturing jobs to the US.[49] But these downgraded manufacturing jobs return from overseas to take advantage of the new deskilled, cheap, nonunion labor in deindustrialized regions. When these laid-off steelworkers, now in their late forties or in their fifties, re-entered the labor market in the 2000s in search of manufacturing jobs, they found that these core jobs were no longer available. Instead, most of the available manufacturing jobs were in this now downgraded sector of manufacturing.

One local employer, exemplifying the low road of downgraded manufacturing, gained international renown as an unsafe and seedy manufacturer. A number of Bethlehem Steel workers went to two pipe foundries in the

Lehigh Valley owned by McWane, Inc. McWane, a large family-owned corporation headquartered in Birmingham, Alabama, was the subject of an award-winning *New York Times* investigative series and *Frontline* expose on poor workplace safety. These series depicted McWane's gross safety violations (resulting in numerous employee injuries and deaths) and lax environmental regulations at its many plants in the US and Canada. From 1995–2003 at least 4,600 injuries, including numerous amputations and nine deaths (from a total of five thousand employees), were reported in McWane's foundries, and the company was cited for more than four hundred health and safety violations.[50] These statistics actually under-estimate accidents, as low-road manufacturers use a number of tactics, ranging from not reporting injuries to rushing workers back on the line after injury to avoid reporting a "missed day," to keep official accident statistics low. Two employee deaths occurred in the Lehigh Valley, at McWane's New Jersey facility, where worker turnover was extremely high. The *New York Times* expose showed the difficulties in enforcing safety standards with underfunded regulatory agencies wielding inadequate sanctions (such as paltry fines) and facing obstacles to criminal prosecution.

In this downgraded manufacturing sector, "what emerged was closer to nineteenth-century traditions of sweated labor than to the postindustrial model that was so widely touted in this period."[51] Abroad, state-supported policies generating new investment patterns supported the growth of manufacturing in less developed and newly industrializing countries, contributing to the loss of manufacturing jobs in the US. At home, an accompanying decline in workplace regulation under neoliberal policies within the US contributed to unsafe working conditions, a decline in wages and benefits, and increasing job insecurity.[52] A decline in safety standards and the reduction of OSHA oversight combined with pressure to work faster resulted in a doubling of US workplace injury rates in the 1980s.[53]

As big factories like Mack Trucks and Bethlehem Steel closed, manufacturing jobs in the Lehigh Valley grew scarce. As other manufacturers left the Northeast for the Sunbelt or less developed countries, these very visible processes undermined the power of labor. Workers followed cases in the local newspapers describing the closing of Durkee, Victaulic, and other manufacturers who used techniques such as pitting US factories against each other or threatening to move jobs outside the US to wring concessions from unions and tax breaks from city governments. Increased spatial mobility of capital, layoffs, aggressive anti-union campaigns, and a reduction in state regulatory agencies weakened workers' power at the same time as immigration and trade policies contributing to increases in cheap immigrant labor provided a ready supply of workers to this sector.

Some of the steelworkers I spoke with found jobs at McWane's pipe found-ries. Manny Vega, a second-generation Bethlehem Puerto Rican steelworker who worked in the coke works, applied for what he thought was a similar job at McWane, but he quit after a short time, describing it as "worse than Bethlehem Steel. It was very dangerous. They didn't care what happened to workers. They've got a lot of major lawsuits against them. They had a union, but it was a union with no clout. The union was very different. It made me realize how good a union we had when I worked there [at Bethlehem Steel]." He left work there and now stays home taking care of his aging mother. Un-like some workers, he was able to walk away from this job because he had a Bethlehem Steel pension and his wife had a job as a medical insurance un-derwriter with a decent salary and very good health insurance.

Matt Hacker, a former manager in the Bethlehem plant, described his dif-ficulties finding a job after his shop closed. When I asked him about work, he pulled an index card out of his wallet with rows of notations of the compa-nies he had worked for after Bethlehem Steel. Matt said since the Bethlehem plant's closing, "I've held so many jobs I keep a timeline." At one point he went to a local McWane foundry and worked there until a 2006 "unexplained" fire burned down the plant. McWane didn't rebuild, so he moved to their Phillipsburg plant. Matt explains that although the company is unionized, "these guys are cupcakes. The union has no teeth. They're afraid, and rightly so. McWane is a private company, so if they say goodbye, the party's over." McWane's Lehigh Valley foundries were organized by two entirely different unions, making collective action more difficult. As a manager in need of work, rather than being critical of this situation, Matt concluded that there are new rules for manufacturing today. "There was a place for the unions in the world at one time. They were beating the guys, management. Not any-more. It's survival now. You've got to work smart." When I ran into Matt two years later, he had left McWane and spoke freely about the dangerous and inhumane work environment in the plant.

McWane's management philosophy was what the *New York Times* describes as one of "disciplined management practices" in which production targets took priority over safety, discipline was used to "suppress union unrest and discourage injury claims," and aggressive cost-cutting measures meant ram-pant safety violations.[54] Even as core industries like General Motors and Gen-eral Electric introduced team management strategies in new and restructured factories, management in the downgraded manufacturing sector became increasingly authoritarian and punitive.[55] This despotic regime of labor control not only coexists with high road factory regimes in contemporary US manufacturing, but often supplies high road manufacturers with important inputs. Will Wagner found a job at McWane after being laid off by Bethlehem Steel. He was very critical of management: "I didn't like the boss I had on night shift, that's why I quit. He was, how would you say, he had his nose up somebody's butt trying to make a name for himself, and the job that I had when I went there the first time was created so it would make his job easier." The high levels of production and cost cutting demanded by the night shift boss, at the expense of safety, ran counter to Will's ideas of how a workplace should be run, and he quit.

Structural insecurity in this sector is high, and without strong union protection, layoffs and closings at these secondary sector plants are frequent and abrupt, often with little intimation of trouble. When Tyler Pipe closed, even though Will was a lower-level manager, he relates,

> we went in one day and the boss said—I don't want to give the exact language. He said, "What the 'f' are you doing here?" I says, "What do you mean? I'm coming to work." We still had to go in [after the fire] to clean up. He said, "You have a meeting at Macungie Park at ten." "Well, nobody told me." My day shift boss said nobody told him either. We hung out until quarter to ten, then we went to Macungie, and by five after ten the boss there told us they were closing.

Workers in this sector found themselves serially downsized and thrown back into a job market in which "people think you bounce from job to job." Workers like Will, who continue working in this sector, are increasingly vulnerable and anxious, "I worry, am I going to have a job tomorrow? . . . Every day I worry about layoffs." Losing their most valuable assets, the skills and experience encoded into Bethlehem Steel seniority, rendered these workers vulnerable to downsizings and layoffs as the new last-hired workers in this downgraded sector of manufacturing.

Ex-steelworkers were not happy working in dangerous, low-paying manufacturing jobs and were disconcerted to find themselves working side by side with new immigrants, the very "other" they sometimes denigrate and even blame for the loss of high paying, unionized jobs. Al Trakas, for example, looked for a job after being laid off from the steel works in 1996, at a bad time when "every steelworker was looking for a job." He took a job in a factory recycling hazardous materials. The job was unsafe ("really a dangerous place"), nonunion, and low-paying, and "half the people couldn't talk English." Don

Booth also correlates a heavily immigrant workplace with unsafe working conditions. At Atlantic Pipes, he says, "ambulances were coming in daily. There were a lot of Puerto Ricans in the furnace. When one got injured, just drag one away. Throw another in his spot. It was horrible." Walt Steckel went from Sparrows Point to a nonunion fabricating shop and described his job, where he works as a crane operator, as "a real sweatshop." Walt says "they have so many illegals working in here, it's unbelievable. They're a union company in their Ohio plant, but not here." He says, in this work environment "they have no respect for anyone. People who have worked in shipyards for twenty-five years, boilermakers, steel, they have no respect. It's like, "Do this, you're lucky you got a job." That shit don't work on a fifty-five-year-old person." Walt attributes this despotic regime, in part, to the availability of low-wage, immigrant labor, "the company likes it because the company doesn't have to pay them benefits . . . those guys are in and out like a revolving door every week."

Undocumented immigrants are often recruited by employers to "break worker solidarity, undermine wages, and heighten profits."[56] Recruitment of immigrant labor and aggressive eviscerating of unions keep labor costs low in downgraded manufacturing. As anthropologist Peter Kwong points out, "the undocumented have given their employers the leverage to force workers to accept many obviously illegal labor practices" such as below minimum wage pay and highly unsafe workplaces.[57] Undocumented immigrant workers are less likely to demand workers' compensation for injuries or to report safety violations due to their precarious status. Ex-steelworkers are aware of these issues and blame undocumented immigrants for undermining unions and lowering wages. Walt Steckel says at his job,

> they do the same jobs as everyone else. . . . That's baloney that they're only supposed to get the undesirable jobs Americans don't want. They're in the trades now, plumbing, electrical, roofing, drywall, mason work, that used to be good paying jobs. I hear, "Don't bitch about what you're getting paid because I can get a Mexican tomorrow for the same work at the same price."

Ernie Lang argues that "these illegals coming over here . . . I can understand, I don't blame them for wanting to come. But hey, it's not right. My dad went through all this hardship [Ernie describes going with his dad to the union hall in the 1959 strike]. For what? To let these guys come over and regress the whole process to 1955?" In Ernie's eyes, undocumented immigrants, willing to work for low wages, constitute a real threat to well-paid union jobs. Ernie's father fought for the union, suffered during the 1959 strike, and helped to bring union power into the industrial workplace. The availability of this low wage, nonunion labor undermines the concept of economic citizenship for Ernie, the idea that through hard work, workers are worthy citizens deserving of middle-class wages.

Contemporary talk among white steelworking families about the undeserving poor elides into discussions of illegal immigration. Therefore, to find oneself in a job, working side by side with undocumented immigrants, is to accept a reality of downward mobility that is a shock to white working-class identity and citizenship. While white steelworkers represent themselves as having worked in an ethnic melting pot at Bethlehem Steel, in reality there were no "new immigrants" working at Bethlehem Steel, as the last major hires had been in 1979 and Puerto Rican workers were mostly second-generation steelworkers. Working side-by-side with the new immigrants who white suburban steelworkers often represent as the undeserving and problematic poor living in the inner cities of Allentown and Bethlehem threatened workers' identities as skilled, middle-class Americans. These ideologies contributed to divisions in the workplace, fragmenting the workforce. White workers often attempted to use their greater social capital, more developed networks, and better access to job training to exit these jobs.

For decades, exclusions built into Fordist working-class solidarity and citizenship rights left those workers that were considered the undeserving poor on the outside. Farm workers, domestics, and the unwaged labor of wives was racialized, ethnicized, or gendered as other and excluded from the public-private welfare rights and benefits attached to economic citizenship. These workers were often characterized as disreputable and undeserving of the same citizenship rights. The Fordist compromise created a schism between the industrial working class and what came to be defined as an "underclass"—a group thought of as radically different than workers.[58] As anthropologist Ida Susser so aptly points out, this underclass is actually a more insecure fraction of the working class, less protected by unions and less supported by the public-private welfare state that provided security to unionized workers.[59] But white workers define this racialized, ethnicized poor as an undeserving, immoral other.

It is, then, particularly disconcerting to the dispossessed and devalued members of the industrial working class to see their increasingly insecure lives as similar to the lives of the undeserving poor. Criticisms of the undeserving poor as lacking a work ethic, taking advantage of the public welfare system, and leading unstable and insecure family lives suddenly seem less distant. The stability of working-class home ownership—being able to plan a future, set aside money for college, have health insurance that ensures health crises don't bankrupt your family, and plan a retirement—can be threatened or decimated through processes of deindustrialization. The ability to delay gratification, to think of one's life as a planned and orderly linear narrative, is shaken. The values of thrift and sacrifice, hard work and commitment, and the work experience and skill honed over time through which one hopes to live a good life are all undermined. The dislocations of deindustrialization replace these with insecurity and precariousness, throwing some workers and their families into the "disreputable" practices of the undeserving poor. But, while ex-steelworkers do not condemn their co-workers for this, they still fail to see the connections between displacement and disreputable practices. Instead, many construct an illegal, disreputable other that can be blamed for undermining wages, degrading jobs, and de-valuing neighborhoods, making illegal immigrants the scapegoats for much broader processes.

Public-Sector Jobs

Many workers looked for jobs in the public sector as these were often the few remaining stable, unionized jobs for workers without a college education. Some workers used their ties to place and local social networks to mobilize support from friends and political representatives in attaining public-sector jobs. Frank Gaskell describes having "one hundred applications out" in 2002 when he returned to the Lehigh Valley after transferring to Bethlehem Steel's Lackawanna plant. He was looking for jobs in trucking or carpentry, but couldn't find any. "They wanted to pay me $7.00 an hour for carpentry jobs, and it wasn't worth it to me." Frank says he figured "the future of manufacturing and getting a good job with good pay and good benefits aren't going to happen here in the Valley." So Frank went to see his state representative, saying, "Hey, I'm a steel guy running out of medical. Any state jobs you can help me with?" Using this strategy, he was hired in a maintenance job at a state hospital. The job was a long commute, and paid low wages, but it had benefits, and Frank thought that he could advance on the job. Steelworker Joe Karp ran into friends, other ex-steelworkers working for Lanta (the public bus company), who encouraged him to come in to apply for a job driving bus. Joe says, "They told my road supervisor there that when I worked in Bethlehem [Steel] I had one of the dirtiest, dangerest jobs and I always made it to work. I never took off, never complained. I was a good worker, no drugs, no drink." Joe got the job, a job with much-needed benefits, even though in 2008 he was "making what I used to make in 1998 when the coke ovens shut down. I lost all that ten years to catch up to what I was making." Other workers found public-sector jobs in transportation—driving buses or working on the highways—or worked in state-owned liquor stores, state hospitals, the post office, community colleges, or job-training programs.

But attaining these public-sector jobs was difficult, as a post-Fordist order that denigrates big government and celebrates privatization has reduced the numbers of secure public–sector jobs. Ron Lambert's wife got a job with the post office after fifteen years of working in the Lehigh Valley garment industry, because the "job security and pay were good at the post office." When Ron was laid off from the coke works and awaiting his transfer options, he took advantage of his wife's knowledge of the post office to work as a rural postal carrier. But this job was a contracted temporary position, not a civil service job, as the post office has increasingly outsourced functions. Thus, it was highly insecure and paid only $9 an hour. When Ron returned from his transfer to Bethlehem Steel's Sparrows Point plant, he again wanted to get a job with the post office, but couldn't. He found another job with a company subcontracted by the post office, this time as a truck driver. The subcontracted job is not unionized, but it is regulated by government contract (prevailing wage) rules, leading to a good wage. But the job does not have benefits, there is no overtime, there is no health care, and there is "no advancement there." Although Ron likes his current job, and likes the working conditions, he says, "I prefer having a union backing me up." He is also well aware that his current job lacks the security of a civil-service position.

Workers clearly recognize that public-sector jobs have become increasingly threatened and insecure. Steelworker Chris Szarko was laid off at Bethlehem Steel in the 1980s, then experienced a series of layoffs working for large manufacturers that moved their factories or closed down before finally attaining a public-sector job. But he feels insecure, even in the public sector.

> We all know just by watching the newspaper, state jobs are disappearing. Right now I think the public-sector jobs are in more trouble than the private-sector jobs are. Hopefully, that changes. I would like to stay where I am, I would like to stay in the public sector, and I often think of state-related jobs as secure, but they're not. . . . Those jobs are disappearing.[60]

What had once seemed like a smart move, from private to more secure public-sector work, is increasingly questioned as austerity initiatives are transforming public-sector jobs to precarious work.

While workers wanted the job security and benefits of the public sector, many bridled at the customer-service orientation in these public-sector jobs. Frank Gaskell, who worked directing traffic at a construction site for the Pennsylvania Department of Transportation (PennDOT), disliked interaction with customers, the "public," required on the job. I found "you're not doing a job, you're getting in their [the drivers'] way. I've been called names by women that I've been called by guys." Frank contrasted that to a Department of Transportation job that he enjoyed, snow plowing. "Give me a rig and let me go. That's the only time people are glad to see you." Joe Karp also finds the service orientation in bus driving difficult.

> The people I pick up, 90 percent of them don't even think. . . . You can have [written] across the whole front [of the bus] *Downtown Allentown*. You get sick of it. People ask, "Are you going to Allentown?" Why are you asking me? You get fed up with this crap. . . . You don't know what the person, passenger's next feelings are going to be. It changes from day to day.

Where steelworkers could rely on co-workers' common sense and collaboration to complete the job, providing a service to fickle customers is perceived as unpredictable and irrational.

Workers were also critical of public-sector unions. Even as these unions have increasingly come under attack for being too powerful, ex-steelworkers found them very weak compared to the USW. Andy Vanek said that workers in a public agency were "afraid to fart even in the men's room." It was, he said, "each person for themselves." He describes this as "too big a transition for me. . . . I have a hard time . . . " Al Trakas says, "PennDOT has a union, but it's a weak union. . . . They're all company unions, no teeth to them, compared to what I knew at the steelworkers' union." Frank Gaskell agreed that the union at PennDOT was terrible; "the ACFSME union exists for the sole purpose of collecting dues. The pay scale stinks, the benefits stink," and "the union had nothing to say about promotion and retirement." Just before Frank got his job, PennDOT introduced a tiered system in which new hires had lower salary and benefits. "The union is useless. The Bethlehem union would have been right on that. That was the difference between a union representing people who are producing something versus a service-oriented union." These weak unions undermine popular support for unions, as workers become frustrated with their inability to aggressively represent worker interests.

Workers were also disappointed with promotional opportunities in the public sector. They were accustomed to the very structured ways that seniority governed access to job opportunities at Bethlehem Steel. But with weak unions, patronage and nepotism became important in securing promotions in the public sector. Steelworker William Brown likes his current white-collar job as a career counselor in the public sector, but says "there is no room for advancement." Frank Gaskell also said that he thought he could advance in the public sector: "I thought I can move up and advance, but you don't advance if you have a brain, if you have ambition, if you have common sense. You only advance if you grease some politician's reelection campaign." Dave Campbell also found that "working for the state is political . . . it's very political." Gaining seniority, working hard, and doing one's job well were not enough to ensure career advancement.

White workers also bridle at affirmative action guidelines that they view as favoring racial and ethnic minorities over the white working class. Frank Gaskell said when he applied for promotion, although he had the skills and test scores and was offered the job, a black applicant contested Frank's promotion, saying "they didn't get a fair shake." Frank says the state convened a second search committee and promoted the African American applicant. Frank is angry about this perceived injustice. "If he's more qualified I have no problem, but if there's some other agenda, like you don't have enough black folk, that's not going to fly. The job goes to the best qualified individual. I know my qualifications are better than his." Frank says, "I want that damn job," since the pay is significantly greater. For Frank, the principles of seniority and ability, in one of the few jobs still protected by unions, trump remedies for racial injustices, especially as affirmative action policies recognize racial but not class-based discrimination.

Small Businesses

Another much-esteemed career alternative for steelworkers is running their own small businesses. Small entrepreneurship is respected by steelworkers, and a goal many workers aspired to, incorporating dominant society valuing of entrepreneurialism, the goal of material success, and the ideal of controlling one's own work. Many workers were also well-prepared for this, as many had run their own businesses while working at the steel mill. Milkman's study of GM autoworkers found that a significant percentage of bought-out autoworkers left the factory to start (or continue) their own businesses.[61] As with Bethlehem Steel workers, she found that most small businesses had been started while workers were at GM, often during periods of layoff, and that workers had a strong desire to start small businesses.[62] In Bethlehem steel shops with frequent layoffs, workers often started a small business and kept it as insurance against future slowdowns. Cyclical layoffs in steel encouraged workers to maintain second jobs. "I never depended on Bethlehem Steel. . . . I had something going on the side so I didn't worry about it so much." While working at the mill, steelworkers and their families ran lawn care businesses; worked as farriers; did construction work; ran retail operations; operated gambling rings; ran commercial laundries; and bought and operated convenience stores, pizza places, and restaurants. Some of these businesses even operated inside the steel mill itself, supplementing workers' salaries through the thriving informal economy within the works. There were retail operations inside the mill, with workers selling wristwatches, tires, and other items. There were bookies in the mill, as many steelworkers liked to gamble. There was an active fundraising culture—selling fundraising tickets for community organizations, for example, or pension party tickets for retiring workers—deeply rooted in reciprocal exchanges.

Of course, the small business needed to be tailored to fit the demands of a steelworking schedule, which could vary tremendously depending on what shop the worker was in and what job he had within the plant. The availability of family labor was also an important variable in successful small businesses. Male steelworkers could rely on wives and children to help run restaurants, stores, or real estate ventures. "Hungry" production workers, working swing shift with heavy overtime schedules, had the capital to invest in a small business, but would have to have family labor to effectively run the business. This contrasts with the businesses skilled craftsmen started outside the steel mill, as wives and children were less able to contribute to that work because they lacked those specialized skills.

But valuing entrepreneurial hard work and autonomy did not mean accepting an ideology legitimizing exploitation. These small-business owners continued to hold strong ethics about just and fair treatment of both workers and customers. Their customers, and their employees, were often also working men and might be former steelworkers. After retiring from Bethlehem Steel, Tony Valeri worked for H&R Block doing taxes, as he had always enjoyed doing taxes for his extended family. However, he left the company precipitously to set up his own business when he became disgusted by the outrageous fees they charged their customers. Tony explained, "The money I had to charge was too much. That's the end of that. They wouldn't let us give discounts anymore." Tony had a strong moral code about what constitutes ethical business practices. Ernie Lang, who started up a landscaping business during layoff, feels strongly about the way employers should treat employees: "If I owned a body shop and made $10 million profit . . . I would give [the workers] one hell of a bonus for making that kind of money, a $50,000 check, or better benefits, or up their salary." And Gus Guerrera expressed shock when the real estate clientele he was trying to help treated him unethically. "I wanted to help people, lower paying people that could just about afford a home," but he found that his customers would switch realtors, demonstrating no loyalty to him.

Although small-business ownership was highly respected, the need to find health care coverage after the Bethlehem Steel bankruptcy prevented many steelworkers from pursuing this strategy, pushing them into waged work with benefits. Only those steelworkers with employed wives with family health care plans could afford this expense. Workers like Ernie Lang, who was on his steelworking wife's health care plan, could start a small lawn care business, but when Joe Karp started the same business he had to go without health care coverage for a number of years, finally shutting down his business to move into a public-sector job that provided health care benefits.

FULFILLING POST-FORDIST WORK

As Ruth Milkman found in *Farewell to the Factory*, not all workers regretted leaving steel work.[63] Many workers found work they enjoyed greatly after Bethlehem Steel, although the pay and benefits were seldom comparable. And many workers considered themselves "successful" in transitioning from steel work to other work in the Lehigh Valley's "new economy." Some workers aspired to jobs with greater flexibility; with more perceived opportunity for mobility; in cleaner, healthier, and safer environments; or with less demanding physical work.

Some workers prepared themselves to move into a postindustrial labor market by consciously pursuing their education, even while working at the Steel, taking advantage of tuition reimbursement programs. However, one's ability to exercise this strategy depended on the shifts one worked. Hungry production workers had difficulty continuing their education. Instead, they prepared for a shut down by building up their salary prior to early retirement. And this strategy could be highly effective. Although workers are often faulted in dominant society discourses for not pursuing higher education and positioning themselves for a postindustrial labor market, it is not always clear that this is a more effective strategy than working long hours in the hopes that one can roll into a heftier pension. The latter strategy was effective precisely because of the value of the union-negotiated rules for overtime pay and pension calculations, the highly valuable benefits of the Fordist order. Workers are, however, fully aware of these dominant society critiques, and justify their decisions to hold on to steel work through reference to their salaries. William Brown, who loved steel work, describes the money he was making when he transferred to Sparrows Point: "my son-in-law has all these degrees, but I was making more money than he does." And had he been able to roll into his pension, that salary would have determined his pension payments.

Workers also pursued union positions, thereby acquiring skills that could be valuable in a postindustrial economy.[64] But this also was not a clearly superior strategy for post-steel success. Serving as a union official detracted from one's total earning capacity, thereby reducing the "best five" of the last ten years determining one's pension. Many workers wonder, in hindsight, if they made a mistake by continuing in their union positions, as it eroded their final pensions. "I didn't realize how close to the end it was," union officer Will Brown reflected. These decisions could lead to significant pension differences. Will reflects that "my pension would have been double or more" if he had transferred back to a full time production job—an enormous amount of money when projected over a long retirement. This strategy for earning the most money in the mill, thereby adding to one's pension payments, seemed opposed to mainstream societal values where "mental" labor and continuing education are considered the route to success, but it often proved a superior strategy for workers' security in retirement.

The strategy of pursuing higher education while working in the steel mill could also run counter to a moral economy that valued solidarity in crew work. Some workers began their college degrees while laid off, but found themselves facing difficulties in continuing their education after being called back to work, as swing shift work made attending courses nearly impossible. Some workers, like Louis Moran, who worked day shift in the maintenance department, were able to finish college while working. But other workers, committed to continuing their educations, had to manipulate the rules of work in order to go to school. Hal Rouse "had to leave early sometimes"; he would leave the plant, go to school, and return "clandestinely." "To get out and get back in was sometimes pretty difficult. I flew under the radar for a couple of months, had people cover for me, and people who were behind what I was doing. You got to get an education. A lot of people knew that the place was going to go down soon." Although many might see educational preparation for the demise of the steel mill as individual initiative and foresight, many co-workers saw it as pushing the expectations of collaborative work. Members on Hal's crew resented covering for him, picking up his work while he pursued an individual avenue of social mobility. They expected a member of the crew to pull his own weight, allowing the entire crew to make their incentive, which would be calculated into their salaries and pensions, and to do so safely. And many of these co-workers, who were working hard to extend the life of the Bethlehem mill, thereby preserving steel jobs for everyone, saw this path to individual mobility as a betrayal of the broader collective goals of all Bethlehem steelworkers.

But craft skills, higher education, and union positions could translate into postindustrial opportunities for workers as well. When I visited him at his home, Fred Bauer, an electronics craft worker, showed me a file folder stuffed with training certificates, and credited his extensive on-the-job training at Bethlehem Steel, as well as his experience as a shop steward, for preparing him to work in banking after he left the mill. These mechanical skills could also translate into opportunities in highly skilled industrial work. Many steel-workers went on to use these skills in the remaining steel industry on the plant, Lehigh Heavy Forge, or in electrical or electronics work in construction or the service sector. Some workers moved into jobs where they could use, and enjoyed using, the craft skills they learned in the steel mill. Barry Kirk, for example, worked at a hobby store managing the train department, and did electrical work for a manufacturer in the Lehigh Valley. He valued both jobs, taking satisfaction in his craft knowledge, and in "wiring and the accomplishment of turning it on and watching it work . . . [there is nothing like] getting to see it work."

Other workers relished the cleaner, healthier environment of work in the service sector. Tim Fuchs, who now works maintenance at a college in the area, says his current job is "a whole different world. I don't live in the dirt. It's cleaner, healthier, out in the public. I can go to lunch." Harry Dudek, who used his vacation time to train as a welding inspector, enjoys his job now. "I like it much better than working at Bethlehem Steel. You don't breathe in the fumes. This is much easier, just looking at [the welds]. It's not the same level of pay, but it's enough." Pat Daly finds his job in a large warehouse "easier than Bethlehem Steel, a cleaner job, a cooler job, everything about it is way better. Except the salary is worse than I was making ten years ago." Mark Castor likes his job driving a van doing medical deliveries, although he's only making half the money he was making in steel. "I love the job, they're all friendly to you, you get to know everybody. I love delivering, I'm relaxed, I have a regular run." For some, a cleaner, easier, healthier job is welcome after the hard, dirty, dangerous work at the steel mill.

Differing attitudes about work and identities forged inside and outside the mill also contributed to differing trajectories as workers struggled to redefine themselves, move into other kinds of work, and restructure their lives after the demise of the Bethlehem plant. Some workers maintain their steel-worker identity in a post-steel world—moving into other blue-collar jobs that allow them to support their families. But other workers, particularly some of those who had not primarily defined themselves as steelworkers, struggled to define themselves as members of a professional middle class in the new post-Fordist economy. This required a qualitative shift in the way one thinks about oneself and the world, and it often required a changed morality—the acceptance of the prioritization of self-advancement over the collective re-sponsibilities in the mill.

These workers accepted the reality of the new economy: "you don't have a choice" about these changes, "you can't change it." Many workers defined anger as an ineffective response—"do I want to be a whiner or make the best of this situation and navigate to where I can make more money or do more satisfying things?" Bob Hale defines a new reality: "Time marches on. History, the nation, is replete with places that shut down; life goes on." He contrasts himself to steelworkers who hold on to their working class iden-tities—"Some of these guys, it's the balance of their life is talking about the steel, trying to convey what it's like,"—saying, "I'm too progressive, forward thinking." These workers prided themselves on preparing for the new econ-omy, pursuing higher education while working at the mill, and changing themselves to adapt to this new reality. Dan Torres highlights the importance of self-transformation: "If you don't like the way things are in front of you, you have to change something within you. I really came to understand that perspective and adopt it." He says, "I wanted something better out of life."

But even while positioning themselves for success in the new economy, trying to adopt a new neoliberal persona, these workers continue to express conflicted and contradictory moralities, often seesawing back and forth be-tween the moral economy of the mill and a postindustrial, middle-class mo-rality. Dan Torres, for example, says working in the mill made workers numb, and "it's not possible to plan for the future when all you can do every day is just be numb and avoid thinking about what kind of environment you work in," but "we agreed to give up our rational thinking, put our safety aside, for that security." But in the next breath, he contradicts himself, lauding the se-curity of the steel jobs: "There is a lot of value in job security. . . . There is just an incredible amount of rational thinking that it allows you to have when you don't have to worry about where your next paycheck's coming from . . . that's when you can really become a productive citizen." Hal Rouse, who went to college and redefined himself as an artist post-Bethlehem Steel, also shifts back and forth in conversation, from defining himself as "the working man" to constructing a new professional, middle-class identity. Hal defines his new flexible, freelance artistic work as empowering; "I get to pick and choose" jobs. And he sees himself as having prestige, related to individual accomplishments, in a way that he didn't at Bethlehem Steel, "Bethlehem Steel never acknowledged us as anything more than a number. Even if we had stock. We were never allowed to go in the office buildings." In his relationship with the Sands Casino, he was a proud owner of stock, checking his portfolio on the computer and recommending that I buy some. "I'm an owner in the Sands . . . Sands stock is up, I'm happy." However, he simultaneously recognizes that even though he is an "owner," he lacks control over the casino—"someone else has control, we don't." Hal seesaws back and forth between commitment to and critique of the union; support for stability in employment and a lauding of flexibility and choice; support of a production-based economy and admiration for speculation and financialization. He is caught betwixt and between discourses and identities, struggling to chart a path and to make sense out of a shifting and contradictory new world.

SKILLED STEEL JOBS

A few steel workers moved into the remaining steel jobs carved out of the former plant. In 1992/93, Bethlehem Steel, amid much negotiation, separated two sections of the south Bethlehem works, BethForge and Centec, into distinct subdivisions.[65] The company then entered a partnership with Chavanne-Ketin, a French steel company, to introduce spin caster technology into Centec for production of steel rolls. The partnership was not successful, so Bethlehem Steel bought out its French partner and in 1997 sold BethForge and Centec to West Homestead Engineering and Machinery Co. (WHEMCO), a family-owned business. WHEMCO created the still-functioning Lehigh Heavy Forge and kept Centec going for a few years longer. While Centec closed in 2000, Lehigh Heavy Forge continues as a forger and finisher of huge components for nuclear power plants, the hydroelectric industry, and the military. Lehigh Heavy Forge receives hot ingots shipped by train from Cleveland-Cliff's Steelton plant and forges and finishes large components from this steel. Lehigh Heavy Forge employs almost two hundred workers today, far less than the eight hundred workers that worked at Bethlehem Steel's BethForge Division in the late 1990s.[66] Like the contracts the International Steel Group negotiated with USW after purchasing Bethlehem's mills, the new contracts negotiated with WHEMCO under the cloud of a botched sale and threats of plant closure resulted in broad concessions from the union. These included a decrease in wages and benefits (amounting to an average reduction of $12 an hour), reduced job classifications, and streamlined work rules. Later, profit-sharing was added to the contract. "The company said we'll give you profit sharing in lieu of a raise." Restructured work was combined with a highly skilled work force recruited from Bethlehem Steel. At Lehigh Heavy Forge in the 2000s, there were no unskilled workers. Due to a contract that allows multiskilling, skilled workers run the forklifts, hook the steel, and operate the cranes.

When workers were laid off from the BethForge Division, with the 1997 sale, they were then eligible for retirement, external transfers, and retraining. Some workers were called in for an interview at Centec or Lehigh Heavy Forge. While Henry Hirsch, a union official, says that according to union negotiations, "they were supposed to bring us back in according to seniority," in reality "it didn't exactly happen that way, because some people needed certain skills. Those people may not have had seniority, so we modified it a little." The result of this was that WHEMCO was able to be very selective, hiring only the most-skilled Bethlehem Steel workers who came highly recommended by managers. Eddie Havela, a machinist, said, "They talked to the bosses at the Steel and found out who they wanted. The more skilled workers, the better workers, they picked the cream of the crop." Mitch Roberts agrees: "They wanted to pick their best people. . . . We're a bunch of prima donnas in the machine shop."

While steelworkers were happy to have jobs, the new contract was hard for workers. Eddie says "I took a tremendous pay cut. On direct incentive, our hourly wage [at Bethlehem Steel] was around the mid-twenties [per hour]. . . . From that amount I went down to $14 an hour. The benefits weren't as good." But he took the job. "I knew the situation with the steel closing, LTV, Bethlehem Steel. I was happy to be working. A lot of the guys I formerly worked with at Bethlehem Steel would have loved to have taken a pay cut to be with WHEMCO." Many of the skilled workers coming to work at WHEMCO were senior workers, many of whom already had their Bethlehem Steel pensions. Walt Martelli says, "The money wasn't as good, [but] being as they were older guys, they weren't concerned about the money. They were looking at benefits." WHEMCO benefited from the Bethlehem Steel (and later PBGC) pensions that some workers received to supplement initially low salaries.

However, Lehigh Heavy Forge workers today are very satisfied with their salaries. As a result of profit-sharing, workers have been making good salaries over the past decade, although that often entails working a lot of overtime. Bob Cook says that "people are scared" and will work overtime without question now. John Baxter states "We work way too much, it's a booming business, and that's a good thing. They ask for overtime all the time. I get maybe three days a month off." According to Mitch Roberts, after putting in a number of years at Lehigh Heavy Forge, workers finally "started making profit sharing money . . . like we've never seen before. We're getting $20,000, $30,000 a year profit sharing now, and it's wonderful. I'm making more now than I did at any time in my Bethlehem Steel career." But George Dent does caution workers about profit sharing. "It's been very lucrative for us, but it's not guaranteed. We've been lucky, very lucky. We make very good money [but] . . . profit sharing can go away like that, it can go away." And, while workers are enthusiastic about the money, they are also aware that at Lehigh Heavy Forge, there are "a lot more grey areas in the contract, not in our favor . . . the grey areas were never in our favor."

Workers at Lehigh Heavy Forge are motivated to work flexibly to keep the steel industry going, to continue in steel work, and to make profit sharing monies. Mitch Roberts says, "When we started in 1973 there were fifteen thousand of us. There's two hundred of us left now, but boy are we efficient. We're a lean, mean crew of guys. That's why our profit sharing is the way it is." The new management regime emphasizes self-reliance and personal responsibility, what anthropologist Sharryn Kasmir calls "self-regulating" workers, and workers are given more autonomy to direct their own work, eliminating layers of management.[67] Workers for the most part like this, feeling that their skills and knowledge are valued. Don Booth says, "I love what I do right now. . . . Here, you're your own boss. I know what I have to do, and I do it." And workers were happy to be able to continue doing steel work, "I'm very thankful to be here," it is "the last stronghold of steelworkers." They know that they are doing well in comparison with many of their Bethlehem Steel cohort, they are valued for the skills that they invested so much of their life in learning, and they take pride in the work they do. Mitch Roberts, who could talk for hours about the steel industry, loves the giant press forge. "It's tremendous, and I'm sort of proud of that. I don't know why I should still be a steelworker. It just doesn't make sense with fifteen thousand of us in 1973, and I'm still there, and I actually like my job."

But those highly skilled workers who continue to produce steel in the Lehigh Valley are a whiter and more male work force than at Bethlehem Steel. While I did hear of one Latino worker at Lehigh Heavy Forge, it does not seem that any women work there. In selecting former Bethlehem Steel workers to hire at Lehigh Heavy Forge, or at Brandenburg, in well-paid and skilled jobs, these companies ended up with a much smaller, highly skilled, well-paid, whiter, and strictly male work force. This skilled industrial working class is today much smaller and more homogeneous.

Conclusion

In many ways, steelworkers have come to accept the tenets of the new, post-Fordist economy. But there have been some exceptions to this. While I did not hear many examples of organizing and protest as steelworkers moved to new economy jobs, the example of the casino does stand out. I knew of only a few Bethlehem steelworkers who ended up working at the Sands casino, as security guards and maintenance workers. The casino did not begin hiring until 2009, so these workers had moved from other post-steel jobs into the casino. The low pay of many casino jobs made them unappealing to many and meant workers needed pensions to supplement their salaries. Thus, most of the casino jobs available to local workers were not highly desirable jobs.

But interestingly, it was among the security guards, spearheaded by ex-steelworkers, that a union was formed at the casino. Sheldon Adelson, the head of the Las Vegas Sands Corporation, was renowned for his virulently anti-union stance, something he fought hard to maintain in a union town like Las Vegas. He had a reputation for viciously battling unions, using the legal system to ensure the Sands remained a nonunion company. The *New Yorker* pointed out, a bit tongue-in-cheek, that Adelson "did not shy away from courtroom battles."[68] Adelson's colleague Jason Chudnofsky summarized this approach. "Sheldon's attitude has been: Spend millions on defense and never settle."[69] This was certainly the case when he dragged the Culinary Workers Union through multiyear legal proceedings in Las Vegas over the right to protest on a public sidewalk. The Sands lost their suit at the end, but they successfully exhausted the resources and energy of the union.

Forming and organizing a union was a new experience for ex-steelworkers and Sands security guards. These steelworkers had started at the mill in the 1960s and '70s, entering a plant with a long-extant, powerful union. But when younger security guards voiced discontent with working conditions, workers with union history and experience reached out to organize. Because security guards must organize under security unions (a law written into the Taft Hartley Act), workers had to look outside the Lehigh Valley to find a union, the Law Enforcement Employees Benevolent Association (LEEBA), to initially represent them.

When workers at the Sands voted the union in and then signed their first contract in 2017, it was a shock to the Sands, and the local Sands Bethlehem managers felt the brunt of Adelson's rage. Workers voted for the union even in the face of an aggressive anti-union, Sands-financed campaign. The Sands brought out-of-town union busters in to schmooze with workers (chatting about shared masculine interests in hunting and fishing) in an attempt to influence their vote. But the security workers voted the union in anyway. And in Sheldon Adelson's vast empire of forty thousand workers, stretching from Las Vegas to Macao, this one small group of security workers became the only union in the empire, the thorn in the billionaire's side. Adelson wheeled out his well-honed tactics of appeal, litigation, and further appeal to stretch out the process of union recognition, while simultaneously increasing surveillance and discipline of security guards. The Sands also escalated aggressive anti-union propaganda directed at all new hires. But the union hung on during this long offensive.

A progressive, local community was supportive of this new union, incorporating the union into a coalition of free speech advocates to hold a large-scale public demonstration related to the Sands' restriction of individual rights on the former Bethlehem Steel site in 2012. As a part of the new development on the Bethlehem Steel site, the Sands transferred land to the city for a "Twenty-First-Century Town Square." The deed for this land, however, included restrictive covenants banning events that would "permit labor related entities" to "organize" workers. In Bethlehem, one of the birthplaces of Fordist unionism, this was an affront to many. A broad coalition of activists, including union officials, social movement activists, and ex-steelworkers protested en masse in 2012. The potential for collective action continues, fueled by the strong union history, solidarity, and right to citizenship governing the space of the former steel mill. But unfortunately, when the Sands sold the casino to Wind Creek, tired security workers decertified their union in 2019.

Conclusion

This generation of steelworkers experienced their life trajectories as traversing across the transformation from a Fordist to a post-Fordist US social order. In following a generation of steelworkers across their work experiences, from beginning as young workers in a robust Fordist mill to their long, drawn-out experience of restructuring, disinvestment, downsizing, and eventually closure, bankruptcy, and dissolution, this book explores the meanings of deindustrialization. By tracking workers through retraining programs, transfers to other mills, and moving into new jobs in a post-Fordist political economy, it examines their reintegration as a reshaped working class into a new postindustrial milieu. In part, these steelworkers came to accept the new reality of the post-Fordist order. But simultaneously, workers are also quite critical of the promises and transformations of the new, postindustrial order.

Steelworkers are very critical of some of the assumptions embedded in a post-Fordist dominant ideology. Steelworkers described their choices when they entered the mill in a Fordist Bethlehem and contrast them to the post-Fordist notion of individual choice as freedom. In the post-Fordist system of ideas, the flexible, freely choosing individual builds a resume, easily moving from employer to employer, pursuing lifelong education and training, and best-positioning him- or herself in the contemporary job market. Steelworkers are cognizant that for themselves, and for their children, this new landscape of work constitutes an illusion of choice. They are aware that the contemporary jobs male workers without college educations can "choose" between are lower-paying, less secure, and have fewer benefits than the Fordist industrial jobs. Steelworkers identify a gender dimension to these insecurities, worrying especially about job opportunities for young men, as many available public-sector and service-sector jobs are perceived as feminine. They are also concerned that although women may now have more opportunities for wage work, women's waged work is no longer a "choice," but a necessary support for working- and middle-class families. Today, the real options for steelworkers and their children are limited and diminished when compared to the choices they had as young men in the 1960s and 1970s. Steelworkers contrast contemporary to past options. Beam yard worker Frank Havlicek says, "My dad worked to give us the choice—to go to college or not. Now, you can't pay for college unless you go into the service," as college has become outrageously expensive. Steelworkers are concerned, today, about intergenerational downward mobility. "For most people the outlook of their kids is less. It's diminished. Unless they go to school." And they worry that the more insecure status of their children will affect their grandchildren's opportunities: "I don't see much of a future that they can even help their kids. What about college?" Steelworkers whose children did not finish college are afraid contemporary jobs will not provide the kinds of wages and benefits that will enable their children to realize a "good life."

Even those steelworkers whose children completed college voiced concerns about the changed post-Fordist workplace and labor market. Beam yard worker Bill Markus's oldest son went to college and works at AT&T "making big dollars." But AT&T has cut back, there's no overtime, and Bill is worried about his son's job security. Joe Privsek's college-educated eldest son "moved from company to company," an individualized and "flexible" approach to career that worried Joe, who asked him to consider not simply wages but also the stability of pensions and benefits in his career trajectory. Paul Davis is proud of his daughter—"luckily my daughter is educated" and has a "very, very good position." But he still worries about her job. "She is fighting for less hours, better pay, better benefits. It's a constant struggle for everybody. . . . What do you do when you're faced with this transient-type lifestyle? You go where the jobs are. You can't just find a company and expect to stay with that company. You have to be mobile and adaptable." And Frank Havlicek compares his trajectory at Bethlehem Steel to that of his college-educated brother, whose computer-oriented job is now being threatened as "now they're bringing people from India. . . . Now he's fighting for his job." A college education and a professional middle-class job no longer guarantee job stability, assured benefits, and a secure old age. Those "rights" have been undermined for white-collar as well as blue-collar workers and are now being attacked and eroded in the public sector as well.

Steelworkers are also highly critical of the new US social order that fails to support and value manufacturing. Steelworkers espouse a strong producerist ideology—they condemn the shift in the US economy from manufacturing to service-oriented, are highly critical of the US government for not more actively preventing the decline of the steel industry, and connect robust production of goods with a strong US economy. Steelworkers link this ideology to "economic nationalism" in anti-free-trade sentiments and a buy-American orientation. Historian Dana Frank points to some of the weaknesses in the buy-American ideology—the ease in which it elided into anti-immigrant sentiment, the "near-total silence about labor's role" leading to a situation in which "nationalism trumped class analysis altogether," and the alliance constructed between unions and corporations to fight imports.[1] But the strong commitment to manufacturing, the critique of an economy too heavily dependent on services and speculative financial activity, and the correlation of a decline in manufacturing with an undermining of US economic strength are also salient criticisms of the contemporary post-Fordist US. Steelworkers do not believe a service economy can support US economic hegemony. Workers argue that "you need to be able to make a product. We can't all be service people." "Instead of a manufacturing society, we're turning into a service industry. And there's only so far that can go before even that collapses," and "it will be tough for the next generation. There's a domino effect. We're cutting our own throat with manufacturing going down the drain." This producerist ideology can extend to a serious critique of post-Fordist class relations, questioning the economic and moral value of CEOs and upper-level managers who do not actually labor to produce goods. This is a radical critique: "the idea that labor, not capital, creates real worth."[2] Frank Havlicek, an ex-craneman, articulates this clearly in his criticism of Donald Trautlein, the first Bethlehem Steel CEO who was a financial, rather than a steel, man. "If you took Trautlein and someone kidnapped him for the day, nobody would have to replace him. Everything would continue. But if you took Frank Havlicek out of the crane for the day, they would have to replace me. Nothing would get done. Who was the most important?" For Frank, it is workers making steel, not financiers accumulating profits, whose labor produces a strong economy.

In steelworkers' producerist ideology, industrial working-class jobs are crucially important in creating the country's economic strength. But good jobs and vigorous industrial production are not simply created by an unfettered free market. Job creation and job retention are struggled over, and most steelworkers are aware of the role of unions and of government in this. George Dent, for example, discusses the important role unions played in negotiating longer vacations, for example, as a way to "create jobs, give young guys the opportunity to come in . . . to make money. You don't have that in this country anymore." Union-negotiated policies such as overtime caps, reduction of work time, and leaves of absence help to redistribute work, to create more jobs.[3] Steelworkers were highly critical of Great Recession government bail-out packages that extended credit to financial entities without creating jobs. They were also critical of the Great Recession auto bailout package because, while they were glad to see manufacturing receive governmental support, they felt government monies should have included strong controls designed to prevent plant closings, factory relocation overseas, and auto worker layoffs.

Steelworkers are also skeptical of the social value of many of the new industries in the Valley, such as warehousing and the casino. They feel these industries do not create enough new jobs nor contribute to building a strong US. While the area's expanding logistics industry creates warehouse jobs, its low pay, poor benefits, and heavy reliance on temporary workers is decried, and steelworkers worry about the introduction of future technology to replace dead-end warehouse jobs. The logistics industry is seen as problematic, focused on moving Chinese-produced goods to US markets, rather than on producing goods in US-based union shops. Steelworkers also don't find much value in the jobs and activity of the casino—"I don't think building a casino is the panacea for our future. . . . Is that going to replace an organization like Bethlehem Steel who employed fifteen thousand hourly workers?" They critique the value of these jobs, for workers and society. Joe Karp contrasts steelworker pride in producing steel to build a strong US with casino jobs, arguing that

> the casino will ruin more lives than make lives better. We should have used this property for economic development for the community, for the people, the schools, and some industry. Making shoes or something. Where people can work. Not where people can go down there [to the casino] and become happy for an hour. That's what's going to happen. People go down with $50 thinking they'll come home with $1,200. They're going to lose a lot. Instead of finding a nice place to work and build their lives, they're going to give up their lives and lose it.

For Joe, meaningful work is more than wages and benefits. Steel work was work with dignity, providing a "good life," satisfaction on the job, and the meaning that came from producing goods that were important in building a "good society." As with essayist Cheri Register's working-class parents, work should provide security, but it also "had to have purpose and had to be of some benefit to others, not in any grand metaphysical sense, but useful at its most basic."[4] Warehouse and casino jobs do not do this. While many steelworkers enjoy gambling, they are critical of the paucity of jobs produced and the poor wages and benefits in the casino, and they also decry the lack of dignity and gratification in a job that does not contribute to what they define as a more just American society.

Most Bethlehem steelworkers do not shy away from an explicit discussion of class. Where Joshua Freeman found a "diminishing sense of class" in his study of New York City's working class, steelworkers in Bethlehem are very aware of class.[5] Steelworkers, for the most part, continue to define themselves as middle class, although as their financial security is undermined some contrast their current position as lower middle class, working class, or working poor to the solid middle-class position they occupied as steelworkers. As Andy Vanek says, "It was the good life. . . . We were the cream of the crop of the middle class." They were not an "affluent" middle class, but "we were definitely just middle class. That's just a normal life." But as Halle demonstrated in his study of chemical workers in New Jersey and as we see in this research, while most workers at the steel mill defined themselves as middle class, they also thought of steelworkers as "working men," describing in rich detail the working-class identities, practices, and sensibilities of their work lives at the steel mill.[6]

Today, however, while many steelworkers still define themselves as middle class, they define this class position as highly insecure and threatened in a contemporary US in which the middle class is, as they perceive it, under attack. "I consider myself middle class, but the middle class is going down fast. There's only going to be two classes anymore: rich and poor. It's been happening. The working man takes the brunt of everything, always." And there are a significant number of workers, especially those more battered by the processes of deindustrialization, that now identify as working class or lower middle class. Jerry Schneider, who took a big financial hit with the closing of the steel plant and loss of health care, now depends partly on his children's support. Jerry describes himself as lower middle class, and is highly critical of what he defines as contemporary class struggle, an attack on the middle class: "the wealthy are trying to wipe out the middle class." Danny Moreno also says, "I'm more like in the lower part of middle. That's what I think. Like the song says 'you're stuck in the middle where money gets tight, but I guess we're doing alright.' . . . It seems like the middle class carries everything on their backs." Rob Cuny, who works driving medical deliveries and whose wife is a nurse, describes himself as "working class. You have to keep working so that you can make a living." Norman Brist elaborates on this idea. "I don't believe there is a middle class. There is no more middle class the way I look at it. You're either poor or working poor. Or you're the greed class." Henry Hirsch agrees, and links the evisceration of the middle class to the decline of unions. "I see us as going more and more toward a two class system. Without a union, there's not going to be a middle class. And the middle class fuels the economic engine of this country." And Frank Havlicek articulates a radical ideology: "We need a revolution. We're eliminating the middle class."

For many steelworkers, this struggle, enacted through and resulting in a massive redistribution of resources from the working and middle classes to corporate elites, is linked with values that are destructive to society, that undermine America's basic values of justice, democracy, and respect. Steelworkers point to new values taking their place, values of greed and a self-centered focus, that decimate society and destroy moral social relations. Norman Brist explains, "The poor and working poor try to work with each other and better each other's lives. But for the rich, it's the me society." Steelworkers worry that undermining the middle class erodes the spirit of community volunteerism in the Lehigh Valley, destabilizes neighborhoods, eats away at the time that families can spend together, de-values production, and undermines real and robust economic growth. Without the consumer demand of a strong and healthy middle class, steelworkers foresee enormous problems for the US economy, "Well hell, what can the poor buy? You can't buy a new car." Workers link a dynamic manufacturing sector and strong unions with the robust middle class ("there never was a middle class until industry started opening up") necessary to support a consumerist economy. And they clearly link processes of deindustrialization and economic restructuring to the elimination of the middle class.

These are powerful critiques of the post-Fordist order, nurturing within them the seeds of a strong, oppositional working-class identity. However, there are also broad schisms within what can be defined as a broadly constituted contemporary US working class that present obstacles to collective action.[7] Business unions that fought for private welfare for only their core workers ensured that as jobs and benefits for nonunion workers declined, and as the number of core union workers shrank, broader public support for collectively bargained benefits was eroded. Non-steelworking Lehigh Valley workers resented the better wages and benefits unionized steelworkers received, and cited the high pay and "gold-plated" health care benefits of steelworkers as driving up the cost of living throughout the Lehigh Valley. Steelworkers report of their neighbors complaining with each new union contract that the cost of dental and health services and other consumables would rise in the Lehigh Valley, and that they as consumers would be harmed by the collectively bargained steel benefits. These schisms, mobilized and exacerbated by reports in a local press heavily influenced by Bethlehem Steel management, of recalcitrant unions, lazy workers, and over-the-top benefits, fomented resentment toward steelworkers. Without strong working-class institutions building broader solidarities, fractures and schisms materialized along alternative identities as consumers, shareholders, or taxpayers, fragmenting solidarities even within the white working class. And exclusions along lines of gender, race, and ethnicity complicate this. New Latino immigrants to the Lehigh Valley, for example, have come to be labeled as the new undeserving poor, with antimonies for illegal immigrants eliding with prior anti-welfare discourses. The attack on organized labor, the movement of manufacturing out of the Lehigh Valley, and the disciplining of post-Fordist workers all function to individualize workers, undermining solidarities, heightening antagonisms, and destroying and weakening those institutions, like unions, that support solidarities and empower workers.

Even within a specific industry, like steel, the decentralization of unions, written into the US legal infrastructure created by the Wagner Act, led to unions that often partnered with companies to encourage worker identification with home plants, to frame plants as competing with each other, even within the same company.[8] This intensified with processes of deindustrialization, as local unions and workers fought to save their home plant, rather than developing broader corporation-wide, industry-wide, or class-wide solidarities. In the Bethlehem plant, even as some plant solidarity increased with deindustrialization in the 1990s (the three local unions at the Bethlehem plant, for example, were merged into one in 1995), the competitive environment of downsizing, manipulated by corporate power, pitted one plant against another. One Bethlehem union official describes, for example, how the Burns Harbor, Indiana, plant manager threatened to "burn our [Bethlehem] plant in his furnaces," to literally turn the scrap from a demolished Bethlehem plant into productive steel in the still-functioning Indiana furnaces. The local Burns Harbor union prioritized the success and survival of the Indiana plant and the jobs of Indiana workers at the expense of Bethlehem workers. These competitions ensured that broader working-class solidarities—between transferees and natives and among steelworkers throughout the company, let alone the country, were undermined.

These schisms undermine possibilities for collective action. It is ironic, for example, that while steelworkers recognize the destructive effect of corporate offensives against unions and the massive shift in wealth from what they define as middle-class Americans to corporate and political elites, these same steelworkers often do not actively support the public-sector workers whose jobs, pensions, health care, and rights to collective bargaining are under attack in Pennsylvania and around the country. But as Dudley shows in her discussion of Kenosha, Wisconsin, many teachers, although unionized, had little sympathy for blue-collar workers' struggles with deindustrialization and disorganization. Instead, they felt that workers' individual "bad" choices to forego an education got them into this situation. A professional middle-class morality that values credentialed knowledge, individualized achievement, and upward social mobility while devaluing blue-collar work and experience, judged steelworkers as over-paid. Steelworkers resented this condemnation, highly critical of a morality that prioritized "book knowledge" over "common sense." Many steelworkers believe teachers overemphasize the value of education and do not sufficiently credit labor unions for the wages, benefits, and status of their careers. Steelworker Henry Hirsch argues that "there should be a labor history course taught in school. The teachers are union. Why don't you educate the kids?"

Even as powerful corporate and political elites turn on teachers, attacking teachers' unions and undermining the promise of social mobility and middle-class stability for educated workers in a "knowledge" economy, these long-standing schisms between blue-collar and white-collar work undermine solidarities. Rather than shared outrage about these same tactics being used to eviscerate the teachers' unions, steelworkers perceive an inevitability to this attack. Mitch Roberts, who has a quite radical perspective on many issues ("I think a little bit of socialism is good for all of us") thinks "that's one of the biggest challenges we have is paying teachers' pensions. Oh, is that going to be a headache. And they're going to go through the same thing that all us Bethlehem Steelworkers did when we lost our benefits and pension plan gone to the government. . . . There's no way around it." Instead of solidarity, Mitch perceives hierarchy and competitiveness. "Right now they're at the top of the food chain. For a long time us Bethlehem Steel workers were at the top of the food chain as far as local jobs and everything." And he accepts the decline of unions in this struggle as a new reality: "Unions are dying anyway. . . . The only strong union anymore is the teacher's union, and even their power is starting to go away." While teachers cite the credentials of their own education and the social value of public education as justification for their pay and benefits, steelworkers have never accepted this as a morally superior route into the middle class. Playing on these tensions, politicians often mobilize blue-collar, property-tax-paying support in attacking teachers unions.

And even as steelworker discourse criticizes the contemporary post-Fordist political economy, it also accepts it as a new reality. Mark Nowak points to the decimation of the defined benefit pension system, for example, as a challenge for the next generation of workers. "They're not going to see a thirty years pension. That's like the steel company. That's a dinosaur." The reality is harsh, it is difficult, but it does not seem transformable—there are no rules, no state support, no political party for demanding a more just, egalitarian society. Tony Russo, a former union official, seems fatalistic about this new reality. Unions, he says, "are becoming a thing of the past . . . blue-collar workers are becoming part of history." And Paul Davis describes a new reality. "This is where we are now. You don't have a choice. You can't change it." When asked what the next generation can do to confront these challenges, Mark replies, "I've got two words: 'God bless' or 'Hit the lottery.'" Divine intervention or luck seem to be the only possibilities for transforming society. But what appears to be a fatalistic acceptance may be "the fatalism of acting within the given 'structural options'—rather than imagining, believing in, and organizing to expand the possible options."[9] The new reality is harsh, especially for working-class Americans, but it does not seem transformable—workers do not see recourse in a legal system biased toward corporate power, there are not strong organizations (neither the Democratic party nor the unions) to articulate and represent their interests, and there is no accessible vision for a more just and egalitarian society, for an alternative reality.

Without strong institutions—unions, political parties, educational institutions, and progressive media—that support political action and elaborate a vision or idea of social and economic alternatives, action becomes difficult. The belief that there is no alternative to the contemporary political, economic, and social reality, a result of the squelching of the very idea of labor's power and the imaginary of the Fordist regime under which this cohort of steelworkers entered the steel mill, has been an enormously important effect of the long assault against labor. When these workers began their steel careers, "the hopes of working people for a better life were fueled by the idea that they themselves could develop power in economic and political relationships."[10] Workers felt powerful as employees in the steel mill—through their internal citizenship, solidarity, and union-recognized rights—and through social citizenship granting them a whole bundle of rights outside the mill. And workers had a vision, a belief in a more egalitarian capitalism. This imaginary had to be beaten down and made to seem illegitimate for corporate power to break the back of labor. An enormous component of class struggle and of the corporate offensive of the post-Fordist period has been "the construction of a vast bureaucratic apparatus for the creation and maintenance of hopelessness."[11]

Through brutal processes of dispossession and disempowerment supported by state institutions and policies, workers were bludgeoned into accepting a new, harsh, and diminished reality.

While steelworkers articulate much common sense that is counter-hegemonic and highly critical of the post-Fordist order, it is difficult for them to articulate this into a consistent Gramscian good sense. A cohesive critique is undermined by anti-immigrant sentiments that characterize illegal immigrants as the undeserving poor and blame them for falling wages and degraded working conditions. It is sidelined by patriotic and nationalist sentiments (although every steelworker I spoke with opposed the US military in Iraq) supporting US industry at the expense of industrial workers in other countries. And it is obfuscated by failing to connect these critiques within a broader analysis of class struggle and how class relations are produced through specific institutions, practices, and discourses that have generated neoliberalism. For example, while steelworkers condemn the greed and speculation that contemporary neoliberalism constructs and supports, and they decry the emphasis on finance and services instead of production, they do not clearly link political support for the financial sector to the undermining of American manufacturing, or the offensive against unions to the wholesale restructuring of the global steel industry. They don't clearly see how the post-Fordist regime of flexible accumulation is not actually an economic project to restore productivity, it is a neoliberal political project to restore class power.[12] In truth, neoliberalism has *not* been successful in restoring US economic growth to high levels, but it *has* very effectively restored capitalist class power.[13] But this political project required that the state support and powerful unions that institutionalized steelworkers' power in the early 1970s and the Fordist discourses that fostered a sense of possibility and an attitude of empowerment be undermined and eradicated.

Steelworkers themselves raise a crucially important question: can neoliberalism be successful without destroying the strength of US society and the productive capacities of the US economy? Can the evisceration of working-class power—the redistribution of working-class assets; re-shaping of working-class life with its accompanying increase in financialization, predatory lending, and working-class debt; and the decline of a manufacturing sector that we have relied on to produce goods and jobs—eradicate a robust working class while maintaining US economic strength? Can these processes that have successfully restored capitalist class power, creating a new "gilded age" of extreme inequality, do so without, as Karl Polanyi threatened, destroying the very health, creativity, and productive fabric of US society and the US economy?[14] As the US struggles with economic and political crises at home and imperial wars abroad, this seems a highly relevant question.

Nonetheless, I do not want to imply a powerless working class—decimated, disillusioned, and disorganized into quiescence. There is a broad and growing working class in the US (and globally) today, although it is a reshaped, re-forming working class, different than the working class of the 1970s, with fewer rights but encompassing more women, workers of color, and immigrants.[15] Scholars discuss the resurgence of unions and other forms of worker activism in the US, as unions are emphasizing "organizing" as opposed to "service" models, encouraging democratic participation in the workplace, supporting direct action, and broadening union politics to include a wider working class as well as community- and family-based concerns.[16] In recent times in the US, 2018 was a record year for strikes and organization. What roles do the industrial working class and former industrial workers have in this activism, and what can a new working class learn from them? Bethlehem steelworkers articulate strong critiques of the contemporary political economy; they continue to value solidarity, seniority, and citizenship; they espouse and practice participatory democracy; and they are highly critical of corporate power.[17] These moralities and practices presage real possibilities for social change and opportunities for building broader alliances with this fraction of the working class—the industrial working class and former industrial workers. But there are also, as always, obstacles and difficulties that must be confronted in doing this.

Given these strong strands of counter-hegemonic culture embedded in steelworkers' understandings of the contemporary political economy, it is surprising that these ideas are not more often mobilized in the Lehigh Valley to support collective political action. Frequently, for steelworkers, political action is expressed through advocacy for official Democratic party candidates. The United Steelworkers, and steelworking families in the Lehigh Valley, have long histories of strong Democratic support. However, while most steelworkers of this age cohort identify as Democrats, they are less likely than their parents to consistently vote Democratic, instead stating that they evaluated each individual candidate rather than voting a party ticket. Many steelworkers I spoke with had voted for Republican candidates in the past, including some for George Herbert Bush, and many voted for Donald Trump in 2016. Steelworkers are often frustrated with the declining influence of unions on the Democratic party. "We're totally against free trade. Everybody who ever had a decent job is against that. But every one of your presidents, whether Democrat or Republican, are for free trade." Steelworkers expressed enormous frustration with George W. Bush and overwhelmingly voted for Obama in 2008 and 2012.[18] But a business unionism that relied on its alliance with the Democratic Party and encouraged rank-and-file members to express themselves politically through voting for Democratic candidates now finds itself hard-pressed to deliver alternative forms of political action as labor issues are often ignored by Democratic politicians. Steelworkers were highly critical of Obama's failure to push through the Employee Free Choice Act after he first gained office, and of his support for the Trans Pacific Partnership free-trade agreement in 2014–15. Steelworkers are frustrated that the party that formerly listened to their concerns seems to now give them lip service, not following up with laws supporting unions, although they are hopeful that Biden will deliver more. These frustrations pushed many steelworkers into either Sanders's or Trump's camp in the 2016 lead-up to the election. Both candidates were seen as anti-free trade and supporting workers. Ex–union officials, those with strong union ties, and urban dwellers were more likely to support Sanders and end up voting for Clinton, even though Hillary Clinton was not especially appealing as steelworkers remembered her husband's legacy as the president who signed NAFTA, a free-trade agreement that encouraged corporations to close unionized factories in the US and relocate them in nonunionized locales in Mexico.

While it is not likely, as Silver argues, that the center of labor movements in the twenty-first century will be in the auto and steel industry, these industrial workers are an important fraction of the US working class and potential allies in class struggle.[19] Silver and others ask what industries might be a locus for class struggle—health care, the tech industry, logistics, personal services, education, health care? And where, geographically, will this class struggle arise? Where are the possibilities for strong alliances between these industry sectors and ex- and current industrial workers? What kinds of organizations can facilitate and mobilize those connections? How can strong institutions and connections be built through community or social movement unionism working to construct alliances between unions and other grassroots struggles for economic and social justice?[20] What are the possibilities for building connections between workers' struggles in the US and abroad? These alliances have the potential to link industrial worker critiques and struggles with the struggles of new fractions of the working class, building on the strong union sentiments, the critique of a contemporary economy that prioritizes services and the financial sector over manufacturing, the frustration over both processes of accumulation by dispossession and expanded reproduction, and the anger of the former industrial working classes over what is defined as an attack on the middle class.

In the Lehigh Valley, steelworkers continue to exercise a profound moral claim over the space of the former mill, especially the most historic part of the mill. These claims are rooted in the lives they spent at the mill, the lives that were lost in steel work, and the intimate knowledge and control they exercised over the space of this city. Workers' rights of citizenship to the space of the mill, built up through struggles to increase worker power, can be mobilized to lend moral authority to social movements. Steelworker members of the Steelworkers' Archives, a nonprofit organization founded by ex-steelworkers to preserve the history of steelworkers, have mobilized around three conflicts over the redevelopment of the site of the mill—tearing down a steel building (the Number 8 hammer shop), renaming a steel-site street to advertise a new entertainment venue, and banning speech and activities related to union organizing on a newly constructed public square beneath the blast furnaces. While not successful with preventing demolition of the building, when ex-steelworkers showed up at a city council meeting, wearing plastic hardhats and summoning their experience as steelworkers, to protest the "branding" of a street, people listened. Steelworkers spoke about the significance of the steel site in the history of the community, the nation, and the lives of Lehigh Valley families; they evoked the "hallowed" status of a site in which many workers' lives were lost, and they argued that the street name should reflect the important history of steel work. Those public statements had weight. Steelworkers were able to mobilize the symbolic power of their difficult and dangerous work producing steel in support of their protest, and the street renaming was overturned. Many steelworkers also turned out for a rally protesting the casino's attempt to control activity on what the city has designated as a public space. Steelworkers argued that here, at the historic Bethlehem mill, on the very ground where their ancestors fought to bring in the union, the banning of union activity was an almost sacrilegious affront, and this ban has never been enforced. When workers' moral authority over the space of the mill, mobilized through their strong sense of a right to that space, is evoked, it remains very powerful in the Valley, although as steelworkers age this is threatened.

But this power of inhabitance, like much of Fordist working-class power, is also contradictory. On the one hand, workers feel ownership over the spaces of the mill, empowered by their inhabitance, generating citizenship rights to the spaces of the mill. But on the other, the "gated city" of the steel mill ensured that political action often played itself out within the confines of the space of that internal, private city. Formal political action was directed at the wage relation—the conditions of work, the wages of work, the benefits of work—as recognized by and codified through the union, that would support a "family wage," defined as a desirable middle-class life outside of work. The acceptance of those parameters of working-class identity, the exclusion of alliances outside the gates of the internal city, and the mystery and "privateness" of steel making stifled broader working-class participation and eroded wider support. It built a working-class identity increasingly confined inside the shrinking internal city of core workers in the mill. This allowed the development of a more exploited—and more black, Latino, and female—working class to develop on the periphery of unionized industrial workers, a new working class that had few connections to the industrial working class.[21] The business unionism of this period also failed to prioritize wider community issues and build broader class alliances, and the steelworkers within the city often did not connect the issues of the steel mill city with wider social issues in the public city of Bethlehem. Even today, a steelworker group such as the Steelworkers' Archives becomes active in political issues involving the site of the steel mill but is rarely as a unified group active in broader urban issues.

New alliances will have work to overcome the obstacles to collective mobilization wrought by processes of deindustrialization and post-Fordist restructuring. These include divisions within the working class; individualized and private strategies for survival; and feelings of powerlessness accompanying the acceptance of a new social and economic reality. Worker organization will need to build on extant worker critiques to further educate workers, build alliances, and construct possibilities for democratic action and a vision of a more egalitarian political economy. They will need to overcome divisions and antimonies within the working class, such as those between new immigrants and native-born workers, white and black workers, public-sector "professional" workers and steelworkers, workers abroad and workers at home, and senior retirees and young workers. Strategies of working class inclusiveness, rather than of exclusion, must be consciously implemented by unions in alliances with other social movements; institutional connections through which inclusive solidarities can be built, and imaginings of alternative cultural and economic realities nurtured. But there are possibilities to do this, as the common sense of the contemporary industrial and ex-industrial working class includes a powerful critique of the contemporary post-Fordist order.

NOTES

INTRODUCTION

1. I interviewed more than 120 steelworkers and family members between 2010 and 2020; I use pseudonyms throughout to protect their identities. Comments from steelworkers that are not otherwise cited come from these interviews.

2. Bruce Ward, interview, 2009, Steelworkers' Archives Oral History Collection, Bethlehem, PA. The Steelworkers' Archives is a not-for-profit, 501c3 organization; their oral history collection contains interviews that volunteers have conducted with steelworkers over the last twenty years. Scholars can access the collection by emailing the Steelworkers' Archives and setting up an appointment. For more information, visit the archive's website, http://www. steelworkersarchives.com.

3. Michael Zweig, *The Working Class Majority: America's Best Kept Secret*, 2nd ed. (Ithaca: Cornell University Press, 2000); Robert Perucci and Earl Wysong, *The New Class Society: Goodbye American Dream?* (Lanham, MD: Rowman and Littlefield, 2001); Michael D. Yates, *Naming the System: Inequality and Work in the Global Economy* (New York: Monthly Review Press, 2003).

4. For more on the resurgence of organized working class actions, see Kim Moody, *An Injury to All: The Decline of American Unionism* (New York: Verso, 1997); Beverly J. Silver, *Forces of Labor: Workers' Movements and Globalization Since 1870* (Cambridge: Cambridge University Press, 2003); Jane Collins, "Theorizing Wisconsin's 2011 Protests: Community-Based Unionism Confronts Accumulation by Dispossession," *American Ethnologist* 39, no. 1 (February 2012): 6–20.; Eric Blanc, *Red State Revolt: The Teacher's Strikes and Working-Class Politics* (New York: Verso 2019); Elizabeth Faue, *Rethinking the American Labor Movement* (New York: Routledge, 2017). For analysis of working class participation in the political system, see Dana Frank, *Buy American: The Untold Story of Economic Nationalism* (Boston, MA: Beacon Press, 1999); Ruy Teixeira and Joel Rogers, *America's Forgotten Majority: Why the White Working Class Still Matters* (New York: Basic Books, 2000); Jacob S. Hacker and Paul Piersen,

American Amnesia: How the War on Government Led Us to Forget What Made America Prosper (New York: Simon and Schuster, 2012); Kim Moody, *Breaking the Impasse: Electoral Politics, Mass Action and the New Socialist Movement in the United States* (Chicago: Haymarket Books, 2022). For studies on new sectors of the working class, see Louise Lamphere, "Introduction," In *Newcomers in the Workplace*, ed. Louise Lamphere, Alex Stepick, and Guillermo Grenier, 1–24 (Philadelphia, PA: Temple University Press, 1994), 1–24.; Patricia Zavella, "The Tables are Turned: Immigration, Poverty, and Social Conflict in California Communities," in *The New Poverty Studies: The Ethnography of Power, Politics, and Impoverished People in the United States*, ed. Judith Goode and Jeff Maskovsky (New York: New York University Press, 2001); Peter Kwong, "Walling Out Immigrants," in *The Insecure American: How We Got Here and What We Should Do About It*, ed. Hugh Gusterson and Catherine Besteman, 255–69 (Berkeley: University of California Press, 2010); Kim Moody, *U.S. Labor in Trouble and Transition: The Failure of Reform from Above, the Promise of Revival from Below* (New York: Verso, 2007).

5. Northampton County was one of the 206 US counties that had a majority vote for Obama for two presidential elections and then flipped to Trump in 2016.

6. See David Roediger, *The Sinking Middle Class: A Political History of Debt, Misery, and the Drift to the Right* (Chicago: Haymarket Books, 2022).

7. Ira Katznelson and Aristide Zolberg, *Working-Class Formation: Nineteenth-Century Patterns in Western Europe and the United States* (Princeton, NJ: Princeton University Press, 1986).

8. J. K. Gibson-Graham and Philip O'Neill, "Exploring a New Class Politics of the Enterprise," in *Re/Presenting Class: Essays in Postmodern Marxism*, ed. J. K. Gibson-Graham, Stephen Resnick, and Richard D. Wolff, 56–80 (Durham, NC: Duke University Press, 2001), 63; see also David Harvey, "The Geography of Class Power," *Socialist Register*, no. 34 (March 18, 1998): 49–74.

9. See E. P. Thompson, *The Making of the English Working Class* (New York: Vintage Books, 1963); Eric Hobsbawm, *Workers: Worlds of Labour* (New York: Pantheon Books, 1984); and Eric R. Wolf, *Europe and the People without History* (Berkeley: University of California Press, 1982); or, more recently, Gabriel Winant, *The Next Shift: The Fall of Industry and the Rise of Health Care in Rust Belt America* (Cambridge, MA: Harvard University Press, 2021).

10. Sharryn Kasmir and August Carbonella, "Dispossession and the Anthropology of Labor," *Critique of Anthropology* 28, no. 1 (2008), 5–25; also see Loic Wacquant, *The Invention of the "Underclass": A Study in the Politics of Knowledge* (Medford, MA: Polity Press, 2022).

11. The Steel is used colloquially in Bethlehem by locals to refer to both the Bethlehem Steel plant and the company more generally.

12. Carol Henn, interview, 2013, Steelworkers' Archives Oral History Collection, Bethlehem, PA.

13. Economists define vertical integration as a form of corporate organization which, in steel, connected raw materials to production to sale centers.

14. Michel Aglietta, *A Theory of Capitalist Regulation: The U.S. Experience* (New York: Verso Books, 1976).

15. College became more accessible thanks largely to democratic administrations, elected in part by union members, who pushed through important legislation to expand access to public higher education.

16. Richard Sennett, *The Culture of the New Capitalism* (New Haven, CT: Yale University Press, 2006).

17. Carol Henn, interview, 2013, Steelworkers' Archives Oral History Collection, Bethlehem, PA.

18. Large companies in the Lehigh Valley included Mack Truck, Western Electric, and Bethlehem Steel.

19. Ted Smith, interview, 2013, Steelworkers' Archives Oral History Collection, Bethlehem, PA.

20. Antonio Gramsci, *Selections from the Prison Notebooks*, ed. Quintin Hoare and Geoffrey Nowell Smith (New York: International Publishers, 1971).

21. For example, older workers were more likely to protect their knowledge and skills from younger workers, be more circumspect in the workplace, and advise workers not to become too confident about the security of their jobs.

22. Jefferson Cowie, *Stayin' Alive: The 1970s and the Last Days of the Working Class* (New York: The New Press, 2010), 45.

23. The coke works' union, for example, was not as powerful as the two other plant locals.

24. The steel companies then passed on their increased costs as higher prices to consumers. Matt Assad, Mike Frassinielli, David Venditta, and Frank Whelan, *Forging America: The Story of Bethlehem Steel* (Allentown, PA: Morning Call, 2010), 113.

25. Jack Metzgar, *Striking Steel: Solidarity Remembered* (Philadelphia: Temple University Press, 2000), 42.

26. Lester Brickly, interview, 2014, Steelworkers' Archives Oral History Collection, Bethlehem, PA.

27. Aaron Brenner, preface to *Rebel Rank and File: Labor Militancy and Revolt from Below in the Long 1970s*, ed. Aaron Brenner, Robert Brenner, and Cal Winslow,

xi–xix (New York: Verso, 2010), xiii; Cowie *Stayin' Alive*; Judith Stein, *Pivotal Decade: How the United States Traded Factories for Finance in the Seventies* (New Haven, CT: Yale University Press, 2010).

28. Brenner, preface to *Rebel Rank and File*.

29. Mike Davis, *Prisoners of the American Dream: Politics and Economy in the History of the U.S. Working Class* (London: Verso, 1986), 104; Cal Winslow, "Overview: The Rebellion from Below, 1965–81," in *Rebel Rank and File: Labor Militancy and Revolt from Below in the Long 1970s*, ed. Aaron Brenner, Robert Brenner, and Cal Winslow, 1–35 (New York: Verso, 2010), 12; Nelson Lichtenstein, *State of the Union: A Century of American Labor* (Princeton, NJ: Princeton University Press, 2003), 99.

30. Gregory Pappas, *Magic City* (Ithaca, NY: Cornell University Press, 1989); June Nash, *From Tank Town to High Tech* (Albany, NY: SUNY Press, 1989).

31. Jefferson Cowie, *Capital Moves: RCA's Seventy Year Quest for Cheap Labor* (New York: The New Press, 1999), 6.

32. David Harvey, *The New Imperialism* (Oxford: Oxford University Press, 2003), 144.

33. This lack of success was evidenced by the 2008 Great Recession.

34. David Harvey, *A Brief History of Neoliberalism* (Oxford: Oxford University Press, 2007), 19.

35. Ching Kwan Lee, *Against the Law: Labor Protests in China's Rustbelt and Sunbelt* (Berkeley: University of California Press, 2007); Jane L. Collins, *Threads: Gender, Labor, and Power in the Global Apparel Industry* (Chicago: University of Chicago Press, 2003); Ruth Milkman, *LA Story: Immigrant Workers and the Future of the American Labor Movement* (New York: Russell Sage Foundation, 2006); Pun Ngai, *Made in China: Women Factory Workers in a Global Workplace* (Durham, NC: Duke University Press, 2003); Leslie Salzinger, *Genders in Production: Making Workers in Mexico's Global Factories* (Berkeley: University of California Press, 2003).

36. Sharryn Kasmir, "The Saturn Automobile Plant and the Long Dispossession of US Autoworkers," in *Blood and Fire: Toward a Global Anthropology of Labor*, ed. Sharryn Kasmir and August Carbonella, 203–49 (New York: Berghahn Books, 2014).

37. Cowie, *Capital Moves*, 6.

38. Kathryn Marie Dudley, *The End of the Line: Lost Jobs, New Lives in Postindustrial America* (Chicago: University of Chicago Press, 1994); Pappas, *Magic City*.

39. Christine Walley, *Exit Zero: Family and Class in Postindustrial Chicago* (Chicago: University of Chicago Press, 2013).

40. Harry Braverman, *Labor and Monopoly Capitalism* (New York: Monthly Review Press, 1974); Michael Burawoy, *Manufacturing Consent: Changes in the Labor Process under Monopoly Capitalism* (Chicago: University of Chicago Press, 1979).

CHAPTER 1

1. Roger D. Simon, "Bethlehem Social Elites, 'The Steel,' and the Saucon Valley Country Club," in *Backcountry Crucibles: The Lehigh Valley from Settlement to Steel*, ed. Jean R. Soderlund and Catherine S. Parzynski, 315–28 (Bethlehem, PA: Lehigh University Press, 2008); John Strohmeyer, *Crisis in Bethlehem: Big Steel's Struggle to Survive* (Pittsburgh, PA: University of Pittsburgh Press, 1994).

2. Woodward Christian Carson, *South Bethlehem, PA: Industrialization, Immigration and the Development of a Religious Landscape* (Masters thesis, University of Pennsylvania, 2000).

3. Carson, *South Bethlehem*, 36; Chloe Taft, *From Steel to Slots: Casino Capitalism in the Postindustrial City* (Cambridge, MA: Harvard University Press, 2016), 39.

4. Michael D. Kennedy, "Rewriting the Death and Afterlife of a Corporation: Bethlehem Steel," *Biography* 37, no. 1 (2014): 246–78.

5. Jose Achando, interview, 2009, Steelworkers' Archives Oral History Collection, Bethlehem, PA.

6. Carol Henn, interview, 2013, Steelworkers' Archives Oral History Collection, Bethlehem, PA.

7. Walter Moore, interview, 2013, Steelworkers' Archives Oral History Collection, Bethlehem, PA.

8. Lance Metz, "A Short History of the Bethlehem Steel Corporation," in *Bethlehem Steel*, ed. Andrew Garn, 3–44 (New York: Princeton Architectural Press, 1999).

9. Kenneth Warren, *Bethlehem Steel: Builder and Arsenal of America* (Pittsburgh, PA: University of Pittsburgh Press, 2008).

10. Warren, *Bethlehem Steel*, 142.

11. Strohmeyer, *Crisis in Bethlehem*, 56.

12. Clyde Prestovitz and Kate Heidinger, "The Evolution of U.S. Trade Policy," in *Manufacturing a Better Future for America*, ed. Richard McCormack, 71–104 (Washington, DC: Alliance for American Manufacturing, 2009), 84.

13. Mark Reutter, *Making Steel: Sparrows Point and the Rise and Ruin of American Industrial Might* (Urbana: University of Illinois Press, 1988).

14. John Hinshaw, *Steel and Steelworkers: Race and Class Struggle in Twentieth Century Pittsburgh* (Albany: State University of New York Press, 2002).

15. Frank A. Behum, Sr., Steelworker Interviews. Unpublished manuscript, Bethlehem, PA, n.d.

16. Stein, *Pivotal Decade*, 155.

17. Hinshaw, *Steel and Steelworkers*.

18. Behum, Steelworker Interviews.

19. Robert P. Rogers, *An Economic History of the American Steel Industry* (New York: Routledge, 2009), 125.

20. Hinshaw, *Steel and Steelworkers*. Economists define structural unemployment as long-lasting, resulting from a mismatch between workers' skills and job requirements, and often exacerbated by technological changes.

21. An example of benefits related to layoffs was the increase in supplemental pay accompanying unemployment benefits.

22. Moody, *U.S. Labor in Trouble*.

23. Stein, *Pivotal Decade*.

24. Lance Metz, "A Short History of the Bethlehem Steel Corporation," in *Bethlehem Steel*, ed. Andrew Garn, 3–44 (New York: Princeton Architectural Press, 1999).

25. Ann Bartholomew and Donald Stuart Young, *Bethlehem Steel in Bethlehem, Pennsylvania: A Photographic History* (Easton, PA: Canal History and Technology Press 2010).

26. Bartholomew and Young, *Bethlehem Steel*.

27. Parents worked in industries such as cement, zinc processing, fabricating, and machine shops.

28. Lisa Szarko, interview, 2010, Steelworkers' Archives Oral History Collection, Bethlehem, PA.

29. Marlene Burkey, interview, 2007, Steelworkers' Archives Oral History Collection, Bethlehem, PA.

30. Assad et al., *Forging America*, 126; Strohmeyer, *Crisis in Bethlehem*, 76.

31. Assad et al., *Forging America*, 124.

32. Walter Moore, interview, 2013, Steelworkers' Archives Oral History Collection, Bethlehem, PA.

33. Assad et al., *Forging America*.

34. Assad et al., *Forging America*, 128.

35. Christopher L. G. Hall, *Steel Phoenix: The Fall and Rise of the U.S. Steel Industry* (New York: Palgrave McMillan, 1997); Judith Stein, *Running Steel, Running America: Race, Economic Policy and the Decline of Liberalism* (Chapel Hill: University of North Carolina Press, 1998).

36. Assad et al., *Forging America*, 127.

37. David Harvey, *A Brief History of Neoliberalism* (Oxford: Oxford University Press, 2007).

38. John Hoerr, *And the Wolf Finally Came* (Pittsburgh, PA: University of Pittsburgh Press, 1988), 417.

39. Lisa Szarko, interview, 2010, Steelworkers' Archives Oral History Collection, Bethlehem, PA.

40. Jill Ruch, interview, 2014, Steelworkers' Archives Oral History Collection, Bethlehem, PA.

41. Walley, *Exit Zero*, 63.

42. Davis, *Prisoners of the American Dream*.

43. See Ronald G. Garay, *U.S. Steel and Gary, West Virginia: Corporate Paternalism in Appalachia* (Knoxville, TN: University of Tennessee Press, 2011), 154. For example, US Steel supported allowing cheap imports of semi-finished steel from NIC countries, thus enabling the repayment of NIC loans to large US-based financial institutions.

44. Garay, *U.S. Steel and Gary*, 154.

45. Garay, *U.S. Steel and Gary*, 198.

46. Garay, *U.S. Steel and Gary*, 198.

47. Hall, *Steel Phoenix*.

48. Daniel Madar, *Big Steel: Technology, Trade, and Survival in a Global Market* (Seattle: University of Washington Press, 2009), 55.

49. Warren, *Bethlehem Steel*, 193.

50. S. Paul O'Hara, "Envisioning the Steel City: The Legend and Legacy of Gary, Indiana," in *Beyond the Ruins: The Meanings of Deindustrialization*, ed. Jefferson Cowie and Joseph Heathcott, 219–36 (Ithaca, NY: Cornell University Press, 2003), 201–18.

51. Assad et al., *Forging America*.

52. Hall, *Steel Phoenix*, 304.

53. Strohmeyer, *Crisis in Bethlehem*.

54. Kenneth Warren, *Bethlehem Steel: Builder and Arsenal of America* (Pittsburgh, PA: University of Pittsburgh Press, 2008), 229.

55. The hot end refers to the iron- and steel-making departments, including the blast furnaces, basic oxygen furnace, and electric furnaces.

56. Strohmeyer, *Crisis in Bethlehem*.

57. Perhaps, for example, communities without ties to steel CEOs were more likely to have mills closed.

58. Louis Uchitelle, *The Disposable American: Layoffs and Their Consequences* (New York: Vintage Books, 2007), 138.

59. Hinshaw, *Steel and Steelworkers*, 239.

60. Stein, *Pivotal Decade*; Hinshaw, *Steel and Steelworkers*.

61. Stein, *Pivotal Decade*, 246.

62. Hoerr, *And the Wolf*, 417.

63. Warren, *Bethlehem Steel*; Assad et al., *Forging America*.

64. Frank A. Behum Sr., *30 Years under the Beam: Bethlehem Steel Exposed* (Savannah, GA: Continental Shelf Publishing, 2010), 139.

65. Assad et al., *Forging America*, 58.
66. Young and Bartholomew, *Bethlehem Steel*; Assad et al., *Forging America*.
67. Strohmeyer, *Crisis in Bethlehem*.
68. Assad et al., *Forging America*, 58.
69. Lorenzo Quaryle, interview, 2012, Steelworkers' Archives Oral History Collection, Bethlehem, PA.
70. Behum, *30 Years*, 443.
71. Behum, *30 Years*, 370.
72. Hoerr, *And the Wolf*.
73. Behum, Steelworker Interviews.
74. Behum, *30 Years*, 17.
75. Katherine Newman, *Falling from Grace: The Experience of Downward Mobility in the American Middle Class* (New York: Free Press, 1988).
76. Hinshaw, *Steel and Steelworkers*.
77. Dudley, *The End of the Line*.
78. The "13 weeks vacation" negotiated for senior workers every five years in the 1963 contract is a commonly cited "cause" for plant closure.
79. Metzgar, *Striking Steel*, 183.
80. David Harvey and Eric Swyngedouw, "Industrial Restructuring: Community Disempowerment and Grass-Roots Resistance," in *The Factory and the City: The Story of the Cowley Automobile Workers in Oxford*, ed. Teresa Hayter and David Harvey, 11–25 (London: Mansell Press, 1993), 20.
81. Metzgar, *Striking Steel*, 124.
82. Richard Moytzen, interview, 2007, Steelworkers' Archives Oral History Collection, Bethlehem, PA.
83. Paul Wirth, "Bethlehem Steel Extends USW's Deadline on Job Cuts," *Morning Call* (Lehigh Valley, PA), March 23, 1986.
84. Pensions varied relative to workers' earnings at the Steel.
85. The remaining labor force had fewer workers, doing the same work at sped-up rates.
86. Anthony Winson and Belinda Leach, *Contingent Work, Disrupted Lives: Labour and Community in the New Rural Economy* (Toronto: University of Toronto Press, 2002).
87. I frequently heard this sentiment of an essentialized, racialized work force expressed in conversations, although I also frequently heard this criticized as a racist assumption.
88. Hoerr, *And the Wolf*, 444.
89. Mike Parker and Jane Slaughter, *Working Smart: A Union Guide to Participation Programs and Reengineering* (Detroit, MI: Labor Notes, 1994).

90. Ellen Schultz, "Banks Owe Billions to Executives," *Wall Street Journal*, October 31, 2008.
91. Paul Wirth, "Partnership Working at Steel," *Morning Call*, May 13, 1987.
92. Ruth Milkman, *Farewell to the Factory: Autoworkers in the Late Twentieth Century* (Berkeley: University of California Press, 1997.
93. Parker and Slaughter, *Working Smart*; Moody, *U.S. Labor in Trouble*.
94. Behum, *30 Years*, 128.
95. Milkman, *Farewell to the Factory*, 128.
96. Frank Walton, interview, 2006, Steelworkers' Archives Oral History Collection, Bethlehem, PA.
97. Dave Hrichak interview, 2007, Steelworkers' Archives Oral History Collection, Bethlehem, PA.
98. Assad et al.; *Forging America*.
99. "Steelworkers Know Good Steel Their Hedge against Competitor," *Morning Call*, June 25, 1995.
100. The areas of the plant under consideration for buyout were the combination mills and the coke works.
101. Ed O'Brien interview, 2009, Steelworkers' Archives Oral History Collection, Bethlehem, PA.
102. Metzgar, *Striking Steel*.
103. Beth Forge is now Lehigh Heavy Forge; Centec was a Bethlehem-French joint venture.
104. Lorenzo Quaryle, interview, 2012, Steelworkers' Archives Oral History Collection, Bethlehem, PA.
105. Hayter and Harvey, *The Factory and the City*.
106. Strohmeyer, *Crisis in Bethlehem*.

CHAPTER 2

1. David Harvey, *The Limits of Capital* (Oxford: Basil Blackwell, 1982), 102.
2. Jeff Hoffert, interview, 2010, Steelworkers' Archives Oral History Collection, Bethlehem, PA.
3. Pingyar quoted in Behum, *30 Years*, 236.
4. Hoerr, *And the Wolf*; Kenneth Warren, *Big Steel: The First Century of the United States Steel Corporation 1901–2001* (Pittsburgh, PA: University of Pittsburgh Press, 2001).
5. Hinshaw, *Steel and Steelworkers*.
6. Metzgar, *Striking Steel*.
7. Robert Bruno, *Steelworker Alley: How Class Works in Youngstown* (Ithaca, NY: ILR Press, 1999).

8. Jobs with direct incentive pay would include jobs in the blast furnaces, the mills, the basic oxygen furnace, and shipping the steel. Incentive pay was itself divided into direct and indirect, which included "primary" and "secondary" indirect based on the job.

9. Maintenance skills included, for example, electrical skills, carpentry, pipefitting, bricklaying.

10. Davis, *Prisoners of the American Dream*; Burawoy, *Manufacturing Consent*; Braverman, *Labor and Monopoly Capitalism*.

11. Burawoy, *Manufacturing Consent*; Richard Edwards, *Contested Terrain: The Transformation of the Workplace in the Twentieth Century* (New York: Basic Books,1979); Andy Friedman, "Responsible Autonomy Versus Direct Control over the Labour Process," *Capital and Class* 1, no. 1 (1977): 43–57.

12. Braverman, *Labor and Monopoly Capitalism*, 57.

13. Harvey, *The Limits of Capital*, 110.

14. Thomas J. Misa, *A Nation of Steel: The Making of Modern America 1865–1925* (Baltimore, MD: Johns Hopkins University Press. 1995).

15. Newman, *Falling From Grace*.

16. Richard Sennett and Jonathan Cobb, *The Hidden Injuries of Class*. (New York: W.W. Norton, 1972); Stanley Aronowitz, *False Promises: The Shaping of American Working Class Consciousness* (New York: McGraw Hill, 1973).

17. See Burawoy, *Manufacturing Consent*; critics also include Friedman, *Responsible Autonomy*; Richard Edwards, *Contested Terrain: The Transformation of the Workplace in the Twentieth Century* (New York: Basic Books, 1979).

18. Burawoy defines this regime of scientific management as more of an ideology than a practice.

19. The workshop games involve competitive speed up with other work groups.

20. Bourdieu, *Distinction*.

21. David Halle, *America's Working Man: Work, Home, and Politics Among Blue-Collar Property Owners* (Chicago: University of Chicago Press, 1984).

22. Halle, *America's Working Man*; Burawoy, *Manufacturing Consent*.

23. Carpenters or electricians, for example, could work in the construction industry.

24. See also Karen Olson, *Wives of Steel: Voices of Women from the Sparrows Point Steelmaking Communities* (University Park: Pennsylvania State University Press, 2005).

25. Ching Kwan Lee, *Gender and the South China Miracle: Two Worlds of Factory Women* (Berkeley: University of California Press, 1998); Tamara K. Hareven, *Family Time and Industrial Time: The Relationship between the Family and Work*

in a New England Industrial Community (London: Cambridge University Press, 1982); Carla Freeman, *High Tech and High Heels in the Global Economy: Women, Work, and Pink-Collar Identities in the Caribbean* (Durham, NC: Duke University Press, 2000).

26. This parental structure was often in a gendered context, where the father is seen as providing stricter discipline.
27. Declining a promotion to foreman could be related to family obligations, a second job, or leisure time activities. Often, as one steelworker said, "they'd actually be taking a cut in pay with incentives and things like that."
28. Friedman, *Responsible Autonomy*; Edwards, *Contested Terrain*.
29. Braverman, *Labor and Monopoly Capitalism*; Burawoy, *Manufacturing Consent*; Edwards, *Contested Terrain*; Friedman, *Responsible Autonomy*.
30. Lee, *Gender and the South China Miracle*, 19.
31. Ruth Milkman, *Gender at Work: The Dynamics of Job Segregation by Sex during World War II* (Urbana: University of Illinois Press, 1987).
32. Jane Collins, *Threads: Gender, Labor, and Power in the Global Apparel Industry* (Chicago: University of Chicago Press, 2003); Lee, *Gender and the South China Miracle*; Saskia Sassen, *Globalization and Its Discontents: Essays on the New Mobility of People and Money* (New York: The New Press, 1999).
33. David Harvey, *The Enigma of Capital and the Crises of Capitalism* (London: Profile Books, 2010), 226.
34. Kim Moody, *Workers in a Lean World: Unions in the International Economy* (London: Verso,1997).
35. Ching Kwan Lee, *Against the Law: Labor Protests in China's Rustbelt and Sunbelt* (Berkeley: University of California Press, 2007), 22.
36. Lee, *Gender and the South China Miracle*, 27.
37. Stein, *Running Steel*, 44.
38. This essentially restricted Puerto Rican workers, for example, to the coke works.
39. Dennis C. Dickerson, *Out of the Crucible: Black Steelworkers in Western Pennsylvania, 1875–1980* (Albany: State University of New York Press, 1986).
40. Braverman, *Labor and Monopoly Capitalism*; Burawoy, *Manufacturing Consent*; Edwards, *Contested Terrain*.
41. Newman, *Falling from Grace*, 185.
42. Mike Rose, *The Mind at Work* (New York: Penguin Books 2004).
43. Dudley, *The End of the Line*, 45.
44. See Elijah Anderson, *Code of the Street: Decency, Violence, and the Moral Life of the Inner City* (New York: W.W. Norton, 2000); Willis, *Learning to Labor*; Lois

Weis, *Class Reunion: The Remaking of the American White Working Class* (New York: Routledge, 2004); Ulf Hannerz, *Soulside: Inquiries into Ghetto Culture and Community* (New York: Columbia University Press, 1969); and Freeman, *High Tech and High Heels.*

45. Sherri Ortner, "Reading America: Preliminary Notes on Class and Culture," in *Recapturing Anthropology: Working in the Present*, ed. Richard G. Fox, 163–90 (Santa Fe, NM: School of American Research Press, 1991); Halle, *America's Working Man.*

46. Ortner, *Reading America*, 176; Freeman, *High Tech and High Heels*, 110.

47. Willis, *Learning to Labor.*

48. Richard Sennett, *The Corrosion of Character* (New York: W.W. Norton, 1998); Stanley Aronowitz, *False Promises: The Shaping of American Working Class Consciousness* (New York: McGraw Hill, 1973); Halle, *America's Working Man.*

49. Jack Deutsch, interview, 2009, Steelworkers' Archives Oral History Collection, Bethlehem, PA.

50. Halle, *America's Working Man.*

51. Jack Deutsch, interview, 2009, Steelworkers' Archives Oral History Collection, Bethlehem, PA.

52. Milkman, *Farewell to the Factory*, 118.

53. See William Kornblum, *Blue Collar Community* (Chicago: University of Chicago Press, 1974). This specific, local knowledge was important in the Bethlehem steel mill, as it had some extremely old machinery still functioning in it.

54. Halle, *America's Working Man*; Dudley, *The End of the Line.*

55. David Harvey, *The Condition of Postmodernity* (Cambridge, MA: Blackwell Publishers, 1990), 134.

56. Kornblum, *Blue Collar Community*, 60.

57. Mario Tronti, *Workers and Capital* (London: Verso, 2019), 244; Antonio Negri, *Insurgencies: Constituent Power and the Modern State* (Minneapolis: University of Minnesota Press, 1999).

58. Tronti, "Strategy of the Refusal," 237.

59. Concessions were granted through collectively bargained contracts and informal shop floor relations.

60. Richard Sennett, *The Culture of the New Capitalism* (New Haven, CT: Yale University Press, 2006), 104.

61. Richard Sennett, *The Craftsman* (New Haven, CT: Yale University Press, 2008).

62. The Grey beam was an innovative, continuously rolled wide-flange beam that was stronger than other beams. They became central in building skyscrapers.

63. See also Gay Talese, *The Bridge: The Building of the Verrazano-Narrows Bridge* (New York: Walker Books, 2003).

64. Burawoy, *Manufacturing Consent*.
65. Moody, *Workers in a Lean World*; Davis, *Prisoners of the American Dream*.

CHAPTER 3

1. Assad et al., *Forging America*, 12.
2. See William Cronon, *Nature's Metropolis: Chicago and the Great West* (New York: WW Norton, 1991).
3. Behum, *30 Years*.
4. Bob Shoemaker, interview, 2006, Steelworkers' Archives Oral History Collection, Bethlehem, PA.
5. "Interview with Bruce Ward: Former Steelworker with Bethlehem Steel," 2006, Beyond Steel: An Archive of Lehigh Valley Industry and Culture, Lehigh University, Bethlehem, PA, https://wordpress.lehigh.edu/beyondsteel.
6. Aihwa Ong, *Neoliberalism as Exception: Mutations in Citizenship and Sovereignty* (Durham, NC: Duke University Press, 2006), 199.
7. See Thompson, *The Making of the English Working Class*; James C. Scott, *The Moral Economy of the Peasant: Rebellion and Subsistence in Southeast Asia* (New Haven, CT: Yale University Press, 1977).
8. Alice Kessler-Harris, *In Pursuit of Equity: Women, Men and the Quest for Economic Citizenship in 20th Century America* (Oxford: Oxford University Press, 2001), 12.
9. Judith Shklar, *American Citizenship: The Quest for Inclusion* (Boston, MA: Harvard University Press, 1998), 67.
10. Will Weisner, interview, 2005, Steelworkers' Archives Oral History Collection, Bethlehem, PA.
11. Cynthia Cockburn, *Brothers: Male Dominance and Technological Change* (London: Pluto Press,1983), 122.
12. Dimitra Doukas, *Worked Over: The Corporate Sabotage of an American Community* (Ithaca, NY: Cornell University Press, 2003), 111.
13. Behum, *30 Years*, 486.
14. Eve Weinbaum, *To Move a Mountain: Fighting the Global Economy in Appalachia* (New York: The New Press, 2004); Staughton Lynd, "The Genesis of the Idea of a Community Right to Industrial Property in Youngstown and Pittsburgh: 1977–87," *Journal of American History* 74, no. 3 (1987): 926–58; Dale Hathaway, *Can Workers Have a Voice: The Politics of Deindustrialization in Pittsburgh* (University Park: Pennsylvania State University Press, 1993); Thomas Geoghegan, *Which Side are You On?: Trying to Be for Labor When It's Flat on Its Back* (New York: The New Press, 1991); Tom Juravich, *At the Altar of the Bottom Line: The Degradation of Work in the 21st Century* (Boston: University of Massachusetts Press, 2009).

15. Michael Luo and Karen Ann Cullotta, "Even Workers Surprised by Success of Factory Sit-In." *New York Times*, December 12, 2008.
16. Lynd, "The Genesis of the Idea."
17. Bruno, *Steelworker Alley*, 67.
18. Bruno, *Steelworker Alley*, 67.
19. James B. Lieber, *Friendly Takeover: How an Employee Buyout Saved a Steeltown* (New York: Penguin Books, 1995), 45.
20. Dudley, *The End of the Line*.
21. Gramsci, *Selections from the Prison Notebooks*.
22. Carl Boggs, *The Two Revolutions: Antonio Gramsci and the Dilemmas of Western Marxism* (Boston, MA: South End Press,1984), 79.
23. Walter L. Adamson, *Hegemony and Revolution: A Study of Antonio Gramsci's Political and Cultural Theory* (Berkeley: University of California Press, 1980), 75.
24. Harry Cleaver, *Reading Capital Politically* (Austin: University of Texas Press, 1979); Tronti, "The Strategy of the Refusal."
25. Michael D. Yates, *Why Unions Matter*, 2nd ed. (New York: Monthly Review Press, 2009).
26. Burawoy, *Manufacturing Consent*.
27. Nelson Lichtenstein, *State of the Union: A Century of American Labor* (Princeton, NJ: Princeton University Press, 2003); Moody. *U.S. Labor in Trouble*.
28. Davis, *Prisoners of the American Dream*; Moody, *U.S. Labor in Trouble*; Lichtenstein, *State of the Union*.
29. See Cleaver, *Reading Capital*; Kessler-Harris, *In Pursuit of Equity*.
30. For example, United Steelworker members do not vote to ratify their contracts, they simply vote in their union officers. E. Paul Durrenberger, "The Anthropology of Organized Labor in the United States," *Annual Review of Anthropology* 36, no. 21 (October 2007): 73–88.
31. Stanley Aronowitz, *How Class Works: Power and Social Movement* (New Haven, CT: Yale University Press, 2003).
32. Stein, *Pivotal Decade*, 25.
33. Moody, *U.S. Labor in Trouble*; Lichtenstein, *State of the Union*.
34. Burawoy, *Manufacturing Consent*.
35. Metzgar, *Striking Steel*, 37.
36. Kessler-Harris, *In Pursuit of Equity*.
37. The contract protected these through seniority rules, Article 2B (past practices), Article 14 (safety), and the grievance process.
38. Frank Walton, interview, 2006, Steelworkers' Archives Oral History Collection, Bethlehem, PA.

39. Tom Petro, interview, 2006, Steelworkers' Archives Oral History Collection, Bethlehem, PA.

40. Metzgar, *Striking Steel*, 49.

41. Davis, *Prisoners of the American Dream.*

42. Strohmeyer, *Crisis in Bethlehem*, 23.

43. Strohmeyer, *Crisis in Bethlehem*, 24.

44. Bruce Nelson, *Divided We Stand: American Workers and the Struggle for Black Equality* (Princeton, NJ: Princeton University Press, 2001), 209.

45. Strohmeyer, *Crisis in Bethlehem*, 24.

46. Metzgar, *Striking Steel*, 33–34.

47. See also Cockburn, *Brothers.*

48. Sennett, *Culture of the New Capitalism.*

49. Behum, *30 Years*, 305.

50. John Hinshaw, *Steel and Steelworkers: Race and Class Struggle in Twentieth-Century Pittsburgh* (Albany: State University of New York Press, 2002).

51. Bea Strahler, interview, 2015, Steelworkers' Archives Oral History Collection, Bethlehem, PA.

52. Behum, *30 Years*, 474–75.

53. Metzgar, *Striking Steel*, 114.

54. Behum, *30 Years*, 69.

55. Kornblum, *Blue Collar Community*, 45. In steel mills a *turn* is a shift. Many steelworkers worked swing shifts that rotated them through day, middle, and night shifts.

56. Kornblum, *Blue Collar Community.*

57. Behum, *30 Years*, 270.

58. Chris Szarko, interview, 2010, Steelworkers' Archives Oral History Collection, Bethlehem, PA.

59. Metzgar, *Striking Steel*, 114.

60. Metzgar, *Striking Steel*, 114.

61. See Kessler-Harris, *In Pursuit of Equity*; and Jane Collins and Victoria Mayer, *Both Hands Tied: Welfare Reform and the Race to the Bottom of the Low-Wage Labor Market* (Chicago: University of Chicago Press 2010).

62. Dudley, *The End of the Line*, 115.

63. Dudley, *The End of the Line*, 116.

64. Metzgar, *Striking Steel*, 204.

65. Kornblum, *Blue Collar Community*, 53.

66. Metzgar, *Striking Steel*, 204.

67. Dudley, *The End of the Line*, 122.

68. Kornblum, *Blue Collar Community*.

69. Pierre Bourdieu, *Distinction: A Social Critique of the Judgment of Taste* (Cambridge, MA: Harvard University Press, 1984), 384.

70. Jack Deutsch, interview, 2009, Steelworkers' Archives Oral History Collection, Bethlehem, PA.

71. Jack Deutsch, interview, 2009, Steelworkers' Archives Oral History Collection, Bethlehem, PA

72. Vicki Smith, "Sprinkler Fitter," in *Hard Hatted Women: Life on the Job*, ed. Molly Martin, 143–49 (Berkeley, CA: Seal Press, 1997), 145.

73. Larry James Neff, *Rigger: From High School to High Steel* (Allentown, PA: Blue Heron Books Works, 2014).

74. See John Ogbu, ed., *Minority Status, Oppositional Culture, and Schooling* (New York: Routledge, 2008) on oppositional identity.

75. Willis, *Learning to Labor*, 188.

76. See Paul Willis, "Shop Floor Culture, Masculinity and the Wage Form," in *Feminism and Masculinities*, ed. Peter F. Murphy, 108–20 (Oxford: Oxford University Press, 2004).

CHAPTER 4

1. David Roediger, *Working toward Whiteness: How American's Immigrants Became White* (New York: Basic Books, 2005), 213.

2. June Nash, *From Tank Town to High Tech* (Albany, NY: SUNY Press, 1989), 19.

3. Ira Katznelson and Aristide Zolberg, *Working-Class Formation: Nineteenth-Century Patterns in Western Europe and the United States* (Princeton, NJ: Princeton University Press, 1986), 24.

4. Stein, *Running Steel*, 151.

5. Ruth Needleman, *Black Freedom Fighters in Steel: The Struggle for Democratic Unionism* (Ithaca, NY: ILR Press, 2003), 8.

6. Eugenio "Gene" Rivera, "La Colonia de Lorain, Ohio," in *The Puerto Rican Diaspora*, ed. Carmen Teresa Whalen and Victor Vazquez-Hernandez, 151–73 (Philadelphia, PA: Temple University Press, 2005), 159.

7. Deborah Rudacille, *Roots of Steel: Boom and Bust in an American Mill Town* (New York: Pantheon Books, 2010).

8. Dickerson, *Out of the Crucible*; Paul Taylor, *Mexican Labor in the United States: Bethlehem, Pennsylvania*, vol. 2 (1932; repr., New York: Arno Press, 1970).

9. Roediger, *Working toward Whiteness*.

10. Dickerson, *Out of the Crucible*, 153.

11. Nelson, *Divided We Stand*.

12. Nelson, *Divided We Stand*, 210.

13. Wandalyn Jeanette Enix, "Thirty Years Ago Today: R. Wakefield Roberts and His Community Civic League Respond to History," *Pennsylvania Heritage*, Spring 1994, https://paheritage.wpengine.com/author/wandalyn-enix.

14. Reutter, *Making Steel*; Assad et al., *Forging America*.

15. *The Eighteenth Decennial Census of the United States: Census of Population: 1960*, vol. I, Characteristics of the Population, Part 40: Pennsylvania, United States Census Bureau, https://www2.census.gov/prod2/decennial/documents/17216604v1p40ch02.pdf.

16. Nelson, *Divided We Stand*, 196.

17. Quoted in Nelson, *Divided We Stand*, 196.

18. Nelson, *Divided We Stand*, 196.

19. Strohmeyer, *Crisis in Bethlehem*, 92.

20. Strohmeyer, *Crisis in Bethlehem*, 90.

21. Joseph Loftus, "Bethlehem Puzzled by Dismissal of Steel Aide Over Racial Stand," *New York Times*, March 22, 1964.

22. Taylor, *Mexican Labor*, 13.

23. Taylor, *Mexican Labor*, 210.

24. Stanley A. West, *The Mexican Aztec Society: A Mexican-American Voluntary Association in Diachronic Perspective* (New York: Arno Press, 1976); Assad et al., *Forging America*.

25. Rudacille, *Roots of Steel*, 115.

26. Ronald Takaki, *A Different Mirror: A History of Multicultural America* (Boston, MA: Back Bay Books, 2008).

27. Assad et al., *Forging America*, 84.

28. Dickerson, *Out of the Crucible*.

29. Lourdes Diaz-Soto, *Language, Culture, and Power: Bilingual Families and the Struggle for Quality Education* (Albany, NY: SUNY Press, 1997), 20.

30. Rivera, "La Colonia de Lorain."

31. Peter Antonsen, *A History of the Puerto Rican Community in Bethlehem, PA: 1944–1993* (Bethlehem, PA: Council of Spanish Speaking Organizations, 1997), 32.

32. Edwin Maldonado, "Contract Labor and the Origins of Puerto Rican Communities in the U.S.," *International Migration Review* 13, no. 1 (1979): 103–21.

33. Mary Margaret Fonow, *Union Women: Forging Feminism in the United Steelworkers of America* (Minneapolis: University of Minnesota Press, 2003), 57.

34. Kenneth Durr, *Behind the Backlash: White Working-Class Politics in Baltimore, 1940–1980* (Chapel Hill: University of North Carolina Press, 2003), 184.

35. Walter Moore, interview, 2013, Steelworkers' Archives Oral History Collection, Bethlehem, PA.

36. Stein, *Running Steel*.

37. Stein, *Running Steel*, 174.
38. Strohmeyer, *A Crisis in Bethlehem*, 97.
39. Needleman, *Black Freedom Fighters*.
40. See Roediger, *Working for Whiteness*; and Nelson, *Divided We Stand*.
41. See also Durr, *Behind the Backlash*.
42. Behum, *30 Years*, 195.
43. Ed O'Brien, interview, 2009, Steelworkers' Archives Oral History Collection, Bethlehem, PA.
44. See also Thomas Dublin and Walter Licht, *The Face of Decline: The Pennsylvania Anthracite Region in the Twentieth Century* (Ithaca, NY: Cornell University Press, 2005).
45. O'Brien, interview, 2009, Steelworkers' Archives Oral History Collection, Bethlehem, PA.
46. David Kuchta, *Memoirs of a Steelworker* (Easton, PA: Canal History and Technology Press, 1995), 11.
47. Kutcha, *Memoirs of a Steelworker*, 35; see also Dublin and Licht, *The Face of Decline*.
48. Fonow, *Union Women*, 57.
49. Fonow, *Union Women*, 7.
50. Stein, *Running Steel*.
51. See Milkman, *Gender at Work*; Stein, *Running Steel*.
52. Donna Cooper, interview, 2009, Lehigh University's Beyond Steel Collection, Bethlehem, PA.
53. See Fonow, *Union Women*.
54. Fonow, *Union Women*, 62.
55. Bess King, interview, 2013, Steelworkers' Archives Oral History Collection, Bethlehem, PA.
56. Fonow, *Union Women*.
57. Behum, *30 Years*, 210.
58. Olson, *Wives of Steel*; Rudacille, *Roots of Steel*.
59. Cockburn, *Brothers*, 135.
60. Louise Lamphere, Alex Stepick, and Guillermo Gremier, eds., *Newcomers in the Workplace* (Philadelphia, PA: Temple University Press, 1994); Belinda Leach, "Citizenship and the Politics of Exclusion in a 'Post'-Fordist Industrial City," *Critique of Anthropology* 18, no. 2 (1998): 181–204.
61. Olson, *Wives of Steel*; Rudacille, *Roots of Steel*; Fonow, *Union Women*; Molly Martin, *Hard Hatted Women: Life on the Job* (Berkeley, CA: Seal Press, 1997).
62. Fonow, *Union Women*; Olson, *Wives of Steel*.

63. Fonow, *Union Women*.
64. Ellen Israel Rosen, *Bitter Choices: Blue Collar Women In and Out of Work* (Chicago: University of Chicago Press, 1987), 171.
65. Behum, *30 Years*, 221.
66. Bess King, interview, 2013, Steelworkers' Archives Oral History Collection, Bethlehem, PA.

CHAPTER 5

1. Teresa Ghilarducci, *When I'm Sixty-Four: The Plot against Pensions and the Plan to Save Them* (Princeton, NJ: Princeton University Press, 2008), 241.
2. Mitchell A. Orenstein, *Pensions, Social Security, and the Privatization of Risk* (New York: Columbia University Press, 2009).
3. See Melinda Cooper, *Family Values: Between Neoliberalism and the New Social Conservatism* (New York: Zone Books, 2017).
4. Jeff Hoffert, interview, 2011, *Keystone Steel*, PCNTV. This program is not available on the PCNTV website, but can be obtained by contacting the station.
5. Cowie, *Capital Moves*, 198.
6. Ted Smith, interview, 2013, Steelworkers' Archives Oral History Collection, Bethlehem, PA.
7. Doukas, *Worked Over*, 24.
8. The more commutable Steelton plant, for example, was desirable as workers could continue to live in the Lehigh Valley and commute to their new mill. Later the Coatesville and Conshohocken plants were also desirably close.
9. There was a small minority of exceptions, as some workers who were eligible for retirement still opted for a transfer.
10. Steven High, *Industrial Sunset: The Making of North America's Rust Belt, 1969–1984* (Toronto: University of Toronto Press, 2003), 73.
11. Fred Schneck, interview, 2010, Steelworkers' Archives Oral History Collection, Bethlehem, PA.
12. High, *Industrial Sunset*.
13. Warren, *Bethlehem Steel*; Bartholomew and Young, *Bethlehem Steel in Bethlehem*.
14. Warren, *Bethlehem Steel*, 230.
15. On the one hand, proposed large-scale investments at the Lackawanna plant included a 1976–1978 $200 million investment in the rolling mills, a 1981 galvanizing line expansion, and a 1980s improved coke works heating system, even as shops were closed and workers were laid off.
16. Lorenzo Quaryle, interview, 2012, Steelworkers' Archives Oral History Collection, Bethlehem, PA.

17. In 2010, when Arlen Specter switched parties from Republican to Democrat and was running against USW-endorsed candidate Joe Sestak in the Democratic primary, he mobilized these Lackawanna transferees to support his campaign. One of them, Joe Long, was quoted in a campaign TV commercial saying, "If Arlen Specter could do this for us, imagine what he can do for the rest of the downtrodden and mistreated workers in Pennsylvania." These commercials failed to mobilize sufficient blue-collar vote, and Specter lost to Sestak (who then lost to his Republican competitor).

18. Sennett, *The Corrosion of Character*, 139.

19. This was laid out in the National Labor Relations Board Inland Steel decision and the 1949 Steel Industry Board report.

20. Hoerr, *And the Wolf*.

21. Kevin J. Delaney, *Strategic Bankruptcy: How Corporations and Creditors Use Chapter 11 to Their Advantage* (Berkeley: University of California Press, 1998).

22. Steve Miller, *The Turnaround Kid: What I Learned Rescuing America's Most Troubled Companies* (New York: Collins, 2008), 199; see also Mark Reutter, "Delphi, the Terminator, and the Misuse of Bankruptcy Law," Making Steel, April 12, 2006, https://web.archive.org/web/20060906025849/http://www.makingsteel.com/delphicase.html.

23. Miller, *Turnaround Kid*, 148.

24. Miller, *Turnaround Kid*, 199.

25. Karen Ho, *Liquidated: An Ethnography of Wall Street* (Durham, NC: Duke University Press, 2009), 147.

26. Eileen Appelbaum, Rosemary Batt, and Jae Eun Lee, "Financial Intermediaries in the U.S.: Development and Impact on Firms and Employment Relations," in *Financialization, New Investment Funds, and Labour: An International Comparison*, ed. Howard Gospel, Andrew Pendleton, and Sigurt Volits, 53–85 (Oxford: Oxford University Press, 2015), 62.

27. Ho, *Liquidated*; Randy Martin, *Financialization of Daily Life* (Philadelphia, PA: Temple University Press, 2002).

28. Ed O'Brien, interview, 2009, Steelworkers' Archives Oral History Collection, Bethlehem, PA.

29. Richard Moytzen, interview, 2007, Steelworkers' Archives Oral History Collection, Bethlehem, PA.

30. Reutter, "Delphi, the Terminator," 2.

31. Robert Guy Matthews, "Steel Merger Seems to be Unraveling—Pension Takeover Scuttles Bethlehem's Plan to Entice Employees to Retire Early," *Wall Street Journal*, eastern edition, December 17, 2002.

32. Those who exceeded the PBGC cap would have included some highly paid production workers and Bethlehem Steel salaried workers.

33. Jonathan Tasini, *The Audacity of Greed: Free Markets, Corporate Thieves, and the Looting of America* (Brooklyn, NY: Ig Publishing, 2009); Ellen Schultz, "Hidden Burden: As Worker's Pensions Wither, Those for Executives Flourish," *Wall Street Journal*, June 23, 2006; Ellen Schultz, "Banks Owe Billions to Executives," *Wall Street Journal*, October 31, 2008; Ellen Schultz, "Banks Use Life Insurance to Fund Bonuses," *Wall Street Journal*, May 20, 2009.

34. Schultz, "Banks Use Life Insurance."

35. Gregg Shotwell, "To Delphi Corporation's Robert Miller 'Bankruptcy Is a Growth Industry in America," MR Online, April 19, 2006, https://mronline.org/2006/04/19/to-delphi-corporations-robert-miller-bankruptcy-is-a-growth-industry-in-america. Steve Miller is quite explicit about saying that when workers retired "at age 65 and then died at age 70 . . . the social contract inherent in these programs seemed affordable."

36. Tasini, *The Audacity of Greed*.

37. Ellen Shultz and Tom McGinty, "Pensions for Executives on Rise." *Wall Street Journal*, eastern edition, November 3, 2009.

38. Schultz, "Banks Use Life Insurance."

39. Jill Quadagno, *One Nation Uninsured: Why the U.S. Has No National Health Insurance* (Oxford: Oxford University Press, 2005).

40. Quadagno, *One Nation Uninsured*, 142.

41. Jacob S. Hacker, *The Divided Welfare State: The Battle over Public and Private Social Benefits in the U.S.* (Cambridge: Cambridge University Press, 2002).

42. Hacker, *Divided Welfare State*.

43. Hacker, *Divided Welfare State*.

44. Michael Katz, *The Price of Citizenship: Redefining the American Welfare State* (Philadelphia: University of Pennsylvania Press, 2001).

45. Thomas Geoghegan, *See You in Court: How the Right Made America a Lawsuit Nation* (New York: The New Press, 2007), 129.

46. Richard Moytzen, interview, 2007, Steelworkers' Archives Oral History Collection, Bethlehem, PA.

47. Kathy Chen and Neil King Jr., "Workers Gain in Trade Equation," *Wall Street Journal*, eastern edition, May 13, 2002.

48. Deborah Solomon, "Off the Job," *Wall Street Journal*, March 1, 2007.

49. Michael Luo, "At Closing Plant, Ordeal Included Heart Attacks," *New York Times*, February 24, 2010.

50. Michael D. Yates, *Naming the System: Inequality and Work in the Global Economy* (New York: Monthly Review Press, 2003).

51. Sherry Lee Linkon and John Russo, *Steeltown U.S.A.: Work and Memory in Youngstown* (Lawrence: University Press of Kansas, 2003), 195–97.

52. Annie Case and Angus Deaton, *Deaths of Despair and the Future of Capitalism* (Princeton, NJ: Princeton University Press, 2020).

53. Newman, *Falling From Grace.*

54. Russo and Linkon, *Steeltown U.S.A.*

55. Barbara Ehrenreich, *Bait and Switch: The (Futile) Pursuit of the American Dream* (New York: Metropolitan Books, 2005).

56. Geoghegan, *See You in Court*, 122.

CHAPTER 6

1. "Allentown [Peopling of PA] Historical Marker," ExplorePAhistory. com, accessed June 12, 2023, https://explorepahistory.com/hmarker.php? markerId=1-A-3DE.

2. Claudia Deutsch, "Eastern Pennsylvania Region Recovers by Turning to Technology Companies," *New York Times*, October 7, 1999.

3. "100 Best Places to Live and Launch: 58. Bethlehem, Pa.," *CNN Money*, last updated July 2, 2008, https://money.cnn.com/galleries/2008/fsb/0803/gallery. best_places_to_launch.fsb/58.html.

4. "Best Places to Live: Bethlehem, PA," *CNN Money*, September 2012, https:// money.cnn.com/magazines/moneymag/best-places/2012/snapshots/ PL4206088.html; Michael C. Upton, "The Most Charming Towns and Small Cities in Pennsylvania," *TravelMag*, February 24, 2021, https://www.travelmag. com/articles/towns-small-cities-pennsylvania.

5. Gregory Karp, "A Darkening Outlook," *Morning Call*, April 13, 2008.

6. Jane Collins, "Theorizing Wisconsin's 2011 Protests: Community-Based Unionism Confronts Accumulation by Dispossession," *American Ethnologist* 39, no. 1 (February 2012): 6–20.

7. Sean Safford, *Why the Garden Club Couldn't Save Youngstown: The Transformation of the Rust Belt* (Cambridge, MA: Harvard University Press, 2009).

8. On the "new economy," see Richard Florida, *The Rise of the Creative Class: And How It's Transforming Work, Leisure, Community and Everyday Life* (New York: Basic Book, 2003); Frank Levy and Richard J. Murname, *The New Division of Labor: How Computers are Creating the Next Job Market* (Princeton, NJ: Princeton University Press, 2004); Manuel Castells, *Rise of the Network Society* (Oxford: Blackwell Publishers, 1995).

9. "About LVIP," Home page, Lehigh Valley Industrial Park Inc., accessed March 10, 2023, lvip.org.

10. Safford, *Why the Garden Club.*

11. Lehigh Valley Industrial Park, *LVIP Annual Report to the Community, 2020–2021* (Bethlehem, PA: Lehigh Valley Industrial Park, 2021), http://www.lvip.org/wp-content/uploads/2022/01/LVIP-final-Annual-Report-2021-Single-Pgs.pdf.

12. Lehigh Valley Economic Development Corporation, *2019 Annual Report*, https://issuu.com/lvmadepossible/docs/lvedc_2019_annual_report; Gregory Karp, "Trend of Contraction in Manufacturing," *Morning Call*, December 1, 2004, D2; Safford, *Why the Garden Club*, 21

13. Safford, *Why the Garden Club*.

14. "Bethlehem Struts Its Stuff," *Morning Call*, June 24, 2010, https://www.mcall.com/2010/06/24/bethlehem-struts-its-stuff.

15. Gregory Karp, "Valley Inflation Rate Doubles Nation's," *Morning Call*, November 16, 2007.

16. Spencer Soper, "Casino Battles a Matter of Preservation," *Morning Call*, April 27, 2006.

17. A brownfield is land that has been previously developed, often for industrial purposes, that now contains environmental pollutants that may present barriers to redevelopment.

18. The Lehigh Valley Economic Development Corporation (LVEDC) is a not-for-profit group controlled by Lehigh Valley elite.

19. Jeffrey Parks, *Stronger than Steel: Forging a Rust Belt Renaissance* (Bethlehem, PA: Rocky Rapids Press, 2018), 282.

20. Nicole Radzievich, "It Won't Cost a Roll of Quarters," *Morning Call*, March 31, 2007.

21. Ruth Milkman, *Farewell to the Factory: Autoworkers in the Late 20th Century* (Berkeley: University of California Press, 1997). Ruth Milkman also found that some workers enjoyed their retirement after auto workers' buyouts.

22. Louis Uchitelle, *The Disposable American: Layoffs and Their Consequences* (New York: Vintage Books, 2007).

23. Uchitelle, *The Disposable American*, 158.

24. David Sirota, *The Uprising: An Unauthorized Tour of the Populist Revolt Scaring Wall Street and Washington* (New York: Three Rivers Press, 2008); Frances Fox Piven, *The War at Home: The Domestic Costs of Bush's Militarism* (New York: The New Press, 2006).

25. Thomas Dunk, "Remaking the Working Class: Experience, Class Consciousness, and the Industrial Adjustment Process." *American Ethnologist* 29, no. 4 (2000): 879.

26. Piven, *The War at Home*.

27. Jane Collins, "One Big Labor Market: The New Imperialism and Worker Vulnerability," in *Rethinking America: The Imperial Homeland in the Twenty-First*

Century, ed. Jeff Maskovsky and Ida Susser, 280–99 (Boulder, CO: Paradigm Publishers, 2009).

28. Ted Smith, interview, 2013, Steelworkers' Archives Oral History Collection, Bethlehem, PA.

29. Ehrenreich, *Bright-Sided*, 115.

30. From November, 1995 to September, 1998 1,416 steelworkers went through the dislocated workers program.

31. Wendy Warren, "Displaced Workers Learn to Overcome," *Morning Call*, September 7, 1998.

32. Wendy Warren, "Displaced Workers."

33. Jacob Hacker, *The Great Risk Shift: The Assault on American Jobs, Families, Health Care, and Retirement* (Oxford: Oxford University Press, 2006), 74.

34. Stanley Aronowitz, *How Class Works: Power and Social Movement* (New Haven, CT: Yale University Press, 2003), 103.

35. Ruth Milkman, *LA Story: Immigrant Workers and the Future of the American Labor Movement* (New York: Russell Sage Foundation, 2006), 98.

36. Andrew Ross, *Nice Work if You Can Get It: Life and Labor in Precarious Times* (New York: New York University Press, 2009).

37. Hathaway, *Can Workers Have a Voice*, 150.

38. Hacker, *The Great Risk Shift*, 72.

39. Philippe Bourgois, *In Search of Respect: Selling Crack in El Barrio* (Cambridge: Cambridge University Press, 1995).

40. Pierre Bourdieu, *Distinction: A Social Critique of the Judgment of Taste* (Cambridge, MA: Harvard University Press, 1984), 199.

41. Doukas, *Worked Over*, 111.

42. Belinda Leach, "Citizenship and the Politics of Exclusion in a 'Post'-Fordist Industrial City," *Critique of Anthropology* 18, no. 2 (1998): 181–204.

43. Behum, *30 Years*, 305.

44. Gregory Karp, "Area Unemployment Rises," *Morning Call*, June 27, 2004.

45. Ching Kwan Lee, *Gender and the South China Miracle: Two Worlds of Factory Women* (Berkeley: University of California Press, 1998); Ching Kwan Lee, *Against the Law: Labor Protests in China's Rustbelt and Sunbelt* (Berkeley: University of California Press, 2007); Milkman, *Farewell to the Factory*.

46. See Edwards, *Contested Terrain*; Burawoy, *Manufacturing Consent*.

47. Jane L. Collins, *Threads: Gender, Labor, and Power in the Global Apparel Industry* (Chicago: University of Chicago Press, 2003), 156–57.

48. Moody, *Workers in a Lean World*.

49. See the Obama-backed documentary *American Factory*.

50. See Lowell Bergman and David Barstow, "A Family's Fortune, a Legacy of Blood and Tears," *New York Times*, Jan 9, 2003; Bergman and Barstow, "2 at Hazardous Foundry Tell of Events," *New York Times*, January 16, 2003; Bergman and Barstow, "OSHA to Address Persistent Violators of Job Safety Rules," *New York Times*, March 11, 2003; and Bergman and Barstow, "Pipemaker Is Sued Over Safety Violations," *New York Times*, April 15, 2003; and PBS *Frontline* episode "A Dangerous Business (Revisited)," WGBH Boston and New York Times (season 2003, episode 2), https://www.pbs.org/video/frontline-dangerous-business-revisited.

51. Milkman, *LA Story*, 80.

52. Steven Greenhouse, *The Big Squeeze: Tough Times for the American Worker* (New York: Anchor Books, 2008), 11.

53. Sharon Smith, *Subterranean Fire: A History of Working Class Radicalism in the United States* (Chicago: Haymarket Books, 2006), 239.

54. Barstow and Bergman, "A Family's Fortune."

55. Sharryn Kasmir, "Corporation, Self, and Enterprise at the Saturn Auto Plant," *Anthropology of Work Review* 22, no. 4 (2001): 8–12; Milkman, *Farewell to the Factory*.

56. Hugh Gusterson and Catherine Besteman, "Introduction," in *The Insecure American: How We Got Here and What We Should Do about It*, ed. Hugh Gusterson and Catherine Besteman (Berkeley: CA: University of California Press, 1–26, 2010), 13.

57. Peter Kwong, "Walling Out Immigrants," in *The Insecure American: How We Got Here and What We Should Do About It*, ed. Hugh Gusterson and Catherine Besteman, 255–69 (Berkeley: University of California Press, 2010), 261.

58. Kasmir and Carbonella, "Dispossession and the Anthropology of Labor"; also see Wacquant, *The Invention of the 'Underclass,'* for a critique of the notion of the underclass.

59. Ida Susser, "The Construction of Poverty and Homelessness in US Cities" *Annual Review of Anthropology*, no. 25 (October 1996): 11–35.

60. Chris Szarko, interview, 2010, Steelworkers' Archives Oral History Collection, Bethlehem, PA.

61. Milkman, *Farewell to the Factory*.

62. As also documented in the 1950s by Eli Chinoy, *Automobile Workers and the American Dream* (New York: Doubleday and Company, 1955).

63. Milkman, *Farewell to the Factory*.

64. These skills included advanced training, skills in mediation and negotiation, and knowledge of human resource skills such as safety.

65. Bartholomew and Young, *Bethlehem Steel in Bethlehem.*
66. Assad et al., *Forging America.*
67. Kasmir, "Corporation, Self, and Enterprise."
68. Connie Bruck, "The Brass Ring: A Multibillionaire's Relentless Quest for Global Influence," *New Yorker*, June 30, 2008.
69. Bruck, "The Brass Ring."

CONCLUSION

1. Frank, *Buy American*, 243.
2. E. Paul Durrenberger and Dimitra Doukas, "Gospel of Wealth, Gospel of Work: Counterhegemony in the U.S. Working Class," *American Anthropologist* 110, no. 2 (2008): 214–24, 216.
3. Sam Gindin, Greg Albo, and Leo Panitch, "Capitalist Crisis and Radical Renewal," in *Capitalism and Its Discontents: Conversations with Radical Thinkers in a Time of Tumult*, ed. Sasha Lilley, 105–21 (Oakland, CA: PM Press, 2011).
4. Cheri Register, *Packinghouse Daughter: A Memoir* (New York: Perennial, 2001), 228.
5. Joshua B. Freeman, *Working-Class New York: Life and Labor since World War II* (New York: The New Press, 2000), 333.
6. Halle, *America's Working Man.*
7. Michael Zweig, *The Working Class Majority: America's Best Kept Secret* (Ithaca, New York: Cornell University Press, 2000).
8. August Carbonella, "Beyond the Limits of the Visible World: Remapping Historical Anthropology," in *Critical Junctions: Anthropology and History beyond the Cultural Turn*, ed. Don Kalb and Herman Tak, 88–108 (Oxford, NY: Berghahn Books, 2005).
9. Anthony Melathopoulos and Sam Gindin, "Unionism, Austerity and the Left: An Interview with Sam Gindin," *Platypus Review*, May 6, 2011, www.platypus1917.org/2011/05/06.
10. Frances Fox Piven and Richard Cloward, "Power Repertoires and Globalization," *Politics & Society* 28, no. 3 (2000): 413–30, 413.
11. David Graeber, *Debt: The First 5,000 Years* (Brooklyn, NY: Melville House, 2011), 382.
12. David Harvey, *Spaces of Neoliberalization: Toward a Theory of Uneven Geographical Development* (Munich: Franz Steiner Verlag, 2005); Piven, *The War at Home.*
13. Harvey, *Spaces of Neoliberalization.*
14. Karl Polanyi, *The Great Transformation: The Political and Economic Origins of Our Time* (New York: Farrar & Rinehart, 1944).
15. Michael Zweig, *The Working Class Majority.*

16. Moody, *Workers in a Lean World*; Durrenberger, "The Anthropology of Organized Labor"; Dorothy Sue Cobble, *The Sex of Class: Women Transforming American Labor* (Ithaca, NY: ILR Press. 2007); Jane McAlevey, *No Shortcuts: Organizing for Power in the New Gilded Age* (Oxford: Oxford University Press, 2016).
17. They express these critiques through their local unions and community groups, and by calling and writing local politicians.
18. Critiques of Bush focused especially on the two wars he initiated given his lack of military experience as well as his positions on health care and social security.
19. Silver, *Forces of Labor*.
20. Moody, *Workers in a Lean World*; Steven Henry Lopez, *Reorganizing the Rust Belt: An Inside Study of the American Labor Movement* (Berkeley: University of California Press, 2004).
21. Gabriel Winant, *The Next Shift*.

INDEX

Abel, I. W., 133
Achando, Jose (pseud.), 25
Adams, Dick, 38
Adelson, Sheldon, 204, 243–44
affirmative action and consent decrees,
    71–72, 96, 125, 130–40, 143–46,
    155, 234
Affordable Care Act (2010), 190–91, 193,
    194
African American workers
  characteristics of, 29–30
  consent decree (1974) and, 71–72, 96,
    125, 130–40
  discrimination and exclusion of, 106,
    123–24, 125–27, 128–29
  internal labor market and, 69–72
  seniority and, 106
  solidarity and, 115–16
agency, 63, 72, 78–79
Allen, Bob (pseud.), 214–15
amor fati, 63
Appelbaum, Eileen, 182
apprenticeship systems, 60, 66–67, 110–
    11, 131, 135, 145
Arcelor, 41
Aronowitz, Stanley, 213–14
ArtsQuest, 54, 204, 205, 206

Bachman, Fred (pseud.), 64, 89, 110
Badzar, Joseph, 102–3
Baker, Dave (pseud.), 163, 165, 166
Barnette, Hank, 37, 51

Bauer, Luke (pseud.), 75
Baxter, John (pseud.), 119, 241–42
Becker, Greg (pseud.), 131
Behum, Frank, 38, 39, 42
Ben Franklin Technology Center, 202
BethForge, 54, 240–41
Bethlehem, Pennsylvania
  deindustrialization in, 21–22, 199–
    200
  history and demography of, 7–8, 22–
    25, 126–27
  postindustrial economy in, 54–55,
    199, 200–207
  See also Bethlehem Steel
    Corporation; South Bethlehem
    plant
Bethlehem Area School District (BASD),
    190–91
Bethlehem Iron Company, 25
Bethlehem Steel Corporation
  Chapter 11 bankruptcy and, 2–3,
    17, 40, 160–61, 167, 173, 178–98,
    207–8
  demographics of workforce at, 126–29
  restructuring processes and, 34–41
  rise and crisis of, 7–8, 26–33
  Taylor and, 61, 99
  See also South Bethlehem plant
Bethlehem Works (BethWorks Now),
    204–5
bitterness, 195–97
Blazek, Jerry (pseud.), 169

racial and ethnic stereotypes and,
69–71
role and factors in, 62–69
seniority and, 45–46, 101–7
women and, 69, 71–72
International Steel Group (ISG)
pensions and health care coverage
and, 173, 182, 184, 188
Ross and, 40–41
South Bethlehem plant and, 2, 204
Steelton plant and, 179
IQE, 202

Jaros, Steve (pseud.), 190, 221, 222
Jensen, Tom (pseud.), 183
Johnstown, Pennsylvania, 31,
126–27
Joyce, Charlie (pseud.), 58, 142
Juran, Joseph M., 46–47

Karp, Joe (pseud.), 231–32, 236, 248
Kasmir, Sharryn, 242
Kaufmann, Robert (pseud.), 197
Keenan, Mary (pseud.), 156, 197
Keglovitz, Karol (pseud.), 147, 154
Kennedy, Michael, 24
Keschl, Ron (pseud.), 105, 224
Kessler-Harris, Alice, 87
kin networks, 165–66, 172–73
King, Bess (pseud.), 145, 155
Kirk, Barry (pseud.)
on challenges of postindustrial
economy, 215, 216–17
on citizenship, 90
external transfers and, 169
on health care coverage, 190, 191,
194, 215
as "successful" in postindustrial
economy, 238
Kornblum, William, 79, 114–15
Kosek, Ron (pseud.), 190
Koval, Nick (pseud.), 67

Kovar, Ann (pseud.), 116, 147, 152–53,
155, 157, 177, 189
Kovarik, Cathy (pseud.)
on discrimination and exclusion,
144, 145, 146
on hazing, 121, 149–50
medical deferment and, 177–78
on solidarity, 111–12, 115, 147–48,
151, 152
Kovarik, Howard (pseud.), 109, 115, 145
Kuchta, Dave, 141
Kwong, Peter, 229

Labor and Monopoly Capital
(Braverman), 61–62
labor degradation, 69
labor process
structure of, 57–60
struggle, knowledge, and control in,
79–83
theoretical perspectives on, 60–65
unions and, 82–83
workplace culture and, 72–79
See also incentive pay (piece-rate
pay); internal labor market
Lackawanna, New York
African American workers and, 71–
72, 126, 130
crisis of steel industry and, 31
external transfers and, 162, 165, 166,
168–69, 171–72, 174–76, 178–79
pensions and, 178–79
restructuring and deindustrialization
in, 35–36, 55, 171–72, 173, 178, 199
Lambert, Ron (pseud.), 232
Lang, Ernie (pseud.), 7, 229–30, 235–36
Las Vegas Sands Corporation, 203, 204–
5, 243–44. *See also* Wind Creek
Bethlehem
Latino workers
consent decree (1974) and, 71–72,
96, 125, 130–40

www.ingramcontent.com/pod-product-compliance
Lightning Source LLC
Chambersburg PA
CBHW031409270326
41929CB00010BA/1385